LEADING
LADIES

CANADA

LEADING LADIES
CANADA

by
Jean Bannerman

Mika Publishing Company
Belleville, Ontario
1977

ISBN 0-919303-18-8

FC25.B35 1977   920.071   C77-001398-8
F1005.B35 1977

Mika Publishing Company

Printed and bound in Canada

087135

Her Majesty Queen Elizabeth II
Queen of Canada

Madame Vanier

Madame Léger

CONTENTS

PREFACE

Heroic and dedicated, skilled and colourful, are the women out of more than three hundred years of Canadian history, who fill the pages of Jean Bannerman's *Leading Ladies-Canada*.

Mrs. Bannerman, a graduate nurse, student and author of numerous travel articles and personality sketches, has spent years of research and study on this volume. She presents to readers many new and fascinating insights into the characters and the works of great Canadian women, from the courageous Jeanne Mance and Mother Marie de l'Incarnation; through the famous five, headed by Judge Emily Murphy, who had Canadian women acknowledged as "persons" in the eyes of the law; to the present gracious chatelaine of Rideau Hall, Madame Léger.

Here, in one volume, Jean Bannerman has brought together many of the great and good women of Canadian history. The book is a fine tribute to the women who have helped to develop Canada.

JOHN FISHER

PRELUDE

Gentle nuns came from France to Canada in the seventeenth century leaving behind all they held most dear, braving hardships and death, to bring religion, nursing, succour and education to the New World. Such noble women chose a lonely life, the better to serve humanity.

Most vital contribution women make to any country is bearing and mothering children. But women, as well as men, long for intellectual achievement, and like Milton, lament: "talent, which is death to hide, lodged with me, useless ..."

Canadian women, since earliest days, have been more than wives and mothers. Women pioneers stood shoulder to shoulder with their menfolk in social and economic development of their country . . . in ever-widening spheres of service played leading roles in helping to create, from the wilderness, a great nation.

Two queens, one out of the dead past, one in the living present, have made an invaluable contribution to Canada. It was the vision and generosity of Queen Isabella of Spain that made possible Christopher Columbus's discovery of America. Her Majesty, Elizabeth II, Queen of Canada, this year celebrating her Silver Jubilee, sets an inspiring example, in both private and public life, to every woman.

Through stern struggle against centuries-old tradition, women have flung wide the door of opportunity. In any critical evaluation of how well women measure up to greater opportunities, we must not forget that, less than a century ago, women were considered the inferior sex, classed with criminals and idiots, denied the rights of citizenship. In time of war, women rise to sublime heights of self-sacrifice. Today, courageously, women face the challenge of the Twentieth Century . . . co-operating with men in trying to find a pathway to permanent peace.

My original intention was to write a series of biographical sketches of achievements of outstanding Canadian women from the dawn of nationhood. In early stages of my research, it became evident that such a book might well have been a history of Canada, illustrated with the lives of Canadian women.

Self-knowledge called me to a halt.

I realized I had not sufficient stature, as an author, to do justice to this more ambitious concept, which would require a lifetime spent in research, plus the pen of a Churchill.

The resulting book is a compromise, a series of chapters concerned with the work of women in various fields. I have made no attempt to be profound or philosophical. I have merely attempted to present a factual account of women's contribution to Canada.

In a factual book of this type, although I have checked and double-checked, and have persuaded my more erudite friends who are experts in various fields, to criticize chapters, errors are inevitable. I would consider it a kindness if anyone noting these would send me corrections, complete with sources.

Chapter on the Famous Five tells the story of the victory of those women in finally being acknowledged as "Persons" in the legal sense. While many women in this book are as well-known as Magistrate Murphy, the heroine of that feminist triumph, it has given me particular pleasure to pay tribute to some unsung heroines, such as Dr. Margaret Newton.

Strangers reading most histories of Canada might well believe this country was populated solely by

Madeleine de Vercheres, Laura Secord, and their des-
cendants. While freely admitting and admiring their
bravery, I should like to tell about aspects of their lives
not so generally known, along with stories of many
more less celebrated pioneers.

How many of the millions who visited Expo '67,
or who dined in St. Helene's Restaurant there, will
know the sad story of a girl for whom island and restaurant were named? In 1610, when only twelve, Helene
was married to forty-year-old explorer Samuel de
Champlain. In honour of his child-bride, he named the
island, opposite Montreal, St. Helene Island.

In 1617 Champlain took his apothecary, Louis
Hebert, and his wife, Marie, first white woman to set
foot on Canadian soil, to Quebec. The Heberts had the
first chimney built in Canada in their home.

In 1620, Champlain brought his young wife, with
three maid-servants, to Quebec. First French aristocrat
to brave the dangers of New France, she must have been
horrified at sight of her new home. Champlain, almost
never there, had let it fall into dreadful disrepair — a
terrible contrast to the luxurious French Court. She had
no companionship, except Madame Hebert (with whom
she had little in common), her maids, and her middle-
aged, seldom-home husband. Lonely, terrified of Indians, surely she is a most tragic figure of New France.

Her lonely life resulted in a nervous breakdown
four years later. Champlain took her home to France.
After his death, on Christmas Day in 1635, in Quebec,
Helene sought solace in an Ursuline Convent, where she
soon died.

Canada's Youngest Heroine: A beautiful, golden-
haired young woman, Mme. de Naudiere, stood glaring
menacingly at an Indian brave, holding the tomahawk
she had wrested from his fierce grasp. She had just
knocked him unconscious with it. Without warning,
suddenly, four furious squaws attacked her, tore her

clothes into shreds, started to burn her alive in the roaring fireplace.

"Stop, or I shoot!" shouted her young son, Charles, miraculously coming to her rescue. His quick-witted mother again seized the tomahawk, threatening to scalp the still-stunned Indian. Beseeching mercy, the squaws finally were allowed to carry away their brave.

This was not Mme. de Naudiere's first battle with Indians. Better known to history as Madeleine de Vercheres, in 1692 she held her father's fort, almost alone, against a terrifying Indian attack. Though pictured as a gentle-faced girl, after her marriage in 1706 she was "The man of the manoir!" It was Madeleine who collected rents, and took recalcitrant tenants to court. However, she did help those in real distress.

Tourists today, visiting the Seigniory of Vercheres, still thrill at the sight of the statue of a windblown, girlish figure, grasping a gun. Canada's courageous, youthful heroine typifies the pioneering spirit.

Feminine Paul Revere: Some may be surprised to know that, in the National Archives, Ottawa, a treasure is the first application to operate a ferry boat, between Queenstown and Niagara. It has a woman's signature. That her request was not granted, need surprise no one. Needing money to raise her family, she was forced into the more orthodox role of seamstress. Given the clue that her picture adorns the box of chocolates with which some men patch up marital differences, the name Laura Secord leaps to mind.

On that steaming, hot day in June 1813, when she made her historic, hazardous journey to Beaver Dams, Laura Secord was a woman of thirty-eight, the mother of five children. Clad in a petticoat, yellow kimono and bedroom slippers, driving a cow to disarm suspicion, she plodded twenty weary miles through swamps and swollen streams. Finding one bridge washed out, she crept across the river on a log. Blundering into an Indian encampment, she thought fast. Managing to persuade the leader that the safety of his tribe also depended on the success of her mission, Indians guided her to the headquarters of Colonel James Fitzgibbon. There she blurted out her warning.

Laura Secord has been called "one of the most patriotic and courageous women of any age or race." No official recognition was made of Mrs. Secord's brave deed. When King Edward VII (as Prince of Wales) visited Niagara Falls, he was so impressed that he sent her one hundred pounds personally. A monument in her honour was erected at Lundy's Lane, Queenston Heights, at the request of the Ontario Historical Society. It was unveiled on June 22, 1911 by Mrs. G. W. Ross, wife of a former Premier of Ontario.

Unsung Heroine . . . is Elizabeth Barnett. When some of William Lyon Mackenzie's adherents were planning to recapture Gananoque, then push on and take Kingston, she overheard plans of great military significance, and issued a warning. Her bravery may have changed Canadian history. Few have heard of her, though Laura Secord's story is in every history book.

Leading Lady of Upper Canada 1791-96: Elizabeth Posthuma Simcoe, wife of the first Governor of Upper Canada, cheerfully lived in a canvas tent, until the official residence, Navy Hall, was built, at Niagara-on-the-Lake. An impressive monument there, the creation of Elizabeth Wyn Wood, honours this illustrious couple. The Simcoes graciously entertained visiting foreign dignitaries, settlers and Indians — impartially.

Mrs. Simcoe, an artist, sketched the quaint costumes and vehicles of the day. As busy as Boswell, her diaries and drawings are a valuable record of pioneer life. Her seven daughters designed and cut the glass for the unique stained glass window in the church of St. George-the-Martyr at Jackson's Point on Lake Simcoe, Ontario.

Due to space limitations, I have shortened such

stories and have had to make a rather arbitrary selection of women for inclusion, in order that *Leading Ladies* be representative of the various sections of Canada. My criteria has been pioneers in various fields, worthwhile achievements, acknowledged leaders, unsung heroines, women who succeeded despite special handicaps. The book therefore is a factual account of their contribution, brightened with bits of human interest. This is the first time the story of Canada's outstanding women has been collected in one volume. It is my sincere hope that *Leading Ladies* will prove valuable, both as a reference book and an addition to Canadiana.

"A Small Tribute to Great Women" is one title I considered, for that is what it really is, and, although arduous, my voyage of discovery has been a constant inspiration. I have amassed a wealth of information through interviewing many intensely interesting women, as well as in years spent in research in archives and libraries across the continent.

Bolton's *Lives of Famous Women* was the inspiration for that great humanitarian, Agnes Macphail, to pioneer in the political field, and, through it to campaign for much needed reform. If even one young girl is similarly inspired by these portraits of outstanding Canadian women, the twenty years of my life dedicated to this book will not have been in vain. My confession of faith was perfectly expressed by Magistrate Murphy:

"I believe that never was a country better adapted to produce a great race of women than this Canada of ours, nor a race of women better adapted to make a great country. I believe the women of Canada carry its destiny in the folds of their garments. The men who will in future people it will be the fruit of their body and the fire of their spirit."

Jean Bannerman

Chapter I

Seraphic Troops

Early French Nuns

Marie de l'Incarnation

Alas, is there no charitable lady who will come to this country to gather up the blood of Christ by teaching His Word to the little Indian girls?

The year — 1639. Destination — New France. The terrifying crunch of timbers, scraping against an Atlantic iceberg, sounded above the rattle of rigging and the boom of loose canvas. "We'll perish! We'll perish!" cried Madame de la Peltrie, as she flung her arms about Mother Marie de l'Incarnation.

Despite the bedlam, the calm voice of Mother Marie came clearly: "If we drown, then let us drown with decency." Luckily, fate was kinder. As if in answer to fervent prayer, the ship's captain won success over the iceberg. Slowly the vessel pointed toward its destination which lay many leagues onward along the St. Lawrence River — at the French settlement of Quebec.

With Mother Marie were Mother St. Joseph and Mother Cecile Richer de la Croix; three nursing sisters, Mother Marie de St. Ignace, Anne le Contre de la Bernard, Marie Forestier de St. Bonaventure, all three of Hotel Dieu, Dieppe; also Mme. Peltrie's devoted maid, Charlotte Barré, who later became the first novice of the Ursuline order in Canada.

It was three weary months since the high-decked, wooden sailing ship had left Dieppe on May 4, 1639. Barely beyond sight of land it was discovered that the ship's water had gone bad. A passing warship warned of marauding Spanish galleons and advised a northern route.

Mother Marie suffered prolonged thirst during the journey. When the fare of tough, salted meat and wormy biscuits gave out completely, raw codfish hand-lined up the ship's side from the sea became the dreary menu. Quarters were cramped, dark, stale-aired, hardly bearable with the stench of continued sea-sickness.

Engraven, as a heraldic legend, on the minds of the two missionaries who were destined to become leaders in the work of care and healing, education, teaching and religion, was Father le Jeune's appeal in his *Jesuit Relations*:

> *Alas, is there no charitable lady who will come to this country to gather up the blood of Christ by teaching His Word to the little Indian girls?*

Cannons boomed as the dignitaries of Quebec offered a grateful welcome. Mother Marie and her little band knelt and reverently kissed the earth of New France, praying for strength. Governor Chevalier de Montmagny and his high officials promptly titled the new arrivals: "The Seraphic Troops".

Madame de la Peltrie

Crystal sparkled and well-filled platters were passed at a great banquet that night in the Governor's residence. Merry laughter rang. Later, the weary travellers were escorted from the gala party to a cheerless shed; their temporary quarters. On beds of fir branches thickly covered with crawling caterpillars, sleep was impossible. Good-naturedly, they named the shed "The Louvre".

First Hospital in Canada

Soon work was started on Canada's first hospital, located at Sillery, Quebec, and called "The House of Health."

Terror in the form of an epidemic of hemorrhagic smallpox among the Indians struck soon after the hospital's completion. The sick lay so close together in the overcrowded quarters that it was almost impossible to avoid stepping on them. Coping with more than 200 patients in six months, they used up all linens; even wimples and frontlets became dressings. To Mother Marie, the nuns and nursing sisters, it was only a normal challenge; for the aristocratic Madeleine it was much more. Her colleagues paid tribute: "Madame de la Peltrie . . . set herself with marvellous zeal to do service the most humble and revolting." The heroic Hospitallers declared: "We would prefer death and torture rather than desert our post."

The hospital, renamed Hotel Dieu, was later moved to Quebec City, where it operated effectively until June, 1755, when it was destroyed in a fire set by two sailors. Though all patients were rescued, one nun perished in the flames. So essential had the hospital proved itself that the Bishop of Quebec promptly wrote: "I offer you the full use of my palace . . . if necessary I shall, myself, be the first orderly of the new hospital."

Three beautiful young widows had assisted the Hospitaller Nuns in founding the first small hospital in

1639. The Duchess d'Aiguillon financed it, although she never came to Canada. Beloved niece of Cardinal Richelieu, widowed at 18, she became a novice of the Carmel Order in Paris. However, Her Majesty Queen Anne whom she served as Lady-in-Waiting and the Cardinal, intervened. Her entrance to the cloister was forbidden by papal writ; thereafter, she devoted her life to charity. She sent workmen to build the pioneer hospital, and financed the three nursing sisters. Trained in the Hotel Dieu of Dieppe, they transferred to the New World, the traditions of the Order of St. Augustine, the oldest nursing order in Europe, noted for discipline and service.

Mother Marie de l'Incarnation was the leader. Born Marie Guyart, in Tours, in 1599, her father was a wealthy silk merchant; her mother extremely religious. Serious little Marie preferred "playing nun" to "playing house". The religious revival that swept France in the 17th century affected even children.

At seventeen, in an arranged marriage, she wed wealthy, socially-acceptable Claude Martin. Marie made a strange vow for a bride on her wedding night that, should she have a son, she would dedicate him to the service of God; and should her husband die, she would also consecrate herself.

Marie's son, born a year later, was named Claude for his father, who died within a year of the boy's birth, leaving Marie a widow. Refusing several offers of marriage, beautiful Marie declared: "I shall remain in the world until my son is twelve, then I shall enter a quiet convent." When Claude was twelve, Marie enrolled him in a Jesuit school while she entered the Ursuline Convent. Escaping, the boy ran sobbing through the halls of the convent, screaming: "I want my mother! Give me back my mother!" The other nuns were shocked but Marie apparently remained unmoved and Claude was sent back.

In her lonely cell in the Ursuline Convent, Mme.

Martin , now Marie de l'Incarnation, "heard voices and saw visions" as had Joan of Arc. She pored over the *Jesuit Relations* which told of the hardships, the dangers, and the martyrdoms of the Jesuit missionaries in far-off Canada. She conceived the plan of building a convent there to christianize the Indian girls. Through Father Poncet, a missionary about to return to Canada, she met wealthy Madame de la Peltrie, whom they persuaded to finance the venture. They embarked at Dieppe.

Although she had neither kissed nor caressed Claude from the time he was two, to make their eventual parting more endurable, Marie later wrote to her son from Canada: "It seemed as if my very bones were disjointed and twisted from their sockets, so great was my grief at leaving you." In his teens, Claude saddened his mother with riotous living. Eventually, however, he entered the priesthood, to her intense joy.

Madame de la Peltrie, last of the trio, was a gay, fun-loving French aristocrat — daughter of the wealthy Chauvignys. She might have been expected to spend her days in Paris salons, rather than dedicating her life to serving mankind. Born Madeleine de Chauvigny in Alencon in 1603, she had been reared in the luxury of a Normandy castle and married happily shortly after her formal debut. Heartbroken when her husband was killed in battle, having already lost her only child, a baby daughter, Madeleine became critically ill. Propped up on silken pillows in her palace, she pored over the *Jesuit Relations* as eagerly as Mother Marie in her dreary cell. She made a solemn vow that, if she recovered, she would dedicate her life to service in Canada.

Her anxious father, however, insisted that she remarry. To avoid being disinherited, Madeleine went through a mock marriage with an old family friend, M. de Bernieres. Fortunately her father died without learning of her duplicity. Although deeply religious, she still loved the limelight and made a triumphal tour of France with her pseudo-husband before joining Mother Marie at Dieppe. M. de Bernieres remained in France to look after her business affairs.

First Ursuline Convent

Having helped the Hospitaller Sisters during the smallpox epidemic, Mother Marie then founded the first Ursuline "Convent", an unpretentious two-roomed cottage. Her zeal and Madame Peltrie's money combined to complete by 1641, the first mother-house of the Ursuline Order in Canada. It was an imposing structure, with a chapel at one end and four huge fireplaces which devoured almost 200 cords of wood each winter.

"We roast on one side and freeze on the other," one nun wrote in their *Annales*. They slept in boxed-in beds, like chests, lined with serge. First morning task in winter was to shovel out the snow which drifted through the walls during the night. Food was often frozen and had to be thawed before breakfast. A great favourite with the Indians was sagamite — made of fat, freshly-killed animals (cats, dogs, beavers or bears) boiled with Indian corn and seasoned with raisins and prunes. Sometimes the visitors ate it all and the nuns went supperless to bed. Acrid smoke and the odour of eels (the staple diet), forced the high-born ladies to throw open the doors in sub-zero weather while armies of mosquitoes were summertime miseries.

Despite difficulties, the nuns devoted themselves completely to the service of others. Christian converts were urged to abhor cruelty. Indian girls were taught housekeeping and handicrafts. Mother Marie, who planned to marry her educated Indian girls to French settlers, soon learned they preferred Indian braves. So she co-operated in bringing young women from France "pour peupler les pays" and housed them in the convent. Operating expenses were provided from the generous purse of Madame Peltrie. By official decree, marriageable bachelors forfeited the right to fish and hunt in the woods. Both Mother Marie and Madame Peltrie felt their most important duty was training French-Canadian girls — the mothers of the next generation. At the convent itself, while a few of the novices recoiled from the hardships of nursing in the New World, and renounced the religious life to marry colonists, most spent their lives in its service.

Occasionally, glamorous Madeleine de la Peltrie would gather up her voluminous skirts to dance. Her partners were not elegantly-garbed noblemen at some fabulous ball in Paris, but her pagan pupils, teaching her wild Indian dances. Childless, she loved these brown-skinned children and would hug and kiss them, to the astonishment of their undemonstrative parents.

Jeanne Mance

Fun-loving Madame de la Peltrie was serious Mother Marie's perfect complement. Had she realized how soon she was to lose her, she no doubt would have been deeply depressed. For across the ocean in France, in 1641 — the year the Convent in Quebec was completed — Jeanne Mance learned that Sieur de Maisonneuve was bound for New France, to found a colony upstream from Quebec, to be called Ville Marie, (later renamed Montreal, after Mount Royal).

Two centuries before Florence Nightingale revolutionized the battlefields of the Crimea, Jeanne Mance was nursing compatriots wounded in the war between Alsace and Lorraine in France. The Lorraines invaded Alsace in 1637, killing more than 5,000 people and razing the town. Jeanne's home was demolished. She lived in the streets, tearing up her clothing to staunch bloody wounds and whispering words of comfort to the dying. Jeanne was born in Langres, France, of intellectual, but not wealthy parents. From childhood onward she was deeply spiritual. At seven she took the vows of poverty and chastity but never took the veil.

At thirty-four, Jeanne was a delicate-looking woman with large, dark eyes, long black curls and classically beautiful features. At confession, her priest fired her imagination with tales of service in Canada and read the *Jesuit Relations* to her. "Go thither, in the name of God!" he implored. Jeanne longed to go, yet hesitated because of frail health. However, her conscience gave her no rest.

After consulting Father Lallemand, head of Jesuit Missions in Canada, she decided to found a hospital in the wilderness. The modest young woman was surprised when Queen Anne summoned her to the palace to discuss the idea. The Queen persuaded Mme. de Bullion, a wealthy widow, to help finance the venture.

Maisonneuve, who realized that a hospital would make the difference between success and failure in his new colony, welcomed Jeanne Mance warmly. Jeanne Mance and Madame de la Peltrie soon became close friends, however, the new arrival and Mother Marie were less compatible. A meeting of Sieur de Maison-neuve and Governor Chevalier de Montmagny brought to a head the rivalry of older Quebec with the proposed new colony of Ville Marie. Quebec was jealous, clinging to its primary position. "Stay with us and strengthen the colony," Montmagny urged. "I will go to Ville Marie, if every tree there be an Iroquois!" Maisonneuve retorted hotly.

However, it was clear that the founding of the new colony must await spring. They wintered uneasily in Quebec. Jeanne Mance was lodged in the home that later became Spencerwood, the residence of Quebec's lieutenant-governors. She quickly learned the native language and haunted Hotel Dieu, helping and learning nursing lore from the Hospitaller Sisters. Increasing pressures to force abandonment of Maisonneuve's plan infuriated Mme. de la Peltire and temporarily disrupted her friendship with Mother Marie. She shocked her by accompanying Jeanne Mance to Ville Marie, taking her man-servant and convent furniture. Heartbroken, Mother Marie still gave her blessing to the venture.

When Maisonneuve's colonists arrived at Ville Marie in May, 1642, they knelt in thankful prayer, dedicating the Island to the Holy Family. First Mass was celebrated by the fitful light of fireflies collected in bottles. The women had risen before dawn to gather wildflowers to deck the altar. With the Iroquois as yet unaware of their presence, Maisonneuve quickly set up a palisade, then established the hospital, naming it Hotel Dieu. Although a log building, hastily made and poorly chinked, for Jeanne, it was a dream realized. Before the hospital was completed, blood-curdling war whoops heralded the return of the Indians. Jeanne's first patient, a colonist, scalped by the Iroquois, was treated with the motherly tenderness for which she became renowned.

Often, she and her patients too, had to load muskets for the settlers to beat back Indians.

Despite Indian raids, threats of floods, shortages of food, and epidemics, the tiny settlement of Ville Marie clung tenaciously to the shore of the St. Lawrence River. In 1644, when Madame de la Peltrie returned to Quebec, Jeanne Mance cried bitterly. But Mother Marie welcomed her treasured colleague back. Quebec also had been through trying times, sometimes they ate little, even took their meals standing. Appalled that most of their food was still imported from France, Mother Marie urged settlers to till the soil. Wheat was first sown in Quebec in 1644. From that year on, although still rivals, the two colonies tolerated each other.

Fire was so feared in the colonies that smoking in the street was punished by the cat-o'-nine tails. Every man had to join a bucket brigade during a fire. In 1650, a raging fire broke out in the Quebec convent, levelling it to the ground. Mother Marie braved the inferno to save the papers of her Community and the Blessed Sacrament. Standing in snow, in a worn nightdress, glamorous Madame de la Peltrie sobbed: "We are reduced to the nakedness of Job." Kindly neighbors took the fire victims in. Later they stayed with the Hospitaller nuns. Mother St. Joseph died soon after, probably from exposure.

Mme. de la Peltrie had built a comfortable home, where she housed sixteen persons for more than a year (two centuries later, in 1936, her home was enlarged and modernized and is now the Day School of the Ursuline Convent). However, even her wealth was insufficient to rebuild the convent. Undaunted, the black-robed nuns started rebuilding it themselves. The sight of them at this backbreaking task shamed the settlers and Indians into helping.

By 1653, the colony of Ville Marie was still in constant danger. Men feared to till the fields without armed guards. Maisonneuve was discouraged. Jeanne advised and financed a trip to France for him. He returned with 100 soldiers, additional settlers and Marguerite Bourgeoys. Left to labor alone, Jeanne was delighted by her new companion. Marguerite helped Jeanne to nurse the sick, prepare the dead for burial and comfort their relatives, unselfishly depriving herself of necessities to help others.

Marguerite Bourgeoys was born in Troyes, France, in 1620, on Good Friday, an appropriate birthday for one destined to suffer much in the service of her Master. As a child, she loved playing school. After both parents died, Marguerite went to live with Madame du Chuly, Maisonneuve's sister. Filled with religious fervor, Marguerite tried to join the cloistered Carmelites as well as the Convent of the Poor Clares, but was refused entry. She then turned to teaching in a girl's Sodality attached to the Congregation de Notre Dame.

Through his sister, Marguerite met Maisonneuve, who fired her imagination with tales of adventure in the New World. However, when he asked her to marry him, she replied: "I have taken a vow of chastity and dedicated my life to God." He never married. Marguerite gladly agreed, however, to accompany him to Ville Marie to teach. En route, she washed his ruffled lace sleeves in the sea.

When Maisonneuve gave Marguerite an unused log stable for her first schoolhouse, she said gratefully: "Christ was born in a stable in Bethlehem." As they sang songs of New France, her pupils learned practical lessons in cooking, sewing, knitting and weaving, which Marguerite introduced to Canada. Later, the kindly nuns knit long woolen hose for the kilted Highlanders. Lacking formal education, she would consult the scholarly priests about the three R's.

Marguerite Bourgeoys

First Medical Plan

In 1655, Jeanne Mance's Hotel Dieu started the first medical pre-payment plan in North America. Physicians agreed to dress wounds and prescribe for 30 sous a year. Twenty-six families enrolled in that first plan. Four years later, three Hospitaller nuns of the Order of St. Joseph, Mother Judith de Bresoles, Catherine Mace, and Marie Maillet came to Canada to help Jeanne Mance with the administration of her hospital and to train nurses to staff it. Since Mother de Bresoles also was a trained pharmacist, she was a welcome addition to Hotel Dieu. The same blue bottles she used in the dispensary 300 years ago are used today.

Two years later, Mother Bourgeoys laid the cornerstone of a chapel especially for sailors, the men who brought the lifesaving ships from France to Ville Marie. Maisonneuve fully supported the project. Portraits of both hang in the Church de Notre Dame de Bonsecours.

Deafening war whoops interrupted the peaceful pursuits of the colonists in 1660. Five Iroquois tribes had banded together, determined to exterminate the French. Mother Marie despaired, "My God! Blot out my name from the Book of Life rather than permit the destruction of New France!" To help defend Quebec, the Marquis de Tracy arrived with four companies of the Carignan de Salieres regiment. The saintly sisters felt it a hollow victory, however, since some libertine soldiers ran riot. Mother Marie wrote: "Soldiers . . . have planted wickedness, sin and crime in our soil of Canada, where virtue once stalked the streets!"

Peace restored, in 1669, Mother Bourgeoys built the first convent in Montreal, an uncloistered one — a revolutionary idea! In a travel-stained habit, she stood before the glittering court of King Louis XIV to plead for Royal assent to the founding of the Congregation de Notre Dame in Montreal, the first religious Order of Canadian origin.

Jeanne Mance died in 1673 not long after she laid one of the foundation stones for the Church of Notre Dame where, along with her beloved hospital, she is portrayed in one of the stained glass windows. In 1909, a bronze statue of Jeanne Mance was unveiled on the hospital grounds, in the park named for her. This "Hospital of the Poor" provided free medical aid until 1903. Today, it is noted for research in the treatment of arthritis. No priest, soldier, statesman or explorer had left a more heroic record than "The Mother of Lay Nursing in Canada", who many feel was the true founder of Montreal.

Marguerite Bourgeoys, left alone after Maisonneuve had been recalled to France, sought solace in work. Early marriages were encouraged in this era. The youngest bride on record was Marguerite Sedilot, aged 11½, who married Jean Auchubon of Three Rivers in 1654. This marriage was declared null and void — until she was 12. Large families were subsidized by the authorities in New France. In 1670, the government went a step further and fined a father 150 libres ($30) for every unmarried daughter over 16 and son over 20.

When a shipload of one thousand "Filles de Roi" came out as wives for the settlers, Mother Bourgeoys kept them at the convent and taught them housekeeping. With its sign "Filles à Marier" it was North America's first marriage bureau. These brides sought her advice and named their girl babies "Marguerite".

In 1676, Mother Bourgeoys established an industrial school, La Providence, to teach trades to girls. She founded both the Tabernacle Societies and the Society of Perpetual Adoration. Seven schools were founded by her, personally. Now numbering more than 265 Congregations in North America, it is among the richest and most successful orders of teaching nuns in Canada. Marguerite Bourgeoys joined the company of the Saints in 1700 and was beatified in 1950. College Marguerite Bourgeoys in Montreal was named in her honor. Today, a steel skyscraper stands on the site of her log stable. In one corner is a plaque, depicting Mother Bourgeoys with two little girls, one French, the other Indian, enfolded in her motherly arms.

Mohawk Saint

The names of many Indian women are indelibly etched in Canada's history but none more poignantly than a gentle Mohawk maiden, Kateri Tekawitha. Kateri delighted Mother Bourgeoys when she visited her new school at the Congregation of Notre Dame. The young Mohawk had been baptized a Christian on Easter Day

1676, a vow that netted her savage persecution by fellow-Indians. But Kateri persisted in her beliefs. Orphaned early in life and a victim of smallpox which had left her disfigured and half blind, she not only defied her guardian, but also tried to make reparation for the sins of her tribe through fasts and self-scourgings.

On the second Easter of her conversion, she had been admitted to the Confraternity of the Holy Family, a high honor. Learning that Kateri Tekawitha had taken the vow of chastity, almost unheard of for an Indian, Mother Bourgeoys realized that the years of gruelling labor and self-sacrifice seemed suddenly worthwhile. Kateri continued her life of selfless service until her sudden death on April 17, 1680. Years later she was revered and called a saint.

The mighty St. Lawrence Seaway, nearly three centuries after her death, was slightly rerouted in order to avoid disturbing what generations of Roman Catholics have considered holy ground. Earth from her grave was reputed to have power to heal. Friends of a young soldier blinded in Korea sprinkled dust from Kateri's tomb on his bandages. The next day he could see. A woman dying of cancer contributes her overnight cure to Kateri's dust. The monument over her grave at the St. Francis Xavier Mission at Caughnawaga bears the inscription "The fairest flower to bloom among the Indians."

Vastly different but vitally important to our country were the numerous Indian women who were married, sometimes according to the customs of their tribe and sometimes according to the Christian religion, to the adventurers and officers of the Hudson Bay Company and other trading companies who opened up the Canadian West. Had it not been for these women, who understood the living conditions and the medical herbs that grew in the woods, it is doubtful whether these men could have survived the cruel climate and otherwise hostile natives.

Mother d'Youville

Mother d'Youville

Mother d'Youville, born Marie de la Jemmerais in Varennes, Quebec, in 1701, continued the work of the early French pioneers. The daughter of a French officer, whose premature death left the family poor, Marie was educated by her grandfather, the Governor of Three Rivers, who financed her education at the Ursuline Convent in Quebec.

Marie's marriage to fascinating François d'Youville proved less than ideal. Her husband turned out to be a faithless gambler. Marie's fault-finding mother-in-law lived with them. Before her dissipated husband died after eight years of marriage, Marie had already buried four children. She was left with a $30,000 debt and two sons to educate. Her home and possessions were sold at auction.

Madame d'Youville, of necessity, became a business woman, starting a small shop in her home where she sold piece goods, laces, needles and thread. She also took to sewing, to pay off her husband's debts. She gave her sons, both of whom entered the priesthood, an excellent education. After doing voluntary welfare work at l'Hôpital Général, she and Louise Lasource and Mesdemoiselles Demers and Casson rented a small house as a refuge for needy persons. Misfortunes followed fast. First a knee infection incapacitated Madame d'Youville, then fire destroyed their house. But somehow faith never faltered.

In 1747, the administrators of the almost defunct, debt-ridden l'Hôpital Général handed over control to Madame d'Youville. She and her helpers raised money by making candles for the church, and also in less orthodox ways, by a brewery that earned 1,000 crowns a year, a tobacco plant that earned 2,000, and by doing carting for the government. Her hospital was one of the first places in Canada to care for the insane (the nuns sang to soothe violent patients). Early in 1753, Madame d'Youville opened new wards for incurables, orphans, invalided soldiers and fallen women (derisively nicknamed "Jezebels" by the very men responsible for their condition). In 1753, the community was granted a Royal Charter, officially named the Grey Nuns, Sisters of Charity, and Marie d'Youville became Mother d'Youville. She also was responsible for initiating district nursing, since all the other Catholic nursing sisters belonged to cloistered orders.

During the Seven Years' War, food and fuel were pressing problems. The patients always came first. If no food was left, the nuns said simply: "This is fit time for fasting." The sisters cared impartially for wounded, naked Indians, British Redcoats as well as their French compatriots. All called them "Our Good Mothers". Their records show that they smuggled out two English officers garbed in nun's gray habits to save them from being scalped by Indian patients. When many British prisoners were discharged from the hospital, Mother d'Youville organized Canada's first rehabilitation plan.

Despite her many good works, however, some spiteful persons interpreted "Soeurs Grises" as "Drunken Sisters" and whispered that they drank liquor as well as sold it. She once was heartbroken to be refused communion at church, and members of the order were even pelted by stones in the streets.

Walking quickly one bitterly cold day on some errand of mercy, she suddenly stopped horror-stricken. She had almost stumbled over a tiny baby's head, throat cruelly slashed. Mother d'Youville promptly established the Crèche d'Youville in Montreal, the first foundling asylum in North America, where thousands of unwanted waifs have been cared for.

Mother d'Youville, apostle of the poor, once pelted by stones in the streets of Montreal, reviled as a secret tippler, refused communion by the Recollet Fathers, lived to see the name of "Soeurs Grises" respected and revered. She died in 1771 and was beatified in 1959. The Grey Nuns became the most active order of nursing sisters in the hospital field. They now have 32 houses in Canada and hospitals in the United States, the Arctic and as far away as Japan and Africa.

Then and Now

By 1969, Canada had 212 separate orders of Roman Catholic nuns, most of them teachers or nurses. Mother Bourgeoys and her colleagues would have been amazed by the changes in outlook of the tradition-enforcing Catholic Church during the next three centuries, exemplified by the changes in a nun's habit, from sweeping skirts to short dresses — though stopping short of miniskirts! Sister Corona, head of the English Department at Brescia College, London, Ontario, explains: "We used to wear very medieval outfits. Historically, they were worn by a widow. They symbolized that when you entered the monastery, you died to the world and it died to you. Now the symbolism is no longer relevant."

On the Prairies, the Sisters of Service hired Irish couturier Sybil Connely to redesign their black habit to a smart, knee-length dress, with a white collar and a bowler hat. In Toronto, three members of the Institute to the Blessed Virgin Mary work outside Loretto Abbey and wear ordinary dress. One runs the library for the Catholic Information Center, one does youth social work, and the third teaches at York University.

In Edmonton, more surprising still, a Sister of Misericordia has lectured on sex education to Catholic and Protestants alike, passing along what she has learned in running a provincial home for unwed mothers.

Nuns have been defecting more frequently in the past ten years than in any previous decade. Sister Corona calls it: "A general exodus!", explaining that, after World War II, the Catholic Church campaigned to persuade young girls to join the sisterhoods. "They are now in their thirties," she said, "and I think they should leave while they can, while they still have a chance to get married."

However, the work of Marie de l'Incarnation, Madame de la Peltrie, Jeanne Mance, Marguerite Bourgeoys, Mother d'Youville and their helpers laid a firm foundation for white civilization in Canada. From it have branched out all the humanitarian services in religion, education, nursing, and welfare. Their stores of sublime self-sacrifice form a glorious page of Canadian history.

Chapter II

The Conquering Cross

Religion

Barbara Heck

*More things are wrought by prayer
than this world dreams of.*

(Tennyson)

Through the years they have worked quietly, effectively and almost always behind the scenes, the "guardians of life's intangibles". Although many denominations still bar them from the corridors of church power, nevertheless women have become a significant factor in virtually every religion.

In pioneer days, church work was the only socially acceptable activity for women. Ladies' Aids and Guilds were the first organizations. In the United Church, for example, such organizations later grouped to form the United Church Women now numbering well over 200,000, the largest women's organization in Canada.

To raise funds for charity, for church-building campaigns and to help behind the scenes in a hundred different ways — these have been the tradition-bound, acceptable avenues of participation for women of religion, the backbone of the church but seldom the voice from the pulpit. "There has been an anti-women pessimism in the church which goes back to Genesis," says Colleen La Prairie of Elliot Lake, a Roman Catholic mother of seven. "Women can become Prime Ministers but cannot get into the hierarchy of the church." Mrs. La Prairie failed in a 1961 campaign to persuade the Catholic Women's League to sponsor research into the rhythm method of birth control. The CWL's origins are worth recalling. It sprang into existence as a national organization in Montreal, "the city of churches", at a conference in June 1920. "We may be said to be laying the cornerstone of an edifice that will arise fair and beautifully strong and proud before the eyes of the world . . . gentlewomen, but brave soldiers, holding aloft our banner of patriotism to our beloved country and of inviolable fidelity to our glorious faith," first national president Mlle. Bellelle Guerin said at the conference. Miss L.M. Hart became first editor of the CWL magazine *The Canadian League.*

With the early settlement of Quebec, Roman Catholics had a numerical head start on Protestants in the future Canada. For example in 1774, the year of the Quebec Act, there were 150,000 Roman Catholics compared with 360 adherents of Protestantism. Almost two centuries later in 1966, by a slow steady buildup, the Canadian population was split almost evenly with a 50-50 ratio of Roman Catholics to members of the various Protestant denominations.

The roots of Protestantism in this country can be traced back a couple of centuries to lonely log cabins dwarfed by mighty forests. On sunny Sunday afternoons with the husband nearby, relaxing yet warily watching for Indians, the mother would group her children in their Sunday best to recite Bible verses and catechism while the husband led the singing of familiar hymns.

Later as villages were built, the schoolhouse was borrowed for Sunday School classes, usually taught by women, although probably presided over by a male superintendent. Then, one by one small Protestant churches sprang up.

The power of pioneer women was responsible for establishing the then largest Protestant denomination, the Methodist religion in Canada. Barbara Heck transported the Methodist church from Ireland to New York, then to Canada.

Burning the Devil's Prayer Book

One winter evening in New York, in 1761, Barbara and Paul Heck unceremoniously burst into the parlor of her favorite cousin, Philip Embury, just as four players were finishing a pleasant hand of whist. Barbara's floor-length skirts swished ominously as she snatched the cards from Philip's hands, rushed toward the fireplace and threw them onto the burning logs. "Oh, Cousin Philip," she sobbed. "Hell is paved with this kind of folly!" The others stared in astonishment while Paul soothingly patted his wife's shoulder. "I'm sorry Philip," apologized Barbara tremulously as the flickering candelabra shone upon the strange scene. "But it's so discouraging. We still have no church, no services, no worship of any kind. I'm sure Mr. Wesley wouldn't approve of your incessant card-playing."

"Mr. Wesley is too far away to bother about us. Preaching here is impossible."

"That's not true Philip," Barbara pleaded. "We need only a leader. You were a lay preacher in Ireland. Here we are all backsliding. Philip, preach to us again or we shall all go to Hell together!"

Philip shrugged and stood up. "I'm willing, but where? You know we Wesleyan Methodists have no church in New York."

"Then start in your shop," Barbara suggested. "You preach and I'll provide the congregation."

That dramatic 1761 episode planted the seeds of a far-reaching tree of religious development with the establishment of Methodism in the United States and Canada.

The forefathers of Barbara (Ruckle) Heck had fled to Ireland to escape the fury of King Louis XIV of France, an intractable foe of Protestantism. Barbara was born in 1734 at Ballingrane in County Limerick. As a girl of seventeen she was inspired by the impassioned

preaching of John Wesley who persuaded her to dedicate her life to Christ.

Soon after, she married another Wesleyan convert, Paul Heck. The Methodists met in fields, barns,
homes, wherever people would listen. They placed great
stress upon repentance. Although based upon the 39
Articles of the Church of England, conventional Angli-
cans disapproved of this revivalist type of religion. In
1760 the Hecks, with Barbara's cousin, Philip Embury,
and his wife, Margaret, migrated to New York.

A fully committed Methodist, Barbara naturally
considered card-playing sinful, equally as bad as playing violins (associated with merriment and dancing) in a
church. Concern for the spiritual decline of her cousin
Philip had resulted in her outburst.

Philip did accept her challenge and held the first
service in his small shop with Paul and Barbara Heck,
their Negro maid Betty, Mary Embury, and John
Lawrence, a family friend, as his first congregation. This
was the nucleus of the mighty Methodist Society of
America. More and more colonists came as news of
Philip's preaching spread.

Within seven years the congregation, which by
then included several British soldiers and John Adams
(later second U.S. President), became large enough to
justify the building of a small stone Wesleyan chapel.
Barbara whitewashed the walls herself. John Wesley
sent his best wishes and gifts of money, books and a
large clock. On October 30, 1768 Philip Embury
preached the dedication sermon. The following year
John Wesley sent over several itinerant preachers to
help spread the gospel and by 1773 there were 10 Methodist ministers in the New World — enough to warrant
the first conference.

Philip Embury died before the American Revolution broke out in 1775. Not wishing to support the rebels,
the peace-loving Hecks and Philip's wife, Margaret,

made their way to Lower Canada after angry rebel-supporting neighbors had burned the Hecks' home and stolen their cattle. The trip by boat was long and dangerous with the fear of attack en route by either Indians or rebels. Safely landed in Montreal the Loyalists first lived in tents. Though dedicated to non-violence, Paul decided to join the Loyalist side. "If fight I must, I shall fight for the old flag."

In Loyalist families it was a cold and lonely winter for the women and children far from their army, encamped in deep snow outside Quebec desperately trying to hold off the rebels. Finally, on May Day, the lookout cried: "A sail! A sail!" and rescue ships of the British Navy were loudly cheered. Men hugged each other and burst into hymns of joy. After Paul's discharge from the army (the yellowed copy of his discharge papers is in the Archives of Victoria College in Toronto) the Hecks moved to the village of Maynard near the St. Lawrence. Paul Heck and sons hewed a home from the forest. Margaret Embury had married John Lawrence and lived nearby. The Methodists gathered to worship in the Heck home and later in a barn. Meanwhile Barbara organized the Methodist Society.

Life in their adopted country was simple to the extreme. Mrs. Heck made rag carpets, hooked rugs and knit the family stockings. Social life consisted mainly of sewing bees and birthday and Christmas celebrations. Guests were always warmly received. One sultry summer evening in 1790 a weary horseman, William Lossee, the first ordained Methodist minister in Upper Canada was a welcome sight. Before dismounting he asked Paul: "Tell me first, will you warn the neighbors of the preaching?" "Aye, we will, near and far!" Paul promised gladly. After supper everyone gathered in the parlor to discuss plans for gaining converts in this new locale. There was also quite a settlement of Quakers with whom they were on friendly terms.

Later the first Methodist meeting-house in Upper

Barbara Heck's Monument

Canada was built at nearby Hay Bay, Adolphustown.
Paul Heck died in 1792, as had earlier two of the Heck
daughters. Tired from her labors, Barbara peacefully
passed away in 1804 sitting in her favorite rocking chair,
her old German Bible on her lap. In the church in Ballingrane, Ireland, a marble plaque commemorates her
birthplace and Heck Hall, a memorial built in the Garrett Biblical Institute at Evanston, Illinois, honors her
U.S. work. In the churchyard of the Old Blue Church
near Prescott stands her Centennial monument with the
inscription:

*In memory of one who laid founda-
tions others have built upon. Barbara Heck pitted her brave soul
against the rugged possibilities of
the future and, under God, brought
into existence American and Canadian Methodism, and between these
two her memory will ever form a
most hallowed bond.*

Eventually Methodism became the largest Protestant denomination in Canada. In 1925, its 400,000 adherents joined with the Congregationalists and most of the
Presbyterians to form the United Church of Canada.

Baptist Workers

Woman power proved a hardy element in developing the Baptist movement in Canada. For example, in
1828 six Baptist women trekked 50 weary miles to Wolfville, N.S. to attend a meeting and vote for the formation
of Horton Academy, which became Acadia University.
Some years later in 1867, the first unmarried woman
missionary, Miss Minnie de Wolfe, was sent by Maritime Baptists to Burma. More recently women are filling
high offices. Mrs. Ivan Milne of Ottawa served as first
vice-president of the General Baptist Convention of
Ontario and Quebec. In 1953, Mrs. J. R. MacDonald was
elected president of the Baptist Union of Western
Canada. The Baptist Church has no law which prohibits
the ordination of women. The first, Rev. Muriel Spur-
geon, B.A., B.D., was ordained in 1947 and went to India
as a missionary. One Canadian woman, Mrs. J. Edgar
Bates, R.N., D.C.L., LL.D., feels her most significant contribution to the movement was in strengthening the
organization of Baptist women around the world into
Continental Unions. She visited all six Continental
Unions of the Baptist world alliance between June 1967
and June 1968.

Dean of Women at McMaster University from 1945 to 1965, Mrs. Bates was elected president of the Baptist Women of the World 1960-1970.

Missionary Zeal

No examination of Canada's women of religion could fail to note the missionary movement which moved into high gear in the 19th century with the establishment of the first society, The Female Society for the Propagation of the Gospel. In 1846, Mr. and Mrs. John Geddis became the first missionaries sent from Canada to the New Hebrides by the Presbyterian Church of Nova Scotia.

The Mounties may know how to "get their man" but a woman, Mrs. George McDougall, had a head start on them in the west. In 1862, a full 12 years before the RCMP built a mission near Edmonton at Victoria, practical Mrs. McDougall, wife of the first Protestant missionary sent to the northern wilds of Alberta, nursed the Indians and in 1866 organized the first women's missionary society in Canada, giving the squaws sewing and cooking lessons as well as religious instruction. Until their cabin was built, she and Mr. McDougall roughed it in a tepee. After her husband died in a raging Alberta blizzard, she became one of the first women to homestead in the province.

Such women with little or no specialized training were quiet, vital links to religious development in those early years. Much later it was realized that the wives needed more formal training for their role as ministerial helpmates. Today, for example, wives of ministers may take a preparation course at Union College in British Columbia. As with social work, women who decide to become full-time church workers now back up their intentions with professional training. Miss Helen Turnbull, director of national graduate training for women of the Episcopal Church, before becoming associate secretary of the World Council of Churches explained: "Our department is trying to break down some of the prejudices and traditional barriers against women. Society is impaired if either men or women are excluded."

In the Church of Christ (Disciples) any office, local, provincial or national, is open to women. A woman has been chairman of the National Board for four years and women are eligible to be ordained for the ministry. All overseas missionaries are ordained ministers.

YWCA Expansion

With no irreverence intended, the Canadian branch of the Young Women's Christian Association was inaugurated in Pagan Place. Not long after the YWCA had been founded in England in 1855, a Saint John, N.B. woman, Agnes Blizzard wrote: "A few friends anxious to undertake some definite welfare work gathered at my home, Pagan Place, and decided to start a YWCA. We fixed up two rooms comfortably, made weekly visits to the jail and hospital, started a home for girls and held a weekly prayer meeting."

After the second YWCA was organized in Toronto in 1873, the movement spread rapidly. Its principal aim, to provide Christian home surroundings for girls away from home, remains the same today. Numerous educational and social services were initiated by the YWCA. Its missionary wing came later. One outstanding worker, Caroline Macdonald of Wingham, Ont., became national YWCA secretary for Canada, soon after her graduation from the University of Toronto.

In February, 1903, this attractive intelligent young woman set out for Tokyo as the first YWCA worker in Japan. Enchanted by Japan's pink cherry blossoms, picturesque teahouses, gaily flowered kimonos and colorful lanterns, she was equally appalled by the grim poverty.

In Kobe, confronted by a hostile crowd of 2,000 striking workers, Caroline spoke at the invitation of Japanese labor leaders. Addressing the crowd from a precarious roof-top perch, she talked philosophically about divine love and the ultimate triumph of justice rather than about specific worker grievances. Calmed by her words, the men shuffled back to work. This was one of a number of almost miraculous accomplishments that won Caroline the title "White Angel" among the Japanese.

With $10,000 donated by the Canadian YWCA, she built dormitories for oppressed Japanese factory girls and spread the word of Christianity among prisoners, converting many and comforting all — even prisoners in death row. As her programs of visits gained momentum, prison governors sent her official invitations.

One of her most notable converts was Takish Ishii, a triple-murderer who had been Japan's Enemy Number One. Caroline helped him write a book, *A Rascal Becomes a Saint,* which aroused great interest in prison work and probably influenced Caroline's decision to devote her life to helping criminals. In 1915 she resigned her paid position with the YWCA to work full-time in prisoner rehabilitation.

Soon afterwards "without a sou to my name", as she admitted, Caroline bought a large, expensive house which she called "The House of Friendliness". It became a refuge for prisoners' families as well as for prisoners themselves during their rehabilitation period. She helped more than 7,000 prisoners. It also served as a school for factory girls.

A wealthy New York philanthropist rescued Caroline from financial disaster by providing her with a salary. Donations from friends and missionary societies paid for the house itself. The doors were never locked, as a Canadian visitor nervously noticed one evening before retiring. "What's the use?" Caroline said with a knowing laugh. "There are five burglars sleeping upstairs."

"My work thrives on calamities. Japan is a country of calamities, both natural and manufactured," she wrote to friends.

When the tremendous shock waves of the 1923 Japanese earthquake almost demolished Tokyo, Caroline luckily escaped, although her home was badly shaken. The chimney had fallen across the driveway preventing her from getting out her car which was badly needed for rescue work. The streetcar system was in chaos but dozens of ex-convicts walked miles to her home to check on her safety. Honors were showered upon her. The Japanese department of justice presented her with an engraved gold cup bearing the Imperial crest, a golden chrysanthemum.

When the new emperor was crowned, silver cups "For Distinguished Service" were presented to six foreigners — one of them Miss Macdonald. The delegate from Japan to the International Labor Conference in Geneva requested that Miss Macdonald act as his interpreter and adviser. Her Alma Mater conferred on Caroline the first honorary LL.D. ever given a woman. Felled by an incurable disease in 1931, the "White Angel" returned home to die. She was succeeded by Miss Emma Kaufman of Kitchener, whose mother had been president of the YWCA in that city.

Miss Kaufman helped rebuild and reorganize the Tokyo YWCA which had been destroyed by the 1923 earthquake. After returning home, she helped finance the national YWCA headquarters built in Toronto in 1941. As a member of the world executive of the "Y", she represented Canada at several international meetings. A bronze bust honoring Miss Kaufman was unveiled in the Tokyo YWCA in 1952.

Helping Hand

The Salvation Army has been called the "fluorescent hand shining in the basements of despair". And as often as not that fluorescent hand has been a woman's. Since the Army was founded in England in 1865 by General William Booth women have functioned in complete equality with men waging a war on vice, poverty and despair.

With comparatively few paid officers, the Salvation Army has from the first relied on volunteer workers to take the church to the people, to jails, hospitals, slums, wherever people were in need of help.

General Booth's daughter, Gen. Evangeline Booth, an eloquent orator, became the Army's Commissioner for Canada.

Another woman, Major Blanche Read, known as "The Lady with the Other Lamp" is credited with founding Grave Maternity Hospital in Winnipeg.

Lutie Desbrisay was the first woman colonel in the Salvation Army. Born in Charlottetown, P.E.I., and trained at the Salvation Army Officers' Training College at Saint John, N.B. she was commissioned to Amherst, N.S. In 1896 she successfully organized mission work in Bermuda, gaining more than 500 converts. Later, she organized hospitals in Ottawa, London, Windsor, Halifax, Montreal, and St. John's, Nfld.

During World War I, Major Frances Wagner ran the Maple Leaf Club, where she gave English war brides information about living conditions in Canada and taught them first aid and home nursing. She and her husband later were in charge of the Booth Memorial Home for Children in Calgary. Two of the Salvation Army's national departments in Toronto have been headed by women, the Home League by Brig. Ethel Burnell and the League of Mercy by Col. C. Wiseman. Salvation Army women also command corps, direct

evangelical operationals, and have authority to baptize
babies and conduct weddings and funerals, bearing out
the principle of equality that has held true throughout
the years.

Religion or Circus?

Then there was that one-woman army, Aimee
Semple MacPherson, so volatile she almost defies cate-
gorization. Was she a purveyor of true religion or a one-
woman circus? Even today mention her name and you
can expect a range of responses — most of them con-
tradictory.

Born in Ingersoll, Ontario, the beautiful and
controversial Aimee had taken up evangelism by the age
of seventeen. She toured North America in a rattletrap
car, speaking first to skeptical crowds in tents and living
on the proceeds of hat-passing.

With her brass-colored hair contrasting with
flowing Grecian white robes, she held thousands spellbound, preaching on street corners and in tents, wherever people would listen. Immensely popular by 1922, her
admirers honored Aimee with the Angelus Temple in
Los Angeles. Said to be the most beautiful church in
North America, it was built at a cost of $1,250,000 — the
only church in the world without a mortgage. Flamboyant Aimee founded the International Church of the
Four-Square Gospel which stressed divine healing and
the second coming of Christ. She also owned a radio station, published a weekly religious paper and wrote several books including an autobiography, *The Story of My
Life*. Married three times, she was mysteriously "ab-
ducted" at one point in her flashy career and her
credibility with her admirers was never quite restored.

Conquering The Peak

Drama certainly, but no such element of flamboy-
ance, surrounds those few women who have managed

to reach the last bastion of church power — the pulpit.

For those first women such as Lydia Gruchy, who dared to dream of preaching a sermon from the pulpit of their own church, the path was a perpetual obstacle course all the way.

Dr. Lydia Gruchy

When her beloved brother Arthur, ready for ordination in the ministry, was killed in battle during World War I, Lydia Gruchy dedicated her life to carrying on his work. Similarly, another sister, Florence, became a nurse-missionary in India. Lydia graduated in Arts in 1920 from the University of Saskatchewan with the Governor-General's Gold Medal. Encouraged by the principal, the Rt. Rev. Dr. Oliver, she went on to graduate in Theology from St. Andrew's College, Saskatoon, heading the class of 1923.

Born of English parents near Paris, France, in 1894, Miss Gruchy was one of ten children. When she was eighteen the family migrated to the Canadian West where after graduation she worked first among Western Canada's 12,000 Doukhobors, influencing the parents through their children, and wrote a book entitled *Doukhobors*. One of the Doukhobors' most controversial characters, 230-pound Florence Storgoff, "Big Fanny", led the sect's Sons of Freedom splinter-group in nude protest marches in these early days.

Much of Miss Gruchy's early ministry was among New Canadians, where she used her ability as a linguist to good advantage. Her work took her to Veregin, Kelvinston and WaKaw where she performed all the difficult work of a minister but was barred from administering the sacrament or conducting marriage services. For these, a male colleague had to be imported at great inconvenience and expense.

Tiny Lydia Gruchy clearly refutes the argument that women are not physically strong enough for the ministry. After one day's driving over the rough roads endured daily by Miss Gruchy, Right Rev. James Endicott, then Moderator of the United Church, reported complete exhaustion. Neither the searing heat of prairie sun nor the bone-chilling cold of winter blizzards ever kept the little minister from her duty. When cars, sleighs and horseback failed she would call a western winter taxi — a snowplane equipped with skis. One evening she was the only person who managed to get to the service. Often she would have to start the church stove before donning her black gown to deliver a powerful sermon.

Miss Gruchy's first request for ordination in 1926 was refused although she had served in seven preaching appointments and five Sunday Schools. Two years later, when the General Council of the United Church passed a resolution stating: "There is no bar in reason or religion to the ordination of women in the United

Church of Canada", it was harder to justify the refusal of her second request. However, she found that prejudice died hard. A man applying, who had little education and no theological training whatever, was granted almost automatic ordination. So Miss Gruchy persisted. Every two years she patiently reapplied and requests flooded in from colleagues and members of her various congregations.

Finally the matter was referred to the Presbyteries and General Council revised the United Church manual to allow women to be ordained as ministers of the gospel. In 1936, Lydia Gruchy was ordained in St. Andrew's Church in Moose Jaw, as assistant minister to the Rev. Geoffrey Glover. Among hundreds of congratulatory messages on her unique victory were some disapproving ones. One man wrote: "St. Paul clearly stated in Corinthians 'Let your women keep silent in the church' ". She quoted right back: "Galatians 3:28 'There is neither male nor female, for ye are all one in Christ Jesus!"

Taking one of thirteen vacant charges in Saskatchewan which no man wanted because they were considered hardship postings, Miss Gruchy in 1952 became pastor of the United Church in Cupar, Saskatchewan. Five years later she was called to Neville, where she looked after three small towns and finally had the luxury of running water in the manse. In 1953 her Alma Mater awarded her the honorary degree of Doctor of Divinity, the first ever conferred on a Canadian woman. She retired in 1962, having trod a path which any woman would be proud to follow.

Merry Minister

Kathleen Christopher, United Church minister in Val d'Or, is a clever, studious woman with a zest for life, who enjoys Beethoven and Bach and curling up with a good theology or psychology book. Miss Christopher admits: "In my mid-thirties I felt the lack of children very strongly . . . but that period of my life is over." She thinks a woman minister must be self-possessed and strong. A total extrovert, she has been known to drop in for an impromptu dinner with neighbors in jeans. Miss Christopher now occupies a senior post in the United Church — president of the Toronto Conference.

Career Versus Cradle

Hope Jackson is a United Church minister in Kingston, N.S. while her husband, Arthur, presides at the nearby Aylesford United Church. In the Kingston parsonage, it's liable to be confusing when someone calls to ask for "The Minister". As with other women in the ministry, Hope's ambition is service to others and she willingly accepts her heavy responsibilities. Feeling that marriage presents enough problems for a woman minister, she and her husband (a widower, with grown children by his first marriage) decided to forego a family. Ordained in 1966, Mrs. Jackson says: "I live the most wonderful life in two worlds."

* * *

Since Dr. Gruchy's pathfinding a number of ordained United Church ministers, including Rev. Anne Graham, have performed marriage ceremonies and administered the sacrament on countless occasions. Dr. Graham says with a smile she has no time for romance, although she has married more than 100 couples — all perfectly legal ceremonies.

Apropos marriage legality, it is interesting to recall that before 1831 any marriage performed by clergymen of dissenting sects, such as Methodists, was not considered legal under Upper Canada legislation. This was because the Church of England enjoyed privileges of a state church, although membership was in the minority. A Royal Pew (the only one in any church in the Western Hemisphere) is in the Anglican Cathedral of Quebec.

In 1952 the Anglican Church, the only church other than Roman Catholic to have religious Orders, gave women the right to be elected as lay members to the Diocesan Synod and made them eligible for an appointment to committees. Hilda Hennaby was the first Canadian woman to receive a licentiate in theology and an honorary Doctor of Divinity degree from Vancouver's Anglican Theological College.

Thus, in ever-widening fields and in varying degrees in different denominations, women have come to play an increasingly important role in church work. In December 1954, thirteen year old Rena Slonim of Toronto became the first Jewish woman to read from the Torah Scroll in the seventy year old history of Beth Tzedec Congregations. In March 1957 for the first time, members of Holy Blossom Sisterhood in Toronto participated in the ritual of the Sabbath service assisting the Rabbi. However, a movement to have women appointed as rabbis is so far unsuccessful. Miss Betty Graham of Toronto in 1969 was elected first woman deputy prolocutor of the General Synod. She defeated Arnold Edinborough, publisher of *Saturday Night*, to attain this office.

Hard-line suffragettes used to maintain: "Pray hard enough to the Lord, and *SHE* will answer your prayers!" However, by 1969, Canada had fewer than 75 women ministers — one Presbyterian, three Baptists, and the remainder from the United Church.

Shirley Jeffrey of Englehart, is Canada's first Presbyterian minister. She proved very empathetic — kind but serious — when three parishioners died soon after her arrival. Women ministers often find they have difficulty breaking down the barriers of formality and Shirley Jeffrey is no exception. One of the elders in her church, Ernie Smith, always insists on calling Shirley "Miss Jeffrey", saying: "She's the minister, and she's senior to me."

Most women come to the ministry by way of

teaching. Often attractive, few of them marry because as one said ruefully: "Men don't make passes at their pastor." Carolyn Palmer, a Baptist minister in Truro, N.S. notes: "You're the minister and many people — men and women — never get beyond that barrier to know you." Cheerful Carolyn, the antithesis of a "gloomy Baptist", loves psychedelic colors for her car.

Neither the Lutheran nor the Church of England admitted women to the Ministry of the Word and Sacraments until recently. The Anglican Church, however, did make an exception in the case of Mrs. Goldwin (Nancy) Smith. On Sunday, September 25, 1955, at the morning service at St. John's Anglican Church in York Mills, Mrs. Smith was presented with her academic hood, the symbol of theological degree — a long 16 years after she had passed her final examinations at Wycliffe College. On a later occasion, the suitable subject of her sermon was "Mission in Life", a phrase that aptly describes all the women who have written a page in Canada's religious story.

Pamela Joe McGee, 29, of Kitchener, Ontario was ordained as Canada's first female Lutheran pastor.

The decision to ordain women, taken by the Canadian General Synod in 1973, was finally passed by the Anglican Church's House of Bishops in June 1976. This was vitally important to two women who, as girls, wanted positions in the public eye. Elspeth Alley longed to go to Toronto Conservatory and be a pianist, and Virginia Briant, though terribly shy, wanted to be an actress.

Elspeth's father was an atheist, and her mother "fed up with the church" so deeply religious Elspeth attended church services alone. She married a highly successful lawyer, and waited until she had a husband, three children, four dogs and five tanks of fish before attending theological college.

She found her reception there shocking. She was

not allowed to eat in the dining-room. The first day, a man student said: "For every day you are in this institution, I am going to make your life as miserable as I possibly can." After passing her Christmas exams, Elspeth quit. But, as she said, "God nagged me" and in eighteen months she returned and finished. She didn't consider becoming a deacon until 1970, nor a priest even then.

Virginia had also married and raised two sons, and was a successful businesswoman. Her college career was less difficult, but men students resented her becoming a deacon. Her special concerns are healing services, whereas Elspeth was more interested in counselling young people about to be married.

On November 30, 1976, they and four other women made history by being ordained priests in the Anglican Church of Canada, in Christ Church Cathedral, with Archbishop Somerville officiating.

In an ordination ceremony, there is a part somewhat similar to a marriage service, where the Bishop asks: "Any of you who knoweth any impediment or notable crime in any candidate to come forward." To everyone's astonishment, one man *did*. Rev. James Penrice, rector of St. David's parish in Vancouver. He read a petition objecting to the ordination of women who, he said "by nature and by biology did not qualify." Archbishop Somerville replied: "I know there are those who are wounded by this and who oppose it, and that I am sorry for." The dissident rector angrily rushed out the back door, as joy again reigned in the congregation where many cried for happiness. This ordination ceremony of women was the most dramatic development in the history of their Church since the Reformation, when King Henry VIII took his clergy from the grip of Rome and established the Church of England.

Devout and dedicated is glamorous, red-haired Eveline Gilstorf, with her Irish wit. She served as executive director of the Canadian Interfaith Conference. Eve

(Mrs. Reginald), former fashion model, figure skater, Registrar of Nursing, Civic Hospital, director of women's activities for the Canadian Highway Safety Council, and liaison officer to the Canadian Centenary Council, gladly accepted this challenging position. Projects of the Conference included an official multi-denominational Centennial Hymn, music by Rex Le Lecheur, sung by his choir, an anthology of common prayer and special commemorative services on New Year's Day, July 1, Canada's birthday, and Thanksgiving Day.

Mrs. Gilstorf sees this Conference not only as an ecumenical body which brought together 35 different faiths to co-ordinate religious activities during our action-packed Centennial, but as "a stepping-stone to inter-faith union". Her Committee sent out 22,000 complete kits to religious leaders in Canada. At the historic ceremonies on July 1, Her Majesty, Queen Elizabeth, was present as an observer. She was so impressed that she had arranged a special interfaith service at Westminster Abbey, attended by former Rabbi Levy Becker of Montreal, Conference board chairman.

Mrs. Gilstorf was awarded the Centennial Medal, and in 1975 she received an award for excellence, an honorable mention, by the Ottawa Public Relations Society for her Queensway-Carleton Hospital Project.

Another dedicated woman, Miss Bessie MacMurchy, half a century earlier, in collaboration with the Women's Missionary Society, organized the first World Day of Prayer, held on the first Friday in Lent. From a mere handful of Protestant women, this developed into a powerhouse of prayer. Under the sponsorship of the National Women's Inter-Church Council, World Day of Prayer is now observed in over 142 countries throughout the world, with women praying for understanding and peace, irrespective of their denomination — for all church spires point toward Heaven.

Chapter III

Moulders of the Mind

Education

Dr. Helen Stewart

60

> *From the immature beings in class-*
> *rooms, every teacher must mould*
> *future citizens . . . it is our privilege*
> *as well as our duty to encourage our*
> *pupils to develop the God-given tal-*
> *ents bestowed upon them.*
> (Sister St. Raymond Martyr, C.N.D.)

Women's march from ladle to lectern was a slow one in Canadian history, but the growth of educational facilities was scarcely faster. Under the early French regime, teachers were not allowed to instruct pupils of the opposite sex. Today the public school educational system is co-educational, with provincial rather than federal jurisdiction. Dr. C.F. Cannon, former director of education for Ontario said sarcastically:

"We spend a lot of money on education today, almost as much as on cosmetics, not quite as much as on cigarettes, and a lot less than on liquor!"

Women's first struggle was to gain a place in the classroom — to get themselves educated. This done, they found an MRS. more respected than a Ph.D., so the next battle was to earn a place in academia. Again success followed hard work. As new goals loomed, women rallied, gathered their slates as well as their skirts and struck out, this time scoring individual achievements. Some established schools, often initiating radical courses for their time, some changed curricula, others founded libraries. Women were attributed with educational accomplishments as early as the ninth century in Fez, where Moroccans claim two women founded the world's first university.

In Canada many centuries later, the Maritimes' Grace Ann Lockhart received a Bachelor of Science degree from Mount Allison University, becoming the first woman in the British Empire to receive a degree openly. (Dr. Barry had received a medical degree from Edinburgh University in 1812, disguised as a man.)

First Canadian woman to receive a Bachelor of Arts degree was Harriet Stewart Starr, another alumna of Mount Allison. There was no cap, gown or platform for this pioneer when she graduated in 1882.

When a friend asked: "Did they just hand you your sheepskin?" Miss Stewart replied: "It would be more nearly correct to say that they threw it at me."

In 1878 Queen's University admitted women. In 1884, nine women enrolled at University of Toronto. The same year, eight graduates of Montreal Girls' School applied for admission to McGill University. Two, Grace Ritchie and Rosa McLean, passed with higher marks than any men students, but scholastic brilliance did not eradicate the old prejudices. It was left to Lord Strathcona to facilitate the opening of special university classes for women at McGill with a generous gift of $120,000.

Reforms Follow

"Life is a sort of spendid torch — and I want to make it burn as brightly as possible, before handing it on to future generations," said Dr. Aletta Marty, one of many educational reformers to emerge in the last century.

Born in Mitchell, Ontario, in 1866, Aletta steeped herself in languages, aided by her French-Swiss father and German-Swiss mother. When her older brother asked her to substitute for him at a large, ungraded rural school, Aletta put her hair up, let her skirts down and embarked on her life-long career, teaching by day, studying by night.

A graduate of Queen's, 1894, she taught French and German in high schools in St. Thomas and Ottawa where her methods became a model for Ontario, and she wrote several books on teaching methodology. Her record of achievements is impressive, yet her campaign and the philosophy behind it bear resemblance to that of other women such as Dr. Ada Courtice. Indeed, it was Mrs. Courtice who was her staunchest ally when she faced opposition to her nomination for public school inspector in Toronto. She got the post in 1919.

Dr. Marty urged equality of opportunity and wanted women to enter public life. She was president of the Canadian Home and School Federation, 1927-28. Tragedy struck when Dr. Marty and her sister, Sophia, went to West Rand Circuit, South Africa, as exchange teachers in 1928. Dr. Marty died there a year later and Sophia died en route home. Queen's Alumnae Association honors their memory with a $1,400, Marty Memorial Scholarship.

Another Queen's graduate was Dr. Wilhemina Gordon, who raised $25,000 for the Marty Memorial Scholarship as convener of the alumnae scholarship committee. The daughter of Daniel M. Gordon, principal of Queen's from 1902 to 1917, Wilhemina, wrote her father's biography and became one of the university's first full-time professors, lecturing in English and coaching the girls' hockey team.

Courageous Crusader

"Aunt Hessie" as she was affectionately called, had a strange assortment of pupils, including several homeless vagrants, and some jail birds. When years of pleas by Inspector J. L. Hughes to the Toronto Board of Education for a classroom for delinquents finally brought action in 1880, he chose youthful, pretty Hester How to teach them. Enrolment was 77 by the end of the first year.

Older boys often had to bring babies to school, as their mothers were charwomen. This prompted Miss How to open the first crèche on Emma Street, with a small grant. It later became the Victoria Street Crèche and was the forerunner of Toronto's nursery and day care centres. By 1890 she had 96 pupils, aged three to seventeen, necessitating a move from their church basement to Elizabeth Street School, where Miss How became principal.

Enlisting the help of fellow-citizens, she introduced free dental services, household science and manual training classes. Teachers administered first aid if necessary. In case of serious illness, children were sent to nearby Hospital for Sick Children, in this era before the development of public health nursing services. Miss How also arranged farm summer holidays, thus really initiating Fresh Air Camps. It was among her "bad boys" that she organized the first Anti-Tobacco League branch. Although her classes were surprisingly successful, Toronto still had about 5,000 incorrigible boys and girls. The Truancy Act, passed in 1891, required all children to attend school until the age of fourteen. By regularly taking her problem cases to the judge's chambers at City Hall for help, Miss How was indirectly responsible for the establishment of Toronto Juvenile Court.

In 1912, a new school was built and special classes were initiated — the senior sight-saving class, a speech and hearing clinic, dental and orthodontal clinics, classes for new Canadian Chinese, and a diabetes clinic, unique in Canada. Toronto's most Metropolitan school represented 30 different nationalities. Named the Hester How School, in later years it was torn down and forms part of the site of the latest Hospital for Sick Children, a fate its principal would have probably approved.

Another Pioneer

Edith L. Groves, born in Cornwall, England, was educated in Toronto, and married William E. Groves. A teacher also, her interest in underprivileged children — especially retarded girls — led her to pioneer in this field. She was the first woman chairman of Toronto Board of Education. Her book *The Kingdom of Childhood* was published in 1927, the year of her death. Edith L. Groves School is her memorial.

* * *

Sarah Maxwell, a woman of finely-developed maternal instinct, was principal of Hochelaga School in Montreal. When a terrible fire broke out and spread with devastating speed on a bitter February day in 1907, she managed to save most of her little charges, but died herself in the fiery, smoke-filled inferno. A subscription of $10,000 was raised and used to endow a wing in the Montreal Children's Hospital, in her memory. The Protestant School Commission rebuilt the school, with modern safety devices, and renamed it Sarah Maxwell School.

Home and School Founder

Although more famous for inventing the telephone, Alexander Graham Bell scored another point in history as the organizer of the first parents' club in Baddeck, N.S. However, he was edged out by Ontario's Mrs. Ada Courtice, who is credited with developing the idea of home and school associations on a national scale in Canada.

Born in 1860 in Bloomfield, Ontario, of Quaker parents, Ada (Brown) Courtice excelled in studies, sports and — much to the chagrin of her strict Quaker father — music. Ada's mother, noticing her little girl's keen love of music, spent her savings to buy her an organ. "Thee must have music lessons," she realized.

Disapproving at first, Ada's father realizing how much innocent pleasure music gave his daughter, added a piano to the house.

Ada Courtice

Music proved an avenue to marriage for Ada, after she completed her studies at Whitby Ladies' College. A voice and piano teacher, she also played the organ at a Methodist Church in Toronto. It may have been the music or, more likely, Ada's striking good looks, but the minister, Dr. Andrew Courtice, was so captivated he became Ada's most devoted listener. Each Friday after choir practice, he would wait with his spanking team of horses to drive her home. They were married in 1888. Their frequent moves gave the young wife ample opportunity to compare the different school systems.

With a close friend, Mrs. James Hughes, an outstanding kindergarten teacher, Ada studied child psychology and other modern educational trends, and developed some innovative theories on the teaching of French, art, and physical education. Her only daughter, Adabell, taught this new subject and later, as Mrs. Colin Campbell, was elected president of the national Home and School Association. Frequently, Mrs. Courtice invited parents in to talk over problems.

A visit to the parent-teacher headquarters in Boston in 1912 roused in Mrs. Courtice a dream for a similar organization in Canada. As convener of the education committee of the Local Council of Women in 1914, she was a delegate to the International Council of Women convention in Holland. "I came home with a new impetus for public service." That same year she was nominated, but lost her bid, for Board of Education. In February she organized an important meeting with Mrs. A.M. Huestis as chairman, which resulted in the formation of the Toronto Home and School Council. Mrs. Courtice was elected president, with Mrs. Newton Mac-Tavish vice-president, and her ever-willing assistant. In 1917, Mrs. Courtice closed her school, ran for Board of Education and won. She introduced progressive measures, such as kindergarten and domestic science, but opposed cadet training.

When the Ontario Federation of Home Associations was formed in 1919 Mrs. Courtice became organizing secretary. She died in 1923, but the Courtice memorial slides and library honor and recall her work in contemporary times.

* * *

Maritime history abounds with examples of women who have contributed to the development of education. Six hundred dollars raised by lottery, financed Nova Scotia's first public school in 1780. Throughout settled Canada in pioneer times, tiny schools were financed by students' fees while teacher became a "floating" boarder at the homes of their parents.

A tutor or governess taught the children of wealthy New Brunswick settlers. Elsewhere the usual teaching method was to have advanced pupils instruct the younger ones, called the Madras system. Several Maritime teachers merit attention for their pioneer work in education.

Canada's most famous governess, Anna Leonowens ("Anna" of *The English Governess at the Court of Siam)* used her influence to have 1,000,000 slaves liberated. Few who enjoyed the fanciful musical version of Anna's career in *The King and I* realize that she lived in Halifax 1878-1897, then in Montreal until her death.

Martha Hamm Lewis of Saint John, N.B., was repeatedly refused admission on applying to the provincial Normal School. Her final appeal to the Lieutenant-Governor was successful, but required an order-in-council. In 1850 Martha achieved a teacher's license for Upham parish and for Saint John in 1854, on condition that she always wear a veil and never speak to a male student.

Martha married Alexander Peters. Fifty years later their daughter, Mabel Peters, established the first free kindergarten in Saint John, headed the movement for compulsory education and inaugurated the first public playground for children in Canada.

The pinnacle of Mary Electa Adam's career was her post as principal at Ontario Ladies' College in Whitby. But this U.E.L. descendant had other accomplishments as well.

Born in Westbury, Que., in 1823, she was educated by her parents until age seven, when she was sent to Montpelier School in Vermont, to Ladies' Seminary, Cobourg, Ont., later graduating from an American College with the degree of M.L.A. (Mistress of Liberal Arts). In the early 1850's she became first women's director at

Mount Allison University, Sackville, N.B., and was appointed president of Wesleyan Ladies' College in Hamilton, Ont. in 1861.

Half a century of hard-working battalions of educational suffragettes were needed before the last placard could finally be closeted away for good. Dr. Marty confronted the crisis back in 1894; Dr. Courtice, Anna Leonowens and Mary Adams held ranks; and botanist Carrie Derick led the final charge, in 1912, when she became the first woman professor at a Canadian university.

Of Loyalist ancestry, Carrie was born in 1862 at Clarenceville, Quebec. She won the Prince of Wales Medal at Normal School, graduated from McGill in 1890, winning prizes in classics, zoology, and botany, and the Logan gold medal. In 1895, she took an advanced course in cryptogamic botany at the Marine Biological Station. Appointed a lecturer in botany at McGill, she earned her M.A. in 1896. Dr. Derick often gave expert advice in law writs concerning dry rot in construction lumber.

Dr. Derick was keenly interested in the study of exotic plant names and was a prolific writer. Describing the position of women in the professions in a chapter she wrote for the Canadian Government's official volume at the 1900 Paris Exposition, Dr. Derick noted: "In Canada, elementary education is almost exclusively in the hands of women . . . collegiate education in the hands of men, conditions unfair to the development of the child . . . Women have almost no voice in the decisions which shape the course of higher education, even for their own sex."

In 1912, she became the first woman in Canada to significantly "shape the course of higher education", being appointed a full professor after having served as assistant professor of botany at McGill from 1904. However, when Professor David Pearce Penhallow died, Dr. Derick was not given his chair.

She was elected Fellow of the Botanical Society

of America and a member of the American Association for the Advancement of Science. Her witty lectures on civic reform and botany kept her in demand as a speaker. As president of the Montreal Suffrage Association from 1913 to 1919, she urged that domestic service be given the status of a profession and wanted women to pursue careers in agriculture.

Professor Derick died in 1941. Her portrait, painted by Minna Keene, F.R.S.P., hangs in McGill University.

Career Girls

The weaker sex certainly was not the less active in the pursuit of education. The pages of Canadian education history record the names of numerous early career girls who left an imprint more lasting than chalk and slate.

Mabel Cartwright who managed to graduate from Oxford before they officially granted degrees to women, was Dean of St. Hilda's College University of Toronto, for thirty-three years, then Dean of Women at Trinity.

Distinguished author and professor, Mossie May Kirkwood, M.A., Ph.D. carried on Dr. Cartwright's work. She says, of managing motherhood plus a job: "Nothing remarkable about it. Charwomen have been doing it for centuries." She wrote *19th Century British Thought* and *Women in the Machine Age*. The women's residence, Kirkwood Hall, opened in 1960, was named in her honor.

Dr. Elize Ritchie has two firsts to her credit — Nova Scotia's first woman professor, and first woman appointed to the Board of Governors of Dalhousie University, Halifax, in 1919.

Sister Francis of Assisi was president of one of the few women's colleges in Canada, Mount Saint Vincent College, which recently started admitting a few men. Sister Maura Power, a poet, was professor of English there from 1925-56. She founded the Halifax School of Journalism.

It took a voyage from the United States to Canada for a Dominican Sister, later Mother St. Thomas Aquinas, to make her mark as a teacher, poet and writer.

Born Jeanne Lydia Branda in France, she taught there and in Italy before coming to United States. Moving to Canada, she was an instructor at Jeanne d'Arc House on Ottawa's Bruyère Street, in 1914. Five years later an entirely new congregation was formed on Sussex Street with Mother St. Thomas named as Superior. Her distinguished Ottawa students included Viscount Alexander, then Governor-General, Senator Cairine Wilson and members of the diplomatic corps. She established a small house for homeless girls, providing lessons in reading and writing, and commercial classes — all for the ridiculously low sum of $18. monthly.

A member of the Canadian Authors' Association, Canadian Women's Press Club and a vice-president of Union National Français, Mother St. Thomas used the name Marie Sylvia for her published poetry. In 1956 France presented Mother St. Thomas with La Croix de Légion d'Honneur for outstanding service.

Inveterate traveller Mlle. Mariana Gendreau is another French woman known for her teaching. Diplomats' families in Canada's capital may learn any of 20 languages from her. She also has donated five scholarships for language study.

Another spirited educationist, Quebec's Laure Gaudreault dedicated her life to improving the lot of the rural teacher. Born in 1891 in La Malbaie, Mlle. Gaudreault founded L'Association Catholique des Institutrices Rurales in 1936 in the tiny village of Clermont. The following year similar associations were set up throughout the province as a result of Mlle. Gaudreault's efforts. She is president of the Federation of these associations which by 1946, had grouped more than 8,000 members. An activist, who lobbied with politicians, the clergy, spoke at countless meetings and wrote scores of articles in the federation's magazine *La Petite Feuille* as well as other publications, Mlle. Gaudreault won her point — achieving salary and pension plan improvements for the underpaid over-worked rural teacher in her province.

Modern Methods

Studying and teaching were only basic interests for several Canadian women who succeeded in establishing schools or courses in fields hitherto untapped.

"If the devil himself gave me an idea...I'd use it," says Mattie Norton, and the words typify the woman. A teacher of perceptually handicapped children, she was among the first to do so in Toronto.

The children have short attention spans, see things backwards, confuse words. Causes range from brain damage at birth to illness during childhood. Mrs. Norton studied speech and later, judo — a useful skill since her students, often frustrated, became hard to handle.

Mrs. Norton is not alone in initiating innovative educational projects. Betty Garbitt, the wife of a high school vice-principal, started a venture by which unwed teen-age mothers could continue their education and receive training as well in economics and prenatal exercises. About 450 young unwed mothers each year in Calgary take advantage of the program, says Mrs. Garbitt.

* * *

Cecile Grenier took an enormous jump in physical education instruction when she introduced graceful rhythm techniques in male and female gymnastics, discarding earlier awkward methods of physical jerking. A Montrealer, who was educated in France, Toronto and Montreal, Miss Grenier, was the first teacher to organize physical education for girls in Quebec in 1937. She also conducted many training courses for teachers in her field and lectured for several years at McGill and the Quebec Drama Conservatory.

Her decision at the age of 25 to exchange the classroom for the gymnasium was one she never regretted. "In a few years you'll be out of a job," her school principal warned her. "They want young girls for that kind of teaching." Miss Grenier proved him wrong and stacked up more than 20 years in the arduous physical education sphere.

Quebec Post

Mlle. Thérèse Baron, a long-time teacher, was appointed deputy-minister of education in October 1967 in Quebec Province. She had been appointed a principal of the Montreal Catholic School Commission, has been vice-president of the Quebec Teacher's Association and president of the Quebec Educational Association. Mlle. Baron thinks that academic reform must be integrated into the educational system through the combined efforts of government, teachers and parents.

* * *

Dr. Grace Maynard was appointed to the External Aid Office in Ottawa on October 1, 1965 as Director of Student Services, charged with directing the over 2,000 students and trainees arriving in Canada each academic year, under auspices of the external aid program. In September 1967 she went to St. John's College, University of Manitoba, before taking a position with the Royal Commission on the Status of Women. She is now with the Extension Department of Carleton University.

* * *

Dr. Mary Quayle Innis, a graduate of University of Chicago, is former Dean of Women at University College, University of Toronto. A well-known author and editor, she edited The Clear Spirit, the Centennial project of the Canadian Federation of University Women and, more recently, *Mrs. Simcoe's Diary.* Of student unrest in universities, she says: "It seems to me both exaggerated and stimulated by the press and electronic media. Student rebellion has become almost a fashion. Students and administration . . . can compose their differences . . . if they are allowed to, without outside interference."

Guidance Leader

An awareness of the needs of the individual child was the fulcrum of Olive Diefenbaker's approach to teaching.

An educator and leader in the field of guidance counselling before her marriage to Rt. Hon. John Diefenbaker in 1953, she had been acting director of guidance for the Ontario department of education and, prior to that, assistant for eight years.

Widowed in 1937 after four years of marriage to H. F. Palmer, she had a daughter, Carolyn, who benefitted greatly from her mother's understanding of the guidance field — always oriented to the needs of the individual child. "I first began specific work in guidance in Owen Sound," the late Mrs. Diefenbaker recalled. "Six months after the formation of the first guidance branch in a provincial department of education, I went to the department to supervise guidance work in Ontario schools."

Born in Roland, Manitoba, of U.E.L. stock, Olive Freeman graduated from Brandon University in Manitoba. She held honorary degrees as well, from both Brandon and Acadia universities. Her unique background proved an invaluable asset on the political hustings with Mr. Diefenbaker during free-wheeling campaigns and in the corridors of power when he was prime minister. Gracious and charming even under the stress of recurring pain from a back injury acquired during the couple's whirlwind political years, Olive Diefenbaker had a phenomenal memory for names and faces — a factor which proved a public relations winner on countless occasions both on and off the hustings.

Stargazers

The stars are the limit for two contemporary professors, Dr. Helen S. Hogg and Dr. A. Vibert Douglas.

Stargazing is a most pleasant profession for Dr. Hogg. "Stars are so beautiful . . . fascinating to watch." She started astronomy systematically as a doctoral student at Radcliffe and has seldom looked earthward since. Her catalogue of stars became the standard reference work in dozens of astronomical libraries. This calm, blue-eyed, widowed grandmother, lectures in astronomy at University of Toronto and has served as president of the Royal Astronomical Society. She tallies about 1,000 miles a month travelling to scientific gatherings. The Royal Canadian Institute elected her president, the first woman to hold the office.

Montreal-born Dr. Douglas studied in Canada and England, earning her Ph.D. from McGill while lecturing there in physics and astrophysics. In 1939 she succeeded Dr. Winnifred Kydd as dean of women at Queen's University, where she was also professor of astronomy. She was international president of the Federation of University Women from 1947 to 1950.

* * *

Teaching and writing have gone hand-in-hand for a number of Canadian women whose textbooks have hit best-seller lists. Since the first school history textbook in Canada was written in 1847 by Miss Jennet Roy, typewriters always have been busy.

Miss Eileen Garland of Winnipeg was for many years an outstanding school principal, and is the author of *Canada — Then and Now* and several other well-known texts on Canadian history.

Donalda Dickie, on the Faculty of Education at University of Alberta, was a member of the committee of three who introduced the enterprise system of teaching. Her standard books for teachers, *The Enterprise in Theory and Practice*, and *The Teacher's Omnibus*, were well received in academic circles. Born in Hespeler in 1883, she attended Queen's University, Oxford and Columbia Universities, receiving a Ph.D. in 1918. She taught in Alberta Normal Schools 1910-45. Dr. Dickie has written more than 60 textbooks, mainly on history. Dr. Dickie's *Great Adventure* won a Governor-General's Award in 1950. She was honored with a Ph.D. in history from University of Toronto, also an honorary LL.D, in 1952.

While Dr. Dickie advocated radical change, Dr. Hilda Neatby favored a more traditional route to change. "Fighting Words", a national television program on which she appeared, aptly describes those used in her 1953 book *So Little for the Mind*, a scathing indictment of modern education. Dr. B. K. Sandwell considered Dr. Neatby's book the most important ever written on the subject. "It may goad the public into demanding a satisfactory solution to this problem from the government," he wrote.

History has been Hilda Neatby's life. She majored in History and French at University of Saskatchewan, where she lived with her Scottish family from 1904 onward. Friends dubbed the clever Neatby family "Books with feet". Receiving her Ph.D. in 1934, Hilda became associate professor in history and later head of the department at University of Saskatchewan.

"Canadian universities will not engage women if they can get men," she maintains, and also feels that "Young Canadians receive recognition sooner in almost any other country."

She was the only woman appointed to the 1949 Massey Royal Commission on arts and letters and received her LL.D. from University of Toronto in 1953.

University Club

It is worth noting that by 1907 there were enough women university graduates across Canada to warrant organization. Evelyn Farris, a graduate of Acadia University, Wolfville, Nova Scotia, wife of Senator John Wallace de B. Farris, envisioned a world federation of women graduates. She called a meeting of seven college graduates at her home in Vancouver and formed Canada's first University Women's Club, a small but solid beginning. One year later, when Vancouver members wrote university graduates across Canada urging them to form similar clubs, the suggestion was received with enthusiasm. The Canadian Federation of University Women was organized in 1919 with Mrs. R. F. McWilliams of Winnipeg as first president. Today more than 100 clubs with a membership of over 10,000 have donated more than $150,000 in scholarships.

In 1912 Mrs. Farris, first woman in Canada elected to the governing body of a university, began an active thirty years' association as a member of Senate and Board of Governors of the University of British Columbia. Later she was awarded an LL.D. by Acadia University and UBC "for services rendered higher education".

Book People

Libraries are halls of higher learning as well as escape routes to another world for the average man. And librarians traditionally have taken the lead in advancing adult education.

Canada's first library can be traced back to 1779 when Governor Frederick Haldimand established one at Quebec, stocked with $2,500 worth of books. Although called a public library, members were required to pay a $25 admittance fee plus $10 annually.

The YWCA established libraries in Montreal in

1874 and Quebec in 1875. Ontario's first public libraries were established in Toronto, Hamilton and London in 1882, following the passage of the Ontario Free Public Libraries Act.

Nineteenth century society raised an eyebrow if a woman even sat down in a library to read a book, as Miss Margaret Faller attempted to do in 1830 in the staid Boston public library. Today in Canada 90% of librarians are women and the history and development of libraries in this country are inextricably linked with such names as Dr. Helen Stewart, Lillian H. Smith and Dr. Mabel Dunham.

Dr. Helen Stewart, a tiny, dynamic woman, took libraries to the people. Born in 1879, she received her training in New York in 1908 and in 1911 was appointed assistant librarian at Victoria Public Library. She became head librarian the following year. In the next twelve years she organized a children's department and a reference library and increased the circulation sixty times. She and John Ridington, the University Librarian, drew up the Public Libraries Act in 1919, which provided the framework for public library organization in Canada. In 1929, when the Carnegie Foundation of New York donated $100,000 for regional library service in British Columbia, Helen Stewart organized branches and book mobiles throughout the Fraser Valley. She cheerfully changed flat tires and did such a superb public relations job that taxpayers voted to have her carry on her work in a Depression year. Her "union libraries" served as models throughout North America, attracting librarians from the four corners of the globe to study her methods.

While weeding her radish patch in 1939, Dr. Stewart was hurried off by cablegrams to Port-of-Spain, Trinidad on a Caribbean crash education program. Before long she had set up a central book pool and organized library training courses to combat widespread illiteracy. She even established a branch library in a still, with the astonished distiller pressed into service as librarian. In 1944, her techniques were adopted by the British Council. Two years earlier a refresher course at Columbia had proved to be the stimulus she needed to complete her B.Sc., M.A. and Ph.D.

Lillian H. Smith, another pioneer with Toronto Public Library, taught and trained most of the children's librarians in Canada. She started the first boys' and girls' departments in a corner of the circulating department of Toronto Public Library, which still houses a valuable collection of 1,800 books for children published since 1700. In 1937, she founded the Canadian Association of Children's Librarians and assisted in founding the Canadian Library Association. Asked by the American Library Association to write a book on the standards of literary criticism in the evaluation of children's literature, Miss Smith titled it *The Unreluctant Years*. She was succeeded at the Toronto Library by Miss Jean Thomson.

The first trained librarian in Ontario was Dr. Mabel Dunham, who established a model children's department at Kitchener Public Library and instituted the first picture collection in an Ontario library. From 1930, she lectured on library science at Waterloo College. Her many books of local history included: *The Trail of the Conestoga, The Grand River, Towards Sodom* and *The Trail of the King's Men*. In 1947 she received an honorary Doctor of Literature degree from the University of Western Ontario, the first woman librarian so honored. A year later she received a medal from the Canadian Association of Children's Librarians for the best child's book of the year, *Kristlie's Trees*.

Powerful Adult Educators

The practical experience of women librarians has made a deep imprint on development of Canadian library work. Mary J. Black, long-time librarian at Fort William combined with Dr. George Locke of Toronto, and John Ridington of Vancouver to undertake a complete report of library service in Canada which was published in 1933.

Freda Waldon, writer, lecturer and long-time chief librarian of the Hamilton Public Library, was given an LL.D. from McMaster University in recognition of her work, both locally and nationally. She was first president of the Canadian Library Association, and chairman of the joint committee of five learned societies and the Canadian Library Association, which prepared the report resulting in the establishment of the National Library in Ottawa by the federal government.

In Toronto in 1909, Winnifred Barnstead became joint head (with Miss Edna Poole) of the catalogue department of the Public Library. Later, as head, her work took her to the United States as well as Europe. Miss Barnstead was first director of the University of Toronto Library School, and established high standards for librarians.

Another travelling Torontonian, bibliographer Marie Tremaine, a serious scholar, started in the Toronto Library's reference division in 1929 and received the first Canadian Fellowship from the Carnegie Foundation for study abroad. She wrote *Canadian Imprints 1751-1800*, edited the 800-page *A Bibliography of Canadiana* (with Miss Frances Station, head of the reference division) and in 1940, helped organize an exhibition of printing and graphic arts to celebrate the invention of printing from moveable type. Her impressive bibliography of Arctic research, *Arctic Imprints of North America*, was completed in 1947.

In the Maritimes, Elizabeth Morton, born in Trinidad, graduated from Dalhousie University and organized the library at Saint John Vocational School. Author of *Libraries in the Life of the Canadian Nation*, she received the Canadian Merit Award in 1960. First executive director of the Canadian Library Association, as its king-pin for two decades, she was honored at a testimonial dinner in Ottawa's Skyline Hotel in 1968, attended by librarians from all over North America. Dr. Kaye Lamb, former National Librarian, paid tribute to Miss Morton's energy, saying that through the years she had done the work of three people.

Montreal's Dr. Kathleen Jenkins, chief librarian of the Westmount Library got a sample of the Morton brand of energy during her stint as president of the Canadian Library Association. "Many times, at the end of an exhausting day, my duty as president seemed to be to see that Elizabeth Morton got some sleep!" she once exclaimed. Lecturer in Library Science at McGill and executive director of the "Canadian Library Week", she was a founder of Canadian Library Association, and served as president 1949-1950. Dr. Jenkins wrote the book *Montreal — Island City of the St. Lawrence.* In 1962 she was given an award for community service, and received the Centennial Medal.

Other outstanding chief librarians of Montreal include: Miss Sybil Grimson of Mechanics Institute, who entertains budding authors and visiting VIPs at her historic library, which formerly served as a concert hall; and Miss Margery Trenholme of Fraser Hickson Library, an active member of the Women's University Club.

Margaret Armstrong Beckman, Waterloo, chief librarian at the University of Guelph, was among twenty-five Ontario women honored at a Dinner given by the Ontario Government in 1975, Women's Year. She has a distinguished record in library science, being the only woman among the Chief Librarians of the fifteen major academic institutions in Ontario.

Out west, Margaret Clay, daughter of a strict Presbyterian minister, remembers reading *Anna Karenina* by the light of Christmas candles secreted in a clothes closet. Her love of reading led her to become chief librarian of Victoria Public Library in 1924. Eclectic in her selection of reading material for the library, she was criticized for making available books about the horrors of war and concentration camps. "Hell's bells! If Canadian soldiers can endure them, readers should," she retorted. Margaret fostered the arts, helping Emily Carr gain recognition. She was active in the "Big and Powerful", as she termed the Business and Professional Women's Club.

As first supervisor of school libraries in Canada, Regina's Lyle Evans, got a broad sampling of the Canadian scene as she travelled across the country. She is now with the University of Saskatchewan.

Miss Simmoine Chiasson, chief of the reference department in the Library of Parliament has been with the Department of Trade and Commerce for 14 years. In 1958 she was in charge of the library of the Canadian Pavilion in Brussels. Prince Philip asked to see some books on humour, and was amused to find the books fastened down. Canadian books had proved just too popular!

Margaret Gill started her career in Vancouver Public Library and is now librarian of the National Research Council, where she ensures that NRC's large collection of scientific material is always within easy reach of Canada's top scientists. She literally put the NRC Library on the map as a national institution. She received two Centennial Medals.

In the McLuhan era, with its often voiced prediction that print media are doomed and that reading itself will soon be superseded by more tactile, visual education and information devices, the words of University of Toronto's Mary Quayle Innis are a worthy warning: "We should insist on an enrichment of the humanities program. If we lose concern for literature, art, history and philosophy, our civilization has suffered the ultimate defeat."

Chapter IV

In the Name of Humanity

Nurses

Agnes Sniveley, R.N.

> *Nursing is an art; for what is having
> to do with dead canvas or cold mar-
> ble compared with having to do
> with the living body, the temple of
> God's spirit?*
>
> (Florence Nightingale)

Although they did not realize it at the time, those pathfinding ladies of the lamp led by Florence Nightingale signalled the start of history's most complete occupational coup.

Nursing had been the exclusive preserve of male members of religious orders until Miss Nightingale revolutionized military nursing in the Crimea. With funds given her by the British people in gratitude for her Crimean war work she established the Nightingale Training School in St. Thomas's Hospital, London, based on the Nightingale system that nursing schools must be under the direction of a trained nurse. Bellevue in New York, modelled after St. Thomas's graduated the first nurse trained in North America, Miss Linda Richards, in 1873.

That same year, Dr. Theophilus Mack started Canada's first training school for nurses in his small hospital in St. Catharines, Ontario. Perhaps lured by the prospects of life in a huge metropolis Agnes Sniveley and her friends Louise Darch and Isobel Hampton chose Bellevue with its established, excellent reputation instead of the Canadian school. The trio smiled tolerantly when bewildered friends asked: "Why nursing? Did you get religion or were you disappointed in love?"

Fresh from graduation at Bellevue in 1884, Miss Sniveley was sent be the hospital's head nurse, a Miss Perkins, to Toronto General Hospital which had put in a request for a nursing superintendent. The financing of Toronto General in this era was as unorthodox as had been the case with Canada's earliest hospital at Louisburg, N.S. Port dues of 10 codfish daily from each vessel in port had sustained the fortress hospital. In Toronto, the Loyal and Patriotic Society of Upper Canada used surplus funds augmented by the sale of unawarded medals for veterans of the War of 1812 to build the hospital which opened in 1830.

Disgraceful conditions prevailed in most hospitals throughout North America in these early days. Vermin flourished, plumbing was primitive and sanitation almost non-existent. Morgue tables doubled for operations and dropped instruments were used without rewashing by surgeons whose gowns were reminiscent of butchers' aprons. At Toronto General nurses received board and lodging, (each girl carried her cutlery in her pocket) and a daily ration of beer. After working from 4 A.M. until 10 P.M. they uneasily slept on straw beds in frigid bedrooms, always ready to spring to attention if needed. The diningroom in the cellar next to the furnace room proved too noisy for table talk.

Youthful and charming Agnes Sniveley brought sympathy and courage to her work. First she successfully appealed to the Hospital Board for a Nurses' Residence. Matron of the hospital as well as superintendent of nurses, she taught nursing and nursing ethics using full-scale written examinations and arranged lectures by visiting doctors. Although initially she encountered much opposition from the medical staff, soon she had their cooperation. Her own devotion to duty and humanitarian ideals inspired her nurses and attracted superior candidates. Agnes Sniveley gave Canadian nursing an amazingly improved status.

On December 1, 1909 at the Alumnae Association

reception held in her honor many distinguished guests paid her tribute. Her nurses presented her with an illuminated address and a cheque for $1,000 in a silver purse. For years she had denied herself every luxury to help others. On her resignation, the Hospital Board also gave her an annuity.

Miss Sniveley's crowning achievement was the organization of the Canadian Nurses' Association. She was its first president from 1908 until 1912. Linda Rogers Struthers, known throughout North America as the organizer of the public school nursing system, became editor of their magazine *The Canadian Nurse*. Miss Sniveley was also a founding member of the International Council of Nurses and its first honorary treasurer.

In 1933, after her death, The Canadian Nurses' Association created the Mary Agnes Sniveley Memorial Medal. Her life was a true example of Toronto Nursing School's motto: "To be is greater than to acquire."

Tradition Continued

Dr. Jean Gunn, LL.B., O.B.E., carried the traditions established by Miss Sniveley a further quarter century. As chairman of the eight-hour day committee of the Canadian Nurses' Association Dr. Gunn lobbied continually to improve working conditions. She was a member of the 1922 committee which brought about the registration of nurses and ensured uniform educational standards and government recognition of nursing as a profession.

Recognition of Dr. Gunn's services came with a Rockefeller Foundation Scholarship in 1925 to study nursing conditions in Europe. Her other honors included the first Agnes Sniveley Memorial Medal, a French government medal, and the Florence Nightingale Medal. On January 13, 1954 the Jean I. Gunn Memorial Library was presented to University of Toronto School of Nursing as a gift of the Toronto General Hospital Alumnae Association.

86

While her contemporary, Agnes Sniveley, was quietly laying foundations of one of the world's great hospitals, Nora Livingston, R.N., O.B.E., was conducting a one-woman revolution on the depressing conditions at Montreal General Hospital. She returned to work in Canada after completing her training in the United States. Her declaration of war on hospital conditions followed swiftly after that historic day in 1890 when she made her first tour of inspection.

Nora Livingston, R.N.

Patients lay two, sometimes more, in the same bed on straw mattresses with no bedsprings, just an iron frame beneath. One little girl desperately ill with diphtheria was not isolated. Delirious, thirsty patients crawled out to drink milk from cats' saucers on filthy floors. Gynecological patients, scorned by nurses, were carelessly treated by ward maids. Urinalyses were done on the wards. Miss Livingston was horrified to discover a corpse wrapped in newspapers. Little wonder the wards smelled vile!

Driven to despair by such conditions the Hospital's first two superintendents had resigned. In 1875 Miss Maria Machan arrived with two other nurses. Nurses were assigned the worst wards as sleeping quarters. Often after a blizzard, their beds would be wet with snow. One nurse, Maria Rice, died of typhoid and Miss Machan's fiance, Dr. Jack Cline on the medical staff, died of diphtheria. Miss Machan resigned and was followed briefly by Miss Anna Maxwell. She found a dearth of essential equipment but discovered that hospital funds were being used to buy champagne to fortify operative patients instead of less expensive ether, which had been discovered some 40 years earlier. Nurses were mainly of the Dicken's Sairy Gamp type — unkempt, untrained, often drunk, sometimes immoral, "sworn at by surgeons, grumbled at by patients, insulted if old, seduced if young". Many disgusted doctors were so determined to have formally trained nurses that a Dr. Stephenson fought a duel with another doctor who bitterly opposed this innovation.

Montreal General was a hospital with a tradition. By 1815, except for the jail, the small Hotel Dieu was Montreal's *only* public institution. When 5,000 hungry refugees from Europe's Napoleonic Wars swelled Montreal's normal population of 16,000, the situation became desperate. The old, the ill and the unemployed, along with vagrants and criminals roamed the streets, homeless. Mrs. Beniah Gibb with other ladies "of the first respectability" organized the Female Benevolent Society and started a soup kitchen. This was the humble beginning of the mighty Montreal General Hospital.

Within six years, the soup kitchen developed into a House of Recovery (near McNab's Tavern). Patients crowded into its four beds and slept on condemned barracks bedding which the ladies bought at a bargain. The House was fairly independent with its own shoemaker, cow, pig, and chickens. Denied a grant to enlarge the hospital by the government, the ladies successfully appealed to the public for funds, to open the first Montreal General Hospital with 24 beds.

Citizens were grateful for the enlarged hospital in 1831 when Montreal's population of 30,000 was decimated by cholera. Smallpox was also a terrible menace. As late as 1869 Montreal had more than one hundred cases, one being the famous Sir William Osler. In 1882 a still larger hospital of 72 beds was built on Dorchester Street. Associated with it was the first School of Medicine in Canada, later the Faculty of Medicine of McGill University. At the banquet celebrating the hospital opening, the 22nd toast was "To the ladies!"

Nora Livingston's revolution at the General was far from quiet. Filthy wards were scrubbed, proper bedding was laundered when soiled, and a fire alarm system installed.

Nurses who formerly were treated like servants were addressed by their surnames by Miss Livingston — a custom which survives. She taught them to administer medicine and take temperatures (pocket thermometers had been invented by Albutt in 1868) and organized the first hospital diet kitchen in Quebec with her sister Grace in charge of special diets and of teaching cooking to the nurses.

Miss Livingston was a stern, though kind disciplinarian whose motto was: "Nurse the patient, always the *patient* first". Since, in early days, public hospitals existed solely as public charities for the care of the indigent poor (who regarded admission to hospital as a death sentence) this idea was revolutionary. She established the first three-year training course in North America and was the first to have a distinguishing uniform for probationers. She said quite rightly: "Nurses should be grateful to me for I have done much for them and their profession."

She warned her first graduating class: "You are pioneers in the field of professional nursing. It will be your duty to blaze the trail for those who will follow. Be dignified and wise." However, she found it exceedingly difficult to educate the public. Most people felt that a nurse's fee of $2.00 a day was exorbitant, and her duties should include some sewing and housework.

Nurses resented the rigid rule forbidding dates with interns even more than chronic sore feet and red-ringed necks from tight collars. When one nurse eloped with an intern, headlines screamed: "Mothers fear to send their sons to McGill, lest they be trapped by wily nurses!"

Miss Livingston died in 1927. When the golden anniversary of the training school was celebrated in 1940 the Alumnae Association donated funds for a monument and for the Nora Livingston Scholarship Fund. The Nurses' Residence became Livingston Hall.

When the new $20,000,000 Montreal General Hospital opened in 1955 one doctor referring to the hand-carved doors of the Library salvaged from the old hospital noted: "Every hospital should take some of its ghosts with it." Surely the ghost of Nora Livingston walks the wards and her spirit of service still dominates this vast modern "House of Recovery".

Professionalism

With the advent of nursing schools many practical nurses feared the end for them had come. One of these, Mrs. Mary Gowdy on staff at St. Mary's Hospital in British Columbia, needed to be convinced by the provincial medical examiner Dr. J. S. Fagan: "You have forgotten more about nursing than any school can teach anyone." He gave her a nurses' diploma — the first ever awarded to a practical nurse. Many years later Elizabeth Martens of Morden, Manitoba, received the Canada Nurse Award in 1954 — another first for a practical nurse.

In the early days small nursing outposts — the hardship stations — tested the endurance and the abilities of scores of quiet heroines who did whatever had to be done. Sister Marie-Elmire, a practical nurse who went to Albany at James Bay in 1929, for example, performed surgery 15 times in as many years, extracted more than 500 teeth, and never lost a patient! To the Indians she was "The White Angel".

Another angel of mercy, Sadie Stringer of Kincardine, Ontario, put her pre-marital nursing training to good use when her husband, Bishop Isaac Stringer, was posted as a missionary to the west Arctic coast in 1896. The Stringers' home, Igloopuk or Big House, became headquarters for solving physical as well as spiritual problems. The medicine men were furious with this encroachment on their preserve, but the Stringers worked to overcome the hostility and inherent superstition of the Eskimos. A young Eskimo man, Okpit, became the test case. Okpit, who had been abandoned in a snowbank by the medicine man to die of pneumonia and exposure, recovered completely after weeks of careful nursing in the Stringer home, establishing Sadie's supremacy.

Ray Freedman, nurse in charge of the Grenfell Mission hospital at Happy Valley, Labrador, encountered similar psychological problems in helping the native peoples. Often simply to get a pregnant woman to enter a hospital required the persuasion of the RCMP. Miss Freedman became dentist, midwife and doctor —

whatever the occasion demanded — caring for Indian, Eskimo and white patients in this far away outpost.

Lord's Cove, Newfoundland, got itself a gregarious helper when practical nurse Mrs. Dinah Hillier arrived on the scene. In addition to her own sixteen children, she adopted six orphans and cared for an invalid husband while nursing townfolk of Lord's Cove. In 1953 after the children became independent, Mrs. Hillier moved to Lamaline. With no town doctor or nurse there, she took a maternity course at the Salvation Army Grace Hospital to cope with the burgeoning population.

Such emergencies would have been a natural for Miss Jane Pushie of Antigonish, Nova Scotia. Legend has it that she delivered a whopping 1,000 babies in her career, losing none.

Then there was "Mother Foster", a Negro practical nurse in Nelson, British Columbia. A jovial 200-pounder who was known as the "Midnight Nurse", she was charged double by the livery man whenever she rode in his carriage. But "Mother Foster", who served as the village laundress, had her small revenge. She used to charge him double for her "special" service.

However, for some the ending was less fortunate. In Rock Bay near Vancouver a Miss Sutherland, the first nurse at this station assisted only by a housekeeper and an orderly, actually died from her heavy workload.

Stamped on History

Starting with Jeanne Mance and continuing in an almost unbroken line, the history of Canadian hospitals is indelibly stamped with woman power. When Jean Drever, after a whirlwind courtship, married Rev. William Cyprian Pinkham, her wedding ring was cut from a five-dollar gold piece by the tinsmith. Mrs. Pinkham calmly embroidered while rebels searched their home (during the Riel Rebellion) which concealed Loyalist guns. With $100 as a nucleus (a bequest from a dying

Chinese man) she raised funds to build Calgary General
Hospital in the 1890s.

Elizabeth McMaster, R.N.

Concern for Children

Elizabeth McMaster's tender concern for youngsters transformed an impossible dream into reality —
the first Canadian hospital devoted exclusively to the
care of sick children, in Toronto. A mother of four children whose invalid husband, Samuel, left her a widow
at the age of 38, Elizabeth McMaster organized a ladies'
hospital committee from among her friends to help establish a hospital for children. Starting out with $10 in
coins and a great deal of faith they advertised in a

Toronto newspaper and soon attracted additional helpers, food, furniture, money and equipment. Number 21 Avenue Street, a rented building with space for six cots, became the first Hospital for Sick Children. A badly-scalded little girl of three was the first patient.

Need for the hospital proved so great that many moves to larger quarters followed. While summering at The Moorings, Center Island, Mrs. McMaster interested her neighbor John Ross Robertson, publisher of the *Toronto Telegram*, in the project. It soon became his greatest interest also and he gave generous financial help. It was decided in the late 1880s to build an even larger hospital. Friends felt that Mrs. McMaster should be its superintendent.

She set out to acquire the training needed, enrolling as a student nurse at Illinois Training School in Chicago and graduating in 1891 with high honors. She spent the summer studying many other children's hospitals and finally in the autumn of 1891 took over as superintendent of the Hospital for Sick Children. On May 6, 1892 when the new College Street Hospital was formally opened by Mrs. McMaster, assisted by Mr. Robertson, she said: "May the doors of this new building swing widely open at the cry of any suffering child and the same spirit of love and sympathy rest within."

The combined strain of training and building the hospital provoked a breakdown forcing Elizabeth McMaster to move to California for her health. The Good Samaritan Hospital in Los Angeles and later the Children's Home in Schenectady were the results of her stay in the U.S. Her health improved, she returned to Toronto and started the original First Aid Courses before her death in 1903. Her Hospital for Sick Children became the largest and best equipped in North America with the opening of a modern complex in 1951.

Children were the lifelong concern of four other Toronto nurses, Hannah Cody, Sarah Annie Kinder,

94

Louise C. Brent and Florence J. Potts, who were responsible for the oldest pediatric school of nursing in North America at the Hospital for Sick Children. A stained glass window designed by Yvonne Williams, was installed in their honor by the Alumnae Association.

* * *

The school of nursing at University of Toronto, which she organized and administered for 30 years, is a monument to nurse Kathleen Russell of Windsor, Nova Scotia. Florence Emory, author of *Public Health Nursing in Canada*, was her capable assistant. Miss Russell developed a degree course combining an excellent general university course with professional nursing training. Toronto is internationally recognized as a model school.

She then persuaded the Red Cross and the Canadian Nurses' Association to jointly finance two experiments, the metropolitan demonstration school for nurses in Windsor, Ontario, with director Miss Nettie Fidler, and one at the Toronto Western Hospital, directed by Miss Gladys Sharpe and Mrs. Blanche Duncanson. Later Mrs. Duncanson was appointed director of the Nightingale School of Nursing established in Toronto in 1960 to provide a streamlined two-year course in nursing. She furthered her academic career six years later with her appointment as associate professor of the University of Toronto School of Nursing.

In Vancouver, Sister Charles Spinola brought fame to St. Paul's Hospital with her invention of the St. Charles ether apparatus, patented in 1920 and still used today. Another nurse, Sister Denise Lefebvre, director of nursing education at Montreal's Institute Marguerite d'Youville and co-author of the 1947 book *L'art de Soigner*, became the first member of the Canadian Nurses' Association to receive a doctorate in pedagogy in 1956.

Wartime Service

In war as in peace nurses through the years have waged a never-ending battle against disease and injury and death. In Canada the unbroken line of service extends from the Riel Rebellion, the Boer War, through two World Wars and the Korean confrontation to contemporary times. Mother Hannah, the first woman ever awarded a medal for nursing services, was typical of the hardy breed of nurses who headed into the thick of battle. When the Riel Rebellion broke out, she and several sisters volunteered for service in the Moose Jaw military hospital. Fresh from her work of organizing Canada's first women's surgical hospital, St. John's in Toronto, Mother Hannah found the west different indeed. En route, finding it a nuisance, she cut off her long black hair, throwing it into Lake Superior and possibly starting the fashion of bobbed hair. On arrival the nurses found their beds were occupied by hordes of red ants, so the volunteers slept with their skirts clutched protectively around their knees while the ants rested somewhat more comfortably in the beds.

The Boer War proved an even harsher testing ground. Wearing the blue uniforms that earned them the name "Bluebirds", Misses Forbes, Russell and Affleck served with their matron, Georgina Pope of Prince Edward Island in an Imperial hospital in South Africa. Other Canadians, including Margaret C. Macdonald of Bailey's Brook, N.S., joined the group, all of whom had the rank and pay of lieutenants — a sore point with male military nurses today, who still are not given officer status in the army.

Frances Upton's World War I exploits were, to say the least, mind-boggling. She narrowly escaped death on a British submarine torpedoed shortly after she had lunched aboard. In the Middle East when more than 60,000 soldiers were felled by malaria she nursed 'round the clock for many wearying days, took care of gas war-

96

fare victims and helped fight Britain's flu epidemic in 1918. More pleasant memories of the war were meeting Lord Kitchener; and acquiring a flock of turkeys she fattened behind British lines to give Canadian soldiers a traditional Christmas dinner.

Col. Elizabeth Smellie, R.N.

After the war Miss Upton established a tuberculosis sanatorium at Ste. Agathe, Quebec and organized the first course of treatment for that disease in Canada. (Back in 1887 three other women, Georgina and Leontine Genereaux and Algaee Laberge, had founded Montreal's first tuberculosis hospital, Le Sacre Coeur). Frances Upton received the Royal Red Cross and the Agnes Sniveley medals in 1942.

Evelyn (Mrs. W.D.) Chambers, a U.E.L. of Montreal, was a grandniece of Hon. George Brown, one of the Fathers of Confederation, and mother of Egan Chambers, former M.P.

During World War I, Evelyn Chambers was the first woman to drive for the Canadian Army Service Corps in England, and like her mother, she served overseas. Evelyn was with the First Aid Nursing Yeomanry in France and was awarded a military medal in 1917.

France Calls

World War I took Edith Rayside to Le Treport, France, where she became Matron at No. 2 Canadian General Hospital in 1915 and later transferred to Moore Barracks, Shornecliffe. A graduate in nursing from Ottawa Civic Hospital and in arts from Queen's University, Miss Rayside peaked a brilliant career with two senior jobs — matron-in-chief at Military Headquarters, Ottawa and superintendent of nurses at Hamilton General Hospital. Her University of Toronto Master of Household Science honorary degree seemed slightly incongruous.

Miss Rayside's colleague Elizabeth Smellie had a series of firsts to her credit — first woman made a life member of the Canadian Public Health Association, first woman vice-president of the American Public Health Association and the first woman to receive an honorary LL.D. from the University of Western Ontario. War took Elizabeth Smellie overseas in 1915, the same year that Frances Munro became first nurse killed on active duty. By war's end she had served as matron of a military hospital at Shornecliffe, been awarded the Royal Red Cross, First Class, had become the first woman colonel in the Canadian Army and organized the first women's army — a force she expanded from 200 to more than 3,000. Returning home, Col. Smellie was appointed national superintendent of the VON. In 1924 and during the '30s she set out with a Rockefeller Foundation grant on a twelve-country tour to study maternal welfare. With the outbreak of the Second World War, Col. Smellie became matron-in-chief of the Canadian Army's Medical Corps. A warm friendly woman, Col. Smellie enjoyed the chuckles her name sometimes provoked. "Wouldn't you think with a name like mine I'd have tried to change it? And I'm no man-hater either!"

World War II put Marion Macdonald up in the clouds. One of the first RCAF nurses to take parachute training, Flying Officer Macdonald later gained international acclaim for a sensational jump into the frozen Northern Manitoba wilderness to rescue Col. I. McGrew and Capt. Lester Epton, whose jet bomber had exploded in mid-air. Capt. Epton said of his rescuer: "She was wonderful — a real morale builder."

Red Cross

The war record of Red Cross nurses such as Hamilton's Jane McKee in World War I set a bold standard. A winner of the French Croix de Guerre, Miss McKee has held executive posts in a number of organizations, including the Red Cross Society for more than 30 years.

In peacetime or in war, solving emergencies has been the specialty of the Canadian Red Cross. In one three-year period, for example, their cross-country mobile hospital — a railway car donated by the CNR — treated more than 5,000 patients throughout northwestern Canada.

When the Dionne quintuplets were born in Callander, Ontario, Dr. Allen Dafoe sent an SOS for milk to the nearest Red Cross outpost at Bonfield. Nurse A.

Cloutier knew her district well and came up with enough milk to keep the quints alive during those crucial first days.

In the east, when Newfoundland became Canada's tenth province, the Red Cross Society's national director of nursing services, Helen G. McArthur, organized the provincial division. Not long after, she became the first woman appointed associate co-ordinator of relief for the League of Red Cross Societies and was posted to Korea in 1954. Miss McArthur became "Our Canadian Nightingale" to the nurses at the Seoul Hospital, who embroidered a striking wall hanging for her in their off-duty hours. During the war some 117 nurses were kidnapped from the hospital with only 24 safely returned. For her Red Cross work, Miss McArthur was awarded the Florence Nightingale Medal.

Busy Islanders

In Prince Edward Island Dr. Iphigenie Arsenault serves the Red Cross as commissioner for her province, the only woman holding the position in Canada. She is a past president of the province's Business and Professional Women's Club.

Years earlier, in 1923, Miss Mona Wilson, O.B.E., had gone to Prince Edward Island as chief Canadian Red Cross nurse. After graduating from Johns Hopkins School of Nursing and University of Toronto's Public Health Nursing Course, she served in France during World War I, then from 1919 until 1922 worked with the American Red Cross in Siberia, Albania and Montenegro. In 1931, when P.E.I. established a Department of Health, Miss Wilson as director of public health nursing organized camps for crippled children, dental, and public health and maternity clinics. After serving in the Red Cross again during World War II, she carried on her public health work until her retirement in 1961. Miss Wilson was awarded the Florence Nightingale Medal, the highest and only international award in nursing.

Public Health

Like their Red Cross counterparts, public health nurses have walked willingly into emergencies day after day, year after year. Dispelling the traditional cure-oriented approach to medicine and nursing, public health nursing set out to further the concept of disease prevention. Harriet Meiklejohn, who won the Royal Red Cross for her courageous rescue of patients from an overseas hospital during a World War I bombing raid, carved the same kind of reputation in the field of public health nursing.

Back home in Canada after the war, she spent three years in Saint John as director of public health nursing for New Brunswick, organizing and directing public dental and other clinics for treatment of tuberculosis, venereal diseases and eye, ear, nose and throat ailments. On a typical trip to Riley Brook, N.B., she wrote: "We took a clinic up there, commandeered the hotel and performed 49 adenoid operations in one day." Over 80 per cent of the more than 1,000 babies born in the area were helped into the world by midwives. Miss Meiklejohn set up treatment clinics in New Brunswick's luxurious Carvill Hall, where youngsters who seldom even saw a bathtub splashed in a tub originally meant for royalty. After organizing a Victorian Order of Nurses training school for public health nurses, Miss Meiklejohn had the satisfaction of seeing eight of her trainees fan out across the province to lecture student nurses.

An organizer and a builder of institutions, Harriet became superintendent at the General Hospital, St. Catharines, Ontario while it was being rebuilt and from 1927-43 served as superintendent of Women's College Hospital in Toronto. Here, she and Mrs. A. M. Huestis almost single-handedly raised funds for the hospital's new building. A scholarship established by the hospital alumnae honors Miss Meiklejohn's work.

Jean Leask and Lily Turnbull have built on this

solid foundation. Miss Leask won the R.D. Defries Medal for her outstanding contribution as director-in-chief of the VON while Lily Turnbull, whose graduate training was completed at McGill University, was appointed chief nursing officer with the World Health Organization.

Nursing is indebted to the Canadian Mothercraft Society, a volunteer health organization dedicated to the well-being of mothers and babies. Founded in Canada in 1931 by Mr. and Mrs. Irvine Robertson with headquarters in Toronto, the Society literally took wing. "Be a nurse and see the world", became the motto as trained Mothercraft nurses set off for far-flung assignments in the Bahamas, Greece or even Hollywood. Film star Hedy Lamarr at the height of her flaming Hollywood career brought the Society considerable glamor when she asked one of its nurses, Frances Milner, to tend her during a pregnancy. Dorothy Lamour, taking time out from one of the Bing Crosby-Bob Hope "Road" show epics to have a baby, was nursed by Miss Milner's twin sister Dorothy.

An active Ottawa branch of the Mothercraft Society was established in 1944 with Miss Elva Hewitt, R.N., as nurse supervisor and Mrs. Mackintosh Bell as chairman. Mrs. E. S. Brand was the first mother to use the Ottawa Society's services. Nine years later Canada's capital was first to organize a branch of the Education for Parenthood Association. Also in Ottawa, Mrs. C. W. Sheridan, for many years active in hospital work, became president of the Canadian Association of Hospital Auxiliaries, representing nine provinces. In Quebec, Mrs. John Howe headed the Association.

Changing Scene

Sweeping socio-political changes have transformed the face of the nursing profession in the last forty years. The strain of the Depression, when huge numbers of nurses were unemployed and some schools of nursing forced to close their doors, paved the way to change.

When World War II broke out the demand for nurses surged and young women headed into the armed services leaving civilian hospitals short-staffed. In the 1960s, in Canada and around the world, the nursing shortage was so critical it seriously affected and curtailed patient-care. The United Nations Educational, Scientific and Cultural Organization estimated that the world needed about 6,000,000 nurses but had less than 2,000,000. In Montreal alone almost one quarter of the hospital beds were vacant because of a lack of nurses, while thousands of patients awaited admission. Miss Helena Reimer, secretary-registrar of the Quebec Association of Nurses explained: "The serious shortage . . . is of nurses qualified for the higher positions in teaching, supervision and administration." They are the key figures in the whole program she felt. "If we had more teachers . . . schools might be able to absorb more students."

By 1977, nurses again are busy job-hunting, especially the lower echelons. Coping with such changes in the contemporary nursing scene is the task of Helen Mussalem, executive director of the Canadian Nurses' Association, and Alice Girard, past president of the International Council of Nurses. Their frequent travels around the world keep them apace with changes and trends in the nursing profession both at home and abroad. Miss Girard, who was the first Canadian to become president of the 800,000-member International Council of Nurses, says: "Nursing faces a crisis in competition and identification, produced by the greater emancipation and unlimited choice of careers open to girls nowadays." At the International Council of Nurses Congress in Montreal in June, 1969, Miss Girard was host to more than 8,000 nurses from some 70 countries.

A graduate of St. Vincent de Paul Hospital, Sherbrooke, Quebec, Miss Girard also has a B.Sc. in public
health nursing from Washington, D.C.'s Catholic University; a public health nursing certificate from University of Toronto; an M.A. in nursing education from
Columbia University; and a social sciences degree from
University of Montreal, where she was also director of
the School of Public Health Nursing. She was the only
woman member of the Hall Royal Commission on
Health Services, 1961-64.

Nursing Educationalist

Dr. Helen Mussalem, O.C., Ed. D., LL.D., D. Sc.,
executive director of the over 115,000 members of the
Canadian Nurses' Association, also Secretary-Treasurer
of the Canadian Nurses' Foundation, is outstanding in
the field of nursing education. In this position she is
concerned with the expanded role of nurses today, who
are gradually taking over some of the duties formerly
the sole domain of physicians. Problems of pay and
jurisdiction almost inevitably arise.

After active service in the Royal Canadian Army
Medical Corps during World War II, she returned to
Vancouver General Hospital to become Director of
Nursing Education there. She directed the trail-blazing
Pilot Project for the Evaluation of Schools of Nursing in
Canada, which led to great reforms in nursing educa-
tion.

Like Alice Girard, Helen Mussalem brings to her
work the wide experience and knowledge gained from
assignments in far-flung corners of the world, during
the last decade. The U.S.S.R. beckoned in 1966 when
Miss Mussalem served as senior consultant with
twenty-three chief nursing officers from twenty-two
countries on a Travelling World Health Organization
study tour. "I learned much about nursing in other parts
of the world," Dr. Mussalem recalls. Author of many

articles she has written three major works: *Spotlight on Nursing Education, Path to Quality,* and *Nursing Education in Canada.*

Like Alice Girard, who has received an honorary degree from University of Toronto, the Order of Canada, and the Florence Nightingale Medal, to name a few, Helen Mussalem has also won multiple awards, including two honorary degrees, and the Order of St. John of Jerusalem. Dr. Mussalem was the first member of the health professions to be appointed to the Economic Council of Canada in 1971 for a three-year period. In November 1976 she was awarded an Honorary Fellowship of the Royal College of Nursing of the United Kingdom, (R.c.n.)

These outstanding nurses and their predecessors are typical of the women who have raised their calling from despised servitude to the status of a noble profession. Ministering to fundamental human needs, women find in this vocation a sublimation of their maternal instinct. Changing from the apprentice method of education to university degrees, the nursing profession now merits government grants such as those awarded other professions, for example, pharmacy, law and medicine.

The government issued a special stamp in 1958 to commemorate 50 years of organized nursing in Canada. The Canadian Nurses' Memorial in the House of Commons' Hall of Honor is a tribute to Canadian nurses from 1639-1918 and especially to the fifty-three who gave their lives for their country in World War I. This memorial was built: "To perpetuate a noble tradition in the relations of the old world to the new, led by the spirit of humanity across the seas."

The Canadian Nurses' Memorial in the Hall of Honour in the House of Commons is a tribute to Canadian nurses from 1639-1918, in particular to the fifty-three who gave their lives for their country in World War I. This memorial was erected: "To perpetuate a noble tradition in the relations of the old world to the new, led by the spirit of humanity across the seas."

Chapter V

Healing Hands

Doctors

Dr. Emily Stowe

I want to cure, not to comfort.
(Dr. Frederick Banting)

Behind every great man, there's a woman, and for Dr. James Barry, the truth of this statement came to light only after death — he was a woman!

A graduate in medicine from Edinburgh University in 1812, James (Miranda) Barry carried out her masquerade throughout a triumphant though chequered career, crowned by the appointment as Inspector General of Canada's military hospitals, her last posting. The pinnacle of power — Inspector General of military hospitals throughout the British Empire — she could never have reached as a woman in that era.

Slim Dr. Barry, respected professionally but detested personally, was accompanied always by his little dog and Black John, a colored servant, who held a large umbrella over the doctor's head. Dr. Barry flirted with fellow-officers' wives, fought a duel with Sir Josias Cleote, and in 1838, was arrested, sent to England and court-martialed, but exonerated of a charge of carelessness made by a fellow officer. When Dr. Barry died in 1865, his charwoman who prepared the body for burial exclaimed: "My God, it's a woman!" Evidence showed also that she had borne a child, and there were rumors of a royal romance.

The year 1865 was a memorable one in medicine in England, inasmuch as Elizabeth Garrett graduated as the first woman to have taken her training *openly*, albeit with the aid of a police escort to classes.

In Canada, Emily Jennings Stowe pioneered for hundreds of other women in their struggle for acceptance as doctors. In 1852, she had made history as the pioneer woman school principal in Canada. When the University of Toronto rudely refused her admittance, she went to New York to study medicine. Her husband, John Stowe, a carriage maker, had developed tuberculosis, forcing the mother of three to become the family breadwinner.

In 1867, Emily began to practise medicine in Toronto. It was the first round in a fight that her only daughter, Augusta, would carry on. Fees were pitifully small — only 50c a call and, since there were no mails, bills had to be hand-delivered. Dr. Emily became a familiar sight, making rounds in her carriage, drawn by her horse, Barney.

Male doctors complained she was practising illegally since she was not a member of the Ontario College of Physicians and Surgeons. She could not obtain membership without attending a Canadian medical school and, of course, no Canadian medical school would accept a woman. To halt her practice, she was fined but she persisted even when threatened with jail. Persecution always failed with Emily and finally, she was grudgingly told she would be admitted after attending one session in a Toronto medical school. During this session, she had the company of Dr. Jennie Trout. Male students gave the women a rough time, often drawing embarrassing sketches on classroom walls. Thoroughly revolted, the motherly, middle-aged Emily maintained a disturbed silence. Professors intervened and had the classroom walls whitewashed four times during the session. Not until 1880, 12 years after graduation, did Emily Stowe become a full-fledged Canadian doctor.

Encouraged by her first successful operation, Dr. Stowe worked on. In 1882, Emily petitioned the Provincial legislature to permit girls to take the arts course at the University of Toronto. The University still "would not allow skirts within medicated walls". Dr. Stowe headed a group of progressive men and women and, with the help of Dr. Michael Barrett, professor of physiology at the university, organized the Women's Medical College which opened October, 1883. Male citadels were finally beginning to crumble.

Teaching and nursing were thought to be as far as a respectable woman should go in the professions, but Dr. Stowe determined to change the status quo. In 1876, while visiting the United States, she attended a meeting for women's rights — an experience which inspired her to organize the first suffrage club in Canada in 1877. With a bow to public prejudice, it became known as The Women's Literary Club. It was apparent, however, that the club was more concerned with votes for women than culture; it was the nucleus of the woman's suffrage movement in Canada and in 1883 was rechristened Toronto Women's Suffrage Club. At its first meeting, members resolved to win the vote for women and make medical education for women a reality. Dr. Stowe headed delegations to extend the franchise once it was granted to widows and spinsters.

Suffrage Fighter

Mrs. Flora McDonald Denison, a clever remarkable woman, was the Stowes' right-hand in their suffrage battle. She took over the presidency of the Ontario and Dominion Suffrage Associations in 1911, when Dr. Stowe-Gullen became honorary president. A successful business woman (actually barred from the fashionable Heliconian Club for that reason) she generously helped finance the movement. Mrs. Denison, probably unequalled as an avant-garde feminist, wrote a page for the Toronto *Sunday World* for many years. Her pre-World War I articles advocated not only political equality but also equal pay for equal work, the unionization of labor and more liberal divorce and abortion laws.

In 1911 she wrote and directed an influential play: *How the Vote was Won*. This powerful play was performed across Canada as part of the battle tactics. When the Suffrage Bill of 1911 was defeated, Mrs. Denison's indignant letters to the papers, published in booklet form, created a furore. In 1914, Mrs. Denison resigned as head of the suffrage associations. She was succeeded by Dr. Margaret Gordon, who remained until the group's objectives were won. The association disbanded in 1925.

Highly successful author and dramatist Merrill Denison of Montreal recalls his boyhood travels across Canada with his mother. Everywhere her topic was suffrage. Her Bon Echo (on Mazinaw Lake, Cloyne) association produced the Walt Whitman inscription on the Big Rock there, and prompted Merrill to donate Bon Echo as a spacious, beautiful national park to the people of Ontario in memory of his mother and to further conservation and education, two causes to which she was devoted.

Dr. Emily Stowe also pushed the Ontario Legislature into passing the married Women's Property Act; before that even their clothes and jewelry belonged legally to their husbands. Like Adelaide Hoodless, she advocated training schools for homemakers and domestic workers. Her battles against the evils of the sweat shop system forced factories and stores to install sanitary arrangements and shamed shop owners into providing chairs for clerks.

In 1953, a half century after her death, a portrait of Dr. Emily Stowe was hung in Women's College Hospital. Dr. Minerva Reid, the first woman to graduate from the Medical School of the University of Toronto, said, when she unveiled it: "It is difficult to realize the intelligence, energy, perseverance and courage necessary to be and do what Dr. Stowe was and did. Because of the contribution her life has made to Canadian progress along the medical, educational, humanitarian and political lines, Dr. Emily Stowe belongs, not only to her family, but to history."

Dr. Augusta Stowe-Gullen

When feminine, pretty Augusta, "like a piece of Dresden china", enrolled in Toronto School of Medicine, she encountered such antagonism she nearly had a nervous breakdown. Every morning, her brother escorted her to her desk, to remove gruesome specimens from the morgue, placed there by male students. But, when she graduated from Victoria College (then in Cobourg) in 1883, everyone rose and cheered, and Augusta and Emily exchanged triumphant smiles. Inspired by her mother's example, Augusta too contributed to significant social changes in a number of fields. Dr. Augusta Stowe was the first woman to take her complete medical training in Canada, and, when she married her classmate, Dr. J. B. Gullen, it was the first marriage between two Canadian doctors.

When University of Toronto finally decided to admit women to the medical school in 1905, it was another coup for the Stowes.

Montreal Milestone

While this mother and daughter team had a female medical monopoly in 19th century Toronto, in Montreal Dr. Charlotte Ross, graduate of the Philadelphia Women's Medical School in 1875, became that city's first woman to practise medicine. She opted for a rugged practice, heading for western Canada, where she lived in a tent, plagued by grasshoppers, whose favorite snacks proved to be clothes and bedding. Tough trappers and lumbermen were among Dr. Ross' patients. As a woman doctor she had to work hard to win their admiration. One night Dr. Ross rushed to the saloon to attend a man bleeding from an ugly neck gash. Having no instruments with her, she sewed up the wound with an ordinary needle and thread. The patient's weather-beaten skin was so tough, she had to use a poker chip as a thimble. His hard-boiled pals, asked to hold the lantern, fainted one by one! Accidents were so common that it is said Dr. Ross once casually exchanged recipes with other women at the station house while scrubbing up, after skillfully amputating a man's leg crushed under the wheels of a train.

It took a special act of the Manitoba Legislature to enable Dr. Ross to practise medicine there. Her eldest daughter took care of the household and seven brothers and sisters while mother did her rounds, travelling by handcar, canoe, sleigh, ox-team, even on foot. After delivering a baby, she would often stay, clean her patient's house, wash, iron and cook. One night she left her dying four-year-old son (who was beyond help) to attend a confinement case. She walked almost two miles, in knee-high snow, to help another woman — two months before having a baby herself. Like Dr. Stowe, Dr. Ross transmitted love of medicine to her family. Edith, her favorite grandchild, became a physician, won a medal in obstetrics, and established a high reputation as an anaesthetist in St. Boniface Hospital. After Dr. Ross' death in 1916, Dr. Edith Ross gave a medal in obstetrics to honor her grandmother.

North-style Medicine

It became accepted practice for women doctors to combine their professional career with motherhood. Dr. Stowe and Dr. Ross are two examples. Dr. Elizabeth Matheson even carried her youngest child papoose-style on her rounds. The first doctor and coroner in the Northwest Territories, Dr. Matheson cared for her nine children while attending Indian patients. Before graduating, she was a missionary in India for two years, where she married Rev. John Matheson. He persuaded her to finish her medical course. Elizabeth attended University of Manitoba 1895-96, but asked her professor, a gynecologist, to excuse her from classes after Christmas. He wondered why? In March she had her third child, who weighed 13 pounds. Dr. Elizabeth finally graduated in 1898 from Trinity College Medical School, in Toronto (now purely theological).

The Mathesons moved to Onion Lake in Northern Saskatchewan to serve as missionaries to the Indians. Dr. Elizabeth was appointed doctor for the Indians, at a salary of $300. In addition to her own nine youngsters, she legally adopted five other children, acted as teacher to the entire brood and was principal of the Indian School. In 1905, when the Prairies had more white settlers, Rev. Matheson built his wife a small hospital where, helped by their two eldest daughters as nurses, Dr. Matheson fought smallpox and diphtheria epidemics.

Quebec Pioneer

The first French-Canadian woman physician in Quebec was American-educated, Dr. Irma LeVasseur. Born in 1879, Irma graduated from University of Minnesota in 1900, then practised in New York. Anxious to make a contribution to her own country, she applied for permission to take the examinations of the College of Physicians and Surgeons of Quebec. Its constitution had to be amended by the Quebec Legislative Assembly. Dr. LeVasseur, a pioneer pediatrician, opened a children's clinic in 1904, helped found St. Justine's Hospital for children in Montreal and its counterpart in Quebec City.

Fire Hits

On her knees, amidst smoking ruins, a stout woman, sobbing, hands bleeding from broken glass, was rescuing specimens. It was Dr. Maude Abbott.

Fire practically destroyed the McGill Medical Museum and its contents in 1907. "Dr. Maude" was so popular that other museums around the world sent specimens to replace those lost. But seventeen years of irreplaceable notes had gone up in smoke. Dr. Ruttan, registrar at McGill University, one day, had remarked: "McGill's Medical Museum needs a lover!" It found one in Maude, curator from 1900 to 1932.

In the United States, Maude met Dr. William Osler, who said: "A clinical museum is the greatest place I know for teaching students. Pictures of life and death together. Wonderful!" The seed sown by Dr. Osler influenced not only her future career, but that of her students. She organized the Associations for the Proper Education of Women, enlisting support from leading doctors and wealthy women. Many phsyicians did not object to girls studying medicine, but frowned on mixed classes, maintaining they would encourage immorality. However, it was felt that separate classes would be too expensive. The contemptuous attitude of others was crystallized in Dr. F. W. Campbell's sneering: "Women may be useful in some departments of medicine, but in difficult work — surgery, for instance — they would not have the nerve. Can you think of a patient in a critical case waiting while the medical lady fixes her bonnet, or adjusts her bustle?"

McGill remained obdurate, although Maude had won a scholarship to that university, so in 1890 she enrolled at Bishops' College, first institution in Quebec to admit women as medical students. There, Grace Ritchie, an ardent feminist, was finishing her medical course. Grace, who held the first ticket for clinics at Montreal General Hospital ever issued to a woman, urged Maude to apply for one immediately. Only when widespread publicity and sympathy for Maude induced some of the hospital's wealthy supporters to threaten withholding donations, did she receive a ticket — the last issued to a woman. Men students actually stole student case reports from the wards to prevent Maude from graduating. However, despite this she graduated from Bishops' in 1894 with both the senior anatomy medal and the chancellor's prize. (Bishops' amalgated with McGill in 1905.)

Her medical reputation was established by the section she wrote on congenital heart defects (almost unknown until then) for Osler's *System of Medicine*. Her major writing was a massive volume called *Atlas of Congenital Cardiac Disease* (which listed and described 1,000 cases), a classified bibliography of Osler's writings. Hundreds of "blue babies" indirectly owe their lives to the indefatigable Dr. Abbott.

Dr. Maude Abbott

In 1905 McGill appointed Dr. Abbott a research fellow in pathology and in 1910 made her a lecturer. That year, the University also formally recognized her work with the honorary degree of M.D., C.M. — the very degree she had tried to earn back in 1890!

Maude's chequered career, filled with tragedies

and triumphs, did much to break down barriers against women doctors. She became an international authority on cardiac diseases, as well as medical museums. Born in Montreal in 1869, orphaned early (her father deserted the family), Maude and her only sister, Alice, were adopted by their grandparents. In 1898 tragedy befell Maude. She spent a fortune seeking a cure for her sister Alice who, through an illness, became a mental patient.

Maude attended McGill from 1888, graduated with a B.A., then petitioned the McGill faculty to allow her to study medicine. She was curtly refused. Consulting her cousin, the Prime Minister, Sir John Abbott, Maude was advised: "Get the public at your back!" And she did. Unpopular at McGill University and considered a "grind", in later years she was loved by all who knew her. Late in her career, in 1932, at a formal dinner at a medical convention, Maude, having written most of the preceding night, dozed off and snored. Fellow physicians looking on with affectionate amusement, wakened her with rousing hand-clapping. She joined in heartily, but was embarrassed to find the applause was for her! Dr. Abbott won the gold medal, the highest award for her exhibit on congenital heart disease. This exhibit, a summary of years of research, was so valuable it was featured at the centenary meeting of the British Medical Association in London, and was on display at the Graduate Fortnightly in Cardiology at the New York Academy of Medicine in 1931.

After her reluctant retirement in 1936, the Carnegie Foundation in 1940 granted her $2,500 to complete a book on heart disease — her life's work. It was not too little, but it came too late. While sitting for her portrait, painted by a close friend, Mary Bell Eastlake, which was to hang in the medical building of McGill — the first portrait of a woman in that distinguished company — Dr. Maude became exhausted and was taken to hospital. She died of a cerebral hemorrhage on September 2, 1940.

* * *

Dr. Frances McGill didn't always get her man, but that's because she was usually behind a microscope at her job for the Royal Canadian Mounted Police. The first woman ever to become a member of the force, Dr. McGill graduated in medicine from the University of Manitoba and did postgraduate work in laboratory technique.

She was appointed Saskatchewan provincial bacteriologist, then in 1922, director of the Saskatchewan laboratory. From 1928-48, Dr. McGill worked in close collaboration with the RCMP in Regina, handling medico-legal cases and performing autopsies.

* * *

The chance of riding horses, lured Dr. Mary Jackson from England to western Canada where she pioneered in obstetrics. With the biggest event of the week — the mail delivery — she was able to send home letters filled with the excitement of life in Canada. Her courage is legend. While snow clogged streets around her and temperatures dropped to 60 below, she delivered her own son, John, six weeks premature. She staged a one-woman campaign to secure government help when rabid wolves and foxes spread the disease among farm animals in 1952.

Dr. Jackson delivered many babies, but it is another westerner who makes a specialty of it — Dr. Elinor Black, chief obstetrician and gynecologist at the Winnipeg General Hospital and professor at University of Manitoba. The Royal College of Obstetricians and Gynecologists elected her to Fellowship, the first Canadian of either sex to meet the rigid standards of the College. As a pioneer in Canada's medical aid to the Caribbean, Dr. Elinor Black spent a hectic three months in early 1969 at the University of the West Indies.

A province away, Dr. Marion Hilliard headed the department of obstetrics and gynecology at the Women's College Hospital in Toronto for 10 years until 1957. Born in Morrisburg in 1902, she graduated from the University of Toronto medical school in 1927, where she had been a star athlete. She took post graduate work in Europe.

On Christmas Day in 1911, as Women's College Hospital handled its first maternity case, Nurse Dixon worried. "My goodness, this baby hasn't any bed!" "Neither did another baby born on Christmas Day," reminded Dr. Isabella Wood, who delivered the child. The fact that, through the years, in over 6,000 obstetrical cases only one mother died (from an incurable disease) made many people think of Women's College solely as a maternity hospital. Dr. Hilliard's work contributed greatly to its prestige. She delivered over 10,000 babies many named "Marion" after her. She also carried out valuable research on cancer, dying in 1958 from the disease she had worked so hard to combat.

* * *

Dr. Jean Hogarth, a dark, magnetic woman is one of Canada's leading gastroenterologists. Graduating from University of Toronto in 1951, she obtained her B.Sc. in 1953 and became a member of the Royal College of Physicians and Surgeons five years later. She is an associate professor at Toronto Western Hospital.

War work took Hamilton's Dr. Jean Davey to Europe. Born in 1909, the daughter of Dr. J. Edgar Davey, she interned at Toronto Psychiatric Hospital from 1935 to 1936 and when war broke out, became senior medical officer to the Women's Division of the RCAF, stacking up an O.B.E. for distinguished service. In 1950 she became chief of medical services at Women's College Hospital.

Dorothy Frances Graham, when chairman of the

Board of Governors of the Women's College Hospital, was honoured by her father C. L. Burton, who established a Research Fellowship there in her name in February 1956. Misses H. M. G. Macmorine and N. Farrell of Toronto, were members of the original teams that in April 1955, developed Salk vaccine to prevent poliomyelitis. Dr. Elizabeth Garbutt of Calgary did research in England on leprosy. Handsome Dr. Edith Mankiewicz, born in Germany, obtained her licence to practise medicine in Canada in 1959 and passed the P.Q. Certification as microbiologist in 1960. Since 1962, she has been director of laboratories at Royal Edward Chest Hospital, with which her sister, Dr. Margaret Kunstler, a clever and sympathetic G.P., is also associated. Dr. Mankiewicz made an important discovery which reduces by three weeks the time needed to find out whether a patient has active tuberculosis. She is also professor of bacteriology at McGill and Montreal Universities.

Dr. Frances Kelsey, Canadian-born pharmacologist, was named to Women's Hall of Fame Gallery at the New York Fair in 1965 for her work with the U.S. Public Health Service. She stubbornly refused to approve the distribution of the fetus-malforming drug, thalidomide. For this service she was given a gold medal by President John Kennedy.

Mary Berglund of Ignace, still a volunteer member of the Ignace Ambulance Service at age 73, and who had provided medical services to the Northwestern Ontario community for more than forty years, was one of twenty-five women honored at a Dinner given by the Ontario Government in October 1975 (Women's Year).

"Prevention is better than cure", believes Dr. Elizabeth Bagshaw, founder and, until 1967, director of Canada's first Planned Parenthood Clinic in Hamilton. Dr. Ellen Verway agrees and she made the startling suggestion at the Vancouver hearings of the Royal Commission on the Status of Women that all males over sixteen should be temporarily sterilized to combat mounting illegitimacy.

During the Depression the poor received free advice and help at the clinic of Dr. Bagshaw, who daily risked jail for violating the law. A Kitchener man sold them birth control supplies at cost. However, the Roman Catholic bishop dubbed them "devils" which, of course, drew attention to the clinic and doubled the clientele. Having graduated in 1905 from University of Toronto, Dr. Bagshaw practised medicine for seventy-one years, during which time she delivered over 3,000 babies. Retiring aged ninety-six, she was honoured at a Testimonial Dinner. She was one of eight doctors who founded the Federation of Medical Women of Canada, of which Dr. Abbott was first president. Dr. Bagshaw was the only woman to be made an honorary member of the Ontario Medical Association, and in June, 1969, was honored with a senior membership in the Canadian Medical Association.

* * *

Dr. Henrietta Banting (Ball) born in Nova Scotia graduated in medicine from the University of Toronto in 1945 (following the death of husband, Sir Frederick Banting, co-discoverer of insulin). She specialized in obstetrics and gynecology and became director of the Cancer Detection Clinic, the first in Canada, at Women's College Hospital. It started in 1948 with Dr. Florence McConnery as first director. This hospital was responsible for another innovation, its sterility clinic, which was set up to help childless women. Dr. Elizabeth Stewart, Canada's first woman radiologist, and a staff member for 43 years, wrote its history.

Dr. Ethlyn Trapp, a 1927 McGill University graduate in Medicine, worked in Vancouver as a diagnostic and therapeutic radiologist despite a serious congenital handicap. During World War II, when she directed the

B.C. Cancer Institute, she was the only radio-therapist in the province.

One of Canada's cleverest women psychiatrists, Dr. Grace Baker of Chatham, Ontario, has carried on a highly successful practise in New York for many years, after graduating from the University of Toronto. She maintains an amazing serenity, despite the numerous attempts made on her life by disturbed patients. She travels to relax from her tension-filled work.

Dr. Mary McEwan, a family doctor, followed her children to university for post-graduate psychiatry study, then joined St. Michael's Hospital as staff psychiatrist. In 1969, she became the first woman president of the 62-year-old Toronto Academy of Medicine.

Dr. Laura Coleman Forgues is the daughter of Dr. Ralph Coleman, first professor of bacteriology of UBC. Her mother was a Scottish nurse with titled relatives. Laura has been presented at court. An attractive redhead, slow-speaking but quick-thinking, she is a medical doctor, surgeon and psychiatrist, who studied at McGill, University of London, and Harvard. Dr. Laura worked with the founder of Crease Clinic in British Columbia, was on staff with her American-born husband, Dr. Roland Forgues, psychologist, at Smiths Falls Hospital and has worked in many clinics and hospitals here and abroad.

A perfectionist, Laura entertains beautifully in their combined office-home, and is a gracious guest. But she will leave instantly whenever a patient needs help — "Right Now".

"The drug problem is nothing new," she maintains. "I have seen a five-year-old glue sniffer, and nine to 13 year-olds on drugs in Vancouver. The pushers are the worst offenders." Her ambition is to have schools teach classes in family living. Childless herself, she has helped thousands of young people across Canada, and saved some from suicide.

Somehow she makes time for hobbies of music, stamp and coin collecting, and does considerable lecturing. A member of seventeen different medical associations, she is past president of the Federation of Medical Women of Canada.

Dr. Forgues is at present a consulting psychiatrist for regional headquarters at the prison for women at Kingston Penitentiary.

* * *

Dr. Jessie Boyd Scriver, wife of a doctor and chief of pediatrics at Montreal's Royal Victoria Hospital, became the first woman president of a specialist section of the Canadian Medical Association. Dr. Norma Ford Walker, for years associate professor of human genetics in University of Toronto's zoology department, also director of genetics at the Hospital for Sick Children, undertook detailed research into the root causes of mental retardation.

* * *

Another busy researcher, Dr. Madge Macklin for 24 years taught histology and embryology at University of Western Ontario. Internationally-known for research in human heredity, in 1957 she received the Elizabeth Blackwell Citation. Her colleague, physicist Dr. Elizabeth Laird, was given an LL.D. in 1954. Dr. Vibeke Engelbert, professor of zoology at University of Toronto for 22 years, managed to explode a long-standing text-book theory about blood formation, with her discovery that when nuclei of blood cells, called lymphocytes break up, it results in the formation of new blood cells, rather than a process of degeneration.

* * *

The first woman to attain a masters degree in surgery, Dr. Jessie Gray, in 1939, has a long list of firsts to her credit and a reputation for inspiring confidence in all her patients. During a lull in a business meeting, it is reported that one young executive pointed to the smiling face of Dr. Jessie Gray in the morning newspaper, saying: "Now there's a woman I'd let operate on me!" "Bet you five you wouldn't!" one man exclaimed. "Bet you 25," said another. When the executive had an emergency appendix, he decided to collect.

This sense of confidence that "Dr. Jessie" inspires in everyone is backed by a brilliant academic and professional record. Daughter of Catherine Allebach and Alex Gray, she was born in 1910 and graduated in medicine from University of Toronto in 1934, first woman gold medallist in the medical school. She spent several years interning with famous surgeons and was the first woman resident surgeon at the Toronto General Hospital. In 1941 she was the first woman to secure (by examination) the degree of Fellow of the Royal College of Surgeons.

She commenced her practise as associate chief of surgery at Women's College Hospital and in 1945 was appointed surgeon-in-chief. Dr. Gray specialized in breast, thyroid and abdominal surgery. One morning as she was removing a patient's gallstones, she heard that a young woman had just died while being anaesthetized for a minor operation. Snatching up a sterile knife, she hurried to the girl, opened her chest, and massaged her heart back to life.

In 1951 Dr. Gray was made Fellow of the American College of Surgeons, without examination, and she also received an Elizabeth Blackwell Citation. Following a heart attack, Jessie officially retired in 1965, but was the only woman appointed to the Science Council organized in 1967.

Dentists

Although women entered the dental profession soon after crashing the medical profession, today,

Canada has only a few women dentists. In European countries most dentists are women. Josephine Wells, mother of Mr. Justice Dalton Wells, was the pace-setter. She entered the profession when her husband, a dentist, became ill and she took over his practice in 1893, studying at nights to get her doctorate in dental surgery from Trinity College. She was the first woman to enter institutional work at Mercer Reformatory, Ontario Hospital in Toronto and similar institutions.

Dr. Mabel Connell and her husband, Lorne, of Prince Albert were probably the first husband-wife dental team in Canada. In 1969, the Newfoundland Dental Society elected a woman, Dr. Kira Obrazcova as president.

*   *   *

Though numerically small — only 10% of doctors in Canada are women — compared with 70% in Russia — the healing hands of women doctors have enriched medical profession for more than a century. They have not only helped rebuild broken bodies and minds, but also made discoveries which have helped prevent such tragedies. The courage, ability and tenacity of the advance guard — Emily Stowe, Augusta Stowe-Gullen, Elizabeth Smith Shortt, Charlotte Ross, Elizabeth Matheson and Maude Abbott — smoothed the way for modern women of medicine. Indeed, medical woman power has been an important element of the shock troops battling for mankind's health.

Chapter VI

Ladies Bountiful

Welfare

Mrs. A. J. Freiman

Woman is now emerging as a real force for social change on this continent . . . health and welfare are her babies.

(Dr. Reva Gerstein, Psychologist)

When begging was banned in 1688, the Supreme Council of New France established Le Bureau des Pauvres, thereby laying the foundation of governmental welfare in Canada. The bureau had offices in Quebec, Montreal, and Three Rivers. Almost 100 years later, the Charitable Irish Society was set up in Halifax, followed by the Poor Man's Society in 1820 — all very rudimentary structures for dealing with the complex problem of poverty. It was many years before the idea of charity evolved into the concept of social welfare.

With their gentleness and understanding, women developed their God-given talents in work with the poor as they did in nursing and teaching. Today, they literally dominate the fields. Canada's history has been enriched in human as well as material terms by the continuing army of women volunteers and philanthropists, working to help the less fortunate in our society, often under religious or organizational auspices. Women have contributed to fund-raising for charity as generously as Mary of Bethany poured out her spikenard ointment.

The first charity bazaar in Canada held by English-speaking women was in February, 1829, in Montreal, and it raised 450 Louis ($90.00). That was the precursor of thousands of church and club bazaars and teas through which women have raised millions for charity. For example, on one day in October, 1954, some 2,500 Toronto Jewish women, members of Hadassah, raised $72,000 at a mammoth bazaar in the Automotive Building of the Canadian National Exhibition.

Founded in 1916, Hadassah spends more than $1,-000,000 a year, chiefly for food and clothing, for the relief of the needy in Israel. Some goes to the Children's Village of Hadassim, started by Hadassah after World War II for homeless European waifs; some to youth redemption centers which have rehabilitated more than 65,000 Jewish children since 1933, and some to an agricultural school for 200 boys and girls on reclaimed land by the Sea of Galilee.

Mother of Canada's Jewish People

Mrs. A. J. Freiman, known as "Mother of the Jewish People of Canada", probably was the most prominent national president of Hadassah. Born Lillian Bilsky in 1885, she married Ottawa department-store owner Archibald Freiman in 1903. Their four children, Lawrence, Dorothy (Mrs. Bernard Alexandor), Queenie (Mrs. B. Luxenberg, Toronto), and Gladys, an adopted daughter, carry on the family tradition of community service.

In 1925, Mrs. Freiman was a delegate to the first General Congress of the Child, in Geneva. Nominated one of the three world representatives by La Conference Universelle Juive de Secours, with headquarters in Paris, she raised more than $100,000 to aid Jewish children in Europe. Active in welfare organizations of all denominations, she was the first woman honorary member of the Canadian Legion. Mrs. Freiman was awarded the Silver Jubilee Medal in 1935 and the O.B.E. in 1934, in recognition of her humanitarian work. She died in 1940.

Door Of Welcome

With four of her six sons away in the services, Ottawa's Mrs. Moses Loeb transformed what could have been lonely years into busy, memory-filled times, by opening her doors to visiting servicemen throughout World War II. An active volunteer sewer for the Red Cross, Rose Loeb was also a lady bountiful to a steady stream of transients from Ottawa's Union Mission. They could always find a sandwich at the Loeb house during the hungry '30's. In these years, too, Mrs. Loeb "spent a lot of time in the office," recalls her son, David. The "office" in this case was her husband's business which started out as a confectionery and blossomed into the multi-million dollar Loeb IGA wholesale, tobacco and drug empire, now directed by sons Bertram and Norman and, to a lesser extent, by David, the former owner of the Ottawa Rough Riders Football Club.

As the family expanded and Mrs. Loeb's volunteer work with Hadassah and National Council of Jewish Women increased, she took a less active part in the actual operation of the firm she helped her husband launch. She was, however, a director of the company until her death at the age of 70. The family's philanthropy is strikingly displayed in the form of Carleton University's Loeb Building of Social Sciences — the result of a $500,000 bequest by the family to the university.

Quebec Trio

In Quebec, a trio of outstanding philanthropists, Marie, Justine, and Thais Lacoste, paved the way for welfare breakthroughs in their province. Their father, Sir Alexander Lacoste, Chief Justice of the Quebec Appeal Court, presided at the first meeting of the National Council of Women — a task then thought beyond the capabilities of women. The Council, of course, developed into one of the country's largest welfare organizations.

The eldest Lacoste daughters, Marie and Justine, born in the 1870's and their younger sister, Thais, born in 1886, became tireless workers in the field of welfare, not only in their home province, but also at the national and international level.

Married to a lawyer, Henri Gerin-Lajoie, Marie also studied law so that she could intelligently assist in bringing about reforms on behalf of married women — reforms which resulted in the 1929 revision of the Quebec Civil Code. Marie's 1902 *Treatise on Everyday Law* became a school textbook. Later she headed the French section of the Provincial Franchise Committee, before religious pressure forced her resignation.

Marie became involved in an interesting experiment in bicultural understanding when she helped found the Federation Nationale St. Jean Baptiste, a French-speaking patriotic society, to collaborate with English-speaking Quebec women in welfare work. Mrs. Gerin-Lajoie, who lectured in civics and law at the University of Montreal, had the satisfaction of seeing her daughter, Marie, become the first woman graduate of the University of Montreal in 1911, and later, a lecturer in social sciences at the university.

Justine Lacoste also married a lawyer, Louis de Gaspé Beaubien. With no children of her own, she deployed her considerable energies and wealth in the field of child welfare. The deplorable lack of hospital facilities for infants and young children in turn-of-the-century Montreal was the first of many pressing problems to be tackled.

With a group of other notable volunteers, including Mme. Theodule Bruneau, Mlle. Euphrosine Rolland and Dr. Irma Levasseur, Justine founded St. Justine's Hospital to help ease the critical shortage of beds. The death rate dropped from one baby in four to one baby in 20 during the next 50 years. Twelve tiny patients were accommodated in the rented house on St. Denis Street which served as the hospital's first headquarters. The 11-woman board of directors not only coped with all the problems of renting, but also had a brush with anti-quated Quebec law in the process. They had to persuade the Quebec government to amend the Civil Code so that the board members could conduct hospital affairs with-out the consent of their husbands. The work of Justine Beaubien and her colleagues stood the test of time when a modern 860-bed hospital opened its doors in 1958. Justine, who served as president of the board for more than 50 years, working a regular eight-hour day, was honored by Pope Pius XII in 1949 and was named a C.B.E. for her services.

Thais, the third Lacoste daughter, followed the family tradition, serving as first secretary of St. Justine's Hospital. Married to Charles Fremont in 1910, Thais was a feminine activist, who founded an unemployment bureau for women during the depression and lobbied for wage parity for charwomen working in Quebec's public buildings.

Thais' work took on international dimensions in 1932, when Prime Minister Bennett appointed her a full delegate to the 13th assembly of the League of Nations. For the next three years, she served as vice-president of the League's Society. Back on the Canadian scene in 1937, Thais was the Canadian Welfare Council's repre-sentative in Quebec. During the war years she served on the Women's National Advisory Committee on the Legal Status of Married Women in 1947.

Like the Lacoste sisters, Mrs. Lillian Massey Tre-ble was motivated by a love of humanity. Born in Newcastle, Ontario in 1854, the daughter of Hart Mas-sey (University of Toronto's Hart House bears his name), Lillian earmarked her considerable fortune for welfare work, first as a trustee of the Fred Victor Mis-sion in Toronto, then in 1903 as founder of the Traveller's Aid Society, whose far-reaching arm of assistance reached out to children, immigrants, runaways, and the handicapped. Later she founded and financed the Lillian Massey School of Household Economics.

Pioneer Philanthropist

In the East, Lady Alice Tilley, wife of Sir Leonard Tilley, one of the Fathers of Confederation, was a pioneer philanthropist. She founded Victoria College Hospital in Fredericton, the Seaman's Mission, an Industrial School for boys, a Home for Consumptives in Saint John, and helped found the Chipman Memorial Hospital at St. Stephen, N.B., in 1908. Besides fulfilling exacting social duties, she was vice-president of both the National Council of Women and the Women's Art Association.

* * *

Developments in the contemporary welfare field owe much to the efforts of a long line of hard workers. Florence Gooderham Huestis, Adelaide Mowbray McLaughlin, Maude Keen Riley, Marjorie Bell, Mrs. Kaspar Fraser and Ruth Frankel, to name a few.

As convener of Toronto Local Council of Women's public health committee, Mrs. Florence Huestis had a ready-made platform and the sympathetic ear of the city's newspaper women as a backdrop for her many reform campaigns at the turn of the century. She is credited with helping to purify Toronto's water supply and introducing a superior sewage disposal system which virtually wiped out typhoid fever in the city. She lobbied tirelessly for 50 years for improved housing, more playgrounds, and better care for the mentally retarded. Founding president of the Big Sister's Association, Mrs. Huestis held executive posts in numerous other welfare organizations. Toronto's Women's College Hospital discovered that their board president was also a super fund-raiser when Mrs. Huestis headed the hospital's successful $750,000 building campaign.

* * *

Adelaide Mowbray, born in Kinsale, Ontario, in 1875, was a young school teacher when R. S. McLaughlin, later head of General Motors of Canada, first saw her singing in a church choir. He was so fascintated that he forgot to put in his collection, but slipped a dime to the verger later. They were married in 1898 and settled in Oshawa. The doors of their magnificent home "Parkwood", welcomed scores of servicemen during both world wars. Mrs. McLaughlin received her air raid precautions and St. John's first aid certificates during wartime. Later she was named an officer in the Order of the Hospital of St. John of Jerusalem.

The McLaughlin's annual "Chrysanthemum Tea" was a social highlight for some 1,000 Oshawans. During World War II, the McLaughlins entertained servicemen from around the world. Managing a mansion such as Parkwood might have been a full-time job for some women but Adelaide also managed to raise five charming daughters and hold office in the Red Cross, the Home and School Association, and the National Council of Women, receiving honorary life memberships in the latter two.

Mrs. McLaughlin had helped Mrs. Courtice organize the H. and S. Association. This was recognized officially when she received honorary degrees from both Mount Allison University and Queen's University, and the women of Oshawa organized a Testimonial Dinner in her honor. Proud of her UEL ancestry, which has been called "the aristocracy of Canada", she financed the restoration of the burying ground at Adolphustown, and in her memory, Mr. McLaughlin generously gave them a donation which enabled them to maintain a central office and reading room for members. Interested in the Women's Lyceum Art Association, during her lifetime she allowed them to have their fund-raising parties (for scholarships) at Parkwood. The McLaughlins donated the fine building that became the Oshawa YMCA.

With hardly a pause for breath, Mrs. McLaughlin launched a building campaign to give Oshawa a hospital, just as soon as the mortgage on the church had been paid off. Tossing the fund's initial $5000 into the ring, she mobilized her church women's auxiliary who matched her donation through door-to-door canvassing. President of the Oshawa General Hospital Auxiliary from 1910 until her death in 1958, Mrs. McLaughlin made it a condition to provide the graduating nurses with their crisp white caps, even doing so one year when she was a patient in the hospital.

In Oshawa, Adelaide Street, Adelaide McLaughlin Public School, Adelaide House (YWCA) and Camp Ademac cherish her memory.

* * *

A near-fatal illness in 1909 prompted Maude Keen Riley's intense interest in child welfare. A year later Maude plunged into a number of worthy causes — setting up a baby clinic in 1922, acting as city director of recreation in 1940, helping add policewomen to the city constabulary in 1943, setting up a guidance clinic four years later, and a family court in 1953. Active in the Canadian Welfare Council, Mrs. Riley helped implement the Child Welfare Act. Her spacious home became the Maude Riley Home for Children.

* * *

Children are the main concern of social worker Elizabeth Vera Perlin, whose school for trainable retardates, opened in 1966 in Newfoundland, was the culmination of twelve years hard work. The school's shaky beginnings were in the basement of a United Church orphanage. By 1958, Mrs. Perlin and her associates had succeeded in establishing the Newfoundland Associa-

tion for the Help of Retarded Children, with Mrs. Perlin
as president. A year later a five-classroom school was
organized through public contributions, and Mrs. Perlin
set up branches in seven communities.

During the Second World War, Mrs. Perlin had
co-founded the Home and School Association in
Newfoundland, was a member of the government's
advisory committee on Education, and more recently,
she represented Newfoundland at the Vanier Institute
of the Family, as a member of the Canadian Welfare
Advisory Council. In 1967, the NCJW gave Mrs. Perlin
their award as Newfoundland's outstanding woman.

* * *

Two Torontonians, Marjorie Bell and Mrs. Kaspar Fraser, proved how effectively the professional and
the volunteer welfare worker can complement each
other. As president of the Toronto Welfare Council,
Mrs. Fraser got the professionals on her side in the battle to raise the city's inadequate welfare allowances. As
part of a three-member team investigating the situation,
Miss Bell took a taste of the welfare medicine herself —
two weeks living within the relief allowance budget —
to point up the need for reform. After considerable agi-
tation by the Welfare Council, the investigating team's
recommendations were adopted. Mrs. Fraser later
became first woman chairman of the Canadian Welfare
Council (1949-1952), and in 1954 was chairman of the
International Conference of Social Work, which
brought some 1,800 delegates from around the world to
Toronto. Miss Bell followed up her interest in nutrition
with the VON in Montreal. Her work with expectant
and nursing mothers provided the basis for a study on
the influence of diet on childbirth, carried out by Dr. J.
H. Ebbs of the research department of Toronto's Hospital for Sick Children.

The results, linking miscarriages, premature

births, and childbirth deaths with improper diet, received world-wide attention. In 1952 the British Ministry of Health adopted the study's prenatal diet for use in its maternity clinics. An M.B.E. awarded a year later to Miss Bell honored the research breakthrough which she had initiated.

Three Cheers for Volunteers

Welfare-minded Ruth Frankel of Toronto combines zest with know-how to raise funds for such worthy causes as the Canadian Cancer Society, the YMCA, the YWCA and the Salvation Army. The widow of lawyer Egmont Frankel, Ruth is a sought-after speaker on child psychology and home economics. President of the Canadian Cancer Society for five years and a board member of the Ontario Cancer Research Foundation, Mrs. Frankel has travelled at her own expense to see conditions first-hand in every major cancer treatment center in North America. Her 1956 book, *Three Cheers for Volunteers*, is still very pertinent today. She was awarded the Order of Canada at a Government House ceremony in 1969.

* * *

Lady Clara Kemp's name is synonymous with her special welfare interest — the blind. Active in the women's auxiliary of the CNIB since 1927, she became president of the CNIB in 1954. She was an active worker in other organizations, and generous in loaning her home for any good cause.

Lady Drummond of Montreal, on the other hand, was equally active in many organizations, especially in war work. One day, while rolling bandages at the Red Cross meeting, she received a telegram informing her that her son had been killed in action at St. Julian in April 1915. This heroic mother quietly resumed her work.

Such programs, expanded and carried out in a professional atmosphere by trained personnel, are the basis of social service in the contemporary sense. The field of social welfare has developed to an unprecedented degree from the early church and philanthropic group efforts of the 19th and early 20th century. Government now tends to direct those services which once were provided by volunteers. Today's social worker must have multi-disciplinary training to cope with the complex needs and problems of contemporary society. Although volunteers are still a vital link in the chain, trained graduates of Canada's dozen or so university-based schools of social welfare from the background of the profession ... schools such as the forerunner in Toronto, founded in 1914, or the McGill School for Social Workers set up four years later.

Miss Jane Wisdom was one of the early lecturers at the McGill school, which was brought to a halt in 1932 by financial problems. Social welfare work found an "angel" in the form of the Bronfman family. Gerald Bronfman, son of Ann and Harry Bronfman, sought the advice of Montreal welfare leaders of all races and faiths concerning a project the family might initiate. Generous contributors to many fund-raising projects, Mr. and Mrs. Bronfman marked their 50th wedding anniversary with a $50,000 donation to the Ann and Harry Bronfman Fund for social work and education. Their son serves as honorary chairman.

Mrs. Saidye Bronfman and her husband, Samuel, also have contributed substantial sums to special projects, particularly in the field of art. The new $1,000,000 center for performing arts, education and Jewish studies — the Saidye Bronfman Arts Center — was donated to the Young Men's and Young Women's Hebrew Association by the children of Mr. and Mrs. Samuel Bronfman. In 1968 Saidye Bronfman received the Eleanor Roosevelt Humanities Award for her wide-ranging work with Hadassah, Canadian Save the Children Fund and Youth Alyiah of Canada, of which she is honorary patroness.

* * *

Organized social work training was put on a permanent footing in 1933 when, McGill University cooperated to establish the Montreal School of Social Work. For the next 12 years Miss Dorothy King, the first director, built on this solid foundation and in 1945, it became McGill University School of Social Work. Remembered as a distinguished educationalist, Miss King was also a warm-hearted, experienced social worker who served her chosen field for more than 40 years until her retirement in 1950.

* * *

Miss Bessie Touzel did volunteer work with a Children's Aid Society, before graduating from the University of Toronto School of Social Work in 1928. Her college field work took her to both settlements and family welfare agencies. After graduation, she was a district secretary of the Neighborhood Workers' Association, chief of staff with the Ottawa public welfare department, secretary public welfare division, Canadian Welfare Council and executive secretary of the Toronto and district Welfare Council.

Miss Touzel's work with a federal government cabinet committee studying manpower needs in special war situations, resulted in the Marsh Report on Social Security on which she collaborated with Dr. Leonard Marsh. During the '40's and '50's Miss Touzel held top posts at the Canadian and Ontario welfare councils. In 1956 she became a vice-president of the International Federation of Social Workers. Her work took her to New Brunswick where she conducted a major study of provincial welfare services, and to Winnipeg to direct the emergency welfare services to refugees section of

Red Cross disaster operations during the devastating flood. In 1959 Miss Touzel received Toronto's Award of Merit for distinguished public service.

Jet-Age Angel of Mercy

Dr. Lotte Hitschmanova, the dedicated founder and executive director of Unitarian Service Committee of Canada, travels about 50,000 miles annually to inspect eight USC projects throughout the world. She helps the ragged and hungry, bringing them knew hope. This red-headed firebrand in her distinctive khaki uniform lectures across the country to finance her work of mercy.

"The population of our planet may double in five years," she warns: "We believe so strongly that family planning must take place that we are including it in every program of medical help in India. However, we have been unsuccessful in rural India because of religious prejudices. There can be no progress without planned parenthood." Presently Dr. Hitschmanova is campaigning for $1,300,000, urgently needed.

* * *

Mrs. Irena Ungar came to Canada from her native Poland during World War II and became a Canadian citizen in September 1948. Like other immigrants, she worked first as a domestic, then as an inspector in the Otis Fensom Company in Hamilton. She held increasingly responsible positions, and did much welfare work, especially for Polish people in the post war years. From 1955 until 1967 she was placement officer and counsellor in the settlement section, Department of Immigration, and for several years she worked closely with John Collingwood Read on his radio program "Canadians All" heard over CFRB. Mrs. Ungar helps arrange receptions for new Canadians when receiving their citizenship. Fluency in eight languages has been invaluable. For 15 years she has been vice-chairman of the Polish Welfare Committee, and gives advice to other ethnic groups on how to integrate into Canadian life. In 1968 she received the Medal of Service.

Shift of Interest

"It is not always pleasant to be a pioneer," Elizabeth Smith's diary recorded, during her turbulent years in medical training at Queen's in the 1880's. Like her friend Augusta Stowe who was breaking medical ground at Toronto, Elizabeth also suffered the harsh fortunes of a medical woman invading a man's world. "No one knows, or can know, the furnace we are passing through these days at college. We suffer torment, we shrink inwardly, we are hurt cruelly." When the handful of female students started excelling the men in examinations, the air was even thicker with tension with the women students segregated from the men in separate lecture theatres and dissecting rooms.

Determined to assist other women who wanted to become doctors, Elizabeth in her final year, helped found Women's Medical College in Kingston, similar to Toronto College. A generous donation from Dr. Jennie Trout gave the launching a considerable boost.

In her graduating year, Elizabeth served as a demonstrator there. Her marriage to fellow student Adam Shortt was another happy off-shoot of her studies at Kingston, which of course had smoothed the way for other young women to study medicine. Dr. Shortt's social welfare orientation blossomed when her husband moved the family to Ottawa with his appointment to the federal Civil Service Commission. Indeed Dr. Shortt became so completely immersed in welfare work that daughter Lorraine felt that the three Shortt children were sometimes neglected. Her list of credits, however, was impressive.

She initiated the first organized playground, the nucleus of Ottawa's public recreation system, founded the Women's Immigration Hostel, the Elizabeth Residence for elderly women, helped organize the Ottawa Welfare Bureau (later the Family Service Center) and agitated for segregation of mental defectives, treatment of social diseases, pasteurization of milk, a cleanup of the local market, equal pay for equal work, and women police and factory inspectors. Dr. Shortt helped Lady Aberdeen organize both the NCW and the VON. She held high offices in the NCW, including that of convener of immigration, public health and mental hygiene. She was also an eloquent speaker as well as writer.

Dr. Elizabeth (Smith) Shortt

Despite the amazing range of her activities, Dr. Shortt's interest in medicine never waned. "Often in the early part of the night," she said. "I lay awake and planned a paper. Then, when everyone was asleep, I got up and wrote it." Her 'Historical Sketch of Medical Edu-

cation of Women' is a valuable piece of medical Canadiana. Her 'Some Social Aspects of Tuberculosis' was
aired before the Ottawa Tuberculosis Association in
1912. Dr. Shortt's work in this association, forerunner of
the influential Anti-Tuberculosis League, earned her the
title of "The Fresh-Air Fiend".

Everywoman's World wrote of her, "Undoubtedly, there is no woman in Canada who has so wonderful a grasp of national affairs — she is a marvellous
organizer. Mrs. Shortt is the mastermind amongst
Canada's public women." Firmly believing that every
woman should take a vital part in government, Dr.
Shortt assisted members of the National Council of
Women in their campaign to have government aid given
to widowed mothers to preserve normal homes for their
families. As a result of the campaign, led by Dr. Shortt,
mothers' allowances were established in Ontario in
1920. From 1920 to 1927 Dr. Shortt was vice-chairman of
the commission administering allowances although she
was politically opposed to the government of the day.

In 1919, when Dr. Shortt began her campaign to
have oleo-margarine legalized in Canada, Ottawans said
that Hades moved into Parliament Hill. She and D'Arcy
Scott, counsel for the National Dairy Council, could not
be on the same streetcar without their heated arguments
disturbing the public peace. Dr. Shortt lived to hear the
Supreme Court legalize the sale of margarine. She was
buried on her birthday in 1949.

Helping the Helpless

As an English teacher in Toronto's Jarvis Collegiate Institute in the 1880's Helen MacMurchy, the petite
pretty daughter of the institute's principal Dr. Archibald
MacMurchy, found the sight of the school's handicapped students so distressing, she determined to study
medicine to help them. Her second career spanned the
next 35 years and so improved legislation that a federal

division of child welfare was set up with Dr. MacMurchy as director for 15 years.

Although Helen continued teaching while studying medicine at the Women's Medical College, she graduated with first-class honors in medicine and surgery. She then did post-graduate work at Johns Hopkins Hospital, Baltimore, under Sir William Osler. She had the distinction of being the first woman doctor appointed a resident intern at Toronto General Hospital. Dr. MacMurchy specialized in children's diseases, obstetrics and gynecology. In private practice briefly, she was appointed by the Ontario government as medical inspector of charitable institutions, hospitals and prisons. In 1906, the Ontario government requested her to prepare a census of the feeble-minded — a report which she wrote annually for the next 14 years. She also edited *The Canadian Nurse* from 1905 to 1911, wrote for numerous journals and was elected president of the Charities and Correction Association. Her research was considered so important that she was given periodic grants by the Canadian National Institute on Mental Hygiene.

During a stint as medical inspector of girls for Toronto schools, Dr. MacMurchy's bicycle was a familiar sight along Toronto streets. She became a noted lecturer on public health practices throughout North America and Great Britain and represented the Canadian Government in Baltimore at the first annual conference for the prevention of infant mortality, her chief interest. Dr. MacMurchy and Dr. George Adami of McGill, represented Canada at the Imperial Child Welfare Conference in England in 1914. Five years later she was one of more than 100 women doctors meeting in New York to plan a health program for the women and children of the world.

As medical inspector for auxiliary classes in Toronto public schools from 1915 to 1920, her reports on her mentally and physically handicapped charges were as practical as they were full of compassion.

In one appeal to the Board of Education she stressed: "I see these children, and I hear them, day and night. There are many physically handicapped children in Toronto. Many of them will be beggars or dependents if we don't give them a chance. To do so would be cheaper and wiser and kinder than not to."

Gentle by nature, but fierce when aroused by injustice, Dr. MacMurchy criticized the Toronto superintendent of education and officials for lack of co-operation. In return they angrily demanded her resignation. She refused. After six months of intensive work outlining what should be done she left in 1920 to take over as director of a federal department of child welfare for which she wrote best-selling books on child care. The *Canadian Mother's Book* which sold over 800,000 copies and her *Little Blue Books* were the bibles of millions of mothers.

Regretfully retiring at an energetic 72, she spent the next 20 years writing and lecturing. In 1939 she was elected a life member of the Academy of Medicine. The Federation of Medical Women of Canada of which she was honorary president, held a dinner in her honor in 1940 and donated her portrait, painted by Marion Long, to the Academy. She was made a C.B.E. and in 1949 was awarded the Elizabeth Blackwell citation as one of 12 leading physicians of the western world. When she died in 1953 her legacy to Canada was a magnificent heritage of healthier, happier homes.

Lady Bountiful

Elizabeth Ann "Lily" Brown's concern for animals was very much in keeping with family tradition. Her father, M.D. Adam Brown, postmaster in Hamilton, founded the Hamilton SPCA in 1887.

Following her glamorous, storybook marriage to Col. William Hendrie in 1901, "Lily" plunged into a busy round of community service. Her huge home "Gateside" threw open its doors to host scores of fund-raising events over the years. Particularly active in Girl Guides, St. John's Ambulance and SPCA work, Mrs. Hendrie was the first person awarded the Nora Frances Henderson Memorial Award in 1950.

The Humane Society honored her with a bronze medal of service in 1965 and in a ceremony at Government House in Ottawa Queen Elizabeth invested her as an officer sister of the Most Venerable Order of the Hospital of St. John of Jerusalem — a crowning touch to a lifetime of service to others.

Mother to Millions

With sympathetic understanding and devotion, Adelaide Sinclair reached out to 800,000,000 children the world over. As UNICEF's deputy director of programs, Mrs. Sinclair had the gigantic $24,000,000,000 task of helping the helpless — the two out of three children around the world doomed to die without outside assistance.

"It's unbelievable," she says "the colossal job done by UNICEF during the last 10 years" — anti-tuberculosis vaccinations, milk-drying plants throughout Europe and wonder drug shipments, to name only three projects.

Widowed after eight years of marriage to the late Donald Sinclair, slim, green-eyed Adelaide was born in Toronto in 1900, the daughter of Adelaide Sullivan and Dr. O. T. Macdonald. Her grandmother, Mrs. Grant Macdonald, organized Ontario's first Children's Aid Society in 1893. Educated at Havergal College and University of Toronto, where she graduated in honors political science in 1920, Mrs. Sinclair completed her postgraduate training in Berlin and the London School of

Economics, then began lecturing in economics at University of Toronto in 1927.

After her husband's death in 1938, Mrs. Sinclair was international president of her fraternity, Kappa Alpha Theta for several years. She resigned to do welfare work, and in 1942 was called to Ottawa as an economist with the Wartime Prices and Trade Board. A year later she was appointed head of the women's division Royal Canadian Navy. She once introduced herself at a fraternity dinner with these words: "I am Adelaide Sinclair, Sigma Chapter, and I have more children than any of you, because I am mother WREN." She rose to the rank of a captain, and was awarded the O.B.E. (military division). Retiring in 1946 Capt. Sinclair was appointed executive assistant to the deputy minister of welfare, Dr. George Davidson (president of the CBC). Really retiring in 1967 to home in Ottawa, she became president of the CIIA and the first woman elected to the Council of Rockcliffe Park Village.

Her career with the UN and its various agencies which began in 1947, gave her the broad background needed for her 1957 appointment as deputy director of programs for UNICEF. In her work with the UN body, Mrs. Sinclair held firmly to the self-help approach. "Each government knows best its most urgent and pressing problems", she says. "We must get away from the old theory of 'Lady Bountiful' and help others help themselves. It's much sounder. It is impossible to isolate yourself behind national boundaries in the world of today," she maintains. "First you have humanitarianism, and if you have money you have a moral obligation to relieve suffering."

Mrs. Sinclair's self-help theory of social welfare meshes well with the changing approach of contemporary social service, emphasizing rehabilitation and development of the individual as a viable member of his community.

Chapter VII

Modern Portias

Lawyers

Judge Helen Kinnear

> *"Bad laws are the worst sort of tyranny."*
>
> (Burke)

"Women are discriminated against (legally) in a thousand ways," maintains New York judge, Catherine Laut. "There is no country in the world where women have equal rights with men, unless one thinks back to ancient Egypt."

In Canada, for example, not only does the legal status of the sexes differ, but there is a unique system by which the laws of the Province of Quebec are drawn from the same source as the Napoleonic Code, while the other provinces follow British Common Law Procedure. Women have had a long, difficult struggle, first to be considered legally as "persons", then to break through legal and psychological barriers to become lawyers, judges and humanizers of cruel laws.

For example, in Quebec in 1649, a girl of sixteen was executed for theft. In 1722, two unmarried women, who tried to conceal their pregnancy, were sentenced to death. In 1739, a twenty-year-old Jewish girl came to Quebec disguised as a man acting as messenger for the Jesuits. Her impersonation discovered, she was deported, as Jews were barred during the French regime. And pity a poor housekeeper! In 1816 a Quebec woman, convicted of having an untidy house, was imprisoned for three months, then exposed to view on the market place pillory for one-half hour daily.

Even a century later, a little girl of 11, after spending two weeks in a penitentiary in the company of prostitutes, alcoholics and murderers, was sent to a reformatory. Her crime? Stealing a gooseberry from a garden. A young lad, Alex Lafleur, sentenced to Kingston Penitentiary, was brutally flogged thirty-four times, first on Christmas Eve. Why? For breaking the rule of silence by singing a carol. Another lad was so savagely beaten he became insane.

By the Mines Act of Saskatchewan and Nova Scotia, boys of twelve could work underground ... "Chained, belted, harnessed like dogs to a go-cart, saturated with sweat, the children went down into coal pit passageways where adults could not squeeze."

A Royal Commission on child labour, appointed around 1885, noted: "In cotton factories, penned in narrow lanes, they leap and reach and tie, among acres and acres of looms. Always a snow of lint on their faces, always the thunder of machines in their ears." The *Washington Post* commented: "The average life span of children after they go into the mills is four years. It would be less cruel to have them put to death."

Prior to the Factory Act of 1889, children under eleven could be employed around dangerous machinery; and employers could "chastise" them, so long as no "permanent injury" was inflicted.

The Poor Relief Act of Nova Scotia provided for the binding of children of poverty-stricken parents as apprentices (virtually a form of slavery) and was not abolished until 1900.

Until 1886, whipping of females, abolished *two centuries* earlier by Denmark, was legal in Canada as a means of forcing co-habitation on unwilling wives. As late as 1891, it took a writ of habeas corpus to free a Mrs. Jackson, a marital escapee, who had been recaptured and kept under guard by her husband.

These, and other inhumane laws have been torn from the statute books largely as the result of the efforts of women. Frequently, they had lobbied collectively, through such powerful organizations as the Business and Professional Women's Clubs and the National Council of Women, to have laws rescinded, or created and passed. Thus women have swayed the destiny of nations.

Long Lobby

In one major case on record, one of the early "loners" changed an archaic Canadian law. In the early 1880's Susan Wiggins of New Brunswick advocated a measure to legalize the marriage of a man with his deceased wife's sister. Church opposition was understandably strong, since the proposal ran counter to ecclesiastical law. Using the pen-name "Gunhilda", Mrs. Wiggins countered such religious objections in forceful letters, which through their "felicity of expression, cogency of reasoning, fierceness of invective and piquancy of style", caught the imagination of the press across Canada. In 1883, as a one-woman lobby in Ottawa, she out-talked four bishops of the Anglican Church — her own church ironically. When the bill received second reading in the Senate, the Speaker invited Mrs. Wiggins to sit at his right — an honor never before, nor since, granted any woman except the wife of the Governor-General. A statue of the lovely "Gunhilda" once stood in the Parliamentary Library, but mysteriously disappeared. Despite "Gunhilda's" success, and the power of national organizations, women realized that, in order to reform laws, they would have to get into the arena — study law, practise law, become judges. It was a long uphill assault on the male legal bastions.

* * *

Modern women lawyers owe much to the pioneering spirit of Clara Brett Martin, first woman lawyer in the British Empire. Guests arriving at a dinner given by the Women's Law Association in Toronto in 1919 almost ignored a small, simply-dressed woman quietly rocking in a corner of the cloakroom. One guest said patronizingly: "One of the cloakroom attendants — tired, poor dear." The shock waves came later when the "attendant" headed for the podium as the guest speaker. Without Miss Martin there might never have been a Women's Law Association.

Clara Brett Martin

Born in Toronto to Elizabeth (Brett) and Abraham Martin, Clara was educated by private tutors, and attended Trinity College. A pretty, serious and studious girl, she taught for a time, then decided she really wanted to be a lawyer — an impossible dream in an era when the Upper Canada Law Society prohibited women from being called to the Bar. When Clara first applied for admission to the law course, Benchers of Ontario refused on the familiar grounds that she was not a "person". Clara countered this initial rebuff with a formal petition for admission as a student-at-law. Meanwhile, her case sparked heated arguments and discussion pro and con in the newspapers. Her petition, which came up for reading at the Easter term 1891, was referred to a special committee which dragged on for a year, finally resulting in an Act on April 14, 1892, permitting the Law Society of Ontario to admit women to practise as solicitors.

However, Clara still had not won the war. The Law Society *could* but *would not* admit women to its ranks.

Five months later on September 13, 1892, Convocation's acting secretary wrote her: "Convocation . . . is of the opinion that it is inexpedient to frame rules for admission of women as solicitors." In desperation, Clara appealed to the Attorney-General of Ontario, Sir Oliver Mowatt. He moved, on December 9, that Convocation frame rules to admit women as solicitors.

On June 26, 1893, the legal education committee recognized Clara's victory. She became a student-at-law, received her B.C.L., was admitted to the Bar of Ontario in 1897. At first only allowed to act as solicitors, three years later women were granted permission also to act as barristers. In 1899, Miss Martin became the first Canadian woman admitted to the degree of LL.B. (Bachelor of Laws), by the University of Toronto. The legal firm of Shelton and Walbridge welcomed her as a partner.

By 1900 Miss Martin was still Canada's only woman lawyer, although there were one hundred and twenty-one women doctors. Before her death in 1923, all provinces allowed women to study and practise law. The Island of Newfoundland granted this right in 1933. Clara Brett Martin's admission to the Bar preceded that of Ivy Williams, first woman lawyer in Great Britain, by twenty years. In 1926 the Women's Law Association

152

established a scholarship, in perpetuity, to honor Clara Brett Martin.

Her success gradually opened other doors. On July 1, 1916, officials, lawyers, defendants, witnesses and spectators rose to their feet in an Edmonton Court while Emily Murphy, the first woman police magistrate in the British Empire, walked to the dais and seated herself on the bench.

Judge Helen MacGill

A deep desire to right injustices and a passionate sympathy for the helpless, were dominant forces in Judge Helen MacGill's life. In July, 1917, she was named Judge of the Juvenile Court in Vancouver. As with Mrs. Murphy, a distinguished career in voluntary welfare work in British Columbia preceded the appointment.

Judge Helen MacGill

Helen MacGill was born in Hamilton, in 1864, to socially-prominent Silas Gregory and Helen O'Reilly Gregory. Her mother, who inspired Helen, was one of Canada's first feminine activists in the field of welfare work; daughter was a successful pioneer in several widely-different careers. Her parents encouraged her ambition to be a concert pianist.

Seeking new worlds to conquer, Helen determined to take a B.A. and M.A., although universities still were closed to women. Persistence and her grandfather's influence helped her become the first woman student at Trinity College, Toronto. Helen, a petite, pretty blonde, was called by classmates, "The Pocket Venus". One professor, who threatened to resign over her admission, later boasted of Helen as his fair-haired girl. She graduated in 1889 (first in her class in the most difficult course, Mental and Moral Philosophy) and obtained her M.A. the following year.

While travelling in the United States, Helen met the editor of *Cosmopolitan Magazine*, who assigned her to go to Japan to report on the new national constitution and bicameral parliament or Diet. Canadian Prime Minister Sir John A. Macdonald, a family friend, suggested that she travel via Vancouver and contribute a series of articles on foreign settlements in the Western provinces to newspapers in Toronto and Saint John. In the West, Helen met Lee (Frederick) Flesher, whom she secretly married after a whirlwind courtship.

When she sailed for Japan, Helen was pregnant, but refused to postpone her trip. During a nightmarish three-week voyage, she fell down a companionway and broke her leg, but remained undaunted. Through letters of introduction from her influential family, she had entrée to many fascinating phases of Japanese life. She returned laden with exquisite gifts and enough material for dozens of articles, which were widely circulated, in several countries. Her style was terse, interesting. Her self-taught typing, however, was so terrible that editors begged her to write in longhand!

The difficult journey subsequently caused Helen's health to break down and she went to California to recuperate. When her 12-pound baby, Eric, was born, Helen almost died. The agony this small woman endured, with no anaesthetic plus an incompetent doctor, prompted her husband to study surgery. Until he graduated in 1893, Helen and her mother financed the family by publishing two small papers, *Society* and *The Searchlight*.

A second son, Freddie, was born in 1894. Seven years later, after a lingering illness, Dr. Flesher died. Helen married again in 1903 to James MacGill, her college sweetheart, with whom she had kept up a friendly correspondence through the years. James, a graduate in both law and theology, was also a newspaperman. They moved to Vancouver. The MacGills added two daughters, Helen and Elsie. Elsie jokingly said: "We were sometimes called 'Helnelsie' like a team of horses!" Helen became a professor of Sociology in the United States and Elsie an engineer, the first woman engineer in the British Commonwealth.

Mrs. MacGill, active in church, club and welfare work, headed a committee of club women who visited women's prisons to examine first-hand shocking conditions. Consulting leaders in Children's Aid Societies, in churches and settlement work, she wrote a report placed before Government. Her committee petitioned for prison reform, sterilization of unfit degenerates, and supervised probation. She campaigned for youths incarcerated in detention schools to be given practical training. An example of this included the free business courses provided by Mrs. Anna Sprott, owner of the Sprott-Shaw Business College.

Mrs. MacGill once averted a riot in a girls' industrial school by talking over grievances with ringleaders. Her voluntary work was rewarded by her appointment, in 1917, aged 53, as a Justice of the Peace and Judge of the Juvenile Court. Judge MacGill said: "All who engage in Juvenile Court work realize that yesterday's neglected child is today's juvenile delinquent, tomorrow's criminal. This court works to keep child offenders out of jail."

The 1917 B.C. Equal Guardianship of Infants Act was a great triumph for Judge MacGill. It was modelled on a United States law she had seen in a legal periodical, making the necessary changes to adapt to Canadian conditions. From her notes, Attorney-General MacDonald formulated the Act, acknowledged as a model and copied by other Canadian provinces and Great Britain. Judge MacGill implemented her beliefs by urging Children's Aid Societies to form unpaid Juvenile Court Committees to help child offenders re-establish in society. "Placing a green seventeen-year-old, even a troublemaker, in an adult jail is matriculating him into a school for crime," she warned.

Judge MacGill was chairman, and only woman member, of British Columbia's Minimum Wage Board, first Board of its kind in Canada. In 1918 the Board drew up an act guaranteeing working women a living wage. She was Chairman of the Greater Vancouver Mothers' Pension Board 1920-21, the Provincial Board of Industrial Relations in 1934 and numerous other welfare organizations. A kindly, understanding woman, she studied law so thoroughly she was often consulted by barristers, though she never wrote Bar examinations. During her twenty-three years as a Judge, none of her decisions was reversed — a proud record.

On January 1, 1929, when South Vancouver, Point Grey and Vancouver proper, amalgamated to form Greater Vancouver, appointment of all judges was automatically rescinded. It was a bitter blow to Judge MacGill when she was the only judge not re-appointed. A staunch Liberal, her office was given to a Conservative. Indignant sympathizers immediately formed the

Judge MacGill Reinstatement Committee — ironically most of its members were Conservatives. The Tory Vancouver Province stated: "A woman of broad culture, sympathies and undoubted capacity, Mrs. MacGill has practically devoted her life to improving conditions for women and children in British Columbia." In 1934, she was reappointed. Her small salary was the only payment she ever received for her welfare work.

Active in law societies, she was elected international member of the Juvenile Court Judges' Association at a Conference in Brussels, Belgium, in 1935. In 1937 she was a delegate to the first Canadian Penal Conference in Montreal.

Helen MacGill frankly admitted: "I'm a joiner!" One of her favorites was the Business and Professional Women's Club. So busy, and indifferent to fashion, she once changed in a telephone booth.

Striking a blow at female apathy in Canada and the United States, Judge MacGill's harsh words rang true: "Few of us place sufficient value on our time and effort. We fill our lives with a mass of social and domestic details that keeps us from seeing and attempting bigger things. Women tend to shun public responsibility and limit the scope of other women in business and professional life. Most of us do not attempt to realize a fraction of our capabilities." So zealously had Helen pursued her studying and writing, she was threatened with blindness, complaining: "I have to scour the pages with my nose." Her career was an effective answer to the question asked ad nauseum: "Why give a university education to a girl, when the chances are she will marry?"

She wrote numerous magazine articles and pamphlets on domestic legislation, social conditions, juvenile delinquency, penal reform and child labor among them: *Daughters, Wives and Mothers* (1913), *Laws for Women and Children in B.C.* (dedicated to Lady Aber-

deen) and *How to Conduct Public Meetings in Canada.*
A sought-after public speaker, her easy delivery belied
long, wearisome hours spent in preparation.

In 1938 when the University of British Columbia
wished to confer the honorary degree of Doctor of Laws,
she told her daughter: "It is a very great honor, but one
hundred dollars for a gown is out of the question."
Friends, hearing of this collected the necessary amount
and sent it with a note of appreciation she treasured.

That same year, at seventy-four, she again broke
her leg. In hospital, commandeering a spare table as a
court bench she continued to hold court. Child Welfare
was always her paramount concern. The *Quebec Chron-
icle* said: "No woman in Canada made a greater contribution to social problems of children than Judge
MacGill."

In 1944 ill health forced her to retire from the
Bench. She devoted her waning strength to completing a
comprehensive study of juvenile reclamation. Death
intervened. On May 4, 1947, her friends gathered again
in the library of the University of British Columbia for
the unveiling of a memorial plaque by the Women's
University Club. It read: "Let her own works praise her
at the Gates."

Four Fields

Dr. Margaret Patterson made a four-barrelled
contribution to Canada in — medicine, missionary
work, social service and law. Born at Staffa, Ontario, in
1880, the daughter of Sarah Clements and Robert Norris,
she studied at Ontario Medical College, Toronto; took
her M.D. and C.M. at Northwestern University, Chicago,
1899. After a short period as a house-surgeon, she went
to India as a medical missionary where for seven years,
she was in charge of Seward Memorial Hospital for
Women and Children at Allahabad. In 1901, during an
epidemic of bubonic plague, her untiring work in organ-

izing inoculation depots and isolation hospitals resulted
in her being decorated with the Kaiser-I-Hind Medal at
the coronation of King Edward VII. While in Allahabad,
Dr. Patterson wrote a text book on physiology and
hygiene, adopted in India as a standard volume by the
medical profession there. Later she became Professor of
Obstetrics at Women's Christian Medical College,
Ludhiana. Margaret's marriage to Dominion Meteorolo-
gist John Patterson in 1906 brought together a pair of
brilliant minds.

Back in Toronto in 1910 to concentrate on social
service, organizing more than 300 working Red Cross
circles and teaching St. John Ambulance courses to
some 2,000 women during World War I, she was instrumental in forming a Nursing Division for service in hospitals in Canada and overseas. At the request of the
National Council of Women and the Young Women's
Christian Association, she initiated a nation-wide Moral
Hygiene campaign, establishing a Department of Moral
Health in the YWCA, then lecturing across the country
to women. Yet another epidemic, the devastating 1918
influenza epidemic in Toronto, tested Dr. Patterson's
cool. She trained more than 2,000 nurses to cope with
this crisis.

In 1922 the Federal Government sent her to represent the Province of Ontario at the Pan-American Conference in Baltimore. That same year she became a
magistrate. Through twelve years' service as Convener
of Laws for the Local Council of Women, her interest in
police court cases intensified. Instrumental in bringing
about the formation of the Women's Court in Toronto,
she became its first magistrate. The distinguished records of Magistrate Murphy, Judge MacGill and Magistrate Patterson laid a solid foundation which held firm
for those to follow, including Helen Kinnear, Margaret
Hyndman and Vera Parsons, to name three.

First County Judge

When Helen Kinnear was appointed Judge of Cayuga (Ontario) County Court in April 1943, she became the first woman appointed in the British Commonwealth as county judge. Born in Cayuga, Ontario, Helen graduated from University of Toronto in 1917 with B.A. in English and history; Osgoode Hall Law School in 1920; and was called to the Bar the same year. It was a proud moment when the second "Kinnear" added to the sign outside her father's law office, proclaimed the partnership of father and daughter.

Following her father's death, Helen carried on the practise. Prisoners in court and litigants faced a petite attractive woman, wearing her judge's gown with great dignity. Male colleagues who gave no quarter accorded her respect strictly on grounds of outstanding ability. In 1934 she was first woman named a King's Counsel. The following year she became first woman lawyer to plead a case before the Supreme Court of Canada.

Like many lawyers, Helen Kinnear was keenly interested in politics. Though she won the nomination as federal Liberal candidate for Welland in October, 1941, she stepped aside to let Humphrey Mitchell, for years Minister of Labor, run in the riding. Political activity, of course, ceased with her appointment as judge.

Her logical mind probed the root causes of crime, particularly questions affecting the family. If she felt the situation called for it, she would place a prisoner on probation. In the case of juvenile offenders, a condition often was that they attend church regularly. Judge Kinnear served for two years as President of the Juvenile and Family Court Judges' Association for Ontario, 1952-54. In 1954 she was appointed to a Royal Commission to investigate the law relating to insanity, as a defence in a criminal charge. She moved on to another Royal Commission examining possible amendments to the law relating to Criminal Sexual Psychopaths.

Both appointments took her to all major cities across Canada. "Away from home, I'm Exhibit No. 1," she said, ruefully. At home she was taken for granted by everyone, including her neighbours' small sons who greeted her cheerfully: "Hi, Judge." Judge Kinnear died in 1970.

A Born Lawyer

Born in Palmerston, Ontario, in 1901, graduated from Osgoode Hall and called to the Bar in 1926, Margaret Hyndman, when asked why she chose law as a profession, said simply: "I just never thought of anything else!" Miss Hyndman was first woman director of a trust company in Canada; is director of several industrial organizations. She is on the Regional Advisory Board of the Huron and Erie Mortgage Corporation and Canada Trust Company.

Margaret Hyndman

Canada's second woman Q.C. (1938), authority on corporate and business law, she collaborated with partner, F. W. Wegenast, in writing the book *Canadian Companies*. This became a standard reference work in university law departments as well as legal offices. In 1955 Miss Hyndman was first Canadian woman lawyer admitted to practise before the United States Court for the District of Columbia.

As counsel for the Institute of Edible Oil Foods, she was first woman lawyer to appear before the Privy Council when (also representing the Canadian Association of Consumers) she eloquently appealed the sale ban on oleo-margarine, which was ruled invalid.

One time, a judge in Toronto for an important case, telephoned Margaret, so hoarse he could hardly speak. "I'll fix you up!" she decided. Consulting her cook, Miss Hyndman stewed some onions, took them downtown in a large pot. Sailing through the lobby of the King Edward Hotel, with jaunty red feather in her hat, onion pot nonchalantly swinging, Margaret greeted her judicial friend. After a persuasive chat in the lobby, Margaret made an onion poultice for his throat, enabling him to carry on in Court next day.

Miss Hyndman's war work was outstanding. In May 1939, she initiated and organized the Voluntary Registration of Canadian Women, later became chairman of the executive. This committee composed of representatives of some sixty nationally organized women's associations in Canada, was formed to circulate among the women of Canada a questionnaire designed to record capabilities and willingness of Canadian women to serve their country in any national emergency including acting as war-time foster parents. She was honorary counsel and one of the committee that formed the Canadian Women's Voluntary Service (Ontario Division) and a member of the Toronto VS centre. She also organized and was chairman of the Ontario Wartime Legal Service Committee to the Canadian Bar

Association which provided free legal aid to members of armed forces and dependents, and helped over 6,000 persons.

A well-known hostess in her elegantly-restored century-old residence in downtown Toronto, Miss Hyndman notes: "I collect friends (once including Queen Mary) as some women do jewels." At her summer home at Georgian Bay for the comfort of her visitors, she once provided a special cabin to segregate enthusiastic snorers. Her friends there, the Ojibwa Indians of Cape Croker Reserve are given free legal aid each summer.

For several years she was first vice-president of the Women's College Hospital, and was honored by being chosen first Dean of her legal sorority. Miss Hyndman is a frequent guest speaker. Grounded by bad weather, she once insisted the "Show must go on" and set up a telephone circuit from her Toronto office to the Indiana Federation of Business and Professional Women's Clubs meeting at the Morrison Hotel, Chicago. Delivering her talk about the Hungarian relief problem, she became the first woman to make a public speech by phone.

Equal pay for equal work is one of Miss Hyndman's basic beliefs. She was chairman of the Equal Pay Committee of the National Federation of Business and Professional Women's Clubs when Ontario introduced this law in 1951, warning: "Women must make sure that they give equal work for equal pay!" This aspect of legal equality of the sexes was underlined when a Montreal career woman made history. Convicted of nonsupport of her sick husband, she was ordered to provide for him.

Miss Hyndman organized the Arts of Management Conference sponsored by Toronto B. and P. Club, and continued annually. From 1956-1959 she was the first Canadian president of the International Federation of Business and Professional Women's Clubs. In 1966 she was appointed to the Board of Governors of the Canadian Broadcasting Corporation, her appointment coinciding with the issue of the White Paper on Broadcasting. She was one of the prime movers in promoting the Royal Commission on the Status of Women.

Margaret Hyndman was given a citation in 1946 by General de Gaulle for aid to the Free French; in 1959 the Silver Medal of the City of Paris; and in 1967 the Centennial Medal. The B. and P. Clubs lobbied to have her appointed to the Senate.

Pioneer Woman Criminal Lawyer

The first woman lawyer to defend on a capital charge was Vera Parsons, daughter of a Robert Simpson Company executive. Following private school, she graduated in modern languages from University of Toronto; took her M.A. at Bryn Mawr; went to Rome to complete a doctorate in comparative literature. Tiring of academic life, she returned to Toronto and worked at a settlement house, where she helped Italian immigrants adjust to Canada. Her knowledge of Italian was a great asset.

One day an Italian mother came to her, in tears. Her daughter, who had run away from home had been charged with vagrancy. She begged Miss Parsons to go to court with her. They found the case had already been settled by sending the girl to jail. Miss Parsons hunted out the crown attorney, and pleaded for leniency for the girl, especially since she had had no defense lawyer. He told her the case was closed. That curt treatment made legal history in Canada. There and then Vera Parsons decided to become a criminal lawyer.

Vera enrolled at Osgoode Hall Law School, Toronto, succeeding in being articled to the late W. B. Horkins, who had more criminal cases than any other lawyer in the province. When she graduated, in 1924, with Silver Medal and the Christopher Robin Memorial

164

Scholarship, Horkins made her a junior partner. She brought a ready-made Italian clientele.

"Every person is innocent until proven guilty," was her approach.

During a debate in 1955 by the Criminal Justice Committee of the Canadian Bar Association on the perennial question: "Should a lawyer defend a person whom he knows to be guilty?" Vera Parsons won applause when she rose, supporting her lame leg with a cane, to say: "What counsel believes as to the guilt of the client is irrelevant . . . one never knows a client is guilty until the court rules guilty."

Vera Parsons, the epitome of aristocracy, became a familiar figure at dreary Don Jail. She interviewed criminals with the same politeness as a guest in her luxurious home. She was noted for relying mainly on facts. Occasionally she used auxiliary aids. In 1946 when defending young Georgina Slemensky on a charge of murder, she realized what a bad impression the girl would make in court wearing filthy clothes. She induced a friend to loan her a decent outfit. Georgina was acquitted.

Miss Parsons also defended a man charged with murder, while a colleague defended the wife, jointly charged. In 1947, this young man, his wife and three children were found deeply drugged with sleeping pills. One son was dead. Notes found in the living room, signed by both husband and wife, suggested a suicide pact. He told a terrible tale of misfortune.

Tragedy haunted his first marriage. Two babies died, his wife became partially paralysed from sleeping sickness, then hopelessly crippled following a fire, and finally died. Three children were born of a second marriage, but his wife developed lockjaw, and died in agony.

He married a third time, to make a home for his children. A week before they were found drugged, his wife caught her hair in the washing machine. She was partially scalped. Trying to protect her head, her right hand had been badly crushed. Neither could sleep. Life became a nightmare. Finally, desperate, the husband gave the children enough pills to quiet them, enough to his wife to make her sleep. Then he took 93 pills himself, insisting: "I had no intention of poisoning my wife or children." The charge against the man was reduced from murder to manslaughter, and his wife was freed.

Her male colleague paid tribute: "Miss Parsons is not just a top woman lawyer, but a top lawyer, period!"

Quebec Test

Although they could study law at McGill University, women were not permitted to practise law in Quebec in the early years of the century. In 1915 Annie MacDonald Langstaff completed her law course at McGill, then had the audacity to apply for a writ to compel the Quebec Bar Association to allow her to try its examination. Justice St. Pierre of the Superior Court refused indignantly, stating it would be "a direct infringement of law and order, a manifest violation of good morals and public decency." Mrs. Langstaff, enlisting support of two other women lawyers in the same position, Elizabeth Monk and Mrs. Florence Bell, started a crusade, reinforced by the League for Women's Rights, headed by the influential Madame Thérèse Casgrain, and the Local Council of Women. They held a public meeting and started to lobby for their cause. In 1941, largely due to their spadework, women were admitted to the Bar of Quebec by the narrow margin of one vote. Mrs. Florence Bell certainly relished this hard-won right, still practising law at 80!

* * *

In January, 1942, Elizabeth Monk, Q.C., along with Mrs. Suzanne Filion, was admitted to the Quebec Bar, followed later that year by Miss Constance C.

Short, and Miss Marcelle Hemond Lacoste. Miss Monk, who won the Elizabeth Torrance Gold Medal on graduating from McGill, also scholarships enabling her to study at Oxford, served as an alderman on the Montreal City Council 1940-42. Miss Monk has served for years on the executive of both the CFUW and the IFUW. As legal counsel for the League of Women's Rights in 1938, she had presented a brilliant brief to the Rowell-Sirois Commission, urging an amendment to the British North America Act similar to the Sex Disqualification Removal Act of British Columbia and Alberta. In collaboration with Dr. Jacques Perrault, on February 1, 1947, Miss Monk submitted to the Commissioner appointed by the Quebec Government a masterly brief on the Legal Status of Married Women. In October, 1968, the Graduates' Society of McGill University awarded their Gold Medal to Miss Monk.

Feminine First

"It's perfectly damnable!" exclaimed Mrs. Wilhemina Holmes one morning, angrily banging down her coffee cup. "Imagine having to pay a penalty for getting married." So enraged was she at Quebec's injustice towards married women, that she became a lawyer, and, with Joan Gilchrist, set up the first entirely feminine law firm in Canada. Later, Rose Gaultier joined the firm. In 1956, when Mrs. Holmes' daughter, Diana, articled, they planned to become the only mother and daughter law firm in Canada, but Diana's marriage intervened.

She was the first woman lawyer from Quebec to appear before the Senate Divorce Committee, in 1951. They specialized in domestic disputes and were responsible for the passage of a bill in 1954 forcing deserting husbands to support their families. That same year Holmes and Gilchrist published a booklet, *You and Your Family Under Quebec Law*, which became a best-seller. Mrs. Holmes revised it in 1956.

Pioneer Notary

In early 1957 another allied profession, a separate branch of the law was opened to women in Quebec, who may now become notaries. This established universal professional equality for women in Quebec. It is the only province that requires a four-year university course, followed by two examinations, under the Quebec Chamber of Notaries. Louise Dumoulin, a graduate of Laval University, daughter of a judge, paved the way for this development.

* * *

The first woman judge in Quebec was Mme. Thérèse Lemay-Lavoie, who became a municipal judge in St. Georges-Beauce. First Quebec woman judge with jurisdiction throughout the province was Yvette Dussault Mailloux, of St. Lambert, named judge of the Social Welfare Court for the District of Montreal. She was a founding member of the provincial Association of Women Lawyers, and began practising in 1952.

Miss Burgess was the first woman lawyer in Saskatchewan, registering as a student on January 11, 1913, the very day the Profession Act was amended to allow women to practise law. Mary and Roger Carter were married while attending university, and practised law together until March 1960 when she was appointed judge of the Family Court in Saskatoon. There she had a colleague in Judge Tillda Taylor. Another woman lawyer, Miss J. Jamieson is the Official Guardian of Infants in Saskatchewan.

Judge Mary (Fodchuck) Batten, of Ukrainian origin, once was a legal colleague of the Rt. Hon. John Diefenbaker in his Prince Albert law firm. She was admitted to the Saskatchewan Bar in 1945, and married a solicitor M. C. R. Batten in 1948. From 1956 to 1964, she was the MLA for Humboldt before her appointment to the Saskatchewan District Court. After her chairmanship of the provincial Royal Commission on Accounting

Practises and the Cost Study Commission on consumer problems and inflation, Judge Batten was a logical selection as a member of the Canadian Consumer Council in 1969.

Judge Doris (Mrs. Robert) Ogilivie of Fredericton, N.B., is typical of the new breed of woman in the legal profession. Admitted to the New Brunswick branch of the Canadian Bar Association in 1964, she was appointed deputy judge of the Fredericton Juvenile Court a year later. As a member of the Royal Commission on the Status of Women she travelled across the country hearing briefs from organizations and private citizens.

Like many other lawyers, fresh, freckle-faced little Martha Brewin is interested in politics. Just 23, she ran for the NDP of Etobicoke in the 1967 federal campaign, against political stalwarts, the late Robert Winters and George Hogan. She said: "In the very first campaigning debate, after Winters and Hogan had finished taking each other apart, I got an uproarious laugh when I said I felt there was no need for me to rebut because the two giants had done a good job of slaying each other." Martha is the daughter of Andrew Brewin, longtime NDP member for east-end Toronto. Married now to another lawyer, she is a research assistant with the Royal Commission on the Status of Women, looking into laws affecting women.

By the mid-twentieth century, hundreds of women were practising lawyers in every province of Canada — a legacy of Clara Brett Martin's determined efforts. Many developed careers of remarkable distinction. They tend to work behind the scenes, helping to frame legislation, receiving little recognition. A good many assist organizations lobbying for reforms. For example, Ruth McGill of Regina, a capable lawyer, despite being physically handicapped, was very active in the Canadian Bar Association's development of legal aid for soldiers and dependents. She served two years as an alderman. Nationally known as a past president of the Canadian Federation of Business and Professional Women's Clubs, she was chairman of the committee which secured equal pay for equal work in Saskatchewan.

Eileen Miller, former member of R.C.A.F., Women's Division, and official assistant to the British Columbia Court of Appeals, became the first woman barrister in Canada to do legal research for judges in court, except the Supreme Court of Canada. Among women lawyers prominent in the public service of Canada, Miss Janet Scott is with the Immigration Appeal Board.

Miss Violet King, Calgary, made history in March 1956 as the first Negro woman to graduate in law from the University of Alberta. During a stint in liaison work for the Department of Immigration, Ottawa, she experienced more prejudice as a woman in a man's field than because of her race.

Suzanne Barriere, admitted to Quebec Bar in 1946, went to Ottawa to head the Legal Division's Treaty Section, Department of External Affairs. Edith Lorentsen became Director of Legislation Branch, Federal Department of Labor, and conducted research on labour legislation in both provincial and federal areas.

Human Rights Institute Founder

Marguerite E. Ritchie, Q.C., B.A., LL.B., LL.M., LL.D. (Alberta) studied law in Alberta, Nova Scotia, and Quebec. She was called to the Bar in Alberta, and shortly afterwards went to Ottawa as a lawyer in the Federal Government. Her work included constitutional law, international law, air law, and a wide cross-section of legal problems affecting people in all walks of life.

Miss Ritchie was sent to McGill University by the

Government of Canada (1954-55) to attend the Institute of International Air Law; at the same time she studied general International Law and the law of the United Nations. Her thesis was on *Crimes Aboard Aircraft*. In 1955, the Government sent her as an adviser to the Canadian Delegation to the International Air Conference at The Hague. She became senior advisory counsel in the Federal Department of Justice in Ottawa, and was seconded to two different Ministers of Justice, belonging to two different political parties, and organized various aspects of the work of the offices with the Department itself. She was actively concerned with international law and human rights matters since her entry into the Department of Justice. On November 1, 1972, she became Vice-Chairperson of the Federal Anti-dumping Tribunal, which is legally a Court of Record.

Miss Ritchie has been involved in human rights issues throughout her career. She served as first legal adviser to the Elizabeth Fry Society of Ottawa, and has been President of the University Women's Club of Ottawa, (as well as serving on various organizations at different times).

Miss Ritchie was the first woman to receive a Federal Queen's Counsel. She received the Centennial Medal in 1967; and received a Doctor of Laws, Honoris Causa, from Alberta in 1975 for her work in the field of human rights. In 1976 she was honored by the Government of Ontario, as one of twenty-five outstanding women of the Province.

Miss Ritchie is the Founder-President of the Human Rights Institute of Canada. It is the first "people's Human Rights organization" which is intended to develop a staff which will be able to provide expertise on Human Rights matters to people, organizations, and Governmental bodies on the important issues of the day.

* * *

Mary Lou Lynch, Q.C., of Saint John, N.B., a

prominent lawyer, was the first woman to plead — and win — a case in the Supreme Court of New Brunswick, her home province. Active in community work including hospital and two planning boards, registrar of the Law School, the General Selective Board of Beaverbrook Scholarships, and the Senate of the University of New Brunswick, in 1960 she became the first woman invited to Ottawa to serve on the five-member National Parole Board, a position in which she kept close watch over the files of scores of convicted thieves, fraud artists and dope addicts, housed in prisons across Canada. She retired in Ottawa.

Madame Justice Gabrielle Vallee of the Quebec Superior Court was appointed senior associate chief justice of the court, in 1975.

Battered Babies

Mary Elizabeth Maher, a science honors graduate of St. Francis Xavier University in Antigonish, N.S., first worked on the problems of air and water pollution with an oil refinery in Montreal. Seeking closer contact with people, Miss Maher put in three years of hard study at Dalhousie Law School in Halifax, to become Newfoundland's second woman lawyer (Louise Saunders preceded her by thirteen years). At present with the Justice Department, she hopes eventually to work with family courts.

Miss Maher wrote a startling brief on the *Battered Child Syndrome*, following three months of research. "It was so disturbing to find that huge numbers of children died each year at the hands of their parents," she said. The cases she examined were from all types of homes. The United States has passed legislation making it compulsory for people to report mistreatment of children. This legislation gives them immunity from civil or criminal liability. "Canada does not have such legislation," she noted in the brief.

Powerful Pioneer

Legal history was made in Canada, however, in February, 1969, when Rejane Laberge-Colas was appointed a Judge of the Superior Court of Quebec. Versatile Rejane, after completing her arts degree at the University of Montreal, used her rich contralto voice to good advantage in concert and radio work for the next five years before she decided to study law. She was named the first Miss Quartier Latin of her university and also placed first in the Quebec Bar examinations in 1951.

Through her study of the Criminal Code, she began to realize that the status of women — particularly Quebec women — was in need of reform. She became founding president of the Quebec Federation of Women organized in 1965, concerned with co-ordinating the work of associations lobbying for women's rights.

It is ironical that Rejane Laberge encountered the single case of professional prejudice she can recall from the man she was to marry — lawyer Emile Colas, with whom she crossed professional swords in 1955. Meeting her again in 1960, Mr. Colas saw her in a somewhat different light. Determined not to let the charming Rejane escape this time, he married her within five months. They now have three sons and Emile is one of his wife's most vocal champions.

In her new post, Judge Laberge-Colas deals with separation and divorce cases, as well as cases involving corporation law — her specialties since graduation. "I hope to be humane in my judgements", she declares. Rejane Laberge-Colas's full life skilfully combines her career and Vice-Chairmanship of the Canadian Consumer Council, with marriage, motherhood and her special hobbies, making her very much the modern woman of the law.

In relation to law, modern woman has "come a

long way" to appropriate the popular television jingle to the computer-age career girl. For example, by 1960, Canadian women had long established the right to study law, to be called to the Bar in all provinces, and to practise in accordance with legal custom and procedure.

However, the status of women in Canada has received disastrous setbacks. In 1960 Canadian parliament passed John Diefenbaker's Canadian Bill of Rights, which prohibited discrimination on various grounds, including sex. But in 1972 the Federal Government appealed to the Supreme Court of Canada to set aside a finding of equality which had been won by a young Indian woman, Jeanette Lavell, under a unanimous judgement of the Federal Court of Appeal, with respect to the Canadian Bill of Rights.

The Government was successful, and Indian women were denied the equality guaranteed by the Canadian Bill of Rights. An Indian women's organization, named Indian Rights for Indian Women, has now been established by Indian women, including Jenny Margetts of Edmonton and Mary Two Axe Early of Caughnawaga, near Montreal, seeking equality of Indian women with Indian men.

In recent years a few outstanding women lawyers have been appointed judges of the Lower Courts, and now to the Quebec Superior Court, although none has yet made it to the exalted chambers of the Supreme Court of Canada. As a point of interest, in progressive Denmark, two of the country's fifteen Supreme Court judges are women.

Chapter VIII

The Crusading Spirit

Founders of Women's Organizations

Mrs. Clark Murray

> *The International Council of Women was really the first League of Nations before the other was even thought of.*
>
> (General Jan Christian Smuts)

"The age of women's clubs" is a title often given the 20th century. Cynics may say that committee meetings are "the devil's tools to prevent things from getting done" and some people term volunteer work "voluntyranny", but despite some valid criticism, women's clubs in Canada have achieved miracles. One miracle was the success of the temperance campaign which scored its first victory one crucial night in 1876. A huge, homely woman rose to speak to the provincial legislature in Toronto. She was so nervous that the petition she held, signed by 28,000 Ontario women, rustled audibly. Yet Letitia Youmans spoke as one inspired.

"Gentlemen, I have never visited Ottawa. Therefore, I have never seen the Parliament Buildings. But, in the Parliament Buildings there is a tower, and in that tower, there is a bell, and if that bell were to toll every time a drunkard in the Dominion of Canada passes to eternity ... then gentlemen, you would give us prohibition without our asking for it, because that bell would be eternally tolling." The members were won by her eloquence. The Liquor Act was amended to restrict the number of outlets.

Intemperance was a Canadian social problem as long ago as 1648 when Canada's first temperance meeting was held at Sillery, Quebec. During the 19th century liquor was plentiful and cheap; on paydays when husbands arrived home, often drunk and quarrelsome, many unfortunate women received blackened eyes and bruises instead of money for food and clothing for their families.

The women who led the campaign against liquor in the 1880's and 90's were Mrs. Youmans in Canada and Frances Willard in the United States. "Mother" Stewart of Springfield, Ohio, actually organized the first Women's Temperance League and, in 1872, after a night of prayer, this "whirlwind of the Lord" swept the liquor traffic from 250 towns and villages in 50 days. Women besieged saloon-keepers' doors, pleading and praying. In one town a Mr. Van Pelt drenched them with beer. They continued praying. He rushed at them, brandishing an axe as they calmly continued praying. Suddenly, converted, he electrified them by rolling his liquor casks into the street, slashing the casks with his axe.

Inspired by their example, Mrs. R. J. Doyle of Owen Sound, Ontario, organized the first Women's Christian Temperance Union in Canada in May, 1874. In December Mrs. Youmans organized the second Union — in Picton, Ontario. In her mixed Sunday School class of 90, bruised pupils confided pitiful tales of drunken fathers beating them. Motherly Mrs. Youmans urged her pupils to sign the pledge and organized a Band of Hope. After attending an 1874 Sunday School convention at Chatauqua she had become interested in temperance. Organizing the Central Toronto Union in 1875 Mrs. Youmans got signatures of 1,000 women. When the mayor turned down the petition, advising that it go to the provincial legislature, she engaged in a tornado-like tour through Ontario, adding thousands of signatures. This was the woman so shy as a girl that she begged to be excused from oral compositions at school.

Born Letitia Creighton, in 1827 near Cobourg, Ontario, arduous work on the farm gave her great physical stamina. Witty and fun-loving but a serious student, she often cried herself to sleep, despairing of further education. After graduating from Burlington Academy, she taught school and became a pioneer woman school principal in Picton in 1850. At 23 she married widower-farmer, Thomas Youmans and became step-mother to eight children, the eldest a girl of her own age, the youngest a baby. Often called "The Greatheart of Canada", she combined a brilliant mind with a desire to save humanity from the evils of excessive drink. In canvassing Durham and Northumberland counties in the interest of the Dunkin Act (local option), she spoke to more than 15,000 persons in 50 places. She and Tom laughed heartily at hearing one woman ask: "Does her husband amount to anything, or does he drink?" Irate liquor sellers threatened to "take her to court to scare her and shut her mouth."

When the Dominion WCTU was organized in 1883, Mrs. Youmans was elected president. With Sir Leonard Tilley and Hon. G. W. Ross, she represented Canada at the World Temperance convention in Philadelphia and also a convention in Great Britain. Stricken with agonizing inflammatory rheumatism in 1889, she wrote *Campaign Echoes*. She died in 1891. Flags hung at half-mast in Toronto on the day of her funeral — the first time such civic tribute was paid a woman. The Union she founded flourished for a quarter century after her death. By 1905 the WCTU had secured temperance teaching in schools.

On September 16, 1916, prohibition was won but the victory was shortlived. With attendant evils of "bootlegging", the extreme of prohibition was highly unsatisfactory.

In 1926, Mrs. Sarah Rowell Wright, President of the WCTU, told the premier of Ontario "As soon put a powder keg in Hell and control the damage, as put liquor control in Ontario and control drinking!"

But by an ironic twist, in 1927 — the centennial of

the birth of Letitia Youmans — prohibition *was* repealed. Though one critic remarked: "The WCTU is as old-fashioned as a moustache cup", it filled a desperate need in earlier days and is still active. The pioneer of the "White Ribbon Movement" did not live in vain. Today we still have the problem of alcoholism and a need for clinics and Alcoholics Anonymous.

Patriots in Petticoats

The courageous, colorful RCMP is undoubtedly our first line of defense against Communism. But the Communists freely admit that their Enemy Number Two is a group of clubwomen: the Imperial Order Daughters of the Empire. The Order has an Anti-Communist Committee and Mrs. Clark Murray, the Order's founder, would have approved of this development. She would also have approved the First and Second World War Memorial Funds used for scholarships and bursaries to help educate children of soldiers slain or permanently disabled. Some well-known Canadians helped including the late Matthew Halton, the CBC commentator; Jack Pickersgill, head of the Canadian Transport Commission; Dominion Astronomer Carlyle Smith Beals; Dr. A. Vibert Douglas, former professor of astronomy at Queen's University; Canadian diplomat Benjamin Rogers and pianist Malcolm Troup.

Born Margaret Polson in 1844 in Paisley, Scotland, Mrs. Murray loved music so much that she rose at 5 a.m. on cold, dark winter mornings to practise. Bitterly disappointed because her parents refused to allow her to study in Europe, she retained a life-long interest in music. She married J. Clark Murray, a professor of mental and moral philosophy at Queen's University, Kingston and moved to Canada. She was very popular and the Murray home always overflowed with friends and students.

When Professor Murray went to McGill University 30 years later, Margaret Murray soon learned to speak French like a native, complete with Gallic gestures. She arranged a series of interesting programs for working people at a nominal fee of 10 cents and did much welfare work, particularly in the YWCA, of which she was honorary secretary. Mrs. Murray often contributed articles to magazines such as *Nineteenth Century* and *Contemporary Review*. She helped organize the choir at St. Paul's Church, and saw that her daughter had a good musical education. Founding of the IODE (husbands sometimes facetiously interpret the initials as "I Often Don't Eat") was her greatest achievement.

During the Boer War (1899-1902), while chatting with distinguished visitors from different parts of the world, she recognized the need for greater co-operation among women of the British Empire. They felt patriotism should be expressed in service. Her friend Lady Aberdeen encouraged the idea. In 1900 Margaret Murray sent telegrams to the mayors of capital cities across Canada, urging them to persuade public-spirited women to form patriotic organizations to be called "Daughters of the Empire".

So little enthusiasm was shown that she almost abandoned the project. Then she heard the cheering news that Mrs. John Black, Mrs. George Howie and Mrs. C. Fred Chestnut had formed the first chapter in Fredericton. She persevered and within a year the movement spread across Canada. One of the pioneer projects was supplying comforts to Canadian soldiers fighting in South Africa.

The Order's motto is: "One Flag, One Throne, One Empire." It is allied with the Victorian League in the United Kingdom, Australia, New Zealand and South Africa and even has a chapter in Poona, India, another in Burma and the Bahamas. Stranger still, there are 15 chapters called "The Daughters of the British Empire" in the United States. Chambermaids in the Royal York

Hotel in Toronto once formed a chapter. Chapters are named for outstanding Canadian women, including Pauline Johnson, Marguerite Bourgeoys, Madeleine de Vercheres, Laura Secord, Martha Munger Black, Lady Scott and, of course, Margaret Polson Murray.

The Order's organizing secretary, Mrs. Clementina Fessenden of Hamilton, formed a chapter in Stoney Creek and wrote patriotic pamphlets including "Our Union Jack" and "The Genesis of Empire Day". Largely due to her efforts, Empire Day is observed annually. When Mrs. Murray relinquished the presidency due to ill health, the national headquarters moved to Toronto, with Mrs. Edith Boulton Nordheimer as president.

At the Silver Anniversary celebration in Montreal when the 80-year-old founder appeared on the platform, everyone rose and sang: "For She's a Jolly Good Fellow." Mrs. Murray died in 1927. Her portrait, painted by Kenneth Forbes and donated by Mrs. J. A. Stewart of Perth, hangs in the National Archives.

During World War I the Daughters raised $5,000,-000 and in World War II over $6,000,000 to help the war effort. After the Second World War the IODE had the brilliant idea of buying Queen Mary's carpet and exhibiting it across Canada. The tour of this wool carpet netted the Order over $105,000 for Aid to Britain. One woman who contemplated buying it actually asked to have it sent home on approval! Later the IODE donated the carpet to the National Gallery in Ottawa.

By 1950 about 1,000 chapters had been organized with a membership of 35,000. Today one of their principal interests is assisting in the education of Eskimo and Indian children. Latest project of the Provincial Chapter of Quebec is to raise sufficient funds to equip a modern laboratory for the Kateri Memorial Hospital on the Caughnawaga Reserve.

For Home and Country

Young Adelaide Hoodless knelt by her dead baby's crib, crying bitterly: "Didn't I care for him properly?"

"You did your best," the family doctor reassured her. "It is a pity. He was the most beautiful baby boy I have ever seen."

"But why did he die?" she persisted. "You couldn't know," he answered, "but perhaps the milk you were feeding your baby wasn't safe."

So terrible was her remorse and grief that family and friends feared she might lose her mind. Instead, she developed a more altruistic, mature outlook on life, vowing that she would see that other mothers did not lose beloved children through ignorance. Her first civic service was heading a campaign for pasteurization of milk in Hamilton.

The youngest of 13 children, Adelaide Hunter was born in 1857 at "The Willows", a comfortable farm near the village of St. George, to Jean Hunter whose husband died shortly before the baby's birth. Adelaide had great sympathy as well as love for her mother, whose life — as a widow trying to bring up and educate a large family — was sheer, monotonous drudgery. A beautiful and popular girl, Adelaide married John Hoodless, a successful manufacturer, and moved to Hamilton. While their three children Edna, Muriel and Bernard were at school, Mr. Hoodless was chairman of the board of education. Mrs. Hoodless often said: "Educate a boy and you educate a man, but educate a girl and you educate a family."

She felt that since their work in adult life is usually so different, boys and girls ought not to have exactly the same education. Along with the three R's, she advocated teaching of manual training for boys and domestic science for girls. She firmly believed that the

182

highest possible vocation for a woman is to be a good homemaker and mother.

In 1889 the YWCA was opened in Hamilton and Mrs. Hoodless became its first president. Her work there reinforced her belief that most girls desperately needed training in homemaking. Her advanced ideas met with wide-spread prejudice and even ridicule. Despite the fact that her husband was their chairman, the majority of the board of education scornfully referred to her as "Mrs. Hoodless the Faddist", refusing her the use of school classrooms. Undaunted, she started her first class in domestic science, which included dressmaking and millinery as well as cooking, at the YWCA in 1893. More than 200 girls, including many schoolteachers, crowded into lessons.

In 1893, as Canadian delegate of the YWCA, Mrs. Hoodless attended the World Congress of Women in Chicago where she met Lady Aberdeen. Returning home, she envisaged a national association of YWCA's which, besides helping underprivileged girls would provide classrooms for domestic science training. She personally wrote over 90 letters to YWCA's, already in existence and to towns and cities lacking them, urging organization of more YWCA's and amalgamation. When the National YWCA was organized in 1894 Adelaide Hoodless became vice-president and a year later national president.

After serving as president of Hamilton YWCA for 12 years she had to resign because of other demands, but assured the organization of continuing help and interest. She was therefore shocked and deeply hurt when at the annual meeting, she was not re-appointed to the board of directors. She flounced angrily from the room, exclaiming: "I think this is a disgrace!" Most people agreed with her. Young Mrs. Hoodless was now an acknowledged authority on domestic sciences having visited schools in the United States and written to European countries for information. Concurrently, for 10 years she was treasurer and convener of home economics of the Hamilton Local Council of Women which organized the second V.O.N. in Canada. Speaking at the National Council meeting in 1894, she inspired other delegates with her enthusiasm and persuaded them to work for introduction of domestic science in all Canadian schools.

Adelaide Hoodless

It was a great personal triumph for Adelaide Hoodless when the Ontario legislature finally agreed to add domestic science and manual training to school curricula. Education minister Hon. G. W. Ross asked her to travel across Ontario informing the public about domestic science and to write a book on the subject. She gladly agreed and so became the first woman on the provincial payroll. Between 1894-96 she gave 60 lectures. Though busy with outside interests, Mrs. Hoodless never gave her own family merely the remnants of her time and personality. Her daughter Edna said: "As a homemaker, Mother was an inspiration. "Eastcourt" was always 'open house' and she the gracious centre about whom everything revolved."

In 1897 came her greatest achievement — founding of the world-wide Women's Institutes. The Farmer's Institutes were conducting a campaign. Addressing the annual meeting, she startled the members by exclaiming: "Health of your wives and children, which you are neglecting, is far more important than that of your animals."

Though highly controversial, she proved a popular speaker. Mr. Lee arranged for her to speak at a meeting of farmers' wives. On the fateful stormy night February 19, 1897, Bernard hitched up her favorite horse "Scotty" and drove her to Stoney Creek. They found assembled 101 women — and the lone Mr. Lee.

"Let's get together and start a little club," Mrs. Hoodless suggested. "Life on a farm can be pretty dull and lonely. I know. I was brought up on one."

She envisaged a sort of rural university. Six nights later the first formal meeting was held at "Helderleigh", Winona, the home of Mrs. E. D. Smith, who became the first president. She was interested in anything pertaining to the advancement of women. Mrs. Hoodless acted as honorary president. Senator Smith (a Senator 1913-1945, and Dean of the Senate when he retired) helped Mr. Lee draw up a constitution for the Institutes. Mrs. J. H. McNeilly was elected treasurer and Mrs. M. Nash secretary. Mrs. Rorer, author of a famous cookbook which includes the startling statement: "Tomatoes are not fit for human consumption, being only fit for the birds!" accompanied Mrs. Hoodless. The second Institute was organized in Whitby in 1899 and then the movement spread like wildfire. Pioneer child welfare work soon extended to the schools, resulting in medical and dental inspections and the community benefited by the establishment of recreation centres and more library facilities.

Welcoming immigrants to Canada and helping them preserve their unique culture and customs is another service, and Mrs. Anton Prey of New Denmark in New Brunswick credits the Women's Institute there, along with the local historical society which has built a museum, with combating the young people's loss of interest in their language and community social functions. Within 10 years more than 500 branches were organized and by 1915 every Canadian province had Women's Institutes. Miss Laura Rose, first organizer and lecturer appointed by the Ontario Department of Agriculture in 1899, designed the blue and gold Maple Leaf pin worn by members and suggested the motto "For Home and Country."

Success in getting domestic science taught in Ontario schools was also posing problems; that of obtaining teachers. Chagrined at having to import an American teacher for initial classes, Mrs. Hoodless dreamed of a college to train Canadian women to teach domestic science across Canada and persuaded the Ontario premier to grant money for its maintenance if she could secure the building. While brushing her teeth one day, she rushed out of the bathroom exclaiming: "I've got it, Muriel, I'll go to Montreal and see if Sir William MacDonald (the tobacco millionaire) won't finance the school." At a two-hour luncheon at the Ritz-Carlton,

Adelaide Hoodless used all her powers of persuasion until Sir William protested feebly: "I can't do this for Ontario unless I do something for Quebec."

"Then build one in Quebec too. They need it", said Mrs. Hoodless firmly, and went triumphantly home with the promise of $200,000 for a college. Truly, as Mrs. Walden, an admirer, said: "Adelaide Hoodless was a woman who got things done!"

This generous gift made possible the building of MacDonald Institute, attached to the Ontario Agricultural College of Guelph and opened in 1903. Mrs. Hoodless herself lectured and Miss Mary Watson became head of the home economics department, where courses of varying length were given. The one-year, or "Diamond Ring Course", was always the most popular.

Mrs. Hoodless next dreamed of a university course to give household science instructors still higher standing but had to raise money for the venture. On the eve of her 52nd birthday in 1909, she was scheduled to speak at a meeting of the Federation of Women's Clubs in Massey Hall, Toronto. At dinner she complained: "My head is splitting. I can't drive to Toronto tonight!" Edna reassured her: "Bernard will take you."

She began an inspired speech. Halfway through, while the audience was enthusiastically applauding, Adelaide Hoodless, smiling, took a sip of water. Suddenly the glass crashed to the floor and Adelaide fell back, dead. She had given her life to her countrywomen.

The Women's Institutes were given a federal charter in 1919. Canadian organizers helped start them in the United States. During World War I when Britain feared starvation, Mrs. Alfred Watt of British Columbia and Miss Emily Guest of Ontario had introduced Institutes into England and Scotland to teach women food conservation. Stanley Baldwin said they saved England from revolution. John Buchan once chuckled: "If you see your wife dressed as Cleopatra, or see a group of Arabs with camels on your lawn, you just say: 'Well, well, that's the Women's Institute!' "

The Queen Mother is the national president in England.

In 1930 the Associated Countrywomen of the World was created in 27 countries. With over 6,000,000 members, it is the largest women's organization in the world. Mrs. Watt became president, started the magazine, *The Countrywoman*, and was awarded an M.B.E. In Collingwood, her birthplace, there is a plaque in her honor.

Women's Institutes remain Adelaide Hoodless' gift to the world. Adelaide Hoodless School in Hamilton, the Park named for her near her birthplace which is now an historic shrine, and the Adelaide Hoodless Scholarship Fund at MacDonald Institute all commemorate her work. Her portrait which hangs in MacDonald Hall was unveiled in 1912 by her colleague Mrs. E. D. Smith, first president of the Women's Institute, whose daughter Verna was a student at MacDonald Institute at the time. Another beautiful portrait of Mrs. Hoodless, painted by Marion Long, hangs in Ottawa's National Archives. She is the only Canadian-born woman so honored.

Verna Smith, of U.E.L. ancestry, the daughter of Senator and Mrs. E. D. Smith, and niece of Dr. Elizabeth Smith Shortt, graduated from MacDonald Hall then married Gordon D. Conant, K.C. and moved to Oshawa. Mr. Conant was mayor of Oshawa 1916-1917, then Attorney-General and later Premier of Ontario. Dynamic Mrs. Conant has held high executive office in probably every worthwhile organization in Oshawa, including NCW (of which she is now honorary president), Little Theatre, Canadian Club, Women's Voluntary Services, and Women's Auxiliary of Oshawa Hospital. Renowned as a hostess, she has entertained for most of these organizations at their beautiful estate

"Buenavista" and was a co-founder of Oshawa Museum, where a plaque honors the Conant family.

Lady of the Sunshine

People hurrying home along windswept, rain-drenched streets in Montreal one dreary fall evening in 1896 witnessed a strange scene. Grooms were trying to restrain an injured, frightened horse while, still within reach of its thrashing hooves, a man lay huddled in the gutter. Beside the man knelt a beautiful, kind-faced woman, cradling his head on her bosom. Tenderly she wiped blood from his face with a delicate wisp of lace while whispering words of comfort. That compassionate woman was Lady Aberdeen, wife of the Governor-General and founder of the National Council of Women and the Victorian Order of Nurses. The injured man, a soldier in the Guard of Honor forming the Governor-General's escort, had been hurt when his mount fell on the slippery pavement. Only when he had been taken to hospital did Lady Aberdeen, assisted by her husband's Aide-de-Camp, arise and adjust her tiara. Minutes later she swept regally into the drawing room of Lord Strathcona for a formal dinner in honor of her husband and herself. She appeared quite unconcerned about her mud-stained satin skirt and greeted everyone with the radiant smile that brought her the title "Our Lady of the Sunshine". Friends said: "To know her is to love her." But she had many detractors who called her a revolutionary, high-handed and a strong-minded crank.

Born Ishbel Marjoribanks in London, she was the daughter of Isabel Hogg and Dudley Coutts Marjoribanks, Liberal Member of Parliament. Apparently otherwise blessed by fortune, tragedy touched her life in the death of a favorite brother. Inheriting her father's violent temper, Ishbel sublimated it into a dynamic force to help humanity.

Romance came early. John Gordon, a handsome youth of 21, hunting near their country home Guishachan, sought shelter from a sudden storm. It was love at first sight, despite 10 years' difference in age. When his two elder brothers died, John became sole heir to his father's fortune and also a peer of the realm. He and Ishbel were married in 1877 by the Archbishop of Canterbury and honeymooned in Egypt. By the time Lord Aberdeen was appointed Governor-General to Canada, the vice-regal couple had four children. Dorothea's death in infancy was a great sorrow. "We can thank that grim taskmaster, work," said Lady Aberdeen, "for giving us a solace in anxiety and a refuge in grief." She always felt herself deficient in "small talk", though an excellent public speaker active in welfare work in Great Britain.

Lady Aberdeen

In 1888 the National Suffrage Association of America organized a Congress of Women in Washington, D.C., and invited "achieving women" from foreign countries to attend. Envisioned was a sisterhood of nations to promote vital reforms. Each country was to organize a national council composed of existing women's groups. National councils would unite in an International Council of Women which would meet every five years. Only the American women actually did form a national council in 1888. They decided to hold the next meeting during the World Fair in Chicago in 1893, determined to turn the dream of an International Council into reality.

Twelve countries sent more than 200 official women delegates to Chicago. Lady Aberdeen was representative of several British suffrage societies. The 16 Canadian women attending knew Lady Aberdeen was coming to Canada and persuaded the future First Lady to head the delegation. Hundreds of enthusiastic women jammed meetings to take part in daily discussions on charity, education, industry, religion, philanthropy, law, government, and social reform.

Everyone was attracted by Lady Aberdeen — a tall, regal-looking woman with a round, rosy face, dark hair, hazel eyes and sunny smile. Since they planned to hold the next international congress in London, England, in 1889, the logical choice for first international president was a British woman. Each country had one vote. Lady Somerset, the other candidate, was also very popular. It was a crucial choice. Result of the vote was announced at 10 P.M. on a hot, tiring day with Lady Aberdeen the winner. The Canadians were jubilant. In her acceptance speech, Lady Aberdeen, who subsequently held the position for 36 years, said: "I can only pray that womanhood of the world may indeed rise to the opportunity now presented."

Dr. H. D. Drummond, a close friend, told Lady Aberdeen: "You, who work like a hundred tigers ...

have been working overtime, day and night, for years!"

Scarcely were the Aberdeens settled in Ottawa when, at a meeting in Toronto, Mrs. Hoodless persuaded Lady Aberdeen to take on the presidency of the National Council of Women in Canada. Mrs. Hoodless was elected treasurer and Mrs. Willoughby Cummings corresponding secretary.

Her Excellency's position, as wife of the Governor-General, (His Excellency was once barred from a meeting till the embarrassed chairman realized his identity) was a great asset as national president. It gave her a wonderful opportunity while travelling across the country on vice-regal tours to organize local Councils of Women. Toronto was first. Lady Aberdeen personally organized 19 of the 20 formed during her presidency and donated money to establish a head office in Ottawa with a paid secretary. On one trip to Western Canada, Lady Aberdeen celebrated her husband's 50th birthday by presenting him with a hen — so that he might always have fresh eggs while travelling.

The Golden Rule became the motto of the National Council which initiated worthwhile groups such as the Big Sister movement and the Child and Welfare Committees, which later developed into the Canadian Welfare Council. Membership included all races, classes, creeds and political parties. Mme. Routhier of Quebec persuaded many Roman Catholic societies to join the Council but later the Catholic Women's League resigned because it felt the Council favored birth control. When Pauline Johnson was invited to join as representative of Indian women, her vote was equal to that of the representative of the largest organization. Lady Aberdeen made the National Council of Women of Canada a model for the world.

She suggested national council presidents succeeding her be Canadian women with the wife of the Governor-General acting as honorary president. She inspired Canadian colleagues to carry on her great work. Today National Council is composed of more than 50 different organizations and has a membership of approximately 1,000,000 women. The executive meets annually with the Prime Minister and the cabinet to discuss national problems, offer suggestions and make requests.

Some requests have been: the abolition of the death penalty; the creation of rehabilitation centres of mentally defective adults; the establishment of equal pay for equal work; more favorable succession duties for widows; a federal government report on the effects of radiation on living organisms and increased Canadian support of United Nations and Colomba Plan technical assistance programs.

Lady Aberdeen had no precedent for organizing the International Council of Women. Official duties in Canada prevented her from travelling in Europe. However, her private secretary, Miss Teresa Wilson, had been elected secretary of the International Council so Lady Aberdeen organized councils by remote control sending "my girl Friday" as she called her, abroad. Miss Wilson reported such stormy sessions at some founding meetings that Lady Aberdeen almost despaired. "My one resource was to throw myself unreservedly on the power of the Holy Spirit to guide me . . . dreadful difficulties vanished." During the annual meeting of National Council of Women of Canada in Montreal, Lady Aberdeen read letters from Vancouver and Halifax Local Councils. They told pitiful tales of settlers dying from accidents or epidemics and of women dying in childbirth because no trained help was available. The letters begged for visiting nurses. Lady Aberdeen was familiar with the work of visiting nurses, having discussed it with British MP William Rathbone, the organizer of district nursing in England. In 1897 she conceived the brilliant idea of a "Victorian Order of Nurses" to fill this need while also honoring Queen Victoria on her diamond jubilee. Queen Victoria cabled her delighted approval. The prime minister and the press also were enthusiastic. The Aberdeens themselves started a fund with $3,000 and enlisted support for her plan by lecturing and writing. "It is going to take," she exulted, "and I believe that we may get a government grant."

She had talked over her idea with some prominent Montreal physicians, but made the mistake of not consulting the medical associations. Sir Charles Tupper, a bitter enemy had advertisements published in his newspapers warning people against "these female quacks" and convinced backwoods doctors that the Victorian Order of Nurses would ruin their practices. The Ontario Medical Council displayed violent hostility, calling it "a scheme deleterious to the health of the country." Friends urged Lady Aberdeen to abandon the idea to avoid further humiliation. Her family motto is "Advance with Courage" and she persevered.

She persuaded Dr. Alfred Worcester, founder of a home for district nurses near Boston, to speak to medical associations at Ottawa and Montreal. On their 20th wedding anniversary, the Aberdeens received a welcome telegram from the president of the Ontario Medical Association assuring that all opposition had disappeared. Canadian nurse, Miss Charlotte MacLeod returned from the United States to help Lady Aberdeen organize the now-famous Order, a detachment of which accompanied the Canadian troops sent to keep order in the Yukon during the Gold Rush.

Lady Aberdeen usually wrote far into the night. She kept a diary over 70 years. It records: "Sometimes I fairly sink under the load, trying to help John on public business, to be a companion to the children, to work for the National Council and the Victorian Order all night." She confided on another occasion: "To all of us come times when constant worry, endless toil, perpetual disappointment seem to be our lot."

With her many interests, Lady Aberdeen never neglected the husband she adored, nor the children, nor her social duties. At State dinners two young pages (her sons Dudley and Ian) carried their mother's embroidered train. Her Excellency loved entertaining. The Aberdeens gave a ball in the Senate Chamber in 1896 at which everyone impersonated some character in Canadian history, from the Vikings who landed in Labrador in A.D. 1000 to the United Empire Loyalists who left the United States for Canada in the 1780s. In 1897 their Victorian Ball cost $4,000.

May Day, 1898, marked another milestone in women's clubs. Lady Aberdeen organized the May Court Club of Ottawa to interest society girls in welfare work. Proceeds from their annual ball, one of the highlights of the social season, for years financed a chest clinic and convalescent home. May Court clubs have since spread to other cities.

"More and more, I find that, to keep life in proportion, books are an absolute necessity," said Lady Aberdeen. In order that lonely sailors at sea, lighthouse men and pioneer farmers and prospectors might share her pleasure in reading, she started the Aberdeen Associations which sent newspapers, magazines and books to waiting readers. Lady Aberdeen persuaded the railroad and steamship companies to carry them free of charge. She also founded the Home Reading Unions, small groups which meet to read and discuss worthwhile books; their annual writing contest encourages would-be authors. She herself wrote *Through Canada with a Kodak*, collaborated with her husband in writing *We Twa*, and edited a magazine *Onward and Upward*. Her daughter Lady Pentland wrote *A Bonny Fechter*, a biography of her mother. Lady Aberdeen was the first person to suggest (to Prime Minister Laurier) a National Capital Plan which materialized half a century later.

As they were leaving Canada in November, 1898,

Parliament tendered the Aberdeens a farewell address. When Her Excellency graciously expressed thanks, it was the first time that a woman's voice had been heard in the Senate Chamber. In recognition of her services to this country, Queen's University awarded her the first honorary LL.D. given by that seat of learning to a woman. The Women's Art Association honored her with a historical dinner service. One portrait of Lady Aberdeen is in Rideau Hall; another smiles radiantly at visitors to the Public Archives, the woman of whom the poet Yeats wrote:

> To tread the walks of life she stood prepared
> And what she greatly thought, she nobly dared,
> For she . . . had scorned delights and lived labori-
> ous days.

Lady Aberdeen returned to London in time to supervise final preparations for the first convention of the International Council of Women in June 1899. It was an unqualified success. International Council then included 10 national councils with the promise of 15 more.

Work of the International Council was interrupted by World War I. When the League of Nations Commission was meeting in Paris in 1919 at the end of the war, Lady Aberdeen told Lord Robert Cecil of the British delegation that women should be eligible to serve on the League — forerunner of the United Nations — since at least half the world's population was female. Lord Robert promised to introduce that clause — and did. On April 10, 1919, President Wilson received a delegation of women from several countries led by Lady Aberdeen. They asked support for the Women's Suffrage Movement, suppression of traffic in women and children and the establishment of bureaus of education and health. Today the International Council of Women serves as one of the advisory boards of the United Nations.

Canada's First Lady —
Her Excellency Madame Jules Léger C.C.

Madame Léger, nee Gabrielle Carmel, was born in Montreal. She was brought up in Paris, where she attended the Convent of the Dames de Saint-Maur. She married Jules Léger in 1938. They have one daughter, Helene, and three grandchildren. With her husband, Madame Léger has lived in many countries, England, France (twice), Italy and Belgium, as well as Chile and Mexico. She took the opportunity, during these postings, to travel a great deal and to learn Italian and Spanish. Among her main interests are 18th and 19th Century architecture and furniture, and history. Her Excellency was made a Companion of the Order of Canada on January 14, 1974.

Madame Georges Vanier

Beautiful, statuesque Pauline Archer, born in Montreal, the daughter of Hon. Mr. Justice Charles Archer and Mrs. Archer (Therese de Saleberry) was educated at the Convent of the Sacred-Heart and by private tutors. In 1921 she married Georges Vanier, who was appointed Canadian Ambassador to France in 1939. In 1940, following the outbreak of World War II, they fled from Paris to Bordeaux before the German advance. They entertained French resistance leaders in Algeria. When General Vanier returned to Paris in 1944, French authorities were not allowing wives to return except those in the Services. Mme. Vanier appealed to General Basil Price, head of the Red Cross in London. Borrowing the uniform of a girl on leave, Pauline Vanier triumphantly rejoined her husband as Representative of the Canadian Red Cross, a position she held till 1947. Later, while living again in Montreal, the Vaniers were very active in welfare work.

In 1959 General Vanier was appointed Governor General of Canada, and they proved a very popular choice. They have four sons and one daughter, Therese, who is a specialist in blood diseases. Their son Jean provides a home for the mentally ill in France. Feeling that the family is the basic unit of the nation, His Excellency convened a conference at Government House in June 1964. The delegates unanimously resolved that an Institute of the Family, a research body to study family problems, should be founded. It was named the Vanier Institute of the Family. Madame Vanier's nine Honorary Doctor Degrees include a Doctor of Social Science degree from University of Ottawa, and in 1965 she was appointed first woman chancellor of that institution, as well as Woman of the Year. She was with St. John Ambulance Voluntary Aid Department during the 1914-18 War, and her decorations include Chevalier de la Légion d'Honneur, Dame of the Order of Malta, Dame of the Order of Saint John of Jerusalem, and Companion of the Order of Canada.

Madame Vanier is also on the Board of Directors of Bank of Montreal and Bell Canada, and is a Member of the Privy Council. Widowed now, Madame Vanier lives in France, helping her son Jean with his work for the mentally retarded.

* * *

Mrs. A.F.W. Plumptre of Toronto and now Ottawa, a former president of the CAC was elected president of the Vanier Institute of the Family in 1969. An unusual combination of economist, mother and volunteer welfare worker, she is a member of the Economic Council of Canada, the Ontario Economic Council, and the new Canadian Consumer Council.

While the very outspoken Chairman of the Federal Food Prices Review Board, Beryl was the target of much unfair criticism, but says that she herself never felt discriminated against very much as a woman. Criticism tended to overshadow the real value of her work. Beryl said: "I think that anyone who is doing the type of job I was doing with the Review Board has to be tough."

Then, after she changed to become assistant to Jean-Luc Pepin on the Anti-Inflation Review Board, she was chosen the most newsworthy woman of 1975 (she had also had this honour in 1973). Running a close second to Mrs. Plumptre was Flora Macdonald, and third was Rosemary Brown M.L.A. from Vancouver, the first black woman to sit in a provincial legislature, and who ran second for the national leadership of the NDP, won by Ed Broadbent. International Women's Year naturally led the field as news story for 1975, but food prices took a dominant second spot.

In the summer of 1976 Beryl Plumptre resigned, and is presently doing some consulting work and serving as a director for two companies.

Beryl Plumptre

Slum Fighter

Typical of the public-spirited women who have presided over local councils is Mrs. R.G. Gilbride, who headed many important welfare projects in Montreal, though she protests she has "no time for clubs". She headed the Montreal Presbyterial and was on the national executive of the Progressive-Conservative Party.

As chairman of the national housing committee of the National Council she worked wonders. A desperate father of three small children, evicted from his home, appealed to her. Enlisting the support of 50 Montreal organizations, she campaigned for slum clearance. Mrs. Gilbride took the City Fathers to the worst tenements, and by way of contrast told them about Toronto's Regent Park, a model low-rental housing project. Result was the famous $15,000,000 Dozois Plan for slum clearance in Montreal.

Her daughter, Louise Gilbride, who married Leslie J. Stuart carried on her mother's welfare work. Charming Mrs. Stuart was Coordinator of Women's Events for Expo '67 and is now national president of the Canadian Association for Retarded Children.

* * *

Mrs. Edgar Hardy C.B.E. of Ottawa was president of the NCW from 1941 to 1946. She was the only woman appointed to the Canadian War Finance Board. "I was born an extrovert!" she exclaimed, and during the Great Depression she directed the distribution of food and clothing to the needy, an activity that developed into the Neighbourhood Services, which provides employment for the handicapped. Mrs. Hardy was active also in the YWCA and other organizations.

Founder Honored

When Council celebrated its 60th birthday on

June 20, 1953, it honored the memory of its national founder, Lady Aberdeen (who died in 1939) by a plaque in the International Peace Garden on the Manitoba-North Dakota border; it commemorated her lifelong promotion of international understanding. In 1954 the National Council began another project, the "Lady Aberdeen Memorial Library" of books written by women or about women "in all fields, in all epochs, in all countries". Elizabeth Long is convener of this project. The books, in the library of the University of Waterloo, are available to writers and researchers.

Consumers United

During World War II, the National Council of Women was closely associated with the Consumer Branch of the Wartime Prices and Trade Board. Mrs. W. R. Lang was liaison officer. Successful functioning of the board, the envy of other countries, was due to intelligent support from average Canadian homemakers. Since women do 80% of domestic buying, some similar peacetime organization seemed essential so, in 1947, Mrs. Blanche Marshall called a meeting of national presidents of women's clubs.

Mrs. Marshall, a member of the Royal Commission on Education for Ontario, had a son graduate from university the day her youngest daughter started kindergarten. In 1946 she had accepted the presidency of the National Council of Women, requiring almost incessant travelling and public speaking. She became president of the CAC in September, 1947 but resigned a year later due to ill-health. Under her leadership, jurisdiction for oleo-margarines was handed back to the province.

Mrs. Frank (Kay) Wright, a Queen's graduate with the Gold Medal in political economy, replaced Mrs. Marshall as CAC president. Her marriage to Frank Wright brought her to Toronto where she became a convener of the Local Council of Women, dealing with problems of homemakers in low-income brackets. In 1942 she became an adviser to the Wartime Prices and Trade Board Consumer Branch. During her leadership of the CAC, Parliament passed the Trade Mark and True Labelling Act.

Mrs. William (Dorothy) Walton II, led the consumers group from 1950-53, speaking at more than 50 meetings of businessmen and manufacturers each year. Her recipe for a good speech: "Get up, speak up, shut up!" The credo of the pioneer in consumer economics was simple. "We're doing a job in adult education in economics. An intelligent, well-informed buying public could be one of the greatest stabilizing influences in our economy." In 1951, Parliament made it compulsory for packages of detergents to tell weight and contents. A year later the Department of National Health and Welfare brought in new bread and flour regulations.

Mrs. Walton's presidency terminated the year of Queen Elizabeth's coronation and she received a Coronation Medal, partly for CAC leadership and partly for her work in the IODE. In 1957-58 Mrs. Walton was the only woman on the seven-member Royal Commission on Price Spreads and Food Products, the only woman on its advisory board from 1960 to 1962. She credits sports for her physical stamina. In 1940 she was awarded the Rose Bowl as Canada's outstanding woman athlete and was the only Canadian to win the World's amateur Badminton Singles Championship. In 1965 her name was added to Canada's Sports Hall of Fame.

Policy Planner

Mme. Renée Vautelet C.B.E. of Montreal gave the CAC its policy direction during its organizational months and made innumerable speeches across Canada during her presidency 1953-56. She even made an important speech the day after a minor operation. Her record is 39 speeches in 10 days. In one talk a group of clothing manufacturers was blasted "For the love of Mike, gentlemen, nowadays when we buy a size 5 for a child, we don't know whether he's going to need a shoehorn to get into it, or be smothered in a tent!" The sizes of children's clothes became more uniform shortly after.

Born in 1897 and educated privately, as a debutante she accompanied her father to a Privy Council meeting, held next door to the prime minister's residence in Downing Street, London, the first woman to attend one. Plump, pretty Renée also was the first Canadian woman to be given power of attorney as the representative of a candidate in the 1917 election. Her great-grandfather, Sir A. A. Dorion was one of the founders of the Liberal Party; Minister of Justice, and twice Prime Minister before Confederation. Her father, the late Aime Geoffrion, K. C., was one of the British Commonwealth's leading constitutional lawyers.

Renée fell madly in love and married a gallant officer, Col. Henri Vautelet. She says: "The principle of slavery is rejected by society — except in the case of married women in the home — we give them pay envelopes only when they leave it. Then, often they are criticized, if not ostracized, by their community." When their two daughters were infants, Mme. Vautelet would hurry home from a meeting, feed and burp them, then rush back. When her husband was Honorary Aide-de-Camp to Lord Tweedsmuir and then to Lord Athlone, Renée did her duty as a member of the Vice-Regal "family". "I put feathers and a tiara in my hair, hang a veil and train on me, looking like the *Queen Mary* in full sail. . ."

Always an ardent campaigner for women's rights, and ambassadress of better understanding between English and Frensh-speaking Canadians, she says laughingly: "I think in both languages. What annoys me is when I Anglicize my French!"

Madame Vautelet founded and was president of the Montreal French Children's Library and was a founder and vice-president of the Montreal French Social Service and Family Welfare. During the War, besides running her husband's insurance and brokerage business, she was on the War Savings Certificate National Committee at Ottawa; president of the "Block Plan" for war emergencies; and vice-president of the WVS in Montreal. Only woman member of the post-war Advisory Board of Quebec Province, she was awarded the C.B.E. "For leadership in charitable and patriotic endeavors".

* * *

With such dynamic leaders, and later ones, such as Mrs. Glenora Slimmon, the CAC developed as an organization unique in the world. Their steady output of bulletins, press, radio and TV releases and speeches keep Canadian homemakers informed.

Through the years they have lobbied before government officials in support of laws and regulations that would benefit the consumer. The CAC has developed a good system of feedback with members invited to report problems. Complaints are passed on to manufacturers.

In June 1963, during the presidency of Mrs. A. F. W. Plumptre (1961-66), the Association passed a resolution requesting that the Federal government set up a department of consumer affairs. The following year National Health and Welfare minister Judy LaMarsh announced the formation of a 15-member advisory group, The Canadian Consumer Council, (14 men and one woman) to advise the federal government on consumer affairs. This was followed by a full-scale federal department which became operative in 1968.

Ontario has a unique Women's Advisory Committee of the Ontario Department of Trade and Development, organized in 1963, with chairman Mrs. Lilah Lymburner, and with Mrs. R. B. Hales of Ottawa

also on the executive. The main purpose of the committee is to urge women to "buy Canadian".

Voice of Women

The Voice of Women may well be the foundation
of a world movement of women bent on disarmament
and peace, though since its formation in June 1960,
many influential women like Mrs. Lester Pearson and
Judy LaMarsh have resigned because they felt it had
become Communist-infiltrated and too militaristic.

Founder of the movement was Mrs. Fred Davis of
Toronto, who said: "In any future war, women and children would be in the front line. We'd be slaughtered by
millions. Women are closer to creation than men. We
don't resent dying in the pursuit of life. But we resent
having our entire future in the hands of poker-playing
strategists holding nuclear aces, gambling with our lives.
If every woman in the world gives this movement the
whole-hearted support it deserves she may prevent her
own children from being — as children in A-bombed
Hiroshima were — little flaming torches running
around in the hellish nightmare of death." Soon after
founding the organization, Mrs. Davis and another supporter, Mrs. Douglas Henderson, visited the prime minister and leaders of all political parties in Ottawa to
enlist government support.

Helen, wife of William D. Tucker of Port Credit,
was co-founder of the Voice of Women. Graduating
from the University of Michigan, she studied on a scholarship at the University of Bordeaux, France and took a
degree in speech arts at Toronto's Royal Conservatory
of Music. She lectures in speech communications at the
U. of T. Her whole life has been devoted to national and
international service and she has been the leader of
numerous cultural missions abroad, including the International Travel Mission to ten European countries in
1963, and a huge peace rally in Northern Ireland in

December 1976. Chosen "Woman of the Year" that year
by B'nai B'rith, she was also recipient of the ICY medal
in 1965. In 1966 she was a board member of the Centennial International Development Program and Experiment in International Living. A year later she co-
ordinated the Centennial International Visitors' bureau
in Toronto, and in 1968 was a council member of the
International Year of Human Rights.

Girl Guides

The Boy Scout and Girl Guide movements were
organized by the Baden-Powells in England in response
to young people's demands. After visiting England, Mrs.
T. R. Malcolmson organized the first company of Girl
Guides in Canada at St. Catharines in 1910. In the 1970's
Barbara Clasz of Edmonton became the first female to
be named Queen's Venturer, the highest award attain-
able in the Boy Scout program.

Lady Pellatt, chief commissioner of the guide
movement from 1912 to 1921, held the first Girl Guide
meetings at her Toronto home, Casa Loma. She financed
the movement for the first few years until 1919 when it
received a government grant. With "Happier Homes" as
their motto, guides provide help to members in other
countries in case of national catastrophe. The world-
wide movement makes no distinction of race, color or
creed and the first Indian Girl Guide troop was organized on Christian Island, near Midland, by Mrs. J. M.
Sheane in 1958.

B. and P. Clubs

Following World War I, many active in business
and the professions organized individual women's clubs
in cities across Canada. Eloise Girdleston of Vancouver,
promoted the idea of a federation and finally on June 7,
1930, a much discussed constitution was adopted. The

result was the Canadian Federation of Business and Professional Women's Club, which has as its primary concern the economic status of women.

First national president was Montreal lawyer Miss Dorothy Heneker who was requested six months later by the International Federation to tour fourteen European countries to organize new clubs. Her work in Canada was taken over by vice-president and secretary-treasurer Miss Mary Ethel Thornton of Winnipeg. The National Federation is the official spokesman for various clubs in dealings with the Canadian government, the International Federation and the United Nations. Business Women's Week is celebrated annually in Canada.

Women's Service Clubs

"The Age of Women's Clubs" is the name often given to the twentieth century. "Service is the rent we pay for the privilege of living on earth", someone has truly said, and service is the firm foundation of the service club movement in Canada. Our democratic form of government is made practicable by the work of volunteer organizations which often initiate welfare work later taken over by the government. Practically all our laws for the protection of women and children are thanks to members of groups of the National Council of Women, often referred to as "The Parliament of Women."

Canada has five international classified civic-service organizations for executive and professional women, who have much in common, but interesting differences. April 1917 saw the founding, in the United States, of *Altrusa International,* which later came to Canada. It stresses practical idealism. From 1924 on, it has emphasized vocational guidance, it introduced career conferences into schools, aids older women workers, and organizes hobby centres and Golden Age

Clubs for both men and women. Altrusa's two major projects are Founder Fund Vocational Aid; which enables women to enter the job market; and Inter-American Grants-in-Aid, which build friendship with South America. Miss Marjorie Lamb of Toronto has been an International President.

Quota Club (which means "We Share") was conceived by five women who were invited to a ladies' night banquet by the Kiwanis Club of Buffalo. The fellowship enjoyed by the men inspired them, under the leadership of Wanda Frey Joiner, to form a similar club for women. The first club in Canada was organized in Winnipeg in 1925. Their aims are to serve community and country, to promote high ethical standards, the advancement of women, the development of friendship. Their international project is to finance graduate fellowships for non-Communist women overseas, and in colleges on this continent.

Soroptimist Clubs have an interesting origin. Stuart Morrow, a professional organizer of men's service clubs, discussed the idea of a women's service club, similar to Kiwanis or Rotary, or Kinsmen, with Mrs. Adelaide Goddard, head of a secretarial school in Oakland, California. After six months of research and meetings, the installation of eighty women in evening dress was held in the Oakland Hotel on October 9, 1921, with Violet Richardson as first president.

The movement spread quickly, and in 1925 the first Canadian Soroptimist Club was organized in Vancouver. In June, 1927, the Club bought from Mr. Morrow his rights to organize their clubs for $5,000. Soroptimists must be "one of a kind", hold executive status, and have leadership qualities. They have consultative status on UNESCO, the Status of Women section of the Economic and Social Council, and active participation in UNICEF. The Canadian Foundation has as its goal the raising of $100,000 and is now approaching that figure. Funds provide student and citizenship awards. Dr. Sylvia Ostry and Senator Josie Quart are Honorary Members of Ottawa Soroptimist. Three Canadians have been president of the American Federation, Mrs. Anna Sprott of Vancouver, Miss L. Grace Nicholls of Toronto, and a Miss Crehan of Vancouver.

Miss Helen Cleveland, first president of the Toronto Zonta Club organized in 1927, went abroad in 1929, at her own expense, to establish Zonta Clubs in Europe. First of these was in Vienna, where she had the co-operation of the noted European violinist Nora de Kresz, who later became a member of the Hart House String Quartet of Toronto. Later, Miss Cleveland organized clubs in Germany, Denmark, Norway and Sweden. She became the first international president of Zonta, which gives scholarships and bursaries, such as the Amelia Earhardt Scholarship to further women's study of aeronautics. Dorothy Thompson, librarian at OCE, Toronto, after retiring, organized twenty-seven new Zonta Clubs around the world.

Pilot International was organized in 1921 in Macon, Georgia, U.S.A. and was named after the river boats, "pilot" meaning a leader or guide. It has friendship and service as its basic principles, and encourages high ethical standards among business and professional women. District 17 comprises the Canadian clubs, which are all in Ontario. The organization now has over 80,000 members in more than 550 clubs around the world.

Pilot clubs cooperate with other organizations to improve the welfare of all people, in local communities, provinces and the world. Each club selects its own civic service projects. In Ottawa, in addition to help to hospitals, their major project is helping to finance Alleliua House, a home for retarded adults.

Mrs. Jean (Alastair) Conacher of Hamilton has been the only Canadian president of Pilot International 1956-57. The Salk Institute for Biological Studies in San

Diego, California was the recipient of a $1,000 gift in her honour from Pilot International Foundation. The Foundation also promotes safety projects.

Pilot International Foundation's main project is programs to provide full citizenship for handicapped people. Pilot is particularly concerned with the specific area of convulsive disorders. The Ruby Newhall Memorial Scholarship Fund (part of the Foundation) assists international students majoring in health and welfare fields and returning to their homeland to work with their native people.

For many years in Toronto these five clubs joined forces to hold a Dinner to honour an outstanding Canadian woman. Guests have been women in politics, doctors, and women in the arts. This custom deserves to continue.

Chapter IX

The Famous Five

Murphy, Edwards, McKinney McClung, Parlby

Louise McKinney

> *Women are persons in matters of*
> *pains and penalties, but are not per-*
> *sons in matters of rights and privi-*
> *leges.*
>
> (British Common Law 1876)

Commonwealth Pioneer Woman Magistrate

All eyes in the hushed courtroom turned to the determined-looking woman on the magistrate's bench. Defense counsel Eardley Jackson, enraged by the stiff sentence meted out to a bootlegger, had just shouted at the British Empire's first police magistrate:

"You're not even a PERSON. You have no right to be holding court!"

In the stunned silence Magistrate Emily Murphy of Edmonton, flushed with rage spoke quietly: "Will defense counsel develop his argument?"

Jackson did. "Under British common law, in a decision handed down in 1876, the status of women is this: 'Women are persons in matters of pains and penalties, but are *not* persons in matters of rights and privileges.' Therefore, since the office of magistrate is a privilege, the present incumbent is here illegally. No decisions of her court can be binding."

Jackson angrily stalked from the courtroom without even waiting to gather up his papers.

The date was Dominion Day, 1916. Afterwards Emily confessed to a close friend that this, her first day on the bench, was "as pleasant an experience as running a rapids without a guide!"

Her court decision was upheld but the incident was to have important repercussions for all Canadian women. It was only the first of a series of nerve wracking skirmishes with lawyers and officials who scorned the authority of a woman. Her dignified handling of them concealed a growing indignation.

When Alice Jamieson of Calgary was appointed Canada's second woman magistrate, her authority also was challenged. Though the Supreme Court of Alberta upheld the decisions of its women magistrates, Mrs. Murphy asked herself: "What about the Dominion?"

She determined to clarify the ambiguous and ignominious status of women under the British North America Act. The history of the epic battle, begun in that Edmonton courtroom, raged over two continents and covered a period of 13 years. In 1916, when her personal war was initiated, World War I was devastating Europe. Magistrate Murphy was appointed Convener of the Committee on Peace and Arbitration by the NCW, and a member of the War Council of Women by the Federal Cabinet to mobilize women to help increase food production. Emily toiled tirelessly in her own wartime garden, called "The Rake's Progress".

Mrs. Murphy began by conducting a vigorous press campaign, using as her platform the eligibility of women to sit in the Senate. If they were allowed to do so, they were ipso facto "persons" with attendant rights and privileges. Her opening shot was to persuade the editor of Women's Century (an early magazine for which she wrote and on whose editorial board she served) to advocate the appointment of women to the Senate. In addition she wrote more than 700 letters to influential people.

Presiding at the first national convention of the Federated Women's Institutes of Canada in 1919, she urged women to fight for their rights. "The world loves a peaceful man, but gives way to a strenuous kicker", she told them.

Her enthusiasm was contagious. She persuaded delegates representing 100,000 Women's Institute members to sign a petition to government requesting admission of women to the Senate. She addressed meetings all over the country and her stirring speeches rallied many other women's organizations including the powerful National Council of Women.

Judge Emily Murphy

In January 1921 the Montreal Women's Club sent a delegation to Prime Minister Arthur Meighen requesting Magistrate Murphy's appointment to the Senate.

Meanwhile Magistrate Murphy discussed with a prominent Montreal lawyer the possibility of adding a rider to the British North America Act stating the "persons" include women. He indignantly repudiated her suggestion, adding insult to injury by sending her a bill for $200!

The indifference of five federal administrations convinced Mrs. Murphy by 1927 that waiting and hoping was useless, so she initiated legal action — the most far-reaching litigation undertaken by any Canadian woman. She had discovered that Section 60 of the Supreme Court Act stated that any five interested persons had the right to petition the government for a ruling on a constitutional point, and she determined to test it. She chose the other four appellants carefully; all four could help her arouse public opinion by pen and platform. They were Henrietta Muir Edwards, Louise McKinney, Nellie McClung, and Dr. Irene Parlby. The results of their combined efforts came to be known as "The Persons Case".

Each member of this group of five merits individual consideration. Magistrate Murphy, their leader, stands out as one of Canada's great women. Emily was born in 1868 near Cookstown, Ontario. Her grandfather, Ogle R. Gowan, was a famous politician who founded the Orange Order in Canada. Known in Parliament as "The Father of the House", he worked for 27 years for a united Canada.

With her one sister and four brothers, Emily enjoyed a happy home life. Her future was strongly influenced by her father's advanced views on the sharing of duties and privileges by boys and girls alike. He insisted that in addition to elocution she study penmanship, which proved to be a great help as she never learned to type.

With three of her brothers becoming lawyers, Emily was familiar with the judicial atmosphere long before she became a magistrate.

She graduated from Bishop Strachan School in

Toronto with the Alexander Manning Medal for general proficiency. At the age of 15 she met Arthur Murphy, a tall, blond, 26-year-old theology student. They were married in 1887. Nicknamed "Sunshine", she was a dark, pretty girl bubbling with Irish humor, who experienced great difficulty maintaining the dignity required of a minister's wife. "As a bride of 19", she said, "I had to take Bible classes, be president of the Missionary Society, play the organ, speak at meetings, and organize entertainments and bazaars. I was acquiring experience that fitted me for later duties."

Since Arthur was a travelling missionary for several years, Emily had time to study shorthand and painting and develop her writing talent. Nellie McClung called her "a brilliant student, with a mind like a great encyclopedia." By 1898 Arthur was an outstanding preacher and the Murphys were invited to London, England. During the voyage, fellow-passengers spoke contemptuously of Canadians and Emily's spirited defense earned her the nickname of "Janey Canuck", a title she adopted as her pen name.

Tragedy punctuated an otherwise happy life for the spirited Canadian. She lost one of her four daughters in childbirth after falling downstairs, and a second baby daughter died of diphtheria. Her husband collapsed with typhoid during a speaking engagement at Massey Hall, Toronto, and after nursing him back to health — meanwhile using her writing talents to pay the bills — she contracted the disease and nearly died. Nothing daunted, while convalescing, she wrote *The Diary of a Typhoid Patient.*

In an effort to forget its sorrows, the family moved to Swan Lake, Manitoba, in 1903. Emily wrote book reviews for the *Winnipeg Tribune* and sketches of pioneer life which were collected and turned into a best-selling book *Janey Canuck in the West.*

In 1907 Arthur was called to Edmonton, a fast-growing town of adventurous pioneers, full of "copy" for anyone who could wield a pen. Life was lived at a rare pace and cost. Banquets at the hotel cost $15 a plate and some women wore Paris ball gowns costing $150. With her great zest for life, Emily danced, curled, and went horseriding, winning first prize at the Horse Show.

Despite her own exciting life, Mrs. Murphy sensed the dullness of her neighbours' daily routine. She earnestly believed that women's associations, besides providing social contacts, could help with much-needed reforms. With rare organizing ability she started one club after another, winning public support and enlisting influential backers. She was particularly active in writers' groups, being president of the Canadian Women's Press Club for eight years.

With several others, Mrs. Murphy worked hard to have the Dower Act passed, ensuring that a widow receive at least a third of her husband's estate. For years she actively campaigned for a Children's Protection Act, attending not only Juvenile and District Courts, but the Supreme Court. When the Attorney-General established a Women's Court in Edmonton in June, 1916, Mrs. Murphy was the logical choice as magistrate. Congratulatory letters and telegrams poured in after her appointment was announced. One letter addressed her as "Your Majesty". Several called her "Sir". Harcourt, a lawyer brother, wrote: "Try to temper your decisions with mercy, and do not hand out too much of your own medicine — hard labour!"

Her work on the bench gave her a great insight into the problems of drug addiction and mental health. Her book The Black Candle (the drug addict's name for the opium pipe) was the first comprehensive study of the drug habit ever published. It was used by the Narcotics Division of the League of Nations as a textbook. One drug addict she had helped attempted to murder her.

While rather stern and mannish on the Bench,

Magistrate Murphy showed a good deal of womanly sympathy for some offenders. One frowsy-looking but evidently well-educated woman accused of murdering her husband aroused her personal interest so much that she arranged to have the woman placed in her temporary custody, fixed her a warm perfumed bath and gave her a beautiful outfit to wear. Bursting into tears, the woman unravelled her tragic story. A well-bred teacher, she had married a foreign farmer, whose way of life proved worlds apart from hers. His insistence, for example, that they and the hired man all sleep together on the floor was the worst of a number of degrading situations that ultimately provoked her to desperate violence. One night she murdered him with an axe. Magistrate Murphy managed to get her a light sentence.

Magistrate Murphy's uncompromising attitude that insanity is an illness not a crime is now accepted. But at that time it was as revolutionary as her simultaneous suggestion that the subnormal be sterilized. By her writing and speeches she was instrumental in getting the Alberta Sexual Sterilization Act passed in 1928. For years she advocated establishment of mental health clinics. Her ambition was realized in 1930 when the first was opened in Alberta.

Mrs. Murphy was appointed by the Alberta Government in 1926 to investigate international property laws relating to women and conditions of public institutions. Her critical reports made many enemies. On several occasions her life was threatened, once by an insane woman in court. Her creed was: "We magistrates should use remedial measures. Reform and rehabilitation, not punishment, should be the aim of the courts." Accused once of "swaggering" into court, she retorted: "Better to swagger than to stagger!" When she resigned from Women's Court in 1931 because of ill health, she continued as Magistrate and Juvenile Court Judge for the Province of Alberta.

Her passion for justice had previously left too little time for writing. Now her thought-provoking articles sought to arouse public action against evils resulting in crime such as drug addiction and the propagation of the feeble-minded. She wrote vital, controversial, outspoken articles on venereal disease, and a book on birth control titled, *Pruning the Family Tree*. In 1915, in recognition of both her writing and welfare work, Mrs. Murphy was created a Lady of St. John of Jerusalem. Then in 1927 she was made a Brother of the Most Noble Order of Crusaders — its only woman member — and given a special decoration "for services to mankind and the Empire".

On October 26, 1933, Magistrate Murphy died in her sleep. "Perhaps, if we just love enough, we shall be successes in living", was her favorite saying. Flowers and callers who overflowed her home proved that the love of this great humanitarian was reciprocated. A red rose, the offering of a prostitute, was placed in her hand by her daughters. It was Depression years, but many walked miles to pay their respects. The famous and the unknown, the privileged and the underprivileged were among her mourners.

The day of her death she had visited her former colleagues in the courthouse and had heard lawyer Eardley Jackson say: "We are honored today by the presence of Mrs. Emily Murphy, Police Magistrate and Judge. A feminine note missing from this building . . . is brought back by the kindly, smiling countenance of this beloved lady." No words could have been a more fitting epitaph, coming as they did from her enemy — the man who had disputed her rights as a "person" 17 years before, the man who had unwittingly set in motion the great fight for emancipation for Canadian women.

A Modern Hypatia

A tiny woman with rosy cheeks and snapping brown eyes, the 80-year-old Henrietta Muir Edwards was greeted with enthusiastic applause when she stepped up to the platform and climbed on a chair so she could be seen and heard. The applause quickly died away into respectful silence while she gave a masterly report brightened by the odd flash of humor. The occasion was a convention of the National Council of Women in Halifax, Nova Scotia, in 1929.

Henrietta Muir Edwards

Though dumpy and dowdy at 80, as a girl she had had plenty of feminine allure. Fellow artists raved about her glorious, curly, Titian-tinted hair which remained red to the end. She also possessed freckles and a fiery temper. Usually it was injustice especially towards women, which aroused her wrath, but she was never the militant suffragette type. Enthusiastic applause at the end of her Halifax speech was also a tribute to sheer courage and determination. Mrs. Edwards had journeyed all the way from the Prairies to the Maritimes to attend the convention, despite the fact that train travel always made her deathly ill.

Besides being the convener of laws for the National Council, Mrs. Edwards was president of the Provincial Council of Alberta for several years. Both positions entailed almost constant travelling and public speaking. Though not the brilliant lawyer that she might have been had she lived a century later, she was a persuasive advocate. When she headed a delegation of the Alberta Government in 1896, Premier Brownlee complimented her on her knowledge of law. Often called "A modern Hypatia" (an Alexandrian lady noted for eloquence, learning and beauty), Mrs. Edwards was generally acknowledged to know more about laws affecting women than the Chief Justice.

Thirty-six years earlier, in 1893, Mrs. Edwards had helped Lady Aberdeen organize the National Council of Women and had been Convener of Laws thereafter. Her work as head of this committee was so outstanding that it became the model for other countries. The National Council has been largely responsible in securing every reform in laws affecting women. Mrs. Edwards told her fascinated colleagues of her successful battle with the Federal Government to raise the age of "consent" for girls from sixteen to eighteen years, to grant divorces on equal grounds, to allow equal parental rights, to establish mother's allowances, among many other reforms.

This altruistic woman, who had dedicated her life to the service of her sex, had several interesting facets to her personality. She was born Henrietta Muir on December 19, 1849, into a wealthy Montreal family. She finished her education abroad, had flower paintings exhibited in the Royal Canadian Academy, and painted exquisite miniatures of well-known contemporary figures, including Sir Wilfrid Laurier and Lord Strathcona.

But instead of becoming a society leader or dilettante, she devoted her energies towards the welfare of poor working girls. Having organized the "Working Girls' Associations" in 1875, she opened a home for 60 girls which offered vocational training and help in finding employment. The versatile Henrietta then bought a printing press and began publishing a magazine — *Women's Work in Canada.* She wrote the chapter "Women in Professions and Careers" for the book *Women of Canada,* for the Paris International Exposition in 1900.

Henrietta married Dr. Oliver Edwards in 1876, with Sir William Osler as best man. Neither her marriage nor her hobbies, which included chess, Esperanto, amateur photography and taxidermy, were allowed to interfere with her welfare work. She agitated for prison reform and held prayer meetings for women prisoners.

The Edwards moved to Fort Qu'Appelle, Saskatchewan, in 1883, when Dr. Edwards became the first general practitioner in the Northwest Territories. Henrietta cheerfully left a luxurious home and personal maid to live in a tent near an Indian encampment.

In 1890 they moved to Ottawa where Mrs. Edwards helped Lady Aberdeen found both the National Council of Women and the Victorian Order of Nurses. Returning to the West in 1903, the Edwards settled in Macleod, Alta. Dr. Edwards was physician to the Blood Indian Reserve and his wife acquired a fine collection of Indian artifacts. With commendable patriotism, she sold it to the University of Alberta, resisting better offers from the United States.

Around 1908 Mrs. Edwards compiled a handbook on the legal status of women in Alberta. Later, her *Legal Status of Women of Canada* was published by the Federal Government. Friends teased her for devouring Hansard (the daily report of Parliamentary proceedings) the way most women devour novels. After Dr. Edwards' death in 1915, his widow helped to organize the public library and was a member of the Alberta government's advisory committee on health. After her death in 1931, a brass plaque in her honor was hung in the legislative buildings in Edmonton.

Statesmanlike Stature

In June, 1917, Mrs. Louise McKinney had the distinction of being the first woman elected to a legislative assembly in the British Empire. Her political career was an outgrowth of her real interest — temperance work. Alberta's introduction of prohibition in 1915 meant much more to Louise than her election. Government interested her because she was a public-spirited citizen but she was disgusted with party politicians because of the support both parties received from liquor interests. She termed Alberta "a brewer's paradise".

When the Non-Partisan League was introduced in the province, Mrs. McKinney ran on a prohibition ticket, electioneering over rough roads by cutter and buggy. A woman of statesmanlike stature, she made an excellent Parliamentarian. Some progressive measures she helped introduce during her term of office were laws to help immigrants and the sub-normal, and she needled the government into enacting more effective liquor legislation. She also aroused public opinion against the unjust legal status of widows and separated wives.

Sixth in the Crummy family of ten children, Louise was born on a farm in Frankville, Ontario, in 1868. At school she was an outstanding debater and, frustrated in her longing to study medicine, she became a teacher. She protested: "Even as a child I recognized and resented the disabilities laid upon women." Giving up teaching to become an organizer of the Women's Christian Temperance Union in the United States, she met James McKinney — also an ardent prohibitionist —

and they were married in 1894. They named their only son Willard after Frances Willard, founder of the WCTU. (Rumor has it that once, suffering from a severe cough, Miss Willard found great relief in medicine her doctor prescribed, blissfully unaware of its rather high alcoholic content!).

Returning to Canada in 1903, the McKinneys were pioneer settlers in Claresholm, Alta. Mrs. McKinney helped to organize Northwestern Territories WCTU in Calgary. In 1905, after formation of the two provinces, this became the Alberta and Saskatchewan Union of which she was president for more than 20 years. During that time she succeeded in having temperance education introduced into schools and university extension departments. She loved travelling and attended many temperance conventions as vice-president of the Dominion Union between 1908 and 1930.

The versatile woman could with equal ease edit a newspaper column, make a political speech (she was an expert on procedure), write a temperance pageant, or preach a persuasive sermon. The McKinneys helped to build the Methodist Church, where she taught Sunday School. In 1925 she was appointed a Commissioner for the First General Council of the United Church in Toronto; she was the only woman to sign the Basis of Union.

Louise McKinney died in 1931 — worn out from her temperance crusade. Her portrait hangs in the Parliament Buildings in Edmonton and a plaque in Claresholm honors her memory.

Modern Ruth and Naomi

The first Sunday after she arrived in Manitou, Manitoba to teach, young Nellie Mooney attended the Methodist Church and Sunday School. She admired the Sunday School teacher, Mrs. J. A. McClung, the minister's wife, so intensely that she decided the woman

224

would be an ideal mother-in-law! Hearing that the McClungs had a tall, red-haired son, Wesley, she managed to meet him by squandering her last $3 on a fountain pen at the drug store where he worked, admitting: "He had no chance to escape!" When they married in 1896 she remarked: "That investment paid dividends. The day I married Wes I did the best day's work I have ever done. He lighted all the candles of my mind."

Nellie McClung

Nellie was born in 1873 in Chatsworth, Ontario. At seven she was travelling west by ox-cart with her gay Irish father, John Mooney, and her serious Scottish mother, Letitia. The family settled in a one-room log cabin near Brandon, Manitoba where they were often wakened by the howling of wolves, and Nellie's first playmate was an Indian lad. While herding cows Nellie did arithmetic sums which her elder sister Hannah corrected. She devoured history books and all Charles Dickens' novels which aroused her social conscience. She had no formal education till she was 10, but was a brilliant student, winning the Isbister Prize and her teacher's certificate when only 15.

While at Normal School in Winnipeg, she met interesting writers, including Cora Hind and Agnes Laut, which probably aroused an ambition to write.

Her mother-in-law persuaded her to enter a short-story contest. Nellie didn't win but the editor's letter was encouraging. The story later became the first chapter of the children's classic *Sowing Seeds in Danny*, which sold over 100,000 copies and earned her $25,000. In addition to articles, short stories and verses, Nellie McClung wrote 15 books which earned more than $60,-000. She was active in writers' organizations and was national vice-president of the Canadian Authors' Association from 1935 to 1936.

Her advice to aspiring authors was: "One must be willing to work early and late, to be tired, to be depressed, to see one's fairest inspirations tremble and fade and die — when one tries to capture them in a net of words. One must live before one can write. The essential qualifications of a writer are an understanding heart and a habit of close observation."

Although she considered a well-stored mind a greater asset than beauty, Nellie was a pretty woman with a lovely complexion, dark hair and sparkling brown eyes. She took a feminine delight in dress. One admirer described her as "Vivid as a tiger-lily — never sick, never cross, never worried." Up with the lark every morning, and working half the night, she accomplished miracles.

By 1911, when the McClungs moved to Winnipeg, they had four boys and a girl. Little Mark was taught to say solemnly: "My mother is a suffragette, so I have never known a mother's love," to the amusement of their friends. Fortunately, the Ruth-and-Naomi-like love between the two McClung women continued. The senior Mrs. McClung was a progressive woman, largely responsible for Nellie's interest in both church work and women's suffrage. Nellie was a pioneer member of the Canadian Women's Press Club which helped to organize the Manitoba Political Equality League. She pleaded eloquently with the Legislature to "recognize us (women) as citizens, say by your actions that your confidence in us is as great as your confidence in the least intelligent lad of 21."

Next, with sublime self-confidence, Nellie urged Premier Sir R. P. Roblin to call a Cabinet meeting to allow her to discuss women's suffrage. He indignantly refused, publicly branding her "a conceited young woman, laboring under the delusion that she has a gift of oratory." Although the first round went to Roblin, he bitterly regretted antagonizing Canada's most militant suffragette. She produced throughout the West a side-splitting satire called "The Mock Parliament of Women" which later helped overthrow Roblin's government.

Nellie's Irish humor was always in conflict with her dour Methodism. A born mimic, goaded by Roblin's taunt, she developed her natural histrionic gifts until she was hailed as one of North America's most dynamic speakers. Guest speaker at a men's club, "Mrs. Western Canada" once said: "You men say 'women are angels' and you plead that politics are corrupting . . . therefore you can't get women into public life too soon, since there is a shortage of angels in politics."

Her enemies called her "Windy Nellie", threatened slander suits, physical violence and even burned her in effigy. Nevertheless Nellie attracted enthusiastic crowds with clever speeches full of logical argument spiced with humor. Warm-hearted and witty, she was personally very popular. Her memory was phenomenal.

At a luncheon for 80 women she called all but two by name (yet she nearly broke her father's heart by forgetting his 80th birthday). Her bureau drawers were full of speaking invitations she hadn't time to accept. She addressed more than 400 public meetings in 20 years, often speaking three times a day, and toured the United States and Great Britain as well as Canada, speaking on both suffrage and temperance.

Mrs. McClung's feelings on temperance were deeply rooted in childhood memories of hardships suffered by families of hard-drinking, poverty-stricken neighbors. Once she narrowly escaped death from being run down by a drunken rider. Her maiden speech, a flop, was given at a WCTU meeting. Vested liquor interests called her "Calamity Nell" but didn't find it so funny when the WCTU campaign proved successful; prohibition was introduced in 1916.

Eight years later when government liquor control replaced prohibition, a bitterly disappointed Nellie protested: "Women could have sobered this country...why do we hold life so lightly? We, the women, who pay for it with sweat, blood and tears. How can we be indifferent to the evils which mar our creation?"

The year 1916 saw the realization of another cherished dream when Manitoba became the first Canadian province to grant women full suffrage. Other Western provinces soon followed. This was largely achieved by the quarter-century of devoted work by Nellie and other determined suffragettes.

The first woman to publicly electioneer in Canada (the McClung family had moved to Calgary), Nellie was elected to the Alberta Legislature in 1921 as a Liberal, though she sometimes voted against her party's policies. Her political philosophy was: "Never retract, never explain, never apologize; get the thing done and let them howl." Rather domineering at times, one friend said: "Wherever Nell sits is always the head of the table."

Dramatic Nell often inspired bored parliamentarians to spring to their feet cheering. Carrying on the work begun by her colleague, Mrs. McKinney, Nellie became the spearhead of progressive legislation. She championed public health nursing, mothers' allowances, free medical and dental treatment for school children, and fairer property rights for women. She advocated birth control and divorce, saying of the latter: "Why are pencils equipped with erasers if not to correct mistakes?" It seems paradoxical that while she was so realistic about these controversial problems, she should be so fanatical about liquor dubbing it "one of the devil's devices."

Seeking re-election in 1926, she was defeated by 60 votes, partly because she was such a rabid Prohibitionist and partly because Wes's business had necessitated a move to Edmonton where she was not so well known. Smarting from this public setback, she indulged in a "baking binge" — then devoted her energies to the "Persons Case."

Many high honors were accorded Mrs. McClung. In 1918 she was the only woman appointed by Conservative Prime Minister Sir Robert Borden to the Dominion War Council and the only woman delegate representing Canadian Methodists at the 1921 Ecumenical Conference in London, England. She was the first woman appointed to the Canadian Broadcasting Corporation's Board of Governors (1936-1942) and was Canada's sole woman representative to the League of Nations in 1939.

The McClungs moved to Victoria in 1933. At 75 Nellie retained her youthful spirit, despite painful arthritis. Though life had been no bed of roses her marriage was ideally happy. Nellie McClung could truly say: "I have warmed both hands at the fire of life." The Canadian Government issued a stamp honouring Nellie McClung in Aug. 1973.

Her call to women to preserve their hard-won heritage rings down the years: "Women are our last reserves. If they cannot heal the world, we are lost. For ... the trumpets are calling, the call is for women who ... will lovingly, patiently undertake the task of piecing together the torn mantle of civilization, who will make it so strong, so beautiful, so glorious that never again can it be torn or soiled with human blood. The trumpets are calling our healers who will nurse back to health a wounded world."

Patrician Pioneer

Many years ago in picturesque India, an English baby's Ayab gave her an overdose of a powerful sedative to stop her crying. The little girl almost died, then rallied to live through the reigns of six British sovereigns and to become the second woman cabinet minister in the British Commonwealth.

By birth a patrician, Dr. Irene Parlby considered other members of the "Persons Case" rather narrow in some respects. They, in turn, looked askance at a woman who dallied along the primrose path to the extent of occasionally smoking a cigarette and even taking a drink.

Mary Irene was born in 1868 to Lt-Col. and Mrs. Ernest Lindsay Marryat. Her father was the grandson of the M.P. for Wimbledon, S. Marryat, and a nephew of Capt. Fred Marryat, R.N., the writer of boys' adventure stories. After an exciting childhood in India, Irene was educated in England by private tutors, studying literature, elocution, painting and music. Her father suggested she might study medicine, but she was more interested in acting or writing. Travel in Europe completed her formal education. At 23, she was a fine-featured girl with brown hair and hazel eyes and a self-possession that was a by-product of leisurely maturing and a secure background.

When Irene received an invitation in 1896 to visit friends on a prairie ranch in Alberta, she was delighted. Having read *Settlers in Canada*, she considered the country to be The Promised Land. In Canada she met a young Englishman, Walter Parlby, an Oxford graduate whom she married the next year.

In Alberta, they were the first white settlers in their district. Walter built their log cabin and helped set up a little log church. Later, one neighbour lived in a large well until his cabin was built. Relatives in England, who pictured Irene in buckskins and shirts riding a bronco were bewildered at her requests for pretty clothes and beautiful china. But even in such rugged surroundings, women still must minister to "beauty treasured against gray days."

The young Parlbys became leaders in the community, Walter becoming a Justice of the Peace and president of the United Farmers of Alberta. Irene was concerned with bringing up their son, making a home, and — true to her English heritage — her garden. Seeing a country in the making was a thrilling experience for her. "Perhaps the greatest and most illuminating thing I found in the West was the women are useful and important," Irene discovered. She gloried in making a vital contribution to her adopted land. She never felt lonely but realizing that all the neighboring farm women were not so fortunate she organized the Countrywomen's Club for mutual help and education, and became its president.

When this club eventually became part of the United Farm Women of Alberta, Mrs. Parlby had the difficult task as president of building up the provincial organization. She was vice-president of the Women's Section of the Canadian Farmers of Alberta and the Alberta Red Cross Society. In the latter capacity she was largely responsible for having obstetrical nurses stationed in outlying districts which had no doctors, for the establishment of child welfare clinics and the inauguration of a municipal hospital scheme in Alberta.

Dr. Irene Parlby

She was elected to represent Lacombe, a typical rural constituency, in the provincial legislature in 1921 — the same year Nellie McClung was elected. That August she was appointed Minister without Portfolio in Premier Herbert Greenfield's cabinet, sharing with Mrs. Mary Ellen Smith, who was appointed a few months earlier, the distinction of being first women to hold cabinet rank in Canada. Always dignified and reserved, Mrs. Parlby never degenerated into a tub-thumping politician and was vastly amused when one admiring supporter said: "Mrs. Parlby, you do get commoner and commoner every day!"

An eloquent speaker, she was deadly in debate. Her male colleagues came to admire her well-informed mind, good judgement and humanitarian principles. Dr. Parlby, never a cynic or opportunist, remained a practical idealist. She urged: "If, having, through self-analysis, taken the blinkers from our eyes, we could go forward, a united people, with a great purpose to make Canada what it so well might be — what a happy, prosperous democracy we might arrive at."

She worked hard to ensure better education for every Canadian child and in 1924 made an extensive tour of Europe to study modern methods of teaching. She was awarded the first honorary degree of Doctor of Laws by the University of Alberta. She emerged from the 1930 election campaign exhausted but, at Prime Minister Bennett's request and in the interests of peace and international understanding, she represented Canada at the League of Nations' session at Geneva. She was taken seriously ill on the voyage home and spent several weeks in hospital in Montreal. She managed to finish her term in the Legislature and then thankfully returned to private life. She died in 1965. Dr. Parlby could truly say: "Much have I seen and known, cities of men and manners, climates, councils and governments."

The "Persons Case"

These then — Emily Murphy, Henrietta Edwards, Louise McKinney, Nellie McClung and Irene Parlby — were the "five interested persons" who fought the battle for the emancipation of their sex. All outstanding women, all devoted wives and good mothers, but not persons in the legal sense. Five intelligent feminists, they differed widely in background and upbringing, yet in outlook they thought as one. And when the battle raged they fought as one. They joined forces in the final skirmish of the battle which their leader, Mrs. Murphy, fought for 13 years.

Every effort had been made by 1927 to convince the government that Canadian women had a just grievance. Ottawa turned a deaf ear to pleas and no official action was taken. In desperation Mrs. Murphy called a meeting of the five at her home in Edmonton. They discussed the situation over a cup of tea on a sunny August afternoon. Though less famous an occasion than the Boston Tea Party, in its way it was as historic an occasion because of the far-reaching consequences it had for all Canadian women. Earnestly the five made their plans, drew up the petition and, hopefully, signed it.

The argument was heard in the Supreme Court of Canada on March 14, 1928, their lawyer being the distinguished Newton W. Rowell. Judgement was reserved. The verdict after an interminable wait of five weeks was a bitter disappointment. In the opinion of the Supreme Court, Canadian women along with children, criminals and idiots were not legally "persons." It was a crucial moment in the history of Canadian women. The five met again in a mood of sorrow mingled with anger. They agreed there was only one course left: appeal to the Privy Council in London, England — final court of appeal in the British Empire. It was their last hope.

After 19 anxious months had dragged by, Lord Sankey finally delivered the judicial opinion of His Majesty's Privy Council on October 18, 1929. Mrs. Murphy, wakened at 3 a.m. by a long distance phone call from London, danced excitedly up and down in a pink flannelette nightgown as she announced to her family: "We've won! We've won!" The Canadian Supreme Court decision had been overruled. Throughout the British Empire newspaper headlines declared: "Women are PERSONS!" Canadian women everywhere were proud of their acknowledged legal status, with the same rights and privileges as men. They could now share in every activity including the highest pinnacles of government.

Everyone expected that the next move would be

the appointment of Emily Murphy as Canada's first woman senator, though each of the five had some advocates for this honor. Requests flooded in to Ottawa. However, when Prime Minister Mackenzie King made the appointment in February 1930 it was given to Mrs. Cairine Wilson, a relative of Mr. Edwards. She was a Liberal who had done yeoman service for her party, but she was not a feminist. The only reward Emily Murphy ever coveted was to be Canada's first woman senator. When she heard the news Emily was bitterly disappointed. But all she said was: "Cairine Wilson is a good woman." Her family motto was: "Sweetness out of bitterness." She never mentioned the subject again. All five were disappointed but never once were heard to complain. Their great consolation was their victory. A woman sat in the Senate, and they had made it possible.

Dr. Parlby once said: "Women should remember that they are the guardians of the intangibles of life. They may not be called upon to play a spectacular part, but their quiet influence in maintaining the finer attitudes towards life does influence society." The truth of this assessment cannot be denied, but the story of the "Famous Five" is evidence that, when called upon "to play a spectacular part", women are not found wanting.

Chapter X

Pinnacle of Power

Politics

Senator Cairine Wilson

*The care of human life and happi-
ness, and not their destruction, is
the first and only legitimate object
of good government.*

(Thomas Jefferson)

Women Senators

"You are going to make me the most hated
woman in Canada," Cairine Wilson protested, when
Prime Minister King proposed to appoint her as the first
woman to the Senate. She realized her unenviable position — a target of criticism both by Magistrate Murphy's
admirers and by die-hard Senators who would resent a
woman invading their "Gentlemen's Club".

The *Toronto Star* summed up general feeling: "It
is a piece of irony that the first senatorship given to a
woman has been to one who never raised a finger to win
for women the right to sit in the Red Chamber in
Ottawa."

A Montreal paper protested: "If appointments to
the Senate were made as a reward of merit or for outstanding national service then, on every count Judge
Emily Murphy should have been first woman Senator
... distinguished not only as a judge but as an author,
public speaker, reformer and philanthropist, a pattern in
the domestic sphere, an exemplary mother and devoted
wife."

Cairine Wilson's background was a blueprint for political distinction. Her father, Hon. Robert Mackay, was a wealthy Liberal Senator. In the family home in Montreal leading politicians, one of whom was Prime Minister Sir Wilfrid Laurier, were frequent guests.

In 1909, with her marriage to Norman Wilson, wealthy lumberman and former member of Parliament, Cairine's interest in politics intensified. As a member of the women's committee that helped bring Mackenzie King to power in 1920, Mrs. Wilson organized the National Federation of Liberal Women and became first president. In 1930 she banded her eight children and their friends to form the nucleus of Twentieth Century Clubs, an organization of young Liberals.

During World War II when the Government began to move West Coast Japanese to the interior, Senator Wilson courageously urged justice and fair play. Intensely concerned for refugees, she was chairman of the Senate Labor and Immigration Committee and chairman of the Canadian National Committee on Refugees for ten years.

The welfare work of this millionaire philanthropist, however, extended far beyond national boundaries. She served a term as president of the League of Nations Society. Her interest in The International Save the Children Fund, one of her main projects, was carried on by her daughter, Cairine.

In 1950, Senator Wilson was chosen first "Canadian Mother of the Year" and awarded the French Legion of Honor for work on behalf of French refugee children. In 1956 she became first woman to preside from the Senate Speaker's chair and four years later was the first woman appointed to University of Ottawa's Board of Regents. A statue of Senator Wilson, who died in 1962, stands at the entrance to the Senate.

* * *

Conservative Mrs. Howard Fallis, appointed to the Senate in 1935, was married in 1909 and lived on a farm near Peterborough. Iva Fallis became national vice-president of the Progressive-Conservative Women's Association. In the Senate she served on joint committees on Old Age Security and the Indian Act and on the special committee on Salacious and Indecent Literature. Paying tribute to Canada's "Famous Five" Senator Fallis once noted: "These women made an investment of their time, ability and energy for the women of this country. My colleagues and I are the dividends."

* * *

In 1953 Prime Minister Louis St. Laurent brought three women into the Red Chamber: Mariana Beauchamp Jodoin, Nancy Hodges and Muriel Fergusson. Senator Mariana Beauchamp Jodoin, first French-Canadian woman senator, was the daughter of a distinguished lawyer. In 1926 she founded Wilfrid Laurier Club to educate women in political affairs and study national and international problems. Her presidency of ten major organizations between 1925 and 1953 prompted Montreal women to dub her "The Chairman of Chairmen!"

* * *

"Make way for Madame Speaker!" commanded the Sergeant-at-Arms for the first time in the history of the British Commonwealth on February 14, 1950 as Nancy Hodges, MLA, in black silk gown and tricorne hat, took her place in the Speaker's Chair of the British Columbia Legislature. She had come to Canada from England in 1912 with her journalist husband, Henry Hodges, who became editor of the *Victoria Times*. Asked to "fill in" for a few days Mrs. Hodges edited the Women's Page for more than 30 years and wrote 2,550 columns of "One Woman's Day".

In 1941 she won a seat in the British Columbia

Legislature and was re-elected three times. She succeeded Senator Wilson as President of the National Liberal Women's Federation in 1947 and was named "Woman of the Year" in 1950. Defeated in 1952 and summoned to the Senate in 1953, she agitated for a better deal for domestic labor, protection for deserted wives and improved workmen's compensation benefits.

* * *

Senator Muriel Fergusson

"What woman wouldn't enjoy spending $1,000,-000 a month?" As regional director of Family Allowances and Old Age Security for New Brunswick, Muriel Fergusson found the responsibility exhilarating. Angered by a "Males Only" discriminatory Civil Service application form she got backing from several women's organizations in which she was active and lobbied until she won the job in 1947.

A series of firsts are among her string of credits — first woman judge of a probate court, first woman member of Fredericton city council (later deputy mayor), only woman Regional Enforcement Counsel for the Wartime Prices and Trade Board, and first woman to go to Parliament Hill from the Maritimes.

Born in Shediac, N.B., she graduated from Mount Allison University in law in 1925 and married Aubrey Fergusson, another lawyer, a year later. After her husband's death in 1942 Muriel Fergusson moved to Saint John.

Because of her experience in presenting briefs, she was delegated by women's organizations to appear before Premier Hugh John Flemming and request equal pay for women's work, the right of women to serve on juries and on municipal councils. She also lobbied before Flemming's predecessor Premier John B. MacNair for jail reforms, regional libraries and the appointment of a New Brunswick woman to the Senate. On May 19, 1953, Muriel Fergusson became that woman. Called to the Senate by Prime Minister St. Laurent, she has agitated for fairer succession duties for widows, rehabilitation for women in penitentiaries and removal of unemployment insurance limitations on married women. While Quebec and Newfoundland divorce cases were handled by the Senate she served on the Divorce Committee headed by Senator Arthur Roebuck. Senator Fergusson received an honorary degree from

University of New Brunswick in 1969. In 1972 Prime Minister Trudeau appointed Senator Fergusson the *first* woman Speaker of the Senate, which position she filled with distinction until she retired in May 1975.

* * *

From stagecoach inn to the Senate was a logical step for Florence Elsie (MacDonald) Inman. As owner-operator of "Poole House", originally a stagecoach inn at Montague, P.E.I., Mrs. Inman was active in the booming tourist industry as well as politics in her island province. She was elected president of the P.E.I. Innkeepers' Association in 1955. Born in P.E.I. in 1891, she married G. S. Inman, a barrister and later county court judge in P.E.I. In 1919 Mrs. Inman was a charter member and president of the second Women's Liberal Club established in Canada — the first had been organized by Halifax Liberals.

Active in the early suffrage campaigns, Mrs. Inman tells the story of one convert whose husband promised her a new fur coat if she did not vote, another whose husband threatened to kill her if she did. Friends escorted her to the polls — heavily veiled. With the franchise won Mrs. Inman organized Liberal Women's Clubs throughout the Island and canvassed in twelve election campaigns. She was summoned to the Senate in 1955.

* * *

Senator Olive Irvine born in Holland, Manitoba in 1895, was a teacher before marriage to James C. Irvine in 1920 took her to Winnipeg. Active in war work, church work and women's organizations, she was appointed Manitoba's representative on the National Capital Commission in February, 1929. Having held most offices in Progressive Conservative organizations, she was the first woman named a member of the nominating committee at a national Conservative convention. Prime Minister Diefenbaker called Mrs. Irvine to the Senate in January 1960.

* * *

In 1958, when Canada was elected a member of the twelve-year-old United Nations Status of Women Commission, Josie Quart was a natural choice as Canada's representative. A former co-chairman of the Committee on the Legal Status of Women in Quebec, Mrs. Quart represented Canada at the Commission's sessions in Geneva in 1958, New York in 1959, and in Buenos Aires in 1960, where she was vice-chairman of this UN body established to improve the social, educational, legal and political status of women throughout the world.

Radiating vitality and enthusiasm, Josie can be disarmingly blunt, admitting that her glamorous "original" hats are to detract attention from her substantial figure.

Born in Quebec City in 1899, she graduated from St. Lewis Academy then took post-graduate courses in music and drama at the New England Conservatory of Music in Boston. At seventeen she married contractor Harry S. Quart and became the mother of four sons and a daughter and later grandmother to twenty-four youngsters who affectionately call her "Grandmère a-Go-Go". Mrs. Quart was a District Commissioner of Girl Guides and founding president of the United Nations Association of Quebec. In 1935 she was awarded the George V and Queen Mary Medal for community service.

While her officer sons were overseas during World War II, she served at home as founding president of the Women's Voluntary Service of Quebec and founding president of Quebec's Armed Services Welfare Committee. She was awarded an M.B.E. for her war work.

A long-time Conservative, Mrs. Quart was President of the Quebec Women's Conservative Association,

National President of the Women's Conservative
Association and served as a member of the Canadian
delegation to the 1957 UN General Assembly. On
November 17, 1960, Prime Minister Diefenbaker
appointed her to the Senate.

* * *

From 1919 to 1929 Mary Kinnear of Port Colborne
was shipper at the Canada Cement Company — an unusual prelude to a Senate career. Active in women's
organizations, she became president of the Ontario Liberal Women's Association, president of the National
Federation of Liberal Women and served on the
National Liberal Federation.

Mrs. Kinnear's husband, Robert, died in 1954.
They had no children. A life-long Liberal, she was
appointed to the Senate in 1967. That autumn she was
honored at a dinner by the Greater Port Colborne Chamber of Commerce and presented with their first
Achievement Award. A member of several Senate Committees, Health, Welfare and Science, the Joint Committee on the Library of Parliament and Transport and
Communication, her favorite is the Committee on Science Policy. This committee went abroad in the summer
of 1969 to observe the methods used by other countries
to combat the problems of air and water pollution — the
subject of Senator Kinnear's maiden speech in the Red
Chamber.

Senator Ann Heath Bell (recently married) was
summoned to the Senate in October 1970. She sits on the
Standing Committee on Foreign Affairs. Her special
interests are abortion, consumer packaging and labelling, science policy and transportation.

Senator Margaret Norrie was summoned to the
Senate in 1972. She is a member of the Standing Committee on Agriculture. Special interests are adult occupational training, capital punishment, crop insurance,
education, national parks.

Senator Joan Nieman and her husband practised law together for seventeen years. She was summoned to the Senate in September, 1972. Special interests are penal reform and native rights, and education, although it is a provincial rather than a federal matter. She is a member of the Standing Committee on Legal and Constitutional Affairs, and the Joint Committee on Printing. She also represents the Senate on the Ontario Liberal Caucus and is vice-chairman of the Liberal Caucus of the Senate.

Speaker Renaude Lapointe

Petite, Renaude Lapointe, second woman Speaker of the Senate, complains that she has always suffered from cold feet. But, once persuaded, she's a winner! She was persuaded to leave her job as secretary in a law office in Quebec City, to write for *Le Soleil*, and later joined the reporting staff of *La Presse*, becoming the first woman appointed to their editorial board. While in the Indian Affairs Dept. in 1970 she served on the Canadian Delegation to the United Nations, and again in 1971 and 1972. She has also worked as a correspondent for the CBC International Service and for *Time* and *Life* Magazines. During a brief interlude with *Le Nouveau Journal* she won a Bowater award.

Summoned to the Senate in November 1971 she became a member of the Senate Committee on Foreign Affairs and on Legal and Constitutional Affairs. In the Autumn of 1974 Prime Minister Trudeau appointed her Speaker of the Senate.

Federal Women Members

In the marble corridor which separates the House of Commons from the Speaker's Chambers stands a bust of Agnes Macphail, Canada's pioneer woman member of Parliament. Never a formal feminist, her election in Ontario, the cradle of the suffrage movement, marked the culmination of years of feminist campaigning which, combined with war work, had won Canadian women voting rights granted on Victoria Day, 1918.

Agnes Macphail

Agnes Macphail took her Commons seat as an Independent member on March 8, 1922 — the first woman member of the Green Chamber. A determined woman of 31 with a profile strangely reminiscent of Julius Caesar's, Agnes Macphail was dubbed "The Schoolmarm of Politics". Many members were furious about the presence of a woman as a member of the House, some so rude they left whenever she rose to speak. In debate her caustic wit was a potent weapon. Denouncing one Tory premier she said: "Men of that type — I did not say stripe."

Agnes Campbell Macphail was born in 1890 to Henrietta Campbell and Douglas McPhail (she changed the spelling) in Grey County, Ontario. Her domineering father was a farmer and livestock auctioneer. Agnes idolized her grandmother Campbell with whom she lived while attending high school in Stratford. She changed from Presbyterian to her grandmother's religion, Latter Day Saints. Since the "Saints'" are Mormons, Miss Macphail was accused of favouring polygamy!

Obtaining a teaching certificate, she taught in rural Western schools. Her interest in co-operatives took her to the United States and Europe on a fact-finding visit. Returning to South-East Grey to teach, she became organizer for United Farmers of Ontario, thousands of whom affectionately called her "Aggie". Nominated as U.F.O. candidate in 1921 she won the seat boasting: "I never solicited a single vote nor kissed a single baby."

"Women have to be twice as good to get half as far as men," Agnes complained.

Her campaign clothes were simplicity itself — a blue serge suit, sailor hat and spectacles. "This outfit will take me either to the House of Commons or the House of Refuge!" she quipped. Later she added a cape which became almost her trademark.

The sick and the handicapped aroused her sympathy. When ex-convicts told her tales of sadistic discipline, demoralization, and rehabilitation difficulties, she claimed her right as a Member of Parliament to tour Kingston Penitentiary. Disgraceful prison conditions led to serious riots in Canada's seven penitentiaries in 1930. In 1936 Miss Macphail's campaigning bore fruit when a Royal Commission was set up to investigate the penal system. Although she had done the spade work she was not invited to become a member of the Commission. However, the Archambault Commission's Report of 1938, the basis of widespread reforms, credited her achievement:

A strong supporter of the League of Nations, Miss Macphail served as delegate, a high honor for a member of the Opposition.

For 20 years she helped pioneer much social welfare legislation. In 1932 she helped draft the first manifesto of the CCF and brought her various farm clubs into the movement. In September, 1939, when Parliament met briefly to declare war on Germany, it was a crushing blow to a woman who had devoted her life to promoting peace.

She suffered her first defeat at polls in 1940. A raging blizzard piling up huge snowdrifts, made it impossible for many farmer friends to vote. Honorable Walter Harris (later Minister of Finance) unseated her.

In 1943, Agnes Macphail won a seat — one woman among 90 men — in the Ontario Legislature. Stricken with coronary thrombosis and urged to rest she would not retire. Politics had become her very life.

In 1945 she was defeated but won the York East seat for the CCF in 1948. Defeated again in 1951 and urged to run for a federal seat in 1953, she declined. Ill, almost penniless, she received no help nor any special honor from the country she had served so long and so well other than "The love of the people which I value more than any other".

On her death, flags flew at half mast and glowing tributes in newspapers and parliament flowed in. The Elizabeth Fry Society, which she founded in Toronto to aid newly-released women prisoners, set up an Agnes Macphail Memorial Bursary for students in the field of probation or rehabilitation.

248

* * *

"Isn't it hell to be getting old?" Martha Black noted somewhat bitterly in 1935, when at the age of 70 she joined Agnes Macphail in the House of Commons. She frankly admitted: "I'm just keeping the seat warm for George", (her sick husband) who was the Conservative member from the Yukon from 1921 to 1930 and House Leader from 1930 to 1935. Her blunt speech was a souvenir of her life as a sourdough in the 1898 Gold Rush. Her life reads like an adventure story. As a frightened five-year-old, she experienced the horror of the Chicago fire.

Her marriage to Will Purdy, son of the millionaire president of an American railway ended in divorce despite their two sons. Later, chaperoned by her brother, Martha reached Skagway where her initiation to life in the Yukon was as a witness to a shooting match resulting in the death between a desperado and a vigilante. Settled in Gold Hill, Martha married George Black and gave birth to a third son without medical aid. When her husband became Commissioner of the Yukon in 1912, Martha was chatelaine of Government House. Her beautifully illustrated book *Yukon Wild Flowers* won a prize. She also wrote an autobiography, *My Seventy Years*, when she retired from politics in 1940.

* * *

The commons opened its doors to three more women members during the '40s. Mrs. Doris Nielsen was the United Progressive member for North Battleford from 1940 to 1945. Cora (Mrs. Frederick) Casselman (1941-45) elected in Edmonton following the death of her husband, was the first woman Liberal of the House. An active supporter of measures to improve living conditions for low income groups, old age pensions and health insurance, Mrs. Casselman was the first woman to serve as chairman of the Committee of the Whole and was a member of the Canadian delegation at the meeting which launched the United Nations in San Francisco in 1946. Last of the three was Mrs. Gladys Strum who won a threeway race against veteran politicians, E. E. Perley and General A.G.L. McNaughton to become federal member for Qu'Appelle. She represented the CCF party in the House 1945-48 — the culmination of more than 25 years of political activity.

Mrs Strum, who narrowly missed victory against former Saskatchewan premier, W. J. Patterson in 1944, won a seat for the CCF in Saskatoon in the 1960 provincial election.

The Hon. Ellen Fairclough

Changing Role

In the '50s and '60s as the changing role of women evolved in the post-war years, the level of federal female participation registered a parallel rise with the appointment of the first women to the Cabinet — Hon. Ellen Fairclough, appointed in the Diefenbaker era and Hon. Judy LaMarsh, a volatile presence in the Pearson cabinet.

Canada Needs a Woman's Voice was the slogan on which Ellen Cook Fairclough, P.C. F.C.A. U.E. rode into Federal Parliament in a 1950 by-election victory. As a member of the Commonwealth Parliamentary Association, she was adviser to the Canadian delegation to the United Nations in 1950 and later a delegate to the conference of NATO Parliamentarians.

A substantial contributor in House debate, Mrs. Fairclough averaged 150 speeches a year. Certainly one of her most dramatic moments came during the 1957 Pipeline debate one tension-filled evening when closure was invoked to force the legislation through the Commons. Ellen Fairclough symbolically draped the Canadian ensign over her Tory colleague Hon. Donald Fleming's empty chair (he had been temporarily suspended), rose in the House and registered the mood of the moment: "Today the Opposition has been gagged — discussion has been prohibited — what has been Howe's pipe dream may turn out to be Canada's nightmare."

Born Ellen Louks in Hamilton, Ont., in 1905 of French Huguenot and United Empire Loyalist stock, she ambitiously studied nights to become a certified public accountant. Music is her avocation. Plunging directly into politics Ellen was elected Alderman in Hamilton in 1945 and Controller in 1949 topping the poll to become Deputy-Mayor as did Charlotte Whitton in Ottawa.

Prominent in many clubs, her favourite was Rehabilitation Foundation for the Disabled — the

March of Dimes. Her only son, Howard was stricken with polio.

In Parliament, although her private bills for Equal Pay for Work of Equal Value were defeated four years in a row, Labor Minister Milton Gregg credited her when the Liberals passed a similar bill in 1956. Through her efforts the Unemployment Insurance Act was amended. In 1957 when the Progressive Conservatives came to power Ellen Fairclough was placed in the spotlight as Secretary of State, and first woman to be appointed to the Federal Cabinet in Canada's 90 year history. Ironically, Ceylon, India and Israel all appointed a woman to the highest office, prime minister, in the first decade or so of their establishment as nations.

Between 1958, following the Tory landslide, and 1963, Ellen Fairclough held two other portfolios — Minister of Citizenship and Immigration and Postmaster-General. For two days during the absence of Prime Minister Diefenbaker she even reached the pinnacle of power, Acting Prime Minister. She was defeated in the 1963 election by Lincoln Alexander, first Negro elected to the House. Ellen Fairclough became secretary and director of the Hamilton Trust and Savings Corporation and president of two other firms. In 1965, she was elected a Fellow of the Chartered Accountants of Ontario and in 1969 named Advertising Sales Person of the Year by the Hamilton Women's Ad and Sales Club.

New Arrivals

The '50s generally were years of rising participation by women in federal politics. In 1953, Ellen Fairclough was joined by Liberal Mrs. Ann Shipley and Conservative Miss Sybil Bennett, a petite, delicate woman whose political career ended three years later by death from cancer. Toronto *Telegram* columnist Margaret Aitken also joined the Tory ranks. A forceful early spokesman for the abolition of capital punishment, Miss Aitken became the first woman elected chairman of a Commons standing committee — Standing Orders.

Mrs. Shipley came to Parliament with a distinguished civic background — mayor of Kirkland Lake and former president of the Ontario Municipal and Ontario Mayors and Reeves Association. As Liberal member for Temiskaming, she urged that a woman be appointed to the Civil Service Commission and recommended financial assistance for small industries and gold mining.

The final member of this '50s team Jean Rowe Casselman, was ushered into the Commons in a Tory victory in Ontario's Grenville-Dundas riding in September, 1958, filling the political shoes of her late husband. The daughter of Earl Rowe, who had served in R. B. Bennett's cabinet and was the acknowledged dean of the Commons, Jean joined him to make a political first in Canadian Parliament — a father-daughter team. Mr. Rowe later was appointed Lieutenant-Governor of Ontario while his daughter, who became Mrs. Robert W. Wadds in 1964, continued to hold her Commons seat until the Trudeau sweep of 1968 carried Liberal Gordon Blair to victory in the riding.

On the Decline

The number of women in the Commons decreased steadily in the '60s. Liberal Margaret Konantz (well-known Winnipeger, who, along with Mrs. Monica McQueen, organized the city's central volunteer bureau during the war years — a first for Canada) held a Commons seat from 1963-65. Attractive blonde Margaret Rideout sat in the House from 1962 to 1968. Her defeat at the polls was followed by an appointment as a judge of New Brunswick's Citizenship Court. Dr. Pauline Jewett represented Northumberland riding from 1963 to 1965. Later a professor of political science at Carleton University she recalls: "I loved campaigning, but it's hectic." She also found politics extremely disillusioning and was shocked to find votes still being "sold" in 1962. Her paramount interests while in office were national plan and contributory pension plan legislation and, naturally, education. Dr. Jewett took over as director of Carleton's Institute of Canadian Studies July 1, 1967. Years later, in 1976 Dr. Jewett became President of Simon Fraser University, a position paying over $50,000 annually. Dr. Jewett has been elected President of a new national organization to research the status of women in Canada.

The most vocal and volatile female politician in Canada's history, Hon. Judy LaMarsh shot into the spotlight in this decade with a 1960 by-election win in Niagara Falls. For Judy the next eight years were a melange of accomplishment and frustration which culminated in her decision to retire from politics in the 1968 Trudeau election year. Of the women who entered the Commons in this ten year period, NDP member Grace Woodsworth MacInnis, first elected in 1965 and re-elected in 1968, alone remained in the 265-member House — a rather lopsided balance. She has since retired.

Successes and frustrations seem to be inseparable companions plaguing the woman who reaches the peak of political power. Judy LaMarsh's striking political career certainly had ample doses of both elements.

Bird In A Gilded Cage

Blunt, outspoken Judy LaMarsh can trace her interest in politics to the age of ten, "I recall my grandfather sitting weeping (for joy) the night Mitch Hepburn's Liberal legions first took Ontario." Her father had successfully run Bill Houk's political campaign in Niagara Falls.

During the eight years Miss LaMarsh represented Niagara in the House of Commons, she, too, often wept

— but not always for joy as the loneliness, disillusionment and frustration mounted, and press cartoons of her controversial Parliamentary activities became more cruel than amusing. Dark-haired, plump, vivacious and witty, Julia (Judy) LaMarsh was born in Chatham, Ont. but raised in Niagara Falls. She is proud of her Huguenot heritage. Her beautiful, artistic mother and lawyer-father eloped — the kind of impulsive behavior for which their daughter was to become noted. After graduating from Stamford Collegiate and Hamilton Normal School, Judy became a sergeant in the CWACs from 1943-46, working in intelligence, translating and interpreting captured Japanese documents.

With her veteran's credits she attended Victoria College and Osgoode Hall, graduating in 1950 as president of her year and winning the Gold Key for extra-curricular activities. Joining her father's law firm, Judy specialized in criminal law. Later in Parliament, she advocated retention of capital punishment during the abolition debate.

Elected to the Federal Parliament in 1960 as a back-bencher, Miss LaMarsh set out to master the rules of political gamesmanship. Re-elected in 1963, she was invited to become a member of Lester Pearson's administration — the first woman named to a Liberal Cabinet, with the portfolio of Health and Welfare. Pleased at being handed the "human" department, Judy remarked: "I'd have been damn mad if I hadn't been given an important one." Her firm command of the law proved invaluable in drafting the legislation for the Canada Pension Plan — her greatest single Parliamentary achievement.

An earlier notable LaMarsh legislative achievement had been the drafting of a long and complex copyright law.

At times, however, her more serious accomplishments seemed to be overshadowed by her more flamboyant activities — starting with the infamous Truth Squad in which she participated as it doggedly followed Diefenbaker's campaign across the country in the 1962 election providing "constructive criticisms". The venture backfired on the Liberals.

"I'm publicity-prone, just as some people are accident-prone," Judy discovered. Indeed whatever she did — inside or out of the Commons — became hot copy for the news media. It was major news when the chain-smoking Minister of Health and Welfare quit smoking. Her outspoken comments about "rotten management" in the CBC and the Quebec Federal-Provincial Conference, where she noted that every Minister had his own armed plain-clothes Mountie, reverberated across the nation.

Moving from Health and Welfare to Secretary of State, Judy gave Canada's Centennial the LaMarsh touch as she became Canada's official hostess for the country's year-long 100th birthday party. She logged more than 100,000 miles of travel across Canada during the celebration as she assumed responsibility for Canada's cultural institutions — the CBC, National Gallery, Canada Council, the National Film Board, etc. and entertained visiting VIP's, including Queen Elizabeth and Prince Philip.

Named Canada's Woman of the Year three times, Judy brightened the starchy Ottawa scene with her psychedelic stockings, her many fashionable wigs and knee-high leather boots at public gatherings. Her impersonations of the famous Gold Rush prostitute, "The Lady that's known as Lou", at a Klondike Night benefit in 1963 still sparks a smile in the Capital.

By the time the Pearson era gave way to the Trudeau regime, Judy had seen the political game from enthusiasm through to disillusionment. Returning to private life, Miss LaMarsh turned out a best-seller on her years in Ottawa, *Bird in a Gilded Cage*. McClelland and

Stewart advanced $15,000 in royalties on the strength of
anticipated sales — a safe move since the LaMarsh
memoirs sold more than 35,000 copies in the first
months of publication. LaMarsh the writer and broadcaster promises to be as successful as LaMarsh the politician — and still as uncontrollably publicity-prone.
While happy practising law in St. Catharines, Judy
headed into plans for an interview-type series for CBC-
TV starting in November 1969. Miss LaMarsh is presently Chairman of the Royal Commission on Violence
in the Communications Industry.

* * *

Much less happy in the spotlight — or the hot
spot for that matter — was Grace MacInnis, the only
woman Member of the House of Commons at the end of
the '60's. This quietly firm silver-haired woman was
destined to enter politics. Her father, J. S. Woodsworth,
was founder of the CCF movement, the precursor of
today's New Democratic Party. *A Man to Remember,* a
biography of her father, a minister and welfare worker
before he turned to politics, won Grace a Governor-General's award.

Born in 1905, Grace's nickname as a child was
"Yeller Kid" — a reference to her healthy lung power, a
useful attribute for a future politician. As a child, she literally "slept between statistics". Large cotton charts —
souvenirs of welfare work — were thriftily laundered
by Mrs. Woodsworth and used as sheets. One washday,
young Grace noticed neighbours intently eyeing one
sheet which announced in bold, black type — "last year
we buried 500 babies". Tutored by her bilingual mother,
Grace later graduated from the University of Manitoba
and won a French government scholarship.

Her bilingualism has proved invaluable. In her
youth she was her father's secretary on Parliament Hill,
where she met his right-hand man, Angus MacInnis, an
MP from 1930 to 1951. They were married in 1932, the
year her father organized the Co-operative Com-

monwealth Federation movement. Mrs. MacInnis
became secretary of the CCF, did campaign work and
party publicity and was parliamentary correspondent
for a group of weekly newspapers. Plunging directly
into politics, Grace was elected to the British Columbia
Legislature 1941-1945 on a rising tide of Socialism. She
was a member of Federal Government Committee on
Post-War Reconstruction and in 1946, one of six Canadian delegates to the International Association of
Women, representing 55 countries and headed by Eleanor Roosevelt.

Grace MacInnis

A firm advocate of the partnership theory in relationships between the sexes, she put in long years of apprenticeship, first helping her father, then her husband, to attain political success before she fulfilled her ambition to become a Federal member in 1965.

In the House she has lobbied steadily for better housing, nursery schools and adequate wages for mothers who choose to remain home. Childless, she advocated legal abortion: "The choice is shall we have legal, safe abortions, regardless of whether people are wealthy or not, or shall we continue with the backroom, butcher system of abortion?" She feels that legal abortion would help develop "quality population".

Mrs. MacInnis' share of Commons debates takes up a hefty sheaf of Hansard papers presenting her views not only on abortion, but also on housing, finance, and consumer problems — a current pet peeve in this era of rising living costs. "We need a Combines Act that will really work to protect the consumer from business oligopoly," she maintains. A long-time member of the Consumers' Association of Canada, she believes that people are gradually realizing they must get organized as consumers. "Not only must they become thrifty shoppers but they must learn how to bring pressure on government for the kind of legislation they need to protect them."

* * *

Mrs. MacInnis retired before the influx of new women Senators and Members. Prominent among them is Flora Macdonald, who could be sure of a Cabinet post were her party in power. Miss Macdonald, P.C. representing Kingston and the Islands, is a Maritimer who helped Robert Stanfield in his provincial campaign in 1956. That year Flora moved to P.C. headquarters in Ottawa, where she worked for nine years, the last five as Executive Secretary. From 1966 to 1972 Miss Macdonald was an administrative officer and tutor in the department of Political Studies, Queen's University. In 1971 she was the first woman to be chosen for the National Defense College course in Canadian and International Studies.

Miss Macdonald was vice-president of the Kingston and the Islands P.C. Association from 1967 to 1972. She acted as a consultant to both the House of Commons Committee on Electoral Expenses and to the Royal Commission on the Status of Women. She was elected to the House of Commons in 1972 and appointed Conservative critic on Indian Affairs and Northern Development. After her re-election in 1974 she was appointed critic on Housing and Urban Affairs, and sits on the Standing Committee concerned with these matters. Miss Macdonald agitates for more women in politics, thinking they would be particularly concerned with humanitarian affairs. Her lifelong dedication has been to politics. She was an unsuccessful candidate for the leadership of the Progressive Conservative Party in 1975.

In October 1976 Flora was joined by Jean Piggot in the House, a P.C. who had been elected by an overwhelming majority in the by-election to represent Ottawa-Carleton. Mrs. Arthur C. Piggot was President of Morrison-Lamonthe Foods Limited, very active in community affairs and recipient of many awards including the Centennial Medal, the Ottawa Board of Trade Award for distinguished service in the business community, then in May 1975 a citation from the Ottawa Kiwanis Club as Outstanding Canadian Citizen of Ottawa and Ontario. Jean Piggot says: "The fear of Quebec's secession from Canada will become a blessing, forcing us to reassess the future and our priorities for Canada. I refuse to be negative about the future of Canada."

Today not only has the Liberal Party an unprecedented eight women members of parliament, but among them three Cabinet Ministers, Hon. Jeanne Sauve, Hon. Iona Campagnola and Hon. Monique Bégin.

Hon. Jeanne (Benoit) Sauve graduated from the University of Ottawa. She founded the Federation des mouvements de jeunesse du Quebec in 1947, and represented this group at several international conferences. In September 1948 she married Maurice Sauve (Mr. Sauve was Minister of Forests and Rural Development 1964-68). They have one son. In 1952 Mrs. Sauve joined the staff of the CBC as a journalist and broadcaster, until her election to the House of Commons in 1972 as Liberal Member for Ahuntsic. She has gained varied and wide experience from appointments as first Minister of Science and Technology, then Minister of the Environment, and now Minister of Communications. She received an honorary LL.D from University of New Brunswick.

Hon. Iona (Hardy) Campagnola, of Prince Rupert, B.C., Liberal Member for Skeena, completed her matriculation in 1951. After her marriage, she continued her studies through extension courses from University of B.C. and adult education courses in Prince Rupert. She has two daughters. In 1965 she initiated a daily interview program for Skeena Broadcasters Limited, also acting as sales manager and supervisor of creative material and promotions. Mrs. Campagnola became a member of the Board of Trustees of Prince Rupert School in 1966, and in 1972 was elected an alderman. She came to Ottawa as Liberal Member for Skeena in September, 1974. The Prime Minister appointed her Parliamentary Secretary to Judd Buchanan, Minister of Indian Affairs and Northern Development.

In September 1976 Mrs. Campagnola was appointed Minister of State and Fitness and Amateur Sport (she skis and has taught figure skating). Senator Thérèse Casgrain is her special adviser on fitness for the aged. An extraordinary woman, by any standards, Iona

Campagnola becomes totally immersed in whatever her interest is at the moment. Her tenacity is demoralizing to opponents, she is rarely defeated in argument. While being a devoted mother, she is dedicated to her career, and manages to keep in close personal touch with her constituents. The Gitksan Clan made her a member of their Indian family in 1971. Mrs. Campagnola received membership in the Order of Canada in 1973, and was named "British Columbia Broadcast Citizen of the Year" in 1974.

Hon. Monique Bégin, L.M.P. Saint Michel, was born in Rome, but her father was French-Canadian and her mother Belgian. She received her primary and secondary education in Montreal, before attending Normal School in Rigaud. In 1965 she earned a master's degree in sociology from the University of Montreal. She did her doctoral studies at the University of Paris, and took post-graduate courses in the Engineering Faculty of McGill University. Miss Bégin taught for a few years before she became involved in research in the applied social sciences. In 1967 she joined the Royal Commission on the Status of Women in Canada as secretary-general and director of research. In 1971 Miss Bégin became responsible for research at the Canada Radio Television Commission.

In 1972 and again in 1974 she was elected Liberal Member of Parliament for Saint Michel. Monique Bégin co-chaired the national convention of the Liberal Party and now chairs the Services to Constituents Committee of the National Caucus. In 1973 she represented Canada at the Commonwealth Conference in Ottawa and at the United Nations General Assembly. As Minister of National Revenue, Customs and Excise, in a financial portfolio, she is concerned with the rights of citizens, is anxious to explain what is available to them and is happy to correct inequities in the system. She is interested in legal rights of common-law spouses and partnerships, especially small corner store operators.

In the House of Commons Miss Bégin also has special interest in the abortion controversy, the status of women, broadcasting (commercials for children), Bell Canada, reform of rules and procedures. She sits on the Standing Committees on Health, Welfare and Social Affairs, on Broadcasting, Films and Assistance to the Arts, on External Affairs and National Defense, and is vice-chairman of the Standing Committee on Miscellaneous Estimates. Miss Bégin has been active in several organizations — The Canadian Council on Human Rights, and the Women's Federation of Quebec of which she was a charter member and vice-president 1965-67, the American Sociological Association, and the Canadian Sociology and Anthropology Association.

Aideen Nicholson, born in Dublin, after earning a Diploma in Social Studies and a Certificate in Mental Health, worked as a psychiatric social worker in Britain. She immigrated to Toronto, Canada in 1957. She carried on her social service work at Toronto Psychiatric Hospital and later at the Clinic of Psychological Medicine at the Hospital for Sick Children. Miss Nicholson became the director of women's Reformatories and Programme Consultant to Training Schools for the Ontario Department of Correctional Services in 1965. She was appointed Executive Director of Cradleship Creche in 1969. Miss Nicholson ran as the Liberal candidate for Trinity in 1972, but was defeated by Paul Hellyer. However, in 1974 she won that seat. She sits on the Standing Committees on Health, Welfare and Social Affairs, and on Procedure and Organization. She was awarded the Centennial Medal.

Ursula (Carroll) Appoloni, L. York South, after a convent education in Ireland won a scholarship to a secretarial college. From 1948 to 1950 she was a member of the Women's Royal Air Force. She immigrated to Canada in 1952 and worked as secretary in a Calgary oil company and was a freelance radio actress until stricken with poliomyelitis. She took treatments in Edmonton and went to England for rehabilitation. Moving to Italy, she married Lucio Appoloni. They have two sons and two daughters. Returning to Canada in 1965 she worked at Alitalia Airlines and was a freelance journalist. Between 1970 and 1972 she co-ordinated the York Information Centre. Mrs. Appoloni was appointed chairman of the Board of Referees of the Unemployment Insurance Commission in 1973.

Active for years in the Liberal party, she was president of the York South Liberal Association for two years, and worked in her husband's campaign in York South in 1972. She herself won that seat for the Liberals in July 1974. Mrs. Appoloni was a member of the Special Committee on Egg Marketing and sits on the Standing Committee on Labour, Manpower and Immigration and the Joint Committee on Printing. Mrs. Appoloni has been a member of the board of directors of the Family Services Association, the Canadian Mental Health Association and the Canadian branch of UNICEF.

Albanie (Paré) Morin M. P. L. after receiving her primary and secondary education in convents, worked as a secretary of the Aluminum Company at Arvida. In 1945 she married George Morin and settled in Quebec City. They have one daughter and two sons. While her children were growing up, Mrs. Morin taught language and literature at secondary and post-secondary levels, meanwhile earning a certificate of collegial studies, the baccalaureate, a diploma in history and a master of arts (licence).

The Morins were active in the Liberal Party for years at all levels of government. She was elected an alderman in Sillery 1970-74. In 1972, after her husband's death, she won the federal riding of Louis Hébert, and was re-elected in 1974. She sits on the following committees: External Affairs and National Defense, Justice and Legal Affairs, Food Prices and Rules. She was also a member of the Inquiry into Penitentiary Administration. She was appointed deputy chairman of committees in September 1974.

Simma (Milner) Holt took her B.A. at University of Manitoba in 1944. She also took a creative writing course at the University of British Columbia. She is married to Leon Holt. Miss Milner joined the Vancouver *Sun* in 1944 as reporter and feature writer, staying until 1974. She has written three books, and has appeared in such prestigious magazines as *Reader's Digest* and *Macleans*, and has also appeared on national radio and television shows. Mrs. Holt has taught journalism at Western Washington State College.

In 1974 Mrs. Holt was elected to Parliament to represent Vancouver-Kingsway. She is known to have strong views on matters of social concern, and spoke out against the legalization of soft drugs. Mrs. Holt has many awards for writing, including the Memorial Award of the Media Club, the Bowater Award in 1960, the Woman of the Year for Canada in Arts and Letters in 1964, and the Alumni Jubilee Award of the University of Manitoba in 1969.

Simma Holt is a member of the Newspaper Guild. She has served as secretary and vice-president of the local guild and was a Canadian delegate at international conferences of the Guild in 1970 and 1972. She is also a member of the Authors Guild, the Authors League of America, and the Media Club of Canada.

Coline Campbell, born in Liverpool, Nova Scotia, grew up in Digby. She took her B.A. at St. Francis Xavier University with honours in French. She next earned a Bachelor of Education degree at Laval University and taught school for several years. Then she earned a Bachelor of Laws degree at the University of Ottawa and opened a legal practice in Yarmouth, N.S. in 1973. Miss Campbell is a member of the Nova Scotia Barristers' Society and the Law Society of Upper Canada.

Miss Campbell was chosen Liberal candidate for South Western Nova in May 1974 and won the seat in the July election. Prime Minister Trudeau appointed her Parliamentary Secretary to the Minister of National Health and Welfare on September 1974.

Backroom Politicians

In every political party, women behind the scenes — tackle the "joe jobs" which help the party machinery function and often wield a good deal of power. Such women as Hilda Hesson, Elizabeth Janzen (Dreger), Dorothy Downing and Flora Macdonald have been mainstays of Conservative behind-the-scenes organization activity over the years.

Mrs. Hesson, who was a "hero" to her admiring secretary Elrose Mitchell, after a 16-year career with the Manitoba Civil Service and stint as an alderman in Winnipeg, took on the task of organizing Conservative women's clubs into a national organization, during the late John Bracken's era as leader.

Dorothy Downing held a number of minor offices prior to her 1953 appointment as organizer for the PC Women's Association. In 1962 she became Women's National Director. Senator Allister Grosart termed her "one of the outstanding experts in political organization in Canada."

The New Democratic Party has its first woman president Joyce Nash, who was federal vice-president for the last two years.

Mrs. A. L. Caldwell and others contributed the same kind of organizational acumen for the Liberal Party.

Behind-the-scenes political support of quite a different sort was provided by Mrs. M. J. Coldwell whose husband succeeded Grace MacInnis' father, J. S. Woodsworth, as leader of the CCF. Paralysed in both legs and right arm, Norah Coldwell was an amazing tower of strength to her husband and members of the CCF movement through many years of political ups and downs. She died in 1953.

Provincial Politics

As with the federal scene, the road to female participation in provincial politics has been a treacherous one strewn with battle casualties at every turn.

The roots of provincial political activity can be traced to the suffrage movement. Delegations to Ottawa were invariably told that female suffrage must be obtained first at the provincial level. So the suffragettes took their cue. Early political activists encountered general apathy from women and open hostility from many men as they carried their battle across the country to win women the right to vote and hold public office. Bucking the tradition-bound attitude that it was unladylike, if not actually immoral, to participate in politics these early activists accepted slings and arrows from all sides in order to pursue their cause.

It is interesting to note that traditional 19th century Quebec was the first place in the then British Empire where women actually cast a vote. In the fiercely fought election of 1809 Louis Joseph Papineau's mother was among several women who voted orally — as was the custom — in Papineau's campaign. Notaries recorded female votes in their homes, since it was considered indelicate for a woman to appear at the smoke-filled polls. An act in 1849 retracted this early voting right for women and Quebec became the last province to regain it 91 years later.

Among Maritime women, suffrage campaigners never mustered the popular support they received in the West. In Nova Scotia, for example, voting rights for women, granted in 1758, were withdrawn under the New Franchise Act 1851. In this 90-year period no woman had ever cast a vote. "Don't you want to *vote?*" a visiting suffragette asked a farm wife busily doing heavy chores while her husband loafed. The farmer's wife replied with an emphatic: "No, if there's one thing John can do alone, let him do it!"

In Newfoundland the suffrage movement got a boost around 1919, when Mrs. A. G. Gosling organized a club some 30 years before the island became Canada's tenth province. In fitting irony, Lady Squires, whose husband, Liberal premier Sir Richard Squires, opposed female suffrage, was elected first woman member of the assembly serving from 1925-32. In 1925 Sir Richard was defeated by the Conservative opposition who granted women the right to vote and hold office.

Meanwhile more than 3000 miles away in Alberta and British Columbia women had already broken the political sound barrier. In Alberta, Roberta MacAdams and Louise McKinney became the first women elected to a legislative assembly in the British Empire in 1917 — edging out Agnes Macphail's breakthrough at the federal level by more than three years.

Another political first came in British Columbia in March 1921 when glamor girl Mary Ellen Smith was sworn in as a member of the provincial cabinet — the first woman cabinet minister in the world. "Take the Speaker's Chair, Mrs. Smith," Premier Oliver urged. "You'll be the first Madame Speaker in the British Empire." "It is a great temptation, of course," Mary Ellen confided to her close friend Judge Helen MacGill. "But I feel I should stay on the floor of the House to help push through our Bills."

Following the death of her husband Hon. Ralph Smith in 1918, Mary Ellen Smith had decided to become the second politician in the family. She was elected and served the province for the next ten years retiring in 1928. Her legislative credits include bills which improved working hours, gave a minimum wage law for women and pensions for indigent mothers with dependent children. She served as chairman of the B. C. Liberal party until her death in 1933.

In Alberta, Mrs. Edith Gostick, provincial librarian, and Mrs. Edith Rogers were the first women elected to a Social Credit government (1935-40). When Mrs. Dorothy Steeves, CCF, was elected to the British Columbia Legislature in 1937 a telegram reading: "It's a girl!" proclaimed her victory.

Fighting Grandmother

"...I have lost all confidence in the present coalition government and will in future represent my constituency as an Independent Member." These blunt words spoken in the B.C. legislature on March 29, 1951 could have spelled political suicide for anyone other than Mrs. Frederick Rolston.

A Progressive Conservative prior to this declaration, Tilly Jean Rolston, considered loyalty to principle more important than party loyalty and won her point. Not long after crossing the House to join the Social Credit Party Mrs. Rolston became Minister of Education in August 1952. Born 1887 in Vancouver, she taught school until her marriage; had three children and numbered ten grandchildren. Active in many organizations, a director of the Pacific National Exhibition and a member of the Women's Travel Club, she was elected "Woman of the Year" by the Quota Club. In 1938 she was elected to the Vancouver Parks Board. Under her chairmanship the celebrated "Theatre Under the Stars" was organized.

Firmly believing parenthood should come before politics, she violently disagreed with Mrs. Laura Jamieson, CCF, who advocated government nursery schools to enable young mothers to work outside homes. "The time is coming when women will be forced to take a greater interest in politics to save their skins, their homes and their children," Mrs. Rolston maintained. Dubbed the "fighting grandmother", she was a strong supporter of free maternity benefits and family courts. She helped legalize coloring of margarine and stiffly opposed establishment of a provincial sales tax, which she caustically called "a politician's dream, but a housewife's nightmare!" With E. E. Winch (father of MP Harold Winch) she founded the successful New Vista Society rehabilitation centre for women newly released from mental hospitals. In 1953 Mrs. Rolston was defeated by Arthur Laing, B.C. Liberal leader. When she died of cancer, a state funeral honored her. The Vancouver Women's Canadian Club established a scholarship for cancer research in her memory.

Quebec Pace-Setter

Where politics are involved Mme. Thérèse Casgrain showed not a trace of family allegiance. The daughter of former Conservative member of Parliament, Sir Rodolphe Forget, she married a Liberal and herself became the leader of the Quebec CCF Party in 1949. Accused of political expediency when she joined the CCF in 1946 while President of the National Federation of Liberal Women, Mme. Casgrain explained that the CCF takes a more positive approach to social problems. However, she was practically ostracized by lifelong friends.

Born in 1896, Marie Thérèse was educated in the Convent of Sacred Heart. It was a bitter disappointment when her father insisted she study music rather than attend university. At 18 she married Pierre Casgrain, handsome lawyer. Deeply in love, each respected the other's particular interests. Madame Casgrain freely admits: "It took a big man to allow me to go my own way in politics." Her husband later served as Speaker of the House from 1936-1940.

Combining her social position, wealth, and

brains, Thérèse Casgrain worked diligently to improve living conditions for less fortunate women in her province, for better educational opportunities and for protection of neglected children. Since the Quebec Civil Code placed women in the same legal category as "idiots, convicts and minors", Mme. Casgrain realized that the key to improved status for women would be to obtain suffrage.

Madame Thérèse Casgrain

As early as 1909 a Quebec Suffrage Association had been formed. In 1923 Mme. Casgrain became president of the Movement, renamed The League for Women's Rights. She headed the group for the next 14 years steering a steady course toward the goal of female suffrage using every conceivable device from placard-waving marchers to radio broadcasts and political lobbying. The quarter-hour program "Femina" became a weekly feature over CKAC radio from 1930 to '35, directed by Mme. Casgrain and financed by *La Presse*. Later, her weekly broadcasts were heard over both French and English CBC stations as she continued to promote her cause. The Casgrain forces took defeat after defeat between 1928 and 1940. Fourteen Women's Suffrage Bills failed passage in the Quebec legislature. Each time Thérèse's husband sent her a good luck note. Finally in 1940 the bill was successful; and one year later women also were admitted to the Bar in Quebec.

In 1942, Mme. Casgrain tested the Quebec woman's newly-won right to political participation by contesting the family riding as an Independent Liberal. Pierre had been appointed a Superior Court judge that year. Although she ran a strong second, Mme. Casgrain was bitterly disappointed. "The women don't turn out to vote for me ... is that gratitude?" However, in retrospect her defeat probably hinged on her anti-conscription views which made many enemies. Paradoxically she urged her own son to enlist. Later, Quebec women rallied around her again and joined her League of Women Voters organized to teach women to vote intelligently.

Though politics is most important, this complex woman has a wide variety of other interests. She was on the board of the Canadian Association for Adult Education, and vice-president of the French section; a founder of the Societé des Concerts Symphonique; during World War II she was also one of the two organizers of the Wartime Prices and Trade Board. She joined the Voice of Women in 1960, was elected national president in 1962. In 1966 she founded La Federation des Femmes de Quebec to coordinate the work of women's associations; she is president of the League for Civil Liberties, for a third term; also of the Quebec Medical Aid Committee to Viet-Nam; and a member of the Advisory Council on the Administration of Justice in Quebec.

In 1949 as provincial chairman of the CCF she became the first woman to head a provincial party in Canada. She served three terms as provincial leader, and was also one of the vice-chairmen of their national council. As an observer for them, she attended meetings in Bombay, Haifa and Rome. Political setbacks never deterred her. She made six unsuccessful bids for election to the House of Commons, the last in 1958. At the New Democratic Party (formerly called the CCF) founding convention, in 1961, she received a prolonged standing ovation from her colleagues.

Honors have been showered on this altruistic Quebec patrician. She was given the Order of Canada, the O.B.E., given an honorary degree and its Medal of Criminology by the University of Montreal, and a Medal as Woman of the Century in Quebec by the NCJW. Prime Minister Trudeau in 1970 summoned Mme. Casgrain to the Senate, where she sat as an Independent.

* * *

Another Casgrain, attractive Dr. Claire Kirkland-Casgrain, has given Quebec woman power a substantial boost in recent years. Distantly related to Mme. Thérèse Casgrain through her marriage to lawyer Philippe Casgrain, Marie Claire also trained for the law. Born in 1926, she graduated from McGill University's Law School, studied political science in Paris and international law in Geneva. Before her marriage to Philippe she once faced her future husband as the opposing counsel in court and won the case. A standing family joke is that Philippe married Claire to make certain he would lose no more cases.

The mother of three children, Marie Claire Kirkland-Casgrain has two Quebec political firsts to her credit. She was the first woman elected to the Quebec Legislature in a landslide 1962 victory in Jacques Cartier riding, filling the vacancy created by her father's death.

She set another precedent when named Minister Without Portfolio in Jean Lesage's cabinet. In 1964 she became Quebec Minister of Transport. To combat the province's highway death rate — the highest in the country — Mme. Kirkland-Casgrain gave strong attention to promoting highway safety. However, her greatest single achievement before the Lesage Government's defeat in 1966, was Bill 16 designed to ensure that women participate as "full-fledged citizens in Quebec". The key element on the Kirkland-Casgrain Bill is the provision that the wife participate with her husband fully in running their home and family and that a woman may go into business with her husband's consent. Mme. Kirkland-Casgrain termed Bill 16 that first stage in an "overdue overhaul" of the Quebec Civil Code.

Madame Kirkland-Casgrain

* * *

While woman power at the provincial level has never approached its numerical potential, the level of contribution must be considered the plus factor. Names from the past such as Mary Ellen Smith and "Tilly" Rolston are joined by more recent standard-bearers: Buda (Mrs. Don) Brown, B.C. Social Credit member in the '50's; Mrs. Rose Wilkinson, who served as a Social Credit member of the Alberta legislature from 1944 to 1957; Mrs. Gladys Porter of Kentville, N.S. who in the 40's became the first woman mayor in the Maritimes, and later the first woman elected to a Maritime provincial legislature.

In Ontario Mrs. Margaret Renwick joined her husband, James, as an NDP member of the legislature in the 1967 election. They became the first husband and wife provincial team. Re-elected to the Ontario House in 1967 was Conservative Ada Pritchard of Hamilton, who brought a distinguished civic political background to her provincial work. Mrs. Pritchard was an alderman in Hamilton from 1954-56 and topped the polls in 1956 to become vice-chairman. A graduate nurse, she served in France in World War I. Active in clubs and an ardent supporter of Hamilton's philharmonic orchestra, Ada Pritchard has been a strong promoter of better housing for the aged and was instrumental in establishing 16 apartments for senior citizens in her home city.

Civic Politics

If numbers are considered a criterion of success, then civic politics comes out the winner in any count of women who have led the field. Some 15 per cent of all civic political offices across Canada are now held by women. And the contribution has been long-standing and substantial, dating back to 1892 when Augusta Stowe Gullen and Mrs. M. McDonnell became members of the Toronto School Board. Mrs. Edna Ryerson served

13 years on the board. Mrs. H. R. Clark took up duties with the Fredericton School Board in 1896 in what proved to be a lifelong career. In her 25th year of service the city honored her with a silver tray. She stayed on after her husband became Lieutenant-Governor, retiring on the eve of her 50th anniversary to save the city the expense of a gold commemorative tray.

Western Canada

Out in Calgary in 1917, Annie Gale became the first woman elected to a city council in Canada. Mrs. R. F. Margaret McWilliams LL.D. became Winnipeg's first woman alderman in 1932. She attained acclaim as a speaker, serving as president of the Canadian Federation of University Women and later as vice-president of the international federation. Her husband was appointed Lieutenant-Governor in 1940. Skilled as a hostess, she managed to entertain royalty graciously despite the absence of a provincial allowance. Enthusiastic and versatile, Dr. McWilliams collaborated with her husband in writing *Russians in 1926*, and also wrote *Manitoba Milestones, This New Canada*, and *If I were King of Canada*.

Another interesting Winnipeg woman, Mrs. Maude McCreery served as a city alderman and simultaneously ran her florist shop "The Rosery". Active in 20 different clubs, she seldom missed a meeting. In fact, the day she gave birth to a daughter she entertained members of a committee from her hospital bed. An individualist to the core, Mrs. McCreery, a widow, opted out of family allowance payments: "This country was built by people who stood on their own feet."

Further west in Vancouver, Anna Sprott was elected that city's first woman alderman in 1949. Her husband's assistant in operating a chain of commercial radio and wireless schools and developing CKMO, the first radio station west of Winnipeg, Mrs. Sprott carried on as president when he died. She helped found both the Business and Professional Women's and Soroptimist Clubs, and served as president of both as well as head of the American Federation of Soroptimist Clubs. At Vancouver's city hall she headed the Department of Social Service and served on Board of Vancouver General Hospital, Preventorium and Foster Care for Children. She battled to have Vancouver wheat parity with eastern ports restored.

Any list of western women who have become civic leaders must include: Mayor Carrie Gale of North Vancouver, who followed the political example of her husband, John, former B.C. Minister of Labor; Nora Arnold, three times elected as mayor of Prince Rupert; and Alderman Marion Sherman, an active clubwoman and radio commentator. New Westminster's no-nonsense first woman alderman and its first woman mayor, Mrs. Beth Wood, also became the first woman to head the Canadian Federation of Mayors and Municipalities.

In Calgary, Col. Mary Dover, O.B.E. came to the Stampede City council in the 1950s with a broad background. After a war-time stint as a colonel in the CWACS, she lectured across Canada on the subject of women in the army. Mary Dover's family history paralleled Calgary's development. Her mother, Mrs. A. E. Cross, was the first white child born in Fort MacLeod and helped establish Calgary's first hospital. Her grandfather gave Calgary its name and her father was one of four men who organized the popular Calgary Stampede.

Maritime Winner

In the east, Mrs. Henry Drover, Newfoundland's self-named "charwoman mayor" — because she does so many odd chores around the family hotel — was sworn in as mayor of Clarenville in 1957; winner in a stormy session in which most male councillors threatened to resign. Her husband was elected as alderman on the same council, a civic first for Newfoundland.

Quebec's first woman mayor, Mrs. Elsie Gibbons, was elected in 1953 in Portage du Fort. Elsie proved she was a woman who could get what she wanted. She snared a $90,000 modern waterworks system for her tiny community of 500, had the streets and sidewalks repaved and the century-old town hall renovated. In 1959 Mrs. Gibbons became the first woman elected warden of the county of Pontiac. Other Quebec civic winners include: Mrs. Thomas Urquhart of Pointe Claire; Eileen Consiglio of Piedmont; Catherine MacKenzie, who served on the Stanstead Council; and Mme. Eustache Letellier de St. Juste, first woman member of Montreal's 99-member council.

Ontario, with one-third of Canada's population, naturally has contributed the lion's share of women candidates at the civic level, far too many for an inclusive list.

Mrs. Clara Twidale, elected Ontario's first woman alderman in 1922 in Niagara Falls, served 25 years. Her father, a Polish nobleman, had been pressed into the German navy. He deserted and settled in Canada. Naturally she was sympathetic when she found another immigrant, a poverty-stricken widow, hoeing potatoes, helped by her naked little boy. Mrs. Twidale outfitted him for school, and he became an outstanding parliamentarian. She was first chairman of the Mother's Allowance Commission and founded the LCW. Twidale Avenue in the honeymoon capital honors her.

Writer-Politician

Nora Frances Henderson, women's editor of the *Hamilton Herald* from 1918, was elected an alderman in 1932, and to board of control two years later. Topping the poll, she automatically became first woman deputy mayor, a position she held for 13 years. Miss Henderson was relief controller in 1935 when Hamilton, an industrial city, had over 8,000 families on relief. Her exemplary conduct during the 1946 steel strike is still remembered when strikers loudly shouted, outside City Hall: "We'll hang Nora Henderson to a sour apple tree." Resigning from politics to work with the Children's Aid in 1948, she wrote *The Citizen of Tomorrow*. The Nora Frances Henderson Hospital, Canada's first hospital for chronically-ill patients, is her memorial.

Countless others shared the civic spotlight: Mrs. Eunice Wishart, scrappy Councillor for seven years before she became Port Arthur's mayor; Bernadette Smith, alderman for two years, then mayor of Woodstock for five years; Mrs. Jane Forrester, Belleville's record five-time civic winner; Alderman Alene Holt of Peterborough and Wanda Miller, three times elected mayor of Gravenhurst. Not so fortunate was Mrs. Lucy Cole, who in 1955 was defeated in her 24th bid for public office in London, where Mrs. Edwin Fullerton had been elected as the city's first woman alderman.

Mrs. Laura Sabia "the self-styled fighting alderman from St. Catharines" and former national president of the CFUW, thinks that colleges still discriminate against women. She sent a letter to Prime Minister Pearson asking that the government urge the UN to hold a seminar on women's rights in 1966 in Canada. Berating women for meekly accepting a submissive role in a speech at the annual dinner of the Ottawa Public School Teachers' Association, she exclaimed: "We're allowing the government to slit our throats and pick our pockets!" When the government did appoint a Royal Commission on the status of women, outspoken Mrs. Sabia was not appointed a member.

Or how about that mayor for a day — Mrs. Emma Marie Poupore of Gogama, Ontario. Emma Marie had the unique honour in 1939 of serving as Canada's first and only Mayor for a Day. As King George VI and Queen Elizabeth's Royal train edged toward Gogama for a five minute stop-over the citizens of the small Ontario town hurriedly planned a civic reception. Lacking both a mayor and town council, the civic fathers hastily dubbed Emma Marie the mayor for the right royal occasion, temporarily making her Ontario's third woman mayor.

Leamington added Grace to the civic scene — Grace McFarland, who served as deputy reeve and mayor of this Ontario farming community. In 1952 as mediator in a 14-day old strike which threatened to ruin a $1,000,000 tomato crop at the H. J. Heinz Company, Mrs. McFarland saved the crop and sharpened her political reputation by settling the dispute.

"An Ageing Gun Moll Mayor?"

Maggie Campbell is delighted to be called "this irritant" or "an ageing gun moll". Because she insists that the citizens of Toronto, the cosmopolitan capital of Ontario, be kept well-informed, her dream is to have Nathan Phillips Square a sort of modern Roman Forum.

The Toronto election of 1966 showed the force of woman power. Controllers Margaret Campbell and June Marks topped the polls as members of one of Toronto's most criticized administrations. Mrs. Campbell, in fact, polled more votes than William Dennison in his successful mayoralty bid.

Maggie is a handsome, hefty, clever lawyer; a grandmother, a chain-smoker who also enjoys a drink. As Metro's first woman budget chief, she cheerfully tackled the enormous task of up-dating Toronto's archaic financial system by introducing a budget control officer, as a prelude to full-scale reform. A gutsy political veteran with ten years of experience on city council, she counts on considerable support at the polls from both various ethnic groups and male voters. Undaunted by Jean Newman's 1960 downfall, Mrs. Campbell served early notice that she would give Mayor Dennison an exciting run for his money in the December 1969 election.

Slum clearance is June Marks' special problem sphere. In the summer of '65 she sparked a judicial inquiry into Toronto's slums and expropriation procedures. She considers the proposed redevelopment of the harbour area the most important project facing Toronto. Her views on women in the top civic office: "I think a woman has just as good a chance to be elected mayor. The stress is on the individual's ability and performance."

Victory Ride

In Canada's Capital a woman of ability did prove it could be done. Others have taken the victory ride to Ottawa's City Hall — Alderman May Nickson, Cecile O'Regan and Mary Harrison, brainy Ellen Webber on Board of Control and, more recently, Marion Dewar, Deputy Mayor and Controller, Patricia Nicol, Controller, and Toddy Kehoe and Marlene Catterall as aldermen. But none has equalled Charlotte Whitton for colour, controversy and downright ability as the Capital's Mayor. Her life has been a perpetual storm centre. There's a story, possibly apocryphal, that three weeks after birth, baby Charlotte clutched the side of her wash tub as she slipped deeper into the water and literally pulled herself to her feet. The story is symbolic of the fact that Charlotte Whitton has been in and out of hot water ever since.

Born in 1896 in Renfrew, Ont. of an Anglican Yorkshire father and an American-born Irish Catholic mother, Charlotte was built as she puts it: "on good Shetland pony lines". A human dynamo with jutting jaw and charming smile, Charlotte Whitton worked her way through Queen's University receiving a B.A., a masters degree and a host of medals, including the Governor-General's prize.

Charlotte Whitton

For several years she served as secretary to the Hon. Thomas Low, Minister of Trade and Commerce, and during the Depression years travelled across Canada studying social problems. In 1926 she became founding editor of the magazine *Canadian Welfare* and authored several books and articles on welfare and related fields. Her controversial *Liberty* magazine article "Babies for Export", based on a survey into child adoption practices in Alberta which Miss Whitton completed for the IODE in 1947, sparked a Royal Commission inquiry to rectify appalling adoption practices between the U.S. and Canada border, provoked a law-suit for the magazine, and landed Charlotte in jail for a short spell. However between 1926 and 1941 Charlotte Whitton is credited with helping to place social welfare work in Canada on a sound scientific basis, elevating it from casual charity to a respected profession. Under her direction the Council of Child Welfare expanded into the Canadian Welfare Council, a liaison body between voluntary charitable organizations and the provincial and federal governments.

As a result of a speech and a dare, Charlotte plunged into politics. In a talk before the Montreal B. and P. Women's club, she complained that not enough women were in government. "Canadian women rejoice in a life of club activities, instead of community service," she said, referring to women's "resolutionary" rather than "revolutionary" efforts. Firing back, the *Ottawa Citizen* challenged Charlotte to set an example. Her first experiment in political immersion was highly satisfactory — she topped the poll for board of control in the 1950 election, automatically becoming deputy mayor. When Mayor Grenville Goodwin died suddenly, Charlotte Whitton took over as the first woman mayor of a capital city in the British Commonwealth, complete with ceremonial robes and chauffeur-driven Cadillac.

Her first act as mayor was to resurrect a long-disused "official" chair. Friends ascribe her love of pomp to a respect for tradition. She insisted on "robing" reluctant city fathers and, though not interested in personal fashion, gloried in her red velvet robe trimmed with miniver and the ceremonial tricorne hat worn at a jaunty angle — the effect was strongly reminiscent of an English "Beefeater". Incidentally, beefsteak was the food she fortified herself with before council clashes. Her "chain of office", it was rumored, was even worn in the bath!

In politics, her slogan was: "I fight a good fight!"

and so she did with victories in 1952, 1954, 1960 and 1962 elections. Charlotte clashed with controllers, aldermen, heads of civic boards. She has been called "stormy petrel" in a world where most women still suffer from lack of self-confidence. She took a long step in 1958, running as a Conservative in the federal election against George McIlraith, long-time Liberal MP, and lost her one bid for federal politics. In the '60s amid rumors that Prime Minister Diefenbaker would shortly appoint her as Canada's ambassador to Ireland, Charlotte literally blew it. In a battle royal with Controller Paul Tardiff (later Liberal MP for Russell), Charlotte slapped and kicked her opponent and brandished a pistol for full dramatic effect before members of the board of control. It mattered little that the weapon was just a toy pistol once the photo of the encounter hit the news media. It was a memorable battle.

Charlotte met her first civic defeat in 1964, losing her bid for re-election as mayor. She retired quietly to lick her wounds and turned to a daily program on Ottawa television "Dear Charlotte". But politics beckoned again. She won an easy victory that took her back once more to City Hall, as an alderman.

* * *

As Canada headed into the '70s, woman power in politics, whether at the civic, provincial or federal level, was a long way from where it could or should be. "Women haven't fulfilled their responsibilities in public affairs since the pioneer days," insists Dr. Aileen Noonan of Windsor, Ont.

Though conscientious voters and hard behind-the-scenes workers, Canadian women, with rare exceptions, have opted out when it came to taking the political plunge as candidates. Then, too, the brave ones who have tried their luck, often as not, have ended up with the nomination in a riding "where no male candidate wishes to walk the plank for the party's sake," said Charlotte Whitton.

Although half the voting power in this country is in the hands of women, there is no national organization for educating women voters comparable to the U.S. League of Women Voters. It is not idle speculation to contemplate what force women might exert if united behind capable female candidates — reduce the high cost of living, improve the educational system, possibly even change foreign policy in a way that would make Dr. Augusta Stowe-Gullen's utopian prophecy ring true: "When women have a voice in national and international affairs, wars will cease forever."

Chapter XI

Sweet Sounds

Music

Kathleen Parlow

Music is well said to be the speech of angels.

(Carlyle)

Standing knee-deep in flowers, eighteen-year-old Madame Albani wept for joy. In Messina her singing of the title role, Bellini's "La Somnambula" was superb. The highly critical 1870 Italian audience rose, cheered.

Her whole life had been a preparation for this triumph. Born Marie Louise Emma Cecile Lajeunesse in 1847, her mother died when Emma was a baby. Her father Joseph, an excellent musician, was obsessed with ambition for his daughter. She never owned a doll, but was made to practise music — piano and singing — four hours daily almost from infancy. An unhappy, homely girl, firmly under the hand of her father, she pleaded to become a nun. "God has given you a beautiful voice," a Mother Superior told her. "It is your duty to use it."

Her debut at Mechanic's Hall in Montreal was as disappointing as a provincial tour which followed. But she managed to earn enough money to go to Paris to study. It was the start of a flower-strewn career that made her the first Canadian woman singer to attain international fame.

Baroness de Lafitte befriended her — later Prince Poniawski heard Emma sing at one of the Baroness' salons and persuaded first M. Duprez and later the great Lamperti (Milan) to tutor her. Her performances in Russia brought overwhelming acclaim. She was invited there in 1873, where she learned the language and added it to a repertoire of French, German, Italian and English.

Twenty-five curtain calls greeted her the night she climaxed nine operas in Moscow. Gifts flooded in to her among them an emerald butterfly from Prince Dolgourouky, Governor of Royal Theatre.

When she sang *Rigoletto* in St. Petersburg, Czar Alexander II gave personal congratulations, and invited her to sing at the wedding banquet of his only daughter. This proved a nerve-wracking ordeal, since each toast was preceded by a fanfare of trumpets. Following this, her season's fee was raised to 16,000 pounds, most of which she gave to her family. Every programme ended with a rendition of her vocal trademark — Home Sweet Home. It was in Malta that homesick British sailors begged her to sing the song; thereafter, she ended every program with it.

London's leading impresario, Frederick Gye, engaged her to sing in Covent Garden in 1872. It was another triumph, as were her tours of Africa, Australia and New Zealand which followed. Whenever possible, she studied works of living composers with them, numbering Lizst, Brahms and Dvorak (who wrote his *Stabat Mater* for her) among her friends.

Albani did not return to Canada until 1883, where she was greeted by civic and private receptions. She arranged to have all her old friends attend her concert as her guests in her home town of Chambly. When she was told that all seats had been sold, she was furious and refused to sing until her friends were given seats — right on the stage.

Returning to England, she was awarded the Beethoven Gold Medal "for exceptional genius and musical attainments . . ." Lord Tennyson wrote an ode with music by Sir Arthur Sullivan, for her to sing at the 1886 Colonial and Indian Exhibition.

Albani won the title "Queen of English Festivals" for her marvellous performance of Gounod's *Redemption* and *Mors et Vita*. Probably her greatest triumph was Handel Festival, 1877, when over 22,000 people packed the Crystal Palace to hear her sing *The Messiah*. At a Christmas party for newsboys, given by *New York World*, she received a touching tribute. One hungry lad, spellbound, pushed back his plate, whispering: "I'd rather listen to her than eat!"

Family problems overshadowed joys in Madame Albani's life. She had only one child, a boy. After his birth she took the only vacation in her career — a six-month's leave from singing.

Albani's husband, who drank heavily, mismanaged her finances and as the years wore on, too, her voice began to fail. After her husband's death, she was forced to sell her beautiful home and teach singing. Her student, Sarah Fischer, joined with the great Melba in organizing a 1925 benefit concert for her in Covent Garden, scene of former triumphs. The British Government gave a 500 pound annuity. Before her death in 1930, King George V awarded her the O.B.E.

Donalda's Triumphs

As with Madame Albani, it was standard practise for singers to win fame and fortune in Europe before returning, as stars, to their native Canada. Lyric soprano and strong actress, Madame Donalda's voice was heard more often by Europeans than by her countrymen.

Born Pauline Leon Lighthouse in Montreal 1882, she seventeen years later won second prize at L'Academie de Musique de Quebec. She began studying music and arts at the Royal Victoria College.

In 1902 Pauline won a Strathcona Medal and Scholarship, called a "Donalda" in honor of the donor, Sir Donald A. Smith (Lord Strathcona). She took "Donalda" as her stage name, and made it world famous.

In France, at the Paris Conservatoire, Donalda

studied opera with Edmond Duvernoy and acting with Paul Lherie. Her debut as *Manon* (Nice, 1904) was a hit. Its composer, Massenet, coached her in three of his operas. She became a star at the Opera de la Monnaie in Brussels. By May, 1905, she sang Micaela to Emma Calve's historic "Carmen" at Covent Garden, where later, opposite famous baritone Scotti, she created the role of Ah-Joe in Leoni's *L'Oracolo*.

Her Montreal debut was in 1906. She sang in Europe thirty-seven years. Her audiences were as impressive as her voice.

She sang for King Edward VII and Queen Alexandra and the Dowager Empress of Russia. In 1908 she took part in a Diamond Jubilee Concert at Queen's Hall, London, with John McCormack, Edouard de Reszke, Mischa Elman, and the great Patti, whose swan song it was.

At Nice, she created Jennie in Leoncavallo's *Tomasso Chateron;* in 1919 Conception in Ravel's *L'Heure Espagnole*. Her favorite role was Marguerite in *Faust*.

When she returned to Montreal she organized the Opera Guild and Opera School, pioneer projects in Canada. Donalda sang her way through two marriages, the first with baritone Paul Seveillac; second, Harry Haurowitz-Mishca-Leon.

In Montreal, using students of her Opera School she has produced premieres of *Le Coq d'Or, Il Seraglio, Fidelio*.

Her studio is a fascinating place — concert grand piano flanked by golden harp, which she plays. She displays caricatures of herself by Caruso — opera scores autographed by Massenet, Puccini, Ravel. Treasured among many tributes is a studio dedicated to her in Tel Aviv's Cultural Centre; a musical doctorate from McGill University (1954); and Edward Johnson's description of her: "A Canadian artist of international fame, who has devoted talent, career, and life to her native city. Canada may well be proud of her extraordinary achievements."

* * *

Edvina, a contemporary of Donalda's, was born in Vancouver, 1885 and trained in Montreal. Her real name, Mary Martin, was changed three times by marriage, while she used Edvina as a stage name. A dramatic soprano and clever actress, she made her debut in 1908 in Covent Garden as Marguerite in *Faust*.

Following several years with Boston and Chicago Opera Companies, she made a New York debut at the Metropolitan in *Tosca* in 1916.

Beatrice La Palme

Beatrice La Palme, born in 1878 in Quebec, started as a violinist, winning a Strathcona bursary, twice renewed, for study at Royal College of Music in London. However, she also studied singing, and it was as a dramatic soprano that she made a successful debut at Covent Garden. Later she sang at the Opera Comique and at the Century Opera House in New York. Her forte was Wagnerian music. She settled in Montreal where she taught singing until her early death in 1921.

Illustrious Ex-Patriate

Eva Gauthier of Ottawa, a descendant of explorer de la Verendrye, and niece of Sir Wilfrid Laurier, made her debut in Parma, Italy in 1910. She went to the Orient in search of songs and spent three months in the harem of a sultan's palace. First singer to make a trans-Atlantic broadcast, she was also the first to sing jazz and show tunes on the concert stage. In Ottawa in 1927, she helped celebrate the diamond jubilee of confederation. However, she taught singing for many years in New York.

Maureen's Triumphs

Maureen Forrester in 1955 was the first Canadian singer to make a major tour of Europe since Mme. Sarah Fischer. Sponsor was Le Federation Internationales des Jeunesses Musicales. Planned as a three-month tour of ten countries, it was so phenomenally successful that Maureen spent another nine months fulfilling extra concert, radio and recording engagements. "She has a voice with a capital V" wrote Noel Goodwin, *Daily Express.*

"Number please" at her job as telephone operator changed to ovations for "Another number please" by vast audiences. She quit her job as an operator in 1952 when engagements began flooding in.

She secretly married violinist Eugene Kash, had a new stage triumph as well as another baby almost every year. "My own children will finish university if it takes them fifty years," she declared emphatically. Later the Kashes separated.

Her singing career has never halted for an intermission. In 1957, she sang at the Stratford Festival, featuring *Five Songs by Dark Voice* composed for her by Harry Somers. Bruno Walter chose her as soloist with New York Symphony Orchestra in three performances of Mahler's *Symphony Number Two.*

The National Film Board made a movie of her appearance with Casals Festival in Puerto Rico in 1960, she toured in Benjamin Britten's operas *Rape of Lucrece* and *Albert Herring* and in 1966 sang the role of Cornelia in Handel's *Giulio Cesare* at Lincoln Centre. In 1965 she gave seventy-five recitals at a minumum fee of $2,000.

She became head of the voice department of Philadelphia Academy of Music in 1966, received an honorary degree from Sir George Williams University, and appeared in a programme of songs by Canadian composers at the Festival du Marais.

Wrote French critic Jean Cotte: "We have not

heard such a striking voice since Kathleen Ferrier."

Dramatic Voice

Mother of many opera stars whom she discovered and often helped is Sarah Fischer, dramatic soprano who dedicated her life to music and the people who produce it.

A gala anniversary concert in 1969 marked thirty years of helping lesser known artists gain recognition. The popular Sarah Fischer Concerts started in 1939, her "Thank you" to Canada for a Strathcona Scholarship awarded her in 1917.

Her first "find" was Claire Gagne in 1941, who later sang *Cherubino* at the Metropolitan. Others include Maureen Forrester, Arthur Davison, Michele Bonhomme, Pierrette Alarie, Violet Archer and Jacques Lebreque. The Sarah Fischer Scholarship, assisting needy artists, is her memorial to Madame Albani, who befriended and later coached her.

Born in France, Sarah Fischer was brought to Montreal as a baby. She studied at Royal College of Music in London, graduating in 1922.

Her role of Micaela in *Carmen* in 1918 at the Monument National established her stature as a singer, a success repeated in 1922 at London's Old Vic. She created the leading role in Arthur Benjamin's opera *The Devil Take Her* at Covent Garden, sang the title role in *Carmen,* first opera broadcast on television by the BBC from London on July 6, 1934. Miss Fischer also staged and directed the performance. The first Canadian to introduce Canadian folk songs in European capitals, she has sung over 30 leading roles in four languages, besides more than 2,000 lieder and classic songs in recital.

Sarah Fischer was made honorary associate of Royal College of Music in 1928, and in 1968, a scholarship bearing her name was a tribute given this musician by the Concert Society of Jewish People's Schools.

Music has meaning for every Canadian, but, of course, may evoke many different meanings. For Donalda it was an aria in the grand style for royalty of Russia, for Edith Fowke it was the local ditties and country tunes in the development of Canada. The scale is wide and complex but the common bond was simple — music was their life.

Story of Courage

Had the Salk vaccine been discovered earlier, Lois Marshall might have had a happier childhood, but she may not have become a great singer.

Four consecutive times she was chosen "Woman of the Year in Music" — by women editors — "not only for gifts and success as a magnificent singer, but for personal courage in overcoming pain and physical handicap, for generosity in aiding crippled children."

The pattern of one talent brilliantly overcoming a defect is not new, but Lois Marshall's story is disturbingly poignant. Crippled by poliomyelitis as a child, unable to play, she developed her voice by singing along with her brother's fine collection of operatic records.

Numerous, painful operations finally enabled Lois to walk — albeit with a limp. At eight, Lois attended Wellesley Orthopedic School, where Miss Elsie Hutchinson, her music teacher, recognized talent. At 12, Lois won the Toronto Public School singing contest. Her widowed mother, struggling to support seven children, couldn't afford singing lessons but Rotary Club member John Chantler came to the rescue and financed them.

In 1947, she began a three-year course at Toronto Conservatory. A laryngitis attack prevented a debut with the Toronto Symphony Orchestra when Sir Ernest MacMillan invited her. Lois was bitterly disappointed.

Lois Marshall

However, 1950 proved a red-letter year, she won both T. Eaton Company's $1,000 award and Canadian Industries Limited's $1,000 scholarship. She captured every major award in Canada, then won a Naumburg Award, which entitled her to a concert in Town Hall, December 1952.

On the great day, Lois, sick with stage fright, limped painfully across the stage, a lovely picture in a crimson velvet gown. It was an extremely difficult programme of 20 songs in five languages. Stunned silence greeted her phenomenal range, from D below middle C to F sharp above high C, then thunderous applause erupted. Ecstatic critics compared Lois to great Maggie Teyte and Melba, *New York Times* saying: ". . . seems likely . . . a long distinguished career."

Arthur Judson, honorary president of Columbia Artists Management, decided to handle her career himself. An exciting succession of appearances on radio, television, and with major symphony orchestras followed.

Toscanini exclaimed: "Brava! Bravissima!" He chose her as soloist in Beethoven's *Missa Solemnis* (recorded later) at his 1952 Christmas Eve concert in Carnegie Hall.

On stage, dark eyes and hair contrast strikingly with her gardenia-like complexion. She has great poise, though Weldon Kilburn, her accompanist whom she married in 1959, had trouble toning down over-dramatic stage gestures.

Leopold Stokowski selected Lois Marshall as soloist for the first major concert on Canadian music at Carnegie Hall, October 1953.

Perfectionist Sir Thomas Beecham chose Lois for a soprano solo, in Handel's *Soloman*, later she fulfilled a 30 years' dream of his in her role as Constance for his recording of Mozart's *The Abduction from the Seraglio*. He also conducted Royal Philharmonic Orchestra for her British debut (1956) at Royal Festival Hall. Singing extremely difficult *Exultate Jubilate*, composed by Mozart for Rauzinni, a male soprano, she received an ovation.

Next came triumphant tours of European capitals and festivals. In 1958, when she sang seven concerts in the Soviet Union, television technicians cheered. She toured New Zealand and Australia, singing to 50,000 persons at Australia's first Arts Festival in Adelaide. In Moscow, 1960, she received a standing ovation — singer

Zara Dolukhanova paid her the highest tribute when she compared her to Marian Anderson and Elizabeth Schwarzkopf.

As Oscar Wilde wrote: "Out of sorrow have the worlds been built." Suffering has doubtless contributed to the thrilling spiritual quality that distinguishes her singing.

Not A Circus

"People come to hear me because I am a composer who happens to sing my own songs . . . not because I am an Indian," says Buffy Sainte Marie whose real name is Marie Star Blanket. *Until It's Time for You to Go* is probably the most popular of the more than 400 songs Buffy has written. Sometimes her subconscious creates songs while she sleeps. "I'll wake up, and there'll be a song as clear to me as if I just heard it on the radio. I just write it down." Only about five per cent of her compositions are protest songs. In *The Universal Soldier* she despairs about the futility of war. The disturbing lyrics of *My Country 'Tis Of Thy People You're Dying* and *Now that the Buffalo's Gone* arouse the social conscience.

Born at Piapot Reserve, near Regina, Buffy, a Cree, was adopted by a Micmac couple living in Maine. Her guitar playing is self-taught but her knowledge of oriental philosophy was acquired at University of Massachusetts. In New York she played and sang in a gaslight cage and proved so popular she repeated the performance, eventually meeting pianist Herb Gart who became her agent.

Buffy started singing professionally in 1962 and developed into a poet-singer of phenomenal talent. A small, serious, sensible woman, gentle, yet often arrogant (to hide her innate shyness), Buffy sings to a mouth bow, an old, rarely-performed instrument. Doing "fun songs", she stamps the floor with her feet and can almost hypnotize an audience. Standing ovations are frequent at Buffy's concerts. She loves anything Spanish, longs to take Flamenco lessons. Once she joined a peyote-chewing religious ceremony and was hooked on codeine. Her composition *Codeine* is a masterpiece of agony. Deploring the terrible tension singing to strict schedules, she struggles to retain her spontaneity, and hopes to sing forever.

In 1966 her solo concert in London's Royal Festival Hall and at the International Music Festival in Israel enhanced her reputation. Vanguard has put her powerful voice on several albums. Buffy's first record, *It's My Way* in 1964 was followed by *Many a Mile, Little Wheel* and *Spin and Spin* in 1966. Though proud of her Indian heritage, she seldom sings Indian songs, refuses to sing in her native tongue, or wear native dress. "They want me to come on with a feather in my hair, a papoose on my back, and waving a tomahawk. I am not a circus," she says disdainfully.

Cursed with poor health especially in cold weather, she has had recurring bouts of laryngitis — one throat ailment lasted for six months. Of her frequent trips to hospital she says: "I collect medical bills by the thousands. Because of a blood condition, they have to feed me through my veins." At 24, earning about $100,000 annually, Buffy still lived in a New York YWCA. She visits her family annually and still seems interested in helping Indians. One of her projects is to try to save Mistaseni, a sacred rock threatened to be covered by the South Saskatchewan dam. She also held a fund-raising concert to send Indians to law school to study Indian law. "We already have one guy enrolled, and a girl about to enroll. The quality of Indian education is pretty depressing."

Married recently to Dewain Kamai Kalani Bugbee, the couple relax at their farm in Maine between Buffy's singing engagements.

Hitting the Heights

By mid-twentieth century, a number of Canadian women had risen to major heights in operatic and concert music.

Pierrette Alarie was the first French-Canadian to reach the New York's Metropolitan Opera. Born November (1923) in Montreal, she had a head start with a musical family behind her — her father was conductor of the Canadian Operetta Society and her mother was for many years the society's leading soprano.

Her doll was her first audience. She sang *Ma Poupée Cherie* to it one day, determined to be a great singer. At 14 she made her professional debut. With her first cheque she bought the opera score of *Romeo and Juliet*. In 1943 she made her operatic debut in Montreal as Barberina in *The Marriage of Figaro* with a Metropolitan cast. A two-year scholarship with Curtis Institute of Philadelphia led the way to a contract with the Met.

A happy musical collaboration began with her marriage to tenor Leopold Simoneau in 1946. The Simoneaus sang in Montreal's Les Concerts Symphoniques, toured North America two seasons with Theodor Uppman (as Bel Canto Trio). During 1948-49 season, they made an operatic debut in Paris; Pierrette was so successful in *Lakme* they were engaged several seasons and she appeared at most important festivals in Europe. Late in the 1950's the Simoneaus settled in Montreal.

* * *

Teresa Stratas, shared with Lois Marshall the honor of heading a music poll in 1959. Often called "Little Callas" this infuriates her.

Born in Oshawa in 1938, the daughter of a Greek restaurant owner, she received her education there, and sang on local radio. Her brother Nick played the violin and sister Mary sang.

Her velvety voice rang confidently in 1958 when

she debuted as Mimi in *La Bohème* at the Toronto Opera Festival and made a first appearance in America in Empire Music Festival. She sang in *Murder in the Cathedral* in Boston Cathedral in the same year.

Four years later she made still more important debuts. When she sang in Moscow she was greeted with a 20-minute ovation; she debuted at La Scala, Milan as Queen Isabella in the world premiere of Manuel de Fallas' opera *Atlantida*, and at the Cincinnati Zoo Opera.

Her chance for the Met came in 1959 when it advertised vacancy for one apprentice. Teresa played hookey, auditioned with 1,000 other hopefuls and got the apprenticeship. In March, 1960, her great opportunity came when she replaced a sick star, singing the role of Liu in *Turandot*.

Teresa again sang Mimi in *La Bohème* in Covent Garden, London in April 1967. Though in intense pain from a toothache, she sang beautifully, and the performance closed to cheers and 11 curtain calls, in which another Canadian singer shared — Maria Pellegrini, born in Italy, who played the role of Musetta. Maria showed an extremely musical voice, an extremely pretty pair of ankles, and a sense of comedy that literally stopped the show. Maria, a protégée of Daisy Roe Moore, Ottawa pianist and teacher, is married now, and is living and singing in Toronto.

"When I reach my zenith, I want to sing like no one has ever sung before," Teresa explained when she insisted on a sabbatical year in 1968 to restudy singing and appear in many small opera houses in Europe.

Anne Murray: Superstar

An opportunity to record for Capitol Records of Canada proved to be a turning point in Anne Murray's life. Born in Springhill, Nova Scotia, in 1945 she got her B.A. at the University of New Brunswick, then taught physical education for a year in P.E.I. Steadily, singing superseded teaching, till, after *Snowbird* suddenly she was a star! A major hit in Canada, it also reached the top of the American Pop charts and the country hit parade producing a gold record award as a million-seller hit.

The varied styles of songs she selects is shown in her very first LP entitled *Snowbird* with such different selections as Bob Dylan's *I'll Be Your Baby Tonight*; Jose Feliciano's *Rain; Break My Mind* by Nashville's John D. Loudermilk; and Dino Valenti's *Get Together*.

Years of classical training produced a very versatile voice. "I like to mix it up a little," Anne confesses, but her producer, Tom Catalano, points out: "She is the only singer I know who has the vocal equipment to handle all these styles."

Soon Anne found herself in demand as a television performer on both Canadian and American shows, as a regular on the popular Glen Campbell Show for CBS-TV. She also shared top billing with Glen at the International Hotel in Las Vegas for four weeks, and a week at the Greek Theatre in Los Angeles. Glen and Anne worked together for about two years, also cutting a duet album for Capitol.

In Canada, Anne became well-known through her performance in nine CBC-TV specials. Anne was given a place of honour on the Nova Scotia float in the annual Tournament of Roses in Pasadena. She travelled the route singing for thousands lining the route and millions more on TV.

In January, 1973, there was an "Anne Murray Special" on the BBC. Four whirlwind European tours in 1973 ended with concerts at Royal Festival Hall and the London Palladium. In Europe, also, Anne has been seen on Top of the Pops, Saturday Variety, Golden Shot, In Concert, Morcambe and Wise, and the Radio Show, also a pair of Anne Murray Specials for Swedish TV.

Anne won the Juno award as Best Feminine

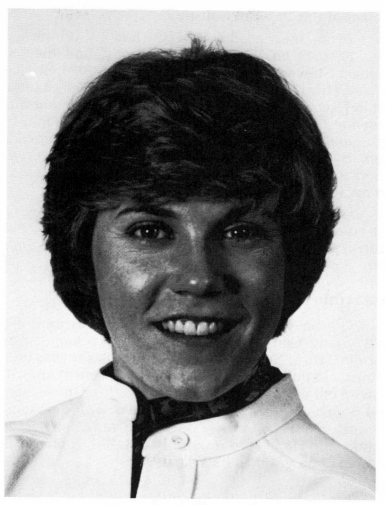

Anne Murray

Vocalist in 1970, '71, '72 '73, and '74 and previously a 1970 Juno award for best single of the year with *Snowbird*. She was voted Britain's top female vocalist for '72 and '73. In 1974 she won a Grammy Award for her *Love Song* album, and in 1975 the Vanier Award, the Broadway Executive Society's Bessie Award as most outstanding Canadian performer, and was appointed an

Officer of the Order of Canada.

Anne married Bill Langstroth, a TV producer on June 20, 1975 on her thirtieth birthday, and their son William Stewart was born on August 31, 1976. She took a "sabbatical" in order to nurse and care for the baby, but in December, '76 returned to the CBC with her ninth hour-long Superspecial entitled *Keeping in Touch*. It is estimated that over three million viewers welcomed her back. By early 1977 Anne was back into the concert and television stage circuit part-time, with engagements as far away as Japan.

As one writer in Toronto said: "If the Grey Cup has come to represent Canada's Super Bowl, then Anne Murray has established herself . . . as Canada's Superstar."

Acclaim Abroad

Portia White, a Negro contralto, was one of the first young Canadian singers to win acclaim abroad. Born in Truro, Nova Scotia, around 1915, she was one of a musical family of 13 children. After a sensational 1944 Town Hall debut, she toured Canada, the United States and South America; later she studied with da Vinci at Toronto Conservatory. Miss White taught singing at Branksome Hall, Toronto, until 1963. She is one of few women photographed by Yousuf Karsh.

* * *

"Composers are not really interesting until they are dead and decomposing", says Barbara Pentland, a widely criticized and as often praised composer. "I just can't help composing."

Born in 1912, daughter of a prosperous Winnipeg family who opposed her musical career, Barbara practised piano after school, and stealthily played her $3.50 pawn shop violin in the basement. She studied composition in Paris with Cecile Gauthier.

Back in Winnipeg, composing incessantly, in 1936 she was awarded a fellowship at Juilliard Graduate School of Music in New York. In 1942 Barbara joined the Faculty of the Royal Conservatory of Music in Toronto. She was influenced greatly by John Weinzweig, professor of composition.

Barbara moved to Vancouver in 1949 and joined the music faculty of University of British Columbia, turning down tempting offers from the United States. She wrote her first symphony before she had even seen a complete symphony orchestra.

"Stark, analytical, unemotional," are descriptions aimed at her compositions. Despite this, her *Studies in Line* (1942) is used throughout Canada in student examinations. Moreover, she was the first Canadian woman to have original, serious compositions published and recorded outside Canada for international distribution. Her resignation from the University in 1963 was attributed to conflict with an imported (American) music department head.

Canadians are just beginning in music to exude vitality of creative thought which activated the arts of poetry and painting much earlier. "Art should be a public utility, like hydro," says Miss Pentland.

A Centennial Medal recognized 50 years of prolific composing.

A Touch Of Genius

Violet Balestreri Archer says that composing is a completely absorbing activity which gives her a feeling of great elation. This internationally acclaimed composer-pianist has produced voluminous quantities of work of superb quality. Her music is often a reflection of world conditions, and as a composer, she represented Canada at the first Inter-American Music Festival of Edinburgh.

Born in Montreal in 1913, she studied all orchestral instruments in order to understand composition. She obtained her Master of Music degree at Yale University. An outstanding pupil of Bela Bartok and Paul Hindemith, she made her Montreal debut as a composer-pianist in 1942 at a Sarah Fischer Concert, playing *Habitant Sketches.* Critic Thomas Archer later wrote of her works . . . " a veritable masculine strength, a loftiness of purpose, an economy of means, and a mastery of musical media. Violet Archer has a touch of genius."

In 1958-59 a Canada Council senior fellowship enabled Miss Archer to devote herself entirely to composing. Her career has been marked by important teaching positions at North Texas State University, University of Oklahoma, and, since 1962, at University of Alberta. Miss Archer received a special citation on Yale's Alumni Day in 1968, is an honorary member Sigma Alpha Iota Sorority, and her name appears in the January 1970 edition of the Blue Book (Leaders of the English-Speaking World).

Another Mood

The reflection of humanity in Violet Archer's compositions is heard again in the work of a contemporary musician entirely apart in style and mood, folk singer Joni Mitchell. A witty soprano from McLeod, Alberta, Joni earned extra money singing her way through Alberta College of Art. Her first job was at a coffee house called "Depression" and her first song, *Day After Day,* was performed at the Mariposa Folk Festival in Ontario. Today, some 60 compositions later, Joni is popular with folk buffs and hit parade fans alike. Her wistful songs such as *I've Looked at Life* have been sung by such notables as Frank Sinatra, Buffy Sainte Marie and Canada's Ian and Sylvia. When a string broke during a guitar tune-up preceding one performance, Joni gamely sang unaccompanied — a feat few would attempt. Her talents at the piano are equally strong.

Hymns

Many hymns, still beloved today, were written by women poets in Canada.

Work for the Night is Coming was created by Anna Louisa Walker, whose poems were gathered in a volume *Leaves from the Backwoods*.

Kathryn Munro, born at Crangedale, Cape Breton, was a reporter at the Nova Scotia Supreme Court. Winner of prizes for poetry, she wrote *O Thou Within Whose Sure Control*, a hymn for travellers.

Mary Suzanne Edgar read her poems and stories by the glowing campfire of her Camp Glen Bernard in Algonquin Park. The nature hymn *God, Who touchest Earth with Beauty*, is her creation.

Minnie Hallowell (Mrs. A. H. C.) Bowen, came of U.E.L. stock. An ancestor, Captain Benjamin Hallowell served under Admiral Horatio Nelson, commanding the *Swiftsure* at the Battle of the Nile. The Bowens lived in Newfoundland, Cobourg, and Sherbrooke, Quebec, where she was active in church and community work and produced two books of poetry. Her best-known poem is *Hymn for Soldiers*.

A Dedicated Teacher

After listening to Dr. Gladys Egbert's students, 13 of whom won top prizes in the 1964 Calgary Music Festival, British adjudicator James Gibb named her as "one of the world's best music teachers." Born in Winnipeg, at twelve Gladys was the youngest person and the first Canadian to win a scholarship to England's Royal Academy of the Royal College of Music.

Renouncing a promising concert career, she returned to Calgary to teach in 1921, making it known as the home of Canada's top pianists. Her students are well-known in musical circles of two continents. In 1938 she was made a Fellow of the Royal Academy of Music,

in 1965 was awarded an honorary degree by University
of Calgary and was one of the founding members of the
Federation of Canadian Music Festivals, a special Dr.
Gladys McKelvie Egbert memorial scholarship was established in her honor.

Conductors

Canada has had a few other musical women leaders. Ann Proctor was probably first woman to conduct a
band in Canada — and she played her own composition
The First Lady of the Land.

Joy Neilson, one-time member of Montreal
Women's Symphony Orchestra, became first Canadian
woman to lead a male dance band.

Flora Goulden, violinist with the Toronto Symphony Orchestra, later was concertmaster of the Ottawa
Symphony Orchestra, and has toured Europe giving violin concerts.

The Women's Opera Committee Toronto Opera
School was founded in 1946 with Dr. Ettore Mazzoleni
as principal and Dr. Herman Geiger-Torel artistic director. Mrs. Floyd S. (Jean) Chalmers was asked to establish a Women's Committee to sponsor productions.
First was Smetana's *The Bartered Bride* at Eaton Auditorium. Weary Committee women, who managed a sell-
out house for three performances, were nicknamed
"The Battered Brides." In 1948 the Royal Conservatory
Opera Company moved to the Royal Alexandra Theatre, producing major productions, then became the professional Canadian Opera Company, moving to O'Keefe
Center. The Canadian Opera Women's Committee had a
distinguished succession of presidents, including Miss
Vida Peane, Mrs. John D. Leitch, Mrs. George M. Milligan, Mrs. John M. Godfrey, and others. Mrs. Chalmers is
one of the trustees of the Floyd S. Chalmers Foundation,
established to support new ventures in the performing
arts.

Successful Tours

The Opera Company has toured several Canadian cities and holds annual Toronto Festivals. Its outstanding singers have included Louise Roy, Irene Salemka, Joanne Ivey, Elizabeth Benson Grey, Joan Hall, Sylvia Grant, Helly Sapinski, at present in Germany. Lilian Sukis with the Metropolitan Opera, Jeanette Zarou now in Dusseldorf, Heather Thomson who sings with both the Canadian Opera Company and New York Opera, Constance Fisher, resident producer, Sadler Wells Opera in London, Milla Andrew, who is with the same company and in addition sings at Covent Garden and the Glyndebourne Festival, and Lois Gyurica of the Municipal Opera, Flensburg, Germany.

* * *

Mary Morrison, wife of composer Harry Freedman, is often called a "Composer's singer" as several outstanding Canadian composers have written special music for her beautiful soprano voice. She has probably done more to popularize contemporary music in Canada than any other singer. After winning two top awards in Manitoba, she studied in Toronto on a scholarship. Her career has been a series of triumphs. An original member of both the Canadian Opera Company and the CBC Opera Company, soloist with leading symphony orchestras as well as active in radio and television, she is also a valued member of the Lyric Arts Trio. In 1968 she was awarded the Canadian Music Citation for outstanding achievement.

While Donalda and Stratas carried on the music of traditional Europe, Edith Fowke was preserving Canada's own music.

A folk song specialist for CBC, she has lectured on recreating history with folk songs and is known for her Folk Songs of Canada in 1954 and Folk Songs of Quebec in 1957.

308

Helen Creighton LL.D. devoted her life to Nova
Scotia folk music and wrote several books. Two serialized for radio were *Folk Songs of Lunenburg County*
1950, and *Bluenose Ghosts,* 1957. She was given grants
by Canada Council and the Rockefeller Foundation and
Mount Allison University granted her an LL.D. Miss
Creighton joined the National Museum staff in Ottawa
in 1940.

Louise Manny of New Brunswick, director of Old
Manse Library in Newcastle, (donated by Lord Beaverbrook) wrote *Memories* and *Ship of Kent.* She used a
recording machine to preserve folk songs of the Mirami-
chi. In 1958 she organized the annual folk festival in
Newcastle. The medal of the National Council of Jewish
Women was awarded her as New Brunswick's Outstanding Woman in 1967.

Separatist Shout

"Vive le Quebec libre!" shouted Quebec chan-
teuse Pauline Julien, as Secretary of State Pelletier
promised Canadian co-operation in building francopho-
nie, at the 1969 conference in Niamey, Niger. "You sing
better than you shout, Pauline," Mr. Pelletier replied.

The Separatist, who in 1965 refused a royal
request to sing before Queen Elizabeth in Charlottetown, organized the successful Poèmes et Chansons de
la Resistance which toured Quebec, raising funds for
legal expenses of convicted terrorists. *Les Gens de Mon
Pays* with which she ends programmes, has become her
trade mark.

* * *

Another French singer, although less political in
her expressions for her native "pays" is Monique Ley-
rac, who left school for factory work at age 13. She spent
half her pay on weekly drama lessons. She struggled
along in amateur contests and night clubs until 1950,

when she went to Paris, met actor and director Jean Dalmain, married him and began a surging career in acting and singing. Her concerts at Montreal's Place des Arts and Ottawa's National Arts Centre in the '60's have provoked standing ovations from sell-out audiences.

Work At Home

While Madame Albani was doing a superb job of public relations for Canada abroad, at home other gifted musicians were performing a vital task founding musical organizations and assisting promising artists.

The Pioneer Club was Hayden Duet Club of Hamilton, founded in 1889 by Miss Ellen Ambrose, with 10 members. By 1964, at the 75th anniversary party, membership had blossomed to more than 300. Many famous musicians have been their guests. Ladies' Morning Music Club in Montreal was founded in 1892 by Miss Mary Bell. Mrs. Arthur Leger, a later president, held salons in the European manner, which helped make Montreal an internationally recognized music center.

Sarah Fischer for many years arranged concerts to help beginners; various clubs were formed across Canada which donated music scholarships. Madame Athanase David, an accomplished musician, with her husband founded Provincial School of Fine Arts and Les Concerts Symphoniques (1934). In 1936 she organized Montreal Music Festivals, of which she was president for 20 years, inspired by Edinburgh and Berkshire Festivals.

In 1936 Miss Marjorie Agnew organized the first Sir Ernest MacMillan Fine Arts Club. They now number more than 100, combined in a federation. Since 1940 it has held an annual festival of arts.

Katharine Burrowes, a composer-educationist, organized Burrowes Piano School and Burrowes Course of Music Study. Miss Evelyn Fletcher, inventor of

Fletcher Music Method (by which students graduated according to ability) used in most conservatories, was an instructor in that method in United States and Europe, as well as Canada.

Favorable Bow

When no one applauded her first concert, violinist Kathleen Parlow almost wept. So she bowed politely, ready to leave. But the Japanese audience rose and bowed back — their traditional acknowledgement of pleasure. Her success in Japan was not the first for the 20-year old woman.

Kathleen was born in Calgary in 1890. She played in public at six, became a protégée of Lord Strathcona. Her musical education began in California and continued in England. At 14, when she played in Bechstein Hall with London Symphony Orchestra, Zimbalist and Heifetz attended. She gave a command performance for Queen Alexandra.

Kathleen went to St. Petersburg in 1906 to study with master Leopold Auer. Then the auburn-haired virtuoso who delighted audiences in European countries, played for King and Queen of Denmark and for King and Queen of Norway, who presented her with a rare violin. Other triumphal tours started in 1910 — she played with virtually every major symphony orchestra.

Because of her mother's illness Kathleen returned to Toronto, where she taught a master class at Royal Conservatory. She organized the Parlow String Quartet there. In 1956 University of Alberta's national award in music was presented to her. It honored her "... as greatest woman violinist in the world ... also for notable contribution to music in Canada."

A pianist, violinist and composer who had made her debut in Berlin at 11, was small, dark, mannish-looking Sophie Carmen Eckhardt-Gramatté. Born in

Moscow, she lived in various European capitals. At twelve she was playing in cafés to support her French mother and sister. A protégée of the Mendelssohns, in 1920 she started a series of successful triumphant European tours in piano and violin.

Her life was chequered with triumphs and tribulations. A happy marriage to Walter Gramatté was marred by neighbours' complaints about a "noisy profession" and they were poor. Stokowski heard her though and was greatly impressed. He arranged an American tour but her husband died and it was postponed.

Despite a triumphant 1930 tour, she renounced her virtuoso career to concentrate on composition. Dr. Eckhardt married her in 1934, but their criticisms of Nazis killed chances of concerts and prompted a move to Vienna. By 1943 she was producing compositions from a dark basement while her husband served as a soldier. She came to Canada when Dr. Ferdinand Eckhardt was appointed director of Winnipeg Art Gallery in 1953, a very valuable musical import.

Violinist, pianist, artist and teacher, Anne Eggleston played on a white toy piano at five. At fifteen she won her first award for Song to the Lute Player sung by Tom Kines. In 1953, Anne won two trophies at Ottawa Music Festival, later she won two scholarships. Her 15 Variations on a Theme of Bela Bartok, with violinist Gail Crossley and pianist Joan Milliken was performed in Ottawa at a concert of the Musical Arts Club, which arranged a Centennial concert of her work at the National Gallery auditorium in 1967.

Career of Promise

In 1932 a peddler sold Mrs. G. H. Grescoe, a poor Ukrainian woman, a cheap fiddle plus a correspondence course. The family's five year old daughter, Donna, two years later, was studying with Dr. George Bornoff, Winnipeg's top teacher. At eleven she won a $5,000 scholarship to American Conservatory of Music, Chicago. She was presented with a violin worth $1,000; she studied with Mischa Mischakoff (Toscanini's concertmaster). At fifteen Arthur Benjamin, adjudicator, awarded her the highest rating ever given in Winnipeg Music Festival, exclaiming: "Hats off, gentlemen — a genius!"

Proceeds of a recital sponsored by *Winnipeg Tribune* bought Donna a Michele Deconnel violin, (Venice, 1754). Winnipegers contributed to a Donna Grescoe Educational Fund, giving Donna four years' study in New York with Mishel Piastro. At 19 Donna, a lovely picture, was thrilling a capacity audience in Winnipeg Civic Auditorium.

The following February she debuted at Town Hall; a year later at Carnegie Hall concert, with Leopold Millman. Successful tours of North America under club rather than concert management were made from 1949 to 1952.

Her profits helped build churches, clubhouses, playgrounds, orphanages and old people's homes. Lyn Cook's book about her, *The Little Magic Fiddler* is required reading in primary schools.

Life of Music

Music for Winnipeg-born Zara Nelsova was part of her life. Her grandfather was an opera singer, her father a flautist. Resourceful M. Nelsova, unable to find a 'cello small enough for his daughter converted a violin into one for Zara.

At five she played to an enthusiastic crowd of 3,500 people. Success was instant. Zara studied at Herbert Walenn Violincello School in London, England. Her magnificent technique today is the result of hated hours of practise. At thirteen she made her formal debut with London Symphony Orchestra. Her teens were crowded with successful world concert tours. She played so sensationally that at one concert blood streamed down the finger board. She finished her concert and said: "After that concert, anything else is apple pie!"

Zara, female Viking type, like her playing, is vibrantly alive. She never smokes, never drinks, is never tired. She swims several times weekly. Zara loves skiing, but feels it is too dangerous.

For several years Zara was first 'cellist with Toronto Symphony Orchestra; she has toured the world in concert. Her Pietro Guarnerius 'cello, made in Venice in 1735, is her favorite. Once it crowded a VIP off a plane, proudly occupying a whole front seat, carefully strapped in with a safety belt. She spent a month in Prades, Portugal with world-renowned Spanish 'cellist Pablo Casals.

* * *

The first woman pianist from Canada to tour Europe was Anom Setab, native of Burlington, Ontario, known internationally as Mona Bates.

During World War I, Mona organized the concert group, Musical Manifesto, which raised $11,000 for war work. In later years her playing was overshadowed by inspired teaching. She trained and directed a ten-piano team of students, which included Mary Mackinnon Shore, Margaret Brown, Madeline Bone and Margaret Ross. Her star student was Virginia Belfer, born 1949 in Galt. A Toronto critic spoke of "The incredible phenomenon of a nine year-old, mature concert pianist."

* * *

Ellen Ballon, petite, world-famous pianist, was also a child prodigy. At three she had perfect pitch, at four performed Bach's Italian Concerto by ear, her first public concert. The mayor of Montreal lifted her onto the piano stool at Windsor Hall where she played a Mozart sonata. At five she was the only pianist to appear on a musical programme when Lord Minto inaugurated McGill Conservatory of Music.

Of Russian parentage, Ellen entered McGill Conservatorium on a Director's piano scholarship, at 5. She studied under Clara Lichenstein, and was McGill's youngest graduate. She studied in New York with Rafael Joseffy during the next seven years. Steinway made special wooden pedals for her — still treasured in Steinway Hall. At ten came her formal debut with New York Symphony Orchestra under Walter Damrosch.

Her tiny hands can still hardly stretch an octave. "I improvise to make up for this handicap," she explains.

A sensational success, guest appearances for her with leading orchestras followed, fitted into six years of strenuous study with Wilhelm Backhaus and Ruben Goldmark. She was the only pupil of Josef Hofmann. In 1938 she broke several bones in her small foot. In hospital, she still kept practising on a portable keyboard, determined that nothing would stop her playing. Leonard Liebling, the great critic, said: "Not since Teresa Carreno's warmblooded performances has such eager, ardent and picturesque playing been heard ..." In 1955 she received an LL.D. from McGill University. She founded the Ellen Ballon Piano Scholarship in 1928; in 1960 she organized Martlet Concert and Ball at the Ritz-Carlton to initiate a $100,000 scholarship Fund for Conservatory. For years she also arranged free lectures by internationally known musicians under McGill Faculty of Music.

Fiddles First

During Christmas celebrations in Quebec in 1645, fiddles were the first musical instruments (other than bagpipes) heard in Canada. By 1664, violins, flutes, clarinets, and organ music accompanied religious services. Ever since the first organ appeared in a parish church — Quebec, 1663 — there have been few women organists. Today there is a shortage of church musicians.

Ethel Stark

316

Exception was Mlle. Victoria Cartier (1867-1955), descendant of Jacques Cartier and of Georges Etienne Cartier. At fifteen she was organist of the church in Sorel, Quebec, also teacher of music at its college. Deeply religious, she entered the Carmelite Order — but after a physical breakdown, re-entered the world. After study in France, Mlle. Cartier gave concerts in Carnegie Hall in New York; one in St. Malo, with proceeds used to erect a monument of Jacques Cartier. After touring Canada as concert pianist, she became organist of a church in Montreal. In 1897 she opened a School of Music and was awarded "Les Palmes Academiques" by the Government of France.

* * *

A few Canadian women, including Mrs. Angus Orr of Ottawa and Catherine Palmer of Toronto, have made the organ a full-time career. When Holy Trinity Anglican Church installed a new baroque organ, Catherine gave the opening recital. In 1956 she became the first Canadian woman elected Fellow of Royal College of Organists. Muriel Gidley Spofford, organist and choir leader of Park Road Baptist Church, Toronto, was first woman president of the College (1956-57).

When violinist, Ethel Stark, in 1940 returned home to Montreal, Madge Bowen urged her to organize a women's string orchestra.

"Never!" Ethel retorted: "But a full symphony — that's a worthy objective."

For $10 the girls bought some second-hand chairs, recruited musicians, rehearsed in basements, warehouses — anywhere free. Six months later, the Montreal Women's Symphony Orchestra played to 4,000 in the Chalet atop Mount Royal, and were praised by Thomas Archer, *Montreal Gazette* music critic — "an admirably disciplined ensemble."

Ethel, born 1910, encouraged by her violinist father, studied at McGill Conservatorium with Alfred de

Seve and Saul Brandt. She was the first Canadian enrolled at Curtis Institute of Music (Philadelphia). Six years' hard study followed. She formed a women's symphonette, which gave 25 concerts between 1937 and 1940. The Montreal Women's Symphony Orchestra included amateurs and professionals. Of their many tours, the highlight came in 1947 with an enthusiastic packed house in Carnegie Hall. It was the first Canadian Symphony to play New York.

Versatile Musician

Pretty Lois Ogilvie Blanchette, born in Ottawa, is singer, violinist, composer and conductor and is now studying the harp. Probably she inherited her musical talent from her parents, as Nelson Ogilvie, former City Clerk, had a fine tenor voice, and her mother was an elocutionist. Lois received her musical education at Royal Conservatory of Music, Toronto, where she was a member of the Leslie Bell Singers. Marrying lawyer Guy Blanchette, Lois moved to Sherbrooke, Quebec. Completely bilingual, she was conductor of The Singing Girls Choir, which appeared frequently on radio and television, singing, among other numbers, Lois's *Echo Song*, one of the selections recorded by Rodeo Record in 1960. Her choir sang twice at Expo '67; earlier in April 1961 they won first prize among 200 entries in the CBC Festival of Choirs.

Trained Many

Emily Tedd, director of music for Toronto public and secondary schools, trained large school bands and choirs.

Ethel Kinley, superintendent of music in Winnipeg schools, trained junior choirs to almost perfect pitch. In one contest her Earl Grey School Choir made 99 out of 100.

318

* * *

Among successful women's musical groups must be noted the Sprigs o'Heather bagpipe band of Moose Jaw and the Macdonald Hundred Pipe band of Gaelic College (Nova Scotia).

Carlotta Fisher, Toronto composer, (*Baroque, One Perfect Rose*) writes: "Woman has helped split the atom and discover radium, she has penetrated the medical field and political world, she has taken an important place in literature and painting. In the creative art of music, she has yet to make her mark . . ."

Vancouver's Jean Coulthard is the antithesis of a musician starving in a garret. Her husband is an interior decorator, her beautiful home is a studio where she has composed more than 30 major works. She is a member of the music Faculty of UBC. Her style is more traditional than that of colleague Barbara Pentland. Among her frequently heard compositions are: *Ballad for Strings, Music on a Quiet Song* for flute and string orchestra. CBC award-winner *Quebec May* and the ballet suite *Excursion* were given world premiere by Vancouver Symphony Orchestra in 1941 and later broadcast to South America and Europe. *Sonata for Piano* in 1947 was played in Carnegie Hall.

Music has been called the highest of fine arts, one which, more than any other, ministers to human welfare and one in which Canadian women have a proud record. Zara Nelsova has some sound advice to aspiring musicians: "One should think very seriously, before making up one's mind to a professional career. Enthusiasm for the instrument is not enough. One should not enter upon such a life without a love of hard work and a willingness to devote all mental, emotional and spiritual resources to the perfection of one's art."

Chapter XII

Silent Arts

Sculpture and Painting

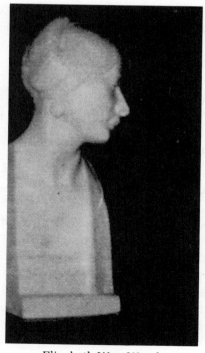

Elizabeth Wyn Wood

> *Art is the elimination of the superfluous.*
>
> (Michelangelo)

Despite the fact that one per cent of the total cost of government buildings in Canada is spent on sculptured adornments, sculpture is still the Cinderella of the arts. Materials are expensive. Trained assistants are difficult to find, and the sculptor must be physically strong. Nevertheless, Canada has produced some outstanding women sculptors. One of the most energetic is a slim blonde who works under the name of Louvin. Until 1966 she was a painter. Then she undertook a mural for the administration buildings at McGill University. The mural, fashioned in fifteen sections, each depicting one of McGill's faculties, weighs a ton and is constructed of self-curing clay which she developed. The clay is her answer to the architect's query: "How can a woman have the physical strength to cover a 32-foot wall?" She sculpted the mural by hand and then painted it.

One of Louvin's contemporaries, Maryon Kantaroff of Toronto, is establishing an international reputation. Already her work is on exhibition in London, Milan, Munich and Toronto. Maryon graduated from university in art and archaeology, specializing in architectural design. Now working in London, England, she hopes eventually to return to Toronto. "Most of my work is abstract and very modern", she says, "though I have done some portraits." She prefers to work in steel, resins and cement, using the recurring themes of love and lovers.

Sculpture preceded other arts in Canada, the earliest recording being of native Indian and Eskimo carving, and the liturgical carving introduced by the School of Art, Cap Tourmente, on the St. Lawrence River in 1620. However, sculpture did not appear in parks and galleries until the late 19th century.

Mildred Peel of London, sister of Paul Peel, R.C.A., was the first woman to decorate public buildings. She erected a series of busts of prominent men — among them Lord Dufferin, Sir John A. Macdonald, Sir Oliver Mowatt, and Sir Sandford Fleming — for the Normal School in Toronto.

Erica Deichmann and her first husband, Kjeld, found New Brunswick clay excellent for making pottery, and their Dykelands Pottery at Moss Glen became world-famous. She modelled, among other pieces, exquisite heads *Madonna Turqoise* and *Sophisticated Sophia,* and her work was displayed at the Canadian Pavilion at the New York World Fair. NFB made a 20 minute film of the Deichmann Family in 1953. Erica is now happily married to Hon. Milton Gregg.

Government Stone Carver

Tall, talented Eleanor Milne was the first woman to be appointed architectural sculptor of the Parliament Buildings in 1962. She and six stone carvers worked the graveyard shift — midnight to seven A.M. weekdays — on the limestone border fronting the foyer's second floor balcony and on a sculptured picture of Canada's development. "It's horrible working at night," she exclaimed, "but I love my work!" Consequently, this friendly artist's social life is nearly negligible.

Born in Saint John, N.B. she studied in Europe and with Sylvia Daoust in Montreal, where she also studied anatomy for a year. Very versatile, she also does gold leaf designs, stained glass windows, steel and wood engravings, oil paintings and water colors. "It was Mestrovic (with whom she studied at Syracuse University, New York) who passed on to me my love of medieval art." The NFB is making a documentary of Miss Milne's work.

Political Art Coup

Pearl Thurston, who studied at the Beaux Arts in Montreal and then with Julien in Paris, was commissioned to do eleven bronze plaques of Canadian prime ministers, and by October, 1932, eight were on exhibition at the National Archives in Ottawa. The Women's Building at the Canadian National Exhibition grounds in Toronto has an interesting relief by Frances Loring on an outside wall. She experimented with a new plastic material — permanent, water-resistant and costing only a fraction of the price of bronze which usually has to go abroad for casting. It is thought her discovery might revolutionize sculpture. Inside the same building is a modernistic mural, representing the arts, by Elizabeth Wyn Wood.

Frances Loring and Miss Wyn Wood also have work exhibited on another Toronto building. The Bank of Montreal edifice, finished in 1960, has 12 panels depicting Canadian industries, and the two women sculptors each completed two. Other women artists involved in the project were Florence Wyle and Jacobine Jones.

"Loring and Wyle"

Frances Loring and Florence Wyle — or "Loring and Wyle" as friends affectionately called them, reversed the usual trek of talent from Canada to the U.S. by settling in Toronto in 1908. They bought a small church in fashionable Rosedale and converted it into a studio which became world-renowned in art circles. They had their initial problems. Models disliked shivering, nude, in a church and could not be tempted even by a huge fireplace. And one saintly-looking man they did find to portray Christ in a memorial window, skipped out with all their portable valuables. Chickens they kept were named for the Group of Seven. However, they apparently resolved their difficulties. *War Records*, among their first works, now rests in the National Gallery and other sculptures can be seen in parks, public buildings and art galleries across Canada. Both women were represented in every major art exhibition until their deaths in 1968.

Florence Wyle was responsible for the Edith Cavell Monument in Toronto General Hospital and *The Sacrifice* — a woman kneeling disconsolately by a dead soldier. The National Gallery, the University of Toronto and the Ontario Museum all have casts of Frances Loring's bust of Sir Frederick Banting; she also won the controversial contest in 1954 for the Sir Robert Borden Monument on Parliament Hill.

At the New York World Fair in 1939, the first time Canadian sculpture was exhibited in the U.S., Dr. Loring and Miss Wyle both entered work: Dr. Loring's *Girl with Torch* and *Eskimo Mother*, now in the National Gallery, were on exhibition, together with Miss Wyle's *Cello* and *Study of a Young Girl*. Both pioneered in art movements, including the National Arts Council, the Federation of Canadian Artists and the Sculpture Society.

In 1952, Dr. Loring was awarded a doctorate of laws by the University of Alberta and in 1955 a similar honor by the University of Toronto; a year earlier she had received the university's national award "for long and distinguished service to art".

Dr. Loring, Miss Wyle — who specialized in wood carving — and Sylvia Daoust were the sculptors chosen to carve the twelve Calvert Regional Trophies for the Dominion Drama Festival, and Miss Wyle's model was chosen for the final Festival Trophy.

Rare Spirit

Elizabeth Wyn Wood seemed destined for sculpture from an early age of two. She sat in her high chair absorbed in fashioning tiny animals, figures, rocks and volcanoes from a mixture of crumbs and milk. Her mother was delighted when she discovered Hurlbut's plasticine — thereafter Elizabeth used that instead of her breakfast for modelling.

Born in 1903 in Orillia, Elizabeth was educated in Toronto and studied at the Ontario College of Art from 1921 to 1926. She financed her lessons in painting, applied art and sculpture by doing commercial art work. At college she won ten scholarships and, in 1924, the Governor-General's Medal. Robert Laurent tutored her in a postgraduate course in sculpture. In 1926 she married one of her teachers — German-born sculptor Emmanuel Hahn — more than 20 years her senior. Hahn's marriage to his star pupil caused a sensation in art circles. But the couple had great respect for each other's work, which helped compensate for the difference in age and tastes. "Mani" died in 1957.

Most original of the 20th century women sculptors, Elizabeth made innovations similar to those of the "Seven" in the painting world, using contemporary materials such as glass, tin and aluminum. Her *Passing Rain* in Orselo stone, won the Willingdon Award in 1929 and that, together with *Negress* in bronze and *Reef and Rainbow* in tin, are in the National Gallery. Her sculpture *Linda* is exhibited in Winnipeg and *Man,* modelled in tin, in Vancouver. Her later work in the traditional fields of portraits, figures and monuments included busts of former Premier Leslie Frost and Narcisse Pelletier. The Central Library in Toronto houses two arresting works — *Man and Woman* and *Old Woman reading a Book.* One of her works *Regeneration* is a heroic study of motherhood. She was well qualified to work on it — while carrying her own child, she slaved

on the granite Welland War Memorial, the biggest
commission she'd undertaken. She worked in limestone
on the fish, owl, Canada goose fountains and leaping
doe reliefs at Niagara Falls, and the Governor Simcoe
Monument at Navy Hall, Niagara-on-the-Lake. In hospital in 1965, dying of cancer, Elizabeth insisted on returning to her studio to finish some commissions.

Elizabeth taught for over 20 years at the Central
Technical School where her most famous pupil
probably was Alan Jarvis, former director of the
National Gallery.

Jacobine Jones

Another woman sculptor whose works decorate
dozens of buildings in Ontario cities is Jacobine Jones.
Born in London, England, she studied in Italy and Denmark and at the Regent Street Polytechnic in London
where she received a gold medal. She exhibited regularly at the British Royal Academy until coming to
Canada in 1932. Settling in Toronto, she since has exhibited regularly at the Royal Canadian Academy and
other Canadian exhibitions. Her stone carving of St.
Joan is in the Kelvin Museum, Glasgow, while her *Circus Pony* in bronze is displayed in the National Gallery
in Ottawa — her work *Stone Torso* is in the Hamilton
Art Gallery.

Miss Jones has done numerous portraits of children. Her portraits in bronze include those of the Hon.
George S. Henry and Dr. William Moffat. Among her
portraits of prize animals is that of a dog, commissioned
by the late Queen Maud of Norway. Her architectural
works include *Hippocrates and Students* and *Aescula-
pius and the Centaur* at Toronto General Hospital,
seven bronze figures at the Bank of Canada in Ottawa,
panels in stone at Hart House Memorial Tower, Toronto
and the South African Coat of Arms at the entrance to
the South African Embassy in Ottawa. From 1951 to

1956, she was a director of sculpture at the Ontario College of Art.

Highest Award

Hamilton-born Elizabeth Bradford Holbrook won the highest award, a gold medal, over 80 other sculptors at the 36th National Sculpture Society Show in New York. Her winning exhibit was a lifesize bronze bust of Dr. James H. Robinson, director of Crossroads Africa. Born in 1913, she studied at the Ontario College of Art and later at the Royal College of Art in London, England. She won an OCA scholarship in 1934 and the Lieutenant-Governor's Medal the following year. A versatile sculptor, she works on memorial tablets, trophies, shields and liturgical sculpture as well as busts; she also paints. She has exhibited at the CNE and art galleries in Hamilton, Toronto, London, and Montreal. Among her works exhibited in public places is a brass portrait of her father-in-law, Dr. J. Howard Holbrook, head of the former Hamilton Tuberculosis Sanatorium, which hangs in Holbrook Pavilion.

World Winner

Anne Kahane has works in major museums and universities across Canada and has exhibited in numerous exhibitions including those at the Canadian Pavilion at the Brussels World Fair, the Venice Biennale in 1958, and Expo '67. Born in 1924, she attended Cooper Union Art School, New York, from 1945 to 1947. She won a cash award for her work *Unknown Political Prisoner* in the First International Sculpture Competition in London in 1953 — she was competing with more than 3,000 other sculptors from 57 countries. In 1956, her sculpture *Ball Game,* now in the Quebec Museum, won a Grand Prix of $1,500 in the Concours Artistiques in Quebec. Five years later the Canada Council awarded her a senior fellowship.

Famous Sculptor in Wood

French-Canada's most outstanding woman sculptor, Sylvia Daoust, initially sketched and painted before turning to modelling. She studied at L'Ecole des Beaux Arts in 1929 and won first prize in the Willingdon Arts Competition for Sculpture and also a scholarship to study in France. In 1932 she embarked on a five-year tour of Belgium, Italy, Spain, Greece and Germany. She became a professor of design and modelling at the Beaux Arts in Quebec City and in 1943 was appointed professor of sculpture in wood at L'Ecole des Beaux Arts, Montreal. Her work includes bronze medals of the Lieutenant-Governors of Quebec and a bust portrait of Senator Mariana Beauchamp Jodoin, but religious statues in wood are her specialty. Her lifesized figure of Saint Michael is in St. Michael's College, Toronto. She exhibited a beautiful Madonna in Montreal in 1955 and made five of thirteen drama festival statuettes, including the special award. She is a member of the Sculptor's Society of Canada.

* * *

Another Quebecer who is well-known in the art world is Sybil Kennedy. Born in Quebec City, she studied in New York and was awarded the third Anna Wyatt Huntingdon prize for sculpture in 1941. She was exhibited at the Walker Galleries in New York, with the National Sculpture Society, New York, and the Sculpture Society of Canada.

* * *

Modernist Dora de Pedery Hunt continually experiments with new materials. Her *Head of an Artist*, a portrait of Frances Loring, was acquired by the National Gallery in 1957, and the same year a sculptured self-figure *The Dreamer* was exhibited in Toronto. She is an exponent of liturgical sculpture. Her *Stations of the Cross* in the new chapel of St. Joseph's College in Toronto proved so modernistic that they aroused inter-

328

est in Europe.

The theme of this work is religion in the noblest sense, the faith that Louis Hubedat proclaimed with his dying breath: "I believe in Michelangelo, Velasquez, and Rembrandt; in the might of design, the mystery of color, the redemption of all things by beauty."

Painting

> *Where the spirit does not work with the hand, there is no art.*
>
> (Leonardo da Vinci)

Canada, or more particularly Ottawa, owes much to painting. An exquisite watercolor by Lady Head, wife of the Governor of Canada, was responsible for the choice of Ottawa as Canada's capital. Her painting of Major Hill, overlooking the Ottawa River, so charmed Queen Victoria that she exclaimed: "That is the place!" — Ottawa became the seat of government in 1857 and Canada's capital 10 years later.

Art was a part of Queen Victoria's life. Her daughter, Princess Louise, was an artist and when she came to Canada with her husband, the Marquis of Lorne, the typical scenes she painted on vice-regal tours publicized Canada in England. While in Canada as wife of the Governor-General, she designed the statue of Queen Victoria at Montreal's Royal Victoria College. In 1880, the vice-regal couple founded the Royal Canadian Academy and National Gallery. Women were eligible for membership, but the constitution had a clause prohibiting "needle work, artificial flowers, cut paper, shell-work, models in colored wax, or any such performance". By the mid-20th century more than one-quarter of the Canadian section of the National Gallery housed the work of women painters and in 1966 the first woman director, Dr. Jean Sutherland Boggs, was appointed.

Women have helped organize art schools and

associations and in 1883 helped drawing become a compulsory subject in public schools. Mrs. Maria Morris Miller of Halifax was the first Canadian woman on record to win international fame — her work *Wild Flowers of Nova Scotia* was published in 1840 and she was granted Queen Victoria's royal patronage. In 1881 she helped establish the first Art College in Halifax.

One of her contemporaries was Mary Dignam; born Mary Ellen Williams in 1860 at Charlotteville (now Port Burwell), Ontario, she studied music and painting in New York and Paris. She married in 1880, settling in Toronto. She showed Canadian landscapes in the Colonial Exhibition in London in 1886 and the Chicago Exposition of 1893, and between 1929 and 1936 held more than 50 exhibitions. Assisting the struggling Toronto Associated Artists' School of Art and Design, she helped found the art department at McMaster University and was director of Moulton College art department from 1890 to 1902.

Twenty members attended the first meeting of the Women's Art Club at her studio in 1886. Six years later the club became the Women's Art Association of Canada, the first women's organization to be incorporated in Canada, and established the Mary E. Dignam Scholarship Fund. Mrs. Dignam was convener of arts and letters for the National Council and convener of fine and applied art on the International Council of Women. But her crowning achievement was the founding of the International Society of Women Painters and Sculptors — the oldest internationally-organized women's club in the world.

In the late 19th century Montreal felt isolated from the world's great art centres. So in 1893 Mary Phillips founded the School of Art and Design and organized art classes for children. A year later Mrs. James Peck, a daughter of Adelaide Hoodless, founded, then became president of, the Women's Art Society. The Canadian Handicrafts Guild, now the Canadian Guild of Crafts, was an offshoot of that society. One early report noted: "Our bank balance was $8.00 but we took our courage in our hands". The women held an exhibition opened by Lord Strathcona, at Morgan's Art Gallery in 1900 — the best exhibit of crafts ever shown in Montreal. It attracted 800 visitors and netted $9,000 for craftsmen and $777.00 for the Guild. Nowadays the Guild meets weekly under President Miss Alice Lighthall.

The Newfoundland Academy of Art was founded by the Shepherd family in 1949. Art pioneer Mrs. Reginald Shepherd painted under the pseudonym of Helen Parsons, and the founding of the academy climaxed the family's years of artistic activity.

Feminine Roll Call

Roll call of a few of Canada's outstanding women painters must start with Charlotte Schreiber; born in England in 1849 she illustrated Chaucer's *Red Cross Knight* and also Mrs. Browning's poem *The Rhyme of the Duchess May*. First woman elected a member of the Royal Canadian Academy, her diploma picture *The Croppy Boy*, hangs in the National Gallery.

In New Brunswick, Mrs. Paul Kane (1867-1905) collaborated with her artist husband in painting a series of Indian pictures and landscapes now in the National Gallery.

Mary Hester Reid, a Torontonian who lived from 1874 to 1921, is renowned for flower pictures. Wife of George A. Reid, president of the Academy from 1906 to 1909 and founder of the Ontario College of Art, she helped him develop Canadian art. After her death the first one-woman show in Canada was held with more than 300 of her pictures exhibited.

Florence Carlyle's best-known painting *The Tiff* first exhibited in Paris, is now owned by the Ontario government. Grandniece of Thomas Carlyle, she studied with Julien Atelier in Paris and won a silver medal for murals at the Chicago World Fair in 1893.

Mary E. Wrinch of Toronto, was art director at Bishop Strachan School and other colleges. She was elected vice-president of the Ontario Society of Artists in 1924 — the first woman officer of an established art society in Canada. She painted exquisite miniatures but is better known for art nouveau paintings such as *Dufferin Terrace*.

Pegi Nicol McLeod of Kitchener, who died in 1949, worked in both watercolor and oils. Her painting *The Log Run* won first prize in the Willingdon Art Competition in 1931.

Best Etcher

Dorothy Stevens (Mrs. de Bruno Austin) had a reputation as Canada's best etcher and also for portraits in oils as well as lifelike nudes and colorful landscapes. Second winner of the Government Travelling Scholarship, she won many other awards. Art curator Martin Baldwin said of her: "She has been a central figure in development of art in this country."

* * *

Virginia Luz, OSA, CSPWC studied at Central Technical School, Toronto, where she was the first woman to head the art department. Her work is in many Canadian Embassies abroad, London Art Museum and other galleries and collections. In addition to exhibiting at major shows, she has had One, Two and Three Man shows in London, Toronto and Hamilton.

Charm of Children

An artist who captures the engaging charm of children on canvas is Elizabeth (Mrs. Gordon) Paterson of Toronto. A graduate of the Chicago Art Institute, she studied in Italy and New York. Her miniatures of famous people include Mr. and Mrs. E. L. Ford of Detroit, Mrs. Wallace R. Campbell and Mrs. F. W. Woolworth. Her painting *The Ghetto Girl* has won several prizes.

* * *

Marion Long, OSA, RCA, is best known for her studies of Canadian workers and her outstanding street scenes and portraits. Some are in the Medical Academy of University of Toronto. She became a full Academician in 1933, the first woman to gain this honor since Charlotte Schreiber's admission 50 years earlier.

Prudence Heward (1896-1947) was a founder-member of the Canadian Group of Painters in 1933 and the Contemporary Art Society in 1939. A Montrealer, she is best-known for figure paintings such as *The Farmer's Daughter* and *Rollande*. She also painted still-life and landscapes and won the Willingdon Art Competition in 1929 with *Girl on a Hill*; that and four other oils painted by her are in the National Gallery.

Portraits of Celebrities

Lilias Torrance Newton of Montreal has portraits of Queen Elizabeth and Prince Philip hanging in the ballroom of Government House in Ottawa; she painted them in 1957. She also painted the Government House official portraits of former Governors-General Vincent Massey and Lord Alexander of Tunis. Other famous Canadians she has painted include Speakers of the House of Commons. A student of Alexander Jacovleff in Paris in the '20's, Miss Newton was a founding member of the Canadian Group of Painters and taught at the Montreal Art Association from 1934 to 1940.

* * *

Two other well-known women painters are Isabel McLaughlin who painted decorative landscapes, and Mabel May who was first winner of the $1,000 Dominion Government Travelling Scholarship established in 1915.

Montreal Leader

Ann Savage — the Montreal-born granddaughter
of A. R. Galt and grandniece of Sir Thomas and Sir
Alexander Galt — was one of the Beaver Hall Group
(eight young girls who shared a studio). The other members were Lilias Torrance Newton, Prudence Heward,
Mabel May, Norah Collier, Mabel Lickenby, Kathleen
Morris and Sarah Robertson; all became well-known
artists. When the Group of Seven expanded into the
Canadian Group of Painters, they all joined.

* * *

Ann Savage studied five years with Will Brym-
ner, then at the Minneapolis Art School. She taught art
at Baron Byng High School from 1922 to 1948. At the
instigation of Helen Bizzell and Dr. Charles Martin
(President of the Art Association), she started children's
art classes at the Montreal Museum in 1937, and also
taught for two summers at Banff. Art supervisor for
Montreal Protestant schools from 1948 to 1953, she organized the Child Art Council for teachers which became
part of the interprovincial "Education through Art" program.

A retrospective exhibition of her work was
arranged by her own pupils, headed by Alfred Pinsky
and Leah Sherman, at Sir George Williams University in
the spring of 1969; sixty of her oils were exhibited. Miss
Sherman, director of Art Education, says: "Miss Savage
taught us the meaning of creativity, of visual experience
and of art." Her paintings hang in all important galleries
in Canada and some are also in the U.S.A. and Great
Britain.

Fifth Generation Artist

Eva (Mrs. Richi) Prager, of Montreal, born in Berlin, Germany, is a fifth generation artist. She received
her art training in Europe and from her father, the
painter Joseph Oppenheimer. Mrs. Prager paints excel-

lent landscapes, seascapes, flowers and other compositions. But, "I like people", she says, and has sketched or
painted many personalities famous in the arts, science
and politics, including a full-page portrait of Prime Minister Trudeau commissioned by *Canadian Magazine*.
Exotically handsome, dark, vivacious, Eva is also
famous as a hostess, and enjoys talking with as well as
painting her interesting subjects. These include Dr. Han
Suyin, Pierre Berton, Col. Alois Podhajsky, and his Lip-
pizaner horses; Yehudi Menuhin, impresario Sol Hurok,
Celia Franca, and a laughing portrait of Dr. Vincent
Macdonald, dean of the law faculty of Dalhousie University. Best known perhaps for her charming portraits
of children of prominent Canadians and Hollywood
stars, she calls these *Motion Pictures* as she prefers
painting her little subjects at play.

Mrs. Prager's work is represented in galleries and
private collections throughout America and Europe.
Intensely interested in child welfare, she has donated
designs and reproduction rights of adorable children's
pictures to various charitable organizations including
the Canadian and English Save the Children Funds,
UNICEF, and the Unitarian Service Committee, which
have helped raise thousands of dollars. She has also
donated murals to the Montreal Children's Hospital.
Eva was particularly proud of having her work represented at Expo '67 and Terre des Hommes saying enthusiastically: "I think Expo is the eighth wonder of the
world ... it will put Canada in the forefront of all
nations."

* * *

Montrealer Ghitta Caiserman-Roth is a stocky,
smiling artist who studied at Parson's School of Design,
A.R.C.P., the Art Student's League and with Moses
Soyer in New York. Her work is in galleries across
Canada including the Vancouver Art Gallery, the
National Gallery and the Confederation Art Gallery in
Charlottetown. She has taught at Queen's University

summer school, Mount Allison summer school, and Sir George Williams University. She won the O'Keefe Award in 1950, a scholarship of $1,500 to study in Mexico, and a Canada Council senior fellowship in 1962. She was awarded a Canadian Centennial Medal in 1967 and the same year held an important exhibition in Montreal. In 1969 she completed a group of murals for the Montreal Children's Hospital.

A Bit of Beauty

Juliette Delavoye A.R.M.S., I.I.C., A.I.C. is currently Canada's only miniaturist and her ambition is to find an apprentice to train in this vanishing art. Born in 1927 in Montreal, she studied drawing and drafting evenings at Sir George Williams College while designing in the drafting room of Canadian Pacific Railways. She practised portraiture and painting in miniature with the American Society of Miniature Painters, New York City and contributed to their annual Exhibits.

First Canadian elected an Associate of Royal Society of Miniature Painters, Sculptors and Gravers of London (1953-77), her exquisite miniatures of young Princess Elizabeth and Princess Margaret were presented to King George VI and Queen Elizabeth during their 1939 royal tour. Her work is represented in the Montreal Museum of Fine Arts by a portrait of the Rt. Hon. Vincent Massey, and also in the beautiful Beaverbrook Gallery (Maritimes). Portraits on ivory of their Excellencies the Governor-General Jules Leger and Madame Leger have been acquired by the National Archives. For the Centennial of 1967 the collection of portraits in miniature on ivories of the Fathers of Confederation was financed by the patriotic generosity of Samuel and Saidye Bronfman. Currently she is painting floral emblems on porcelain, and working on several commissioned portraits, one of an author, for the National Library.

* * *

A co-founder of the Canadian Group of Painters, Yvonne McKague Housser, R.C.A., was born in Toronto in 1898 and studied at the Ontario College of Art and later in Paris and Vienna. While painting she also taught at the Ontario College of Art from 1923 to 1946, as well as several art schools. She was commissioned to paint murals for the Canadian Pacific Railway and exhibited at the Heliconian Club. Her work was in a three-man Exhibition at the Art Gallery of Toronto and a two-man show at the Museum of Fine Arts in Montreal. A member of most art societies, Yvonne Housser's Awards include a C.N.E. purchase award and the Baxter Award from the O.S.A. in 1965.

Powerful Painter

Petite Bernice (Fenwick) Martin CPE, FIAL (Life) Chairman, Presentation Print Committee, member of Society Canadian Painters, Etchers and Engravers is a very versatile artist, and her work has a man-like strength. She studied at University of Toronto, University of Calgary, Toronto Technical Schools, and Ontario College of Art and with J. W. Beatty, Frank Carmichael, and Peter C. Sheppard. An ardent sportswoman, following a heart attack her art became her vocation, and since 1930 her output has been varied and prolific, prize-winning landscapes are her specialty.

Of recent years she has also concentrated on fine art prints, etchings, engravings, and color woodcuts. Mrs. Martin's lectures and demonstrations of color block print making at the CNE Fine Art Gallery in 1968 were a popular art highlight. Bernice has held many one-man shows, and her work is in many major galleries in Canada and abroad. Bernice and her husband Langton, an artist also, and Historian and Librarian of CPE, derive inspiration from travels around the world. Their beautiful, bright studio looks out on a charming

338

Japanese garden.

Protests Moderns

Jean de Coetlagan Forbes was elected an associate of the Royal Canadian Academy in 1945 but resigned in protest of the predominance of modernistic painting in Academy exhibitions. However, she is still a member of the Ontario Institute of Painters. Born in Karachi, Pakistan the daughter of Col. E. A. Edgell and Fanny Williams, she was educated at St. Mary's Abbey, then in France and Germany. She studied art at Camberwell School of Arts and Crafts and the Southwestern Polytechnic in Chelsea. She married portrait painter Kenneth K. Forbes in 1919 and they had one daughter, June, who showed rich promise as an artist, but who died prematurely of cancer. Mrs. Forbes has designed beautiful costumes for Toronto Skating Club carnivals and is well-known for her flower paintings.

* * *

Doris McCarthy ARCA claims to be an Irish peasant at heart, though born in Calgary, was a prize-winning graduate of Ontario College of Art, Toronto in 1930. Primarily a landscape painter in oil and water color, she also does wood carving, engraving, manuscripts and illuminations. Her work is represented in major galleries and private collections. Miss McCarthy has been senior teacher of painting and history of art at Central Technical School since 1933. She served as president of the Canadian Society of Painters in Water Color; as first woman president of Ontario Society of Artists for three years; and first chairman of The Professional Artists of Canada, a federation of the seven senior societies of professional artists. She has enjoyed studying and painting all over the world, but is happiest in the home she built beside a homemade pond, on her spacious estate at awe-inspiring Scarborough Bluffs, petting her cats by the fireplace.

Controversial Cameron

Dorothy Cameron, redhead, clever, controversial, was educated in Toronto and Florence, Italy. Proprietor of "Here and Now", the first commercial art gallery dedicated to showcasing new talent, which opened in 1959, Dorothy has an "in" with the "way-out" world of art. Here Dorothy Cameron's sculpture gallery aroused much public interest. Even more so did her Exhibition entitled *Eros '65,* on the theme of love, in which seven drawings by three outstanding artists were ruled obscene by judges. After two years in the courts, Miss Cameron was fined $350.00.

Since 1966 she has worked as a free-lance art lecturer and consultant. Her first major assignment was *Sculpture '67* at Nathan Phillips City Hall Square. Dorothy Cameron is a sister of blonde television actress and commentator Anna Cameron. Dorothy is on the advisory committeee of Fine Arts of the Canada Council and the Federal Department of Public Works.

* * *

Paraskeva Clark was born in Russia in 1898, studied art there, and came to Canada in 1931. She is represented in most major Canadian art galleries, in New Zealand, and in private collections. She has had several one-man shows and was president of the Canadian Society of Painters in Watercolour in 1949. Among several prizes and awards she has received is a 1967 Centennial Medal.

Sunlight of the Spirit

Small, smiling Kenojuak's cheery optimism illuminates her work, she is probably best-known of Arctic artists. Kenojuak, her husband Johnniebou, and their five children live near Cape Dorset. Speaking of her favourite art subject, the owl, she says: "In the beginning the world was black and only the raven lived.

Then came the owl, and with him light, and things moved and men walked upright." Her "Enchanted Owl", now a collector's item, from the 1960 collection of Cape Dorset graphic art, and her "Complex of Birds" are now in the National Gallery.

Kenojuak and her husband were in Ottawa in late 1967 for a joint exhibition of their prints at the National Library. In a glittering evening gown, she attended a reception at Rideau Hall, where she received the medal of service of the Order of Canada. She was the belle of the ball.

Commissioned to do an enormous 25-panel, green and white mosaic plaster for the Canadian Pavilion at Expo '70 at Osaka, Japan, Kenojuak designed a work with a huge owl as the central motif, surrounded by symbolic interpretations of the sun, igloos, polar bears, and dog sleds. (She does her best work with radio music in the background). Recently Kenojuak has also been doing interesting work in soapstone and she and John-niebou were among a group of Eskimos invited to go to Osaka, Japan to demonstrate the art of soapstone carving at Expo '70. Kenojuak's portrait was printed by Ottawa's Joyce Devlin, and her work has caught the attention of the NFB (National Film Board).

* * *

Mackie Cryderman of London, Ontario, is not only a versatile artist but also an educator and lecturer. She was art director at the H. B. Beal Technical School, taught art at the University of Western Ontario, was on the board of trustees of the London Art Gallery and, since 1966, on the board of governors of Fanshawe College of Applied Arts and Technology. She is a painter in all media, a printmaker, and also works on ceramic murals and carving. One of her prints decorated Habitat at Expo '67 and another was at the Centennial Show at the Montreal Museum of Fine Arts. In addition to one-man shows, she has participated in countless group

exhibitions and is represented in public and private collections here and in Europe. She was named "Woman of
Achievement" in 1964 by the London Business and Professional Women's Club.

Joyous Artist

Erika Helmke Dassel of Ottawa studied to be a
concert pianist, became a successful light opera singer
in Berlin, Germany, and is now an artist. Her husband,
Herbert, also an artist, won her hand by sitting through
36 consecutive performances of Bert Brecht's *Three-
Penny Opera* in Berlin, afterwards greeting her at the
stage door with a bouquet. Herbert's opulently-colored
pictures, called "light paintings" are created without the
use of paint or brush. Erika studied art in Ottawa with
Kay Ide and Robert Hyndman. The beautiful blonde
artist now paints with youthful joie de vivre, specializing in recognizable portraits and powerful landscapes.
Her pictures have been in several exhibitions in Ottawa
and Montreal.

She Walks in Beauty

Margaret Fulton Frame Beatty was born in
Oxford, Nova Scotia, daughter of the late J. Fulton
Frame, K.C. and Mrs. Fulton Frame. For a time the family lived in Regina. Margaret was educated by a governess, then studied art in San Francisco, and exhibited at
the Royal Canadian Academy in Montreal while still in
her teens.

Accompanied by her mother, she then went to
Europe and studied art in London, Italy and Paris for
four years. John Singer Sargent encouraged Margaret to
paint portraits, and those she exhibited in the British
Empire Exhibition in London, 1924 and the Galerie de
Marsan in 1926 created a sensation, *Le Figaro* calling it
"a remarkable debut".

During the 11 years she spent in Europe, friends and acquaintances among artists, writers, and musicians of 53 nations provided many subjects, including His Grace Archbishop Germanos of Greece, Mr. Joseph Hollmann, violincellist, and King Michael of Romania (who had his barber shampoo and cut his hair before each sitting). In 1928, Margaret was presented at court. Her life-size portrait of King George V was for several years in the Canadian Embassy in Paris, then was bought by the Province of Nova Scotia. Her impressive list of portraits, remarkable for their convincing interpretation of character, also includes, among others, Mr. Justice Mellish of Halifax, Hon. W. S. Fielding, Dr. H. M. Tory and General A. G. L. MacNaughton. Favorites with everyone are character studies *The Man with the Pipe*, an Italian peasant, and *Old Austrian Woman*.

An Academician, Margaret was honored by being elected a member of the "Femmes Peintres et Sculpteurs de France". A prolific and passionate painter, she seems equally at home with oils, pastels and charcoal, and has also painted the Roman Forum, Maritime fishing huts, and exquisite flower studies. But this pretty, charming woman was also an art critic and lecturer, an active member of dramatic societies, composed lyrics for songs, and wrote a book of poetry *Phantom Caravan*. During World War II, she helped the war effort by giving concerts and art exhibitions.

Mother at Home is not only an excellent portrait of her beloved mother, for whom she was named, but also of the fascinating apartment they shared. Furnished with beautiful antiques and French tapestries, it contains such treasures as a Buddha in a 700 year-old shrine — a souvenir of Marco Polo's journeys to the Far East — and a church ikon once owned by the Russian Prince Galitzin.

Political Potpourri

Mary Brook-Smith of Winnipeg studied art with Jack Markell there. Later, in Paris in 1950, she studied art with Fernand Léger, and met Jean-Luc Pepin, who was studying politics at the Institut des Etudes Politiques. They were married in Winnipeg in 1952. Both perfectly bilingual and bicultural, their mixed marriage works beautifully. A press clipping tells us that the pretty, left-handed artist prefers her husband's old shirts to smocks as her working clothes:

While Mrs. Pepin works mainly in watercolors, she also does oils and ink washes. Paintings include landscapes, still life and figure studies. In Ottawa she studied with Henri Masson in the early '60s. Mrs. Pepin has exhibited with the Canadian Society of Painters in Watercolor, has twice won the O'Keefe Trophy in Ottawa and has had major shows at Robertson Galleries.

Prize Winning Painters

Hamilton art circles are enriched by the talents of pretty, hard-working Jaunita Le Barre Symington, daughter of portrait artist Charlotte Tutty Le Barre. Her wide-ranging interests include china painting and horticulture. She is director of Art at Appleby College in Oakville, maintains two Hamilton studios and among pupils from seven to seventy-eight years of age numbers a parade of prize winners. Works by this artist are in many galleries, institutions, and private collections as well as in every Hamilton hospital. Internationally known, she has won awards in the New England states and has spent 25 summers at art centres along the Atlantic coast. Four of her landscapes were chosen for the Golden Anniversary Exhibition of Rockport, Mass. in 1970. With daughter, Marjolaine Richardson, and granddaughter, Denise Richardson, now award-winning artists, Jaunita takes pride in four generations of Canadian painters. She is also proud of a framed parchment with names of members who contributed to buy Mrs. Symington's painting of Hamilton for presentation to the Art Gallery. Recently Mrs. Symington has been giving talks on television about painting and china painting.

* * *

Dr. Kathleen Fenwick was persuaded to join the National Gallery staff by the then director, Harry McCurry, when he met her in Europe. He started the Ottawa Gallery's print collection, and Miss Fenwick became curator of the department of Drawings and Prints. She had studied in Paris, and had developed a first-rate lecturing style. For years she was an editor of *Canadian Art Magazine,* author of numerous articles, and co-author of a book on art. Miss Fenwick was a founder member of the Ottawa Film Society, and from 1958-63 chairman of Canadian Film Awards. A member of the selection committee for Canadian art for the Brussels World Fair and director of the fine arts exhibition for Expo '67, she was awarded an LL.D. by University of Toronto. Dr. Fenwick recently retired.

Dynamic Director

The National Arts Centre will probably usher in a new era in the theatre in Canada, just as the appointment of the first woman director at the National Gallery ushered in a not-so-quiet revolution in art.

"It might imply I'm a male in a bilingual country," Jean Sutherland Boggs explained when she dropped the title "doctor" in favour of plain "Miss" on being appointed director of Ottawa's National Gallery on June 1, 1966.

Fiercely ambitious, she had applied for the job in 1959, but was passed over in favor of war artist, Dr. Charles Comfort. Her academic qualifications were excellent — B.A. in Fine Arts from the University of

Toronto, M.A. and Ph.D. from Radcliffe College, Harvard, plus 10 years of teaching experience and work on scholarly publications. But she was young — and a woman.

Jean Boggs lived for a short time in Lima, Peru, where her father was engineer for an oil company; then she attended Alma College, Cobourg, completing two years' work in one. She started the fine arts course at Toronto University at 16. By then, she had decided she was not good enough to make art her career. For two hectic years — 1962 to 1964 — she was curator of the Toronto Art Gallery where her major Picasso and Man Exhibition put both Jean Boggs and the Toronto Gallery on the artistic map. She persuaded the Gallery to buy *The Seated Woman* from the exhibition, saying in effect: "It stays or I go!" It was not merely the acquisition of an important picture but also a triumph of her belief that competent authorities and not wealthy patrons should decide on purchases. She left the Toronto Gallery in September, 1964, to be the first Steinberg Professor of Modern Art at Washington University, St. Louis.

With an annual purchase allowance of $850,000 Dr. Boggs has acquired pictures by important American artists for the National Gallery as well as the special purchase of Rembrandt's *The Tribute Money* for $364,-000. However, she encourages modern art. The French impressionist Edgar Degas is her favorite artist.

Centennial year for Dr. Boggs was a strenuous and exciting time. Besides getting accustomed to a new job and arranging many special exhibits, she gave 19 lectures, attended 20 conferences, starred in a half-hour television program and even managed to make art an "in" thing in staid, civil-service Ottawa. She has three honorary degrees to her credit.

Her work is her life. She loves the contact it gives with interesting people, and the opportunities for travel.

Her stated ambition? "I want, for the Gallery, the finest collection of Canadian art anywhere, a great collection of the art of other peoples, a great centre built around a knowledge of art . . . housed in a new building, which will be a work of art in itself."

Disappointed in her dream of a new art gallery, in 1976 Dr. Boggs resigned to become head of the Fine Arts Department at Harvard University. She was succeeded as curator of the gallery by Dr. Hsio-Yen Shih.

Charming Chatelaine

When charming "Connie" (Mrs. R.H.) Ford became a prize-winning graduate of Macdonald School for Teachers, McGill University, the prophecy for her in the class *Year Book* was that she would "become the head of a large institution." Her husband, a history teacher, was President of the Lachine Society of Regional History and the Lachine Museum Commission, when he died. Mrs. Ford's work in those and many other cultural organizations proved useful when she was appointed Director of the Lachine Museum. The continual research, artistic presentation of historical treasures, and cordial public relations are all fields in which she shines. Mrs. Ford was awarded a Centennial Medal.

Special Techniques

In specialized forms of art, Canadian women have held an important place through the years.

Yvonne Williams, Toronto, has designed stained glass windows, for universities and churches across Canada, including All Saints Cathedral in Aklavik and the chapel at St. John's Convalescent Home, Newtonbrook. She was awarded the Allied Arts Medal by the Royal Architectural Institute of Canada in 1953.

Tutzi Haspel-Sequin of Toronto works in enamels, mosaics and ceramics. She won first prize at the

1965 Canadian National Exhibition for an enamel plaque with a fish and marine motif and in 1962 she was grand prize winner for black-and-white at the Women's International Art Exhibition in Vichy, France.

Yvette Gouin, wife of Senator Leon Gouin of Montreal, is noted for her beautiful work in ceramics. When about 30, she was run over by a streetcar and told she would never walk again. During the year she had to lie flat on her back she began writing plays. By sheer determination, she finally managed to walk normally and even bear another son. Mme. Gouin spent six months in Paris studying theatre, her best known play being *La Reussité* which was produced in Paris. This remarkable woman talks on drama to clubs and literary groups and has organized a home where poverty-stricken old couples can be together.

Curtain Call

Micheline Beauchemin has acquired world acclaim for the glorious colorful $75,000 opera house curtain she created for the National Arts Centre in Ottawa. The curtain took a year to complete and had to be woven in Japan on 45-foot looms, because there was no loom large enough in Canada to handle it. A dedicated artist, she worked night and day, when necessary, "doing her own thing." Another of her striking curtain designs can be seen at Montreal's Place des Arts.

Mlle. Beauchemin studied in Paris and at l'Ecole des Beaux Arts in Montreal, where she lives. She first worked on stained glass windows in Chartres, France, where she lived in a youth hostel for 20¢ a night. Later, in Greece, she experimented with embroidery. Her tapestry idea flowered during a 15-month stay in Kyoto, Japan. Mlle. Beauchemin was responsible for a tapestry which hung in the VIP lounge of the Canadian Pavilion at the 1970 Osaka World Fair, and a modernistic one with a winter theme for the Quebec Pavilion.

* * *

Unique among Canadian artists was Indian Princess Kahasolas (Ellen Neel) of Vancouver — Canada's only woman totem pole carver. In sumer 1956 she gave a demonstration of carving at Stratford Festival. By teaching her children this skill, which she had learned from her grandfather, Charlie James, she perpetuated the oldest art in Canada.

Mildred Valley Thornton, born in Dresden, Ontario, moved west and was on the staff of the art department of Regina Collegiate, later art critic for the *Vancouver Sun*. Mrs. Thornton painted strong, colorful canvases of Indian people and ceremonies, lectured widely on this subject, and wrote *Indian Lives and Legends*. She was a Fellow of the Royal Society of Artists, London, England.

Lonely Genius

Towering above other Canadian women artists, as a Douglas Fir towers above the lesser trees of her beloved British Columbia forests, stands the figure of Emily Carr. Sculptor Elizabeth Wyn Wood said of Emily: "Working all alone, she did in the West what the Group of Seven did for Canadian art in the East." Her bold painting brought her humiliating hostility, just as the Group's stark landscapes shocked many traditionalists, bearing out Graham MacInnes' remark: "Canadians are not addicts of dancing and light wines, but of hockey and rye whiskey!"

In Victoria, one wild winter evening while the wind howled and whistled eerily outside, a chubby little girl, carefully drawing a picture of a dog on a torn brown paper bag with a charred stick pulled from the fire, was too absorbed to notice. This drawing was found among her father's papers, labelled, "By Emily, aged eight." Did he foresee her future fame?

The second youngest of Richard Carr's nine chil-

Emily Carr

dren, she was born December 13, 1871, on a night whose wildness was reflected in her nature. Always a rebel, she hated her father, although he encouraged her in art. Her formal education was at Victoria public and high schools where she was always in disgrace for drawing faces on her fingernails and aprons. She wasn't bright, but she always won the art prizes. Discovering that students learned drawing by copying the plaster casts of lips, noses and hands used by the tombstone-maker, she saved her pocket money to buy them.

At 10 she had a "studio" — a loft in a barn. There she was happy with her drawing and her pets, including a strident-voiced peacock which strutted on the roof. She had few human friends. Her older sisters' teasing that all real artists wore long beards did not deter her from her art work. Her parents died when she was fifteen and though her sisters were unsympathetic to her cause, she was determined to study art. There were no art galleries or exhibitions in Western Canada so she went to art school in San Francisco for two years, arriving there with a straw suitcase and a battered birdcage containing a canary. After her return home, visiting artists convinced her she should study in Europe. Having accumulated enough money from students' fees, she sailed for London and five years' study at the Westminster School of Art. Illness resulted in her return home and the following year, while visiting Alaska, she became greatly interested in Indians and their art. She yearned to paint them and the mighty forests she loved.

In 1910 she went again to Europe — to study at the world-famous Colarosso Academy in Paris. She had two canvases hung in the Salon d'Automne at a rebel Paris showing. On her return home her exhibition of Paris paintings was ridiculed by the conservative Victorians, including her sisters. They told her scornfully: "It is crazy to persist . . . no pupils, no sales . . . go back to your old painting." "I'd rather starve," snapped Emily. She sold pictures for $5 or less, yet today one of her works sells for around $18,000.

To earn a living then she sold pottery to tourists and turned her home into a ladies' boarding house. She wrote heartbrokenly of that time: "I never painted . . . for about fifteen years . . . ". Tragedy touched her also in the one real romance of her life. Emily had been passionately in love and engaged to a soldier, but refused to marry him before he went to war. He was killed. She never loved again.

Eventually, ethnologist Dr. Marius Barbeau of Ottawa became interested in Emily's paintings of Indian Villages and visited her in Victoria. He told National Gallery director Eric Brown about her and they borrowed 50 canvases for an exhibition of West Coast Indian Art in 1927 in Ottawa. Before that Emily had never heard of Eric Brown or the National Gallery. Some of the paintings sold but others were ruined when they were carelessly placed near the steam heat on the train. Emily never forgave those responsible.

After meeting with the Group of Seven during visits to Ottawa and Toronto, she picked up her brushes again with her old enthusiasm, "loving everything terrifically" and finally found fame at fifty-six. In her large studio, callers would stand uneasily eyeing the only chair — occupied by Emily. Suddenly she'd reach out her free hand, give a vigorous yank and a chair would descend from the ceiling. Her pets were ever present.

However, most work was done not in her studio but in a "hideous but darling old caravan trailer" in which she lived in the forest. A truck body fitted up for housekeeping, the trailer was towed into the woods, propped up and covered with a tarpaulin, in case of rain. Edythe Hembroff Scheicher, one of Emily's few friends, occasionally accompanied her on these trips. She complains of having had to undress one night outside in the rain, due to Emily's excessive modesty. A portraitist, Edythe one day insisted they paint one another! Emily agreed, muttering ill-humouredly as she painted: "How I wish you were a tree, Edythe!" Her portrait of Emily (the only one ever painted) has a strange history. Emily threw it into the garbage can, a friend rescued it, and it is in the Memorial Gallery. Edythe also wrote: *Me - A Portrait of Emily Carr.*

Though plagued by ill health after 1930, Emily still painted all day and spent the long, dark, lonely evenings writing. Westerners loved her books as much as they had scorned her paintings. Dr. B. K. Sandwell, then editor of *Saturday Night,* said of her autobiography *Growing Pains* published posthumously: "It is the finest biography, in a literary sense, ever written in Canada."

Emily Carr was awarded the bronze medal of the International Business Machine Corporation "for notable contribution to the art of the world." She established the Emily Carr Scholarship Fund to assist budding artists before she died in 1945. Her best paintings are in

352

the two Emily Carr Memorial Galleries, in the heart of the new Vancouver Art Gallery. Dr. Ira Dilworth's words "I am convinced that Emily Carr is a genius," echo the judgement of most of the world today.

Let all artists heed Emily's warning: "There's words enough, paint and brushes enough, and thought enough. The whole difficulty seems to be getting the thoughts clear enough, making them stand still long enough to be fitted with words or paint. They are so elusive . . . like wild birds singing above your head. Be careful you do not paint or write anything that is not your own."

Chapter XIII

The Power of the Pen

Writers

Catherine Parr Traill

Words are the only things that live forever.

(Sir Winston Churchill)

Canada's bicultural and bilingual elements have given the country a unique place in the world of literature. Both French and English speaking novelists, poets and journalists have contributed a wealth of writings. French-Canadian offerings are noted for their richness of prose, the best known author being Gabrielle Roy, while English-speaking Canadians can sing the praises of Lucy Maude Montgomery, world-famous for her books for young people.

Early writers to a great extent, drew on their experiences and backgrounds as immigrants in a new country. Frances Brooke was the first woman in Canada to write a novel. Her work, *The History of Emily Montague,* described the Canadian scene and was published in England in 1769; it was republished by McClelland and Stewart in 1961. Frances went to Quebec City with her chaplain husband in 1763. She found the people congenial but the climate congealing. After driving about Quebec swathed in sables, she wrote bitterly: "Genius will never mount high where faculties of the mind are benumbed half the year." In England, before her marriage, she edited a magazine, *The Old Maid.* Intimates Fanny Burney, Oliver Goldsmith, David Garrick and Samuel Johnson called her "Queen of the Bluestockings".

Convents and hospitals were understandably the favorite subject of many early factual books by women authors. Françoise Juchereau de St. Ignace published *L'Histoire de L'Hotel Dieu* in 1751, while the previous century Marie de l'Incarnation had inadvertently become an author when her son published her letters in 1677 — the letters are valuable as a historical record.

Julia Catherine Beckwith Hart was the first woman to have a book published in Canada — she was just 16 when *St. Ursula's Convent* was published in Kingston in 1824 by Hugh C. Thomson. There is a commemorative plaque honoring her in Fredericton, New Brunswick.

Literary prodigy Rosanna Mullins of Montreal, was known as the Canadian Jane Austen. At 14 she wrote for *Literary Garland* and at 16 she published her first novel, *Ida Beresford*. Her nine novels helped foster Anglo-French understanding. She later became Mrs. J. L. Leprohon.

Felicite Angers was the first French-Canadian woman to write a novel *Un Amour Vrai*, an important literary event. Laure Conan was her nom de plume. *Angeline de Montbrun* ran into two editions, and *Un Oublié* about the founding of Montreal is still popular. Original in thought, elegant in style, Monsieur l'Abbe Casgrain called her "the Canadian Eugénie de Guérin."

Other early Canadian authors include Lady Edgar who wrote *Ten Years of Upper Canada in Peace and War:* and Kathleen and Robina Lizars who co-authored *Humors of '37, Grave, Gay and Grim,* and *Rebellion Times in the Canadas* published in 1897, and *Days of the Canada Company.* Agnes Maule Machar of Kingston wrote a dozen novels, for which she designed the covers, and considerable poetry.

Prolific Mary Ann Sadlier wrote over 50 books describing the romances of Irish immigrants. Lady Macdonald, wife of Canada's first prime minister, wrote By

Car and Cow-Catcher, On a Canadian Salmon River and *On a Toboggan.*

Trail-Blazers

Two sisters, immigrants from England, penned pioneer classics under difficult conditions.

Susanna and Catherine Strickland were among six of Robert Strickland's nine children who wrote books; their inspiration was the library at Reydon Hall. The children discovered a brass-hinged ancient chest filled with quill pen and paper in the attic and set to writing, despite the fact that their mother often used their precious manuscripts as curl-papers. Catherine began selling at fifteen, when a friend took one of her manuscripts to a publisher, then gave the money to the delighted Catherine. This success inspired the others to persevere.

Her sister, Susanna, born in 1803, married Major John Moodie and Catherine — a kinswoman of Katherine Parr, sixth wife of Henry VIII — wed Thomas Traill, a fellow officer of the Major's in 1832.

Both couples subsequently migrated to Canada — but on different ships. Catherine caught cholera, then raging in Montreal, and nearly died before setting up home near Rice Lake. Milking cows terrified her, but she made a gay adventure out of rural activities — maple syrup-making, candle-making and soap-making. There were no labor-saving devices to brighten life. Water was peddled from house to house at one cent a pail, later, the first water pipes were of wood. Telephones, radios and movies were non-existent. So Catherine wrote for pleasure, informing prospective settlers about conditions in her book *Backwoods of Canada.* Over 50,000 immigrants came during the nineteenth century.

While raising nine children, Catherine wrote nine books including the *Canadian Settlers Guide* and several children's works. She was a pioneer woman botanist and her *Studies of Plant Life and Canadian Wild Flowers* make fascinating reading. She could entertain people of all ages.

Her niece, Agnes Fitzgibbon, illustrated the book with chromolithographs, coloring over 15,000 exquisite plates. She invented a stencil which was later patented.

In 1857 Catherine's husband was killed in a disastrous fire and Catherine was left almost destitute. She was given a pension from the Royal Bounty Fund and continued to write to augment her income and clothe her children. She was 93 when the *Cot and Cradle* stories appeared. She died the oldest and best-loved author in the British Empire.

Sister Susanna had an even harder time. Soon after arrival in Canada, she wrote relatives: "My feeling for Canada is closely allied to that which a condemned criminal feels for his cell." Susanna had a melancholy personality which wasn't helped on her arrival in Montreal by the sullen tolling of the deathbell.

The Moodies lived temporarily in a cattle shed until they could evict an ill-natured tenant from their home. In revenge, the tenant undermined the foundations of the house, girdled the apple trees and left a dead skunk in a cupboard. Scarcely had they settled when Major Moodie became ill with ague. The baby's nurse caught the disease, and on her son's birth Susanna wrote: "I was left to struggle through with a sick husband, sick nurse, sick child and newborn babe."

Intense cold characterized the winter of 1836 and it was then that the Moodie home caught fire. The major was away and Susanna extinguished the flames with pickle brine and snow. The next misfortune occurred when the major foolishly resigned his commission and bought worthless stocks. Existing on half-pay, their lot became worse when neighbors stole their pigs. Their staple diet was potatoes and Susanna roasted dandelion roots to make "coffee".

Susanna Moodie

When her husband — one arm practically useless from a war wound and partially paralysed — volunteered with Thomas Traill to serve against the American Rebels in 1837, Susanna understood why some pioneer women went mad. She was far away from her sister, Catherine, and too snobbish to make many friends. However, throughout her tribulations she continued writing and completed several novels. Finally she penned her most profitable work — an agonized appeal for help to the Lieutenant Governor. Subsequently, her husband was appointed paymaster for militia regiments and later sheriff.

The family moved to Belleville and Susanna began editing *Victoria Magazine*. She wrote prolifically and two of her books, *Roughing it in the Bush* and *Life in the Clearings*, are classics of pioneering. She also painted flower pictures and taught her daughter Agnes, who helped her. Before her death in 1885 she admitted: "Canada has become almost as dear to me as my native land."

Animal Advocate

Marshall Saunders, born in Milton, Nova Scotia, in 1861, became world-famous for animal stories. *Beautiful Joe*, her biography of a cruelly abused mongrel dog, sold over a million copies, was translated into 18 languages and in 1893 won a prize of $200 from the American Humane Educational Society. The author was an ardent supporter of the Society for the Prevention of Cruelty to Animals and the Anti-Vivisection Society, and among the many honors she received was a medal from the French Société Protectrice des Animaux.

Animals throughout the world have cause to be grateful to another Maritimer, Mrs. Hugh John Fleming, wife of the former premier of New Brunswick. In 1959 she established an essay contest for children, the subject being "What is being done for the protection of animals?" Next she organized Kindness Clubs which have become world-wide. In 1964 the Humane Society of the United States chose her as Woman of the Year for her humanitarian work.

Other women writers of animal stories include Mrs. Claude (Gladys) Lewis of Toronto, who wrote *Red Stallion and Black Mare* and many anthologies. Her

Joshua Doane, of Quakers' reaction to the Mackenzie Rebellion, was serialized by the CBC. Barbara May of Ottawa, former editor of *Pony Clubs Magazine,* wrote *Buckle Horse* and *The Five Circles,* and Catherine Anthony Clark whose work *The Sun Horse* was chosen "Book of the Year" by librarians in 1952.

* * *

When the clatter of horses' hooves was being replaced by the chugging of new-fangled automobiles, novelists Dora Duncan, Lily Dougall and Marion Keith were prominent on Canada's literary horizon. Between them they wrote a half dozen books about Scottish rural settlements, including *Duncan Polite.*

Somewhat discredited today, Agnes Laut also wrote books of historic interest. She was the first woman to invade mining camps in the Rockies. She also cruised the Newfoundland coast in a government mail boat, gathering material for unsigned articles. Her books include *Lords of the North* (about the Hudson Bay Company), *Pathfinders of the West, Vikings of the Pacific, Canada at the Crossroads, Romance of the Rails,* and *Heralds of Empire.*

Pearl Packard, wife of famous mystery writer Frank Packard, published *The Reluctant Pioneer,* a family historical novel, at the age of 80.

Mrs. Lena Newman authored *An Historical Almanac of Canada* with quaint illustrations, one of which was used by her publishers, McClelland and Stewart, for their 1968 Christmas card. Her book is being serialized for newspaper publication. Later she wrote *The John A. Macdonald Album.*

Green Gables Story

Lucy Maude Montgomery, author of *Anne of Green Gables* and twenty-one other books, was the modest wife of the Rev. Ewan Macdonald — so modest in fact that many visiting clergymen didn't realize she was an author. "I didn't squeak a word to anyone." Mavor Moore adapted "Anne" into an extremely popular musical.

Born Lucy Maude Montgomery in 1877 at Cavendish, Prince Edward Island, she was raised by her grandparents and pounded out bread-and-butter stories by day while writing *Anne of Green Gables* at night. By popular demand she wrote several sequels to "Anne". *Anne of Avonlea* headed a list of 50 best works of fiction issued in 1909. Her grandmother died in the winter of 1911 and that summer Lucy married Mr. Macdonald and moved to Leaskdale, Ontario.

Her "Anne" series has been translated into foreign languages, made into movies, televised by the CBC in 1959 and is known throughout the world — in Japan, for example it is favorite reading for children. Lucy grew so weary of "Anne" that she remarked privately: "If I'm to be dragged at Anne's chariot wheels the rest of my life, I'll bitterly regret having created her!"

Awarded the King's Jubilee Medal in 1935, she died in 1942 and Leaskdale has honored her with a plaque. Her birthplace, now a national shrine, is part of the national park on Prince Edward Island. Hilda M. Ridley, editor of *Canadiana*, wrote Lucy's biography.

* * *

Though Dr. John McLeish complains: "We embalm our national heroes, rather than describe them!" Canada has had some excellent biographers, including women. Isabel Skelton wrote *The Life of D'Arcy McGee* (1925); also the subject of *The Ardent Exile* for which Josephine Phelan, Toronto librarian, won two awards in 1951. Pearl McCarthy wrote a biography of Leo Smith, cellist. Clara Thomas, professor of English, York University, loves both teaching and writing, specializing in biographies, which include an article

on *Margaret Laurence* and *Ryerson of Upper Canada.*
Elsie Pomeroy gained considerable acclaim for her biography of Sir Charles G.D. Roberts and for *Marquis Wheat Saunders and His Five Sons,* and Lady Eaton, well-known philanthropist, wrote her autobiography *Memory's Wall* in 1956 primarily for her grandchildren.

A great-hearted Montreal woman combined unusual voluntary welfare work with writing. Witty, gay Bluebell Phillips and her husband, the late Rev. Gordon Phillips, Protestant chaplain of a Montreal prison, took newly-released prisoners into their home — an early sort of "half-way house". Among their strange assortment of guests have been gunmen, prostitutes and murderers. Some took advantage of their kindness, but many tried hard and did reform. One girl told Rev. Phillips however: "I'd like to go straight, but how can I? I'll go straight all right — straight to a tavern and a man, to buy me a bit of forgetfulness." Mrs. Phillips wrote their experiences in *Adopted Derelicts* in an effort to persuade others to help give such unfortunates a fresh start. Mrs. Phillips also lectures at Sir George Williams University, but still plays the organ at the prison. In between times she writes poetry, published in many magazines, and two more books *The Fair Promise* and *Something Always Turns Up.*

Proud Heritage

The late Ethel Brant Monture lived on the Six Nations Reserve established near Brantford by Chief Joseph Brant. This was fitting as she is his great-granddaughter, and wrote his biography *Joseph Brant, Mohawk.* She also collaborated with Harvey Chalmers in writing *West to the Setting Sun,* and *Famous Indians.* A well-known expert and lecturer on Indian culture, she is an acknowledged authority on Indian history and problems, and the role of her people in American civilization.

Klondike Days

Laura Beatrice Berton, mother of television personality and writer Pierre Berton, wrote *I Married the Klondike* which revealed a sharp contrast of the gold-rush days. She collaborated with her daughter on another book, *Johnny and the Klondike*. Mrs. Berton tells of Bishop Stringer, invited to an elegant formal dinner, getting lost en route in a blizzard and, ravenous, devouring his boots.

* * *

Jean A. Sweet, for many years a columnist with the Saint John *Telegraph-Journal,* and Dr. Jessie I. Lawson wrote about another part of Canada in *This Is New Brunswick.*

Sheila MacKay Russell, a registered nurse, scored a phenomenal success with *A Lamp is Heavy.* She wrote in the evenings while working for the Alberta Department of Health, and reportedly received a half-million dollars from J. Arthur Rank Company for the television and film rights. Her second book *The Living Earth* had an advance sale of 5,000 copies in England. She insists that being a successful writer-homemaker is simply "the triumph of mind over clatter!" When one prude complained that her books were obscene, sales soared.

Northward My Calling is Mary Hope's memoirs of life as a frontier nurse. The story of a Western nurse was told in *Anna and the Indians,* written in 1954 by Nan Shipley of Winnipeg, who wrote *Frances and the Crees* and six other books, all about Indians.

Constance Tompkinson, a minister's daughter from Canso, Nova Scotia penned the lively bestseller *Les Girls.* After studying drama in New York she authored 15 unsuccessful plays. However, in the 1930's she achieved instant success as a member of the Folies Bergeres in Paris. She saw the film version of her novel *Les*

Girls the night she finished her second book, *African Follies*; the film was chosen for a Royal Command Performance. Constance was following a family tradition when she began writing; her mother Grace Tompkinson, wrote several books, but didn't relate her experiences as a minister's wife, as Nancy Jones did in her humorous autobiography *For Goodness Sake*.

Dr. Wilder Penfield, famous neuro-surgeon, published *No Other Gods* in 1954. His mother had started this story of Sarah, wife of the patriarch Abraham, and when she died he finished it.

Jalna was a Winner

Readers of novels throughout the world associate Canada with the Whiteoaks Family, creation of Mazo de la Roche. The fifteen best-sellers about the Whiteoaks were written laboriously in pencilled longhand by Mazo.

Born in 1879, she was the daughter of Richmond and Alberta de la Roche and lived on a stock and fruit farm at Newmarket, Ontario. She studied art but later changed to writing. Her hard work at first resulted in many disappointments. However, fame and fortune came overnight in February 1927. *Jalna* won first prize of $10,000 in the *Atlantic Monthly* competition. Since then, millions of copies of the book in fourteen languages have been sold.

"My grandmother came from Ireland on a sailing ship," said Mazo. "Granny was the inspiration for *Jalna*. She ran away with the book."

Mazo wrote 29 books and two plays; her last book, an autobiography entitled *Ringing the Changes,* was published in 1957, four years before her death. She was awarded the Lorne Pierce Medal of the Royal Society in 1938, was the only woman member of the Arts and Letters Club, and was awarded an honorary Doctorate of Literature by the University of Toronto for her distinguished contribution to Canadian literature.

* * *

The nostalgia of the Westerner exiled in Eastern Canada was expressed by Mrs. Wilfrid (Lena) Eggleston in *Mountain Shadows*. She also created a number of amusing limericks.

Maida Parlow French, a first-rate artist as well as an author, wrote several interesting novels including *All this to Keep*, the story of her ancestral home near the Seaway, *Boughs Bend Over* and *Apples Just Don't Grow*. Her latest book is a biography of her cousin, violinist Kathleen Parlow. All of Maida's books are pure poetry in prose form.

Doris Parkin Keil of Chatham, whose interests are theatre and historical research, commuted 190 miles weekly to the University of Michigan to study history and creative writing. She is the author of many historical articles and her first book, *The Ploughboy and the Nightingale*, records the visit of Jenny Lind to Chatham.

Martha Ostenso is best-known for *Wild Geese*, published in 1925. It is the sombre, realistic story of pioneer life in Manitoba. She wrote ten books, collaborating with Sister Kenny on *And They Shall Walk*. *Wild Geese* won the Pictorial Review, Dodd-Mead Company and Famous-Player-Laskey Awards.

Katherine Hale (Mrs. John W. Garvin), born in Galt in 1878, mirrored Canadian life in poetry and prose. *Romantic Quebec* was the title of one of Blodwen Davies' fascinating books, set in the era when street lamps burned fish oil (gas wasn't introduced until 1894). Another book about Quebec, *Quebec Today*, was written by Miriam Chapin.

Lyn Harrington of Toronto has written several books, illustrated by her husband Richard, including *Stormy Summer, China and the Chinese, Greece and the Greeks, Ootook, a Young Eskimo Girl, The Polar

Regions, Covered Bridges of Central and Eastern Canada, as well as others under the name of "Evelyn Davis".

Nova Scotia was the subject of several interesting books by Clara Dennis. She also established the Eric Dennis Chair of government and political science at Acadia University in memory of a son killed at Vimy Ridge. The university conferred on her an honorary degree in 1920. She also succeeded in having the City of Halifax charter changed so that women might be elected aldermen or mayor.

Dr. Esther Clark Wright of Ottawa, also wrote several books about the Maritimes and is a well-known lecturer.

The shocks and challenges of two world wars helped to give maturity to the distaff side of Canadian writing. Books were written by Jessie L. Beattie (author of *Black Moses*), Pearl Foley, Winnifred Reeve, Isabel Paterson, Virginia Sheard, the late Dorothy Duncan (Mrs. Hugh MacLennan) also an artist, Isabel Hughes (Toronto book reviewer and novelist) and Ethel Chapman (former magazine editor). Westerner Barbara Villy Cormack wrote a newspaper story, *Local Rag* and *The House*. Margaret Duley of Newfoundland, wrote four first-rate novels including *Cold Pastoral* and *Highway to Valour*. Evelyn Stone, a war correspondent in the Far East during World War II, has written a dozen interesting novels, probably the most popular is *Quietly My Captain Waits*. Her latest book *Go Ask the River* has an Oriental setting. These are just the foundation of an impressive roster.

In *The Viking Heart* Laura Goodman Salvarson tells the story of her Icelandic forebears who settled in Western Canada. Laura, born in 1890, was descended from the last of the Viking nobles. The story was dramatized for CBC by her son, George. Laura could not speak English until she was 10, yet 30 years later her books

Dark Weavers, Confessions of an Immigrant's Daughter, and *Immortal Rock* all won Ryerson Fiction Awards. She wrote another half dozen novels and a book of poems *Wayside Glean.* In 1937 she was awarded the gold medal by the Paris Institute of Arts and Sciences "for maintaining high standards in writing".

A Doctor of Literature degree given by the University of British Columbia to Ethel Wilson was the first conferred on a woman. She wrote her first novel *Hetty Dorval,* at 57; it was followed by three others one of which, *Lilly's Story,* was filmed. Her analytical, sophisticated writing is admired in Europe and her work has been translated into many languages.

Bird-like Montrealer Sophy L. Elliott published *Pioneer Women of North America,* a valuable addition of Canadiana. The writing of it took eight years and, to illustrate it, she learned to paint; her original water colors are now in the National Archives.

Frances Shelly Wees of Stouffville, sometimes called "The Canadian Mary Roberts Rinehart", penned her first five books in bed — she was ill for years following a bad injury in childbirth. Her first novel was published in 1931 by the Mystery League and some 30 other works followed. She plans her work carefully and writes rapidly, aided by copious cups of coffee. *Under the Quiet Water,* written in just four days, was serialized by *Ladies' Home Journal.* Her crime novel *M'Lord, I am not Guilty,* was the first Canadian novel chosen by the United States Crime Club and adapted for radio and television. Another novel, *Where is Jenny Now?,* was the American Crime Club selection in 1958. Recent books include a couple of children's books and *The Last Concubine.*

Mary Leslie of Drumbo, wrote *The Cromaboo Mail Carrier* under the pen-name James Thomas Jones. It was the first Canadian whodunit. She was almost run out of town by irate neighbors for the opening paragraph; "Cromaboo is the most backward village in Canada..."

Another mystery writer, Marion Rippon, had her thriller *The Hand of Solange* published by Doubleday in 1969.

Wings of the Morning, a book reflecting her interest in science-fiction is the work of Adrienne Anderson of Ottawa.

Dynamic, dark-eyed Madge Macbeth of Ottawa, was Canadian by choice. Born in 1881, she was widowed when young and said: "It was the stinging goad of raising my sons that tied me to my desk." The first year she didn't sell a single word and had to bake cakes to pay grocery bills. But in 1921 she was a founding member of the Canadian Authors' Association and their first woman national president from 1932 to 1942. Fifty years of world travel provided her with material for lecturing and writing. Her dozen books include *Boulevard Career,* her autobiography, and *Inside Government House,* the experiences of Col. Willis O'Connor as aide-de-camp to five Governors-General.

The Campbells Came!

Confusion reigned at the Canadian Authors' convention when three "Mrs. Campbell" writers attended. A Campbell panel enabled colleagues to sort them out.

The first was Grace Campbell, born in 1895 and living near Hawkesbury. She married a clergyman and wrote about life in *The Tower and the Town. Thorn Apple Tree* and *The Higher Hill* are idylls of the Glengarry region, while she wrote *Fresh Winds Blowing* as a mother who lost two of three sons in battle.

The second Mrs. Campbell, Marjorie Freeman Campbell, now lives in Burlington. Of United Empire Loyalist stock, she wrote *Loyalist City* for Hamilton's

Centennial Celebration of 1946. Her biography, *Holbrook of the San*, describes the work of the doctor who dedicated his life to developing the largest sanitarium in the British Commonwealth. She wrote other works about the Hamilton and Niagara area as well as two poetry books, also *A Century of Crime* and *Torso, the Evelyn Dick Case*.

The last of the Campbell trio was Mrs. Marjorie Wilkins Campbell, born in Toronto in 1902. She travelled to Saskatchewan, by ox-cart and her first home was a sod shack. Writing *The Saskatchewan*, she maintained she covered as much territory as Alexander Mackenzie. Her travel book on Ontario was published in 1953 and *The Soil is Not Enough* in 1939. Her children's story *Norwesters* was enlarged into *The Northwest Company*, a book of major status. Financed by the Canada Council in 1959, she researched material for a book on William McGillivray, director of the Northwest Company. *No Compromise* is the story of Col. E. A. Baker of the Canadian National Institute for the Blind.

* * *

Jan Hilliard's *The Salt Box*, published in 1951, and Joan Walker's *Pardon My Parka* (1953) won Leacock Humor Awards. Joan was a freelance journalist and editor in England and came to Canada as a war bride. She wrote two fascinating profiles for *Flamboyant Canadians* and her novel *Repent at Leisure* won the Ryerson Fiction Award in 1957.

* * *

Mrs. Roland Michener, wife of a former Governor-General wrote *Maritain on the Nature of Man in a Christian Democracy*, published in 1955. She is also author of a book on protocol, written while her husband was Speaker of the House of Commons, to help wives of new Members of Parliament. Mrs. Michener was born Norah Evangeline Willis in Manitoba. At a young age she moved with her parents to Vancouver, B.C. Graduating from the University of British Columbia in history and economics, she went to Toronto studied and taught piano at the Royal Conservatory of Music. After her marriage she studied philosophy at the University of Toronto and the Pontifical Institute of Mediaeval Studies. She earned both her masters and doctorate degrees and also holds an honorary doctorate of letters from St. Mary's University, Halifax.

Ivory Tower Lighthouse

Evelyn Richardson's phenomenal literary success is inextricably linked with the peculiar place in which she lived — a lighthouse on Bon Portage Island, Shag Harbor. The outbreak of war in 1939 sparked her writing career. Depth charges of anti-submarine patrols rattled their windows, battered ships limped in. While awaiting the coded instructions sent to lighthouse-keepers every four hours to help coastal defense, Evelyn would jot down an autobiography titled *We Keep a Light*. Published in 1945, it won a Governor-General's Award.

Evelyn had no archives, libraries or museums available for reference. But other writers would envy her freedom from aggravating interruption by doorbell or telephone. "I'm an agony writer," she laughs, "I do a lot of revising." *Desired Haven*, published in 1952, was selected by the People's Book Club in March, 1954, and dramatized for the Ford Radio Theatre in 1952; it also won a Ryerson Fiction Award. A sequel, *No Small Tempest*, was published in 1957, and *My Other Island* in 1960. One of her daughters, Betty-Anne, married a lightkeeper at Cape Sable Island and, lacking other means of communication, mother and daughter welcomed the friendly twinkling lights. Evelyn says of her husband, Morrill: "Since I started writing, he's done the dishes. No wife could expect more!" *Living Island* was published in 1965.

Gabrielle Roy

* * *

The Susannah Stories for children were written
by Jessie Muriel Goggins (the late Mrs. Merrill Denison)
and broadcast over radio networks in North America
and Europe. The stories of her childhood in Regina as
the daughter of an RCMP officer so fascinated an American colonel she decided to commit them to paper.
Result: the successful Susannah series of 4 books — as
popular in the States as Montgomery's "Anne" books
are in Canada. By 1959 the Susannah books had gone
into 70 printings, and been translated into five foreign

languages, yet have never been published in Canada.

Canada's RCMP is still a fascinating subject, and William Kelly and his wife Norah make use of his profession in two books they wrote in collaboration: *RCMP, a Century of History 1873-1973* and *Policing in Canada*. They are also in great demand as lecturers on the subject. Norah is engaged now in writing: *I Married a Mountie*.

Lyn Cook, a children's librarian for years, wrote and directed *A Doorway in Fairyland* broadcast coast to coast. She also wrote for the *Sounds Fun* CBC program and the TV series *The Mystery Maker*. For 10 years she taught creative playmaking for the New Play Society. On the Scarborough Public Library staff, she supervises special programs for children. She has written a dozen popular children's books, including *The Brownie Handbook* for Canada's 100,000 Brownies.

The French Fact

"When I set my two feet on the pavement of Paris, I realized two things," said Gabrielle Roy, "First, that I was a writer, not an actress, second that I was French, not English." Nevertheless, she spent two years studying drama in London and Paris. She returned to Canada in 1939, settling in Montreal.

Born in St. Boniface, Manitoba, she was such a sickly baby her parents called her "Little Misery". Like all their daughters she first taught school, but saved her salary to study theatre abroad. Already she had done some writing, and Le Cercle Moliere, the drama group to which she belonged, won the French trophy twice. In Montreal, Gabrielle wrote anything that would sell for nine months each year so that she could devote the other three to work on her first novel, *Bonheur d'Occasion (The Tin Flute)*. It is the story of dreadful living conditions and deep discontent in St. Henri, a poverty-stricken industrial section of Montreal. Published in French in 1945, it was translated into English in 1947. As she sat huddled over her typewriter in a cheap boarding house one day, oblivious to everything else, she was startled by a loud knock on the door. It was a telegram telling her that *The Tin Flute* was the May 1947 selection of the United States Literary Guild. First printing would be half a million copies. Adapted for television, her books proved popular reading also.

Gabrielle has written several other successful novels but says: "People speak of a talent for writing. Talent is infinite patience, coupled with a limitless capacity for sacrifice. Creative writers are the loneliest people in the world." Married to a Belgian doctor, she is a tiny woman, with thin, wistful features. She is shy and rarely speaks in public. Once, when a literary group persuaded her to speak, they invited similar groups and then had difficulty finding a hall large enough. "Why not have the meeting in Union Station?" she suggested: "That's where I've done a lot of writing!"

She has been awarded the French Academy Medal and was the first Canadian to win the coveted Prix Femina.

She Cooks Characters

A tragedy — the death of three-year-old daughter, Lucille — left Germaine Guevremont inconsolable. Worried relatives persuaded her to become local correspondent for the *Montreal Gazette*. She protested while signing the contract: "Nothing ever happens in Sorel!" Then, while she ladled out pea soup for lunch, the church burned down — her first "scoop".

Born Germaine Grignon in Ste. Scholastique, she was handicapped by partial deafness but headed her classes at the convent. After marrying Hyacinthe Guevremont, she moved to Sorel. A reporter on *Le Courier de Sorel*, she chuckled: "I sold advertising, I scrubbed floors, I gathered news, I wrote editorials!" In 1935 the couple moved to Montreal.

"I became a reporter by accident, a novelist by necessity!" she explains. The Great Depression was on when her husband lost his job. Germaine wrote short stories for *Paysana Magazine,* glad to get $5 apiece and was secretary to La Société des Ecrivains. Besides homemaking and bringing up children, Germaine looked after her sick mother-in-law. The first thing Germaine bought for herself with her own money was a dishwasher.

Her book *En Pleine Terre* (The Full Earth), comprising twenty short stories, was published in 1942. Her next two novels, *Le Survenant* (1945) and *Marie-Didace* were published in English as *The Outlander* (Governor-General's Award, 1950). It is a saga of the Beauchemin family who settled in Sorel in 1642. Her books were also popular as television programs.

Germaine says: "When I have a novel in me, it never leaves me. When I'm cooking, I cook my characters. When I'm ironing, I iron them. But, don't think I burn the dinner or scorch the shirts, I don't!"

Mme. Guevremont was the first woman to receive an honorary degree from the University of Ottawa (1960). Her book, also published in France, won the Duvernay Prize, the French-Canadian Award, and the Sully-Oliver de Serres Prize, Paris, the first time it was awarded outside France.

Canadian Mosaic

Canada's colorful history and multi-cultural structure have inspired numerous women writers. Some have contributed sociological studies or "problem novels". *Tanya* by Christine Kristofferson concerning intermarriage with Indians; *Anastasia's Daughter* by Gale Taylor is a story of the Doukhobor way of life; *Yellow Boots* by Vera Lysenko is the story of Ukrainian immigrants in the West; and Luella Creighton, of Brooklin,

Ontario, the wife of historian Donald Creighton, wrote, as first novel, *High Bright Buggy Wheels*, the story of a girl who marries outside her Mennonite faith. Among Mrs. Creighton's other books are *Turn East, Turn West, Tecumseh*, a biography, and *The Elegant Canadians*. Text books she wrote are *Canada, Struggle for Empire* and *Canada, Trial and Triumph*, and children's books *Miss Multipenny and Miss Crumb* and *The Hitching Post*. Born in Stouffville, Mrs. Creighton, after 35 years in Toronto, now lives in Brooklin, where she also grows roses. Mrs. Edna Staebler of Kitchener combined several of her interesting articles into a book *Sauerkraut and Enterprises* about Mennonite life and customs.

Jean Beattie, in 1950, was the first woman and youngest writer to win the Ryerson Fiction Award. *Blaze of Noon* recounts her experience with Communism in New York. At fifteen she was Canada's youngest radio commentator over CKTB, St. Catharines. In 1944, Jean became assistant director of public relations for BBC in New York. *The Ultimate Thunder* came out in 1954.

Mrs. Donald (Isabel) Lebourdais wrote the highly controversial book *The Trial of Stephen Truscott*, about a youth convicted of rape and murder; she believes him innocent even though a Supreme Court decision upheld the conviction. A strange quirk is that her original publishers, McClelland and Stewart, wanted so many changes in the manuscript that she finally had it published in England, but McClelland became her Canadian distributors. Sales were fabulous. The book prompted the Supreme Court of Canada hearing for Truscott. He was paroled, under an assumed name, after 10 years in jail. Isabel's sister, the late Gwethalyn Graham of Montreal, wrote *Swiss Sonata* and *Earth and Heaven* (a plea for racial tolerance) — both won Governor-General's Awards. Her last book was *Dear Enemies*, a spirited dialogue between French-Canadian and English-Canadian women (1963), written in collaboration with Solange

Chaput-Rolland.

Beautiful social worker Adele Wiseman's first book *The Sacrifice* was seven years in preparation. It is a searching account of anti-Semitism and won an award from the National Conference of Christians and Jews for an outstanding contribution to the cause of brotherhood, a $1,000 Beta Sigma Phi Award, the Governor-General's Award, and a Canadian Foundation grant of $2,700. In England it was runner-up for the John Llewellyn Rhys Memorial Prize for the "most memorable work of any kind published in 1956."

Juvenile Books

Juvenile historical books by Marie McPhedran include *David and the White Cat, Golden North,* and *Cargoes on the Great Lakes* (Governor-General's Award-winner). She is now writing a biography of Jeanne Mance. Phyllis Lee Peterson, who has sold every short story she has written is listed in Martha Foley's 1951 collection. She wrote one juvenile book, *The Log Cabin in the Forest.*

Black Falcon, By Paddle and Stream, Red River Shadows are books petite Olive Knox wrote for children. Brought up in a manse, she used that setting for the novel, *Mrs. Minister* which was later adapted for television. Edith Lambert Sharp, Penticton, B.C. won the $1,000 Little-Brown Canadian Juvenile Award for her first work *Nkwala of the Salish.*

Mrs. Sheila Burnford, a doctor's wife from Port Arthur and a mother of three, won the Canadian Library Association's 1962 medal for the best children's book in English. Her winning work was *The Incredible Journey,* the story of a trek by three family pets determined to be reunited with their master. Mrs. Burnford was chosen Woman of the Year in Literature and Art. Her best-seller became an equally popular Walt Disney movie with thousands of North American youngsters and indeed animal lovers of all ages.

Jean Feather of Ottawa specializes in children's stories, and her *Sawtooth Harbour Boy* was published in 1973 and *The Best of Enemies* in 1974.

Prizewinners

Grace (Woodsworth) McInnis, M.P. won a Governor-General's Award for her biography of her father J. S. Woodsworth, *A Man to Remember*, while Joy Tranter's *Ploughing the Arctic* and Ross Munro's *From Gauntlet to Overlord* tied for another. Joy (Mrs. Wilton Tranter) signed this book "J. G. Tranter" and people thought the author was a man. A pocketbook edition of *Plowing the Arctic* was published in Dutch in Holland. This witty Irish-Canadian also wrote a biography *Link to the North*, short stories and poetry, translated Dr. Marius Barbeau's *Roundelays* into English. From 1958-67 she edited *Junior Red Cross Magazine*.

George C. Metcalf honors his wife with the annual "Vicky Metcalf Award," presented to writers who have written at least a half dozen inspirational books for young people. Lorrie McLaughlin was the winner in 1968. Vicky herself wrote a charming children's book *Unwanted Legacy*.

Kathleen Strange's *With The West in Her Eyes* published in 1936, won the Canadian Book Contest, and Suzanne Butler, formerly of Ottawa, had her first two books — *My Pride, My Folly* and *The Vale of Tyranny* — selected by the Doubleday Dollar Book Club.

Constance Beresford Howe, a Montrealer who lectures on writing, has authored several books. *The Unreasoning Heart* (1946) won the Intercollegiate Literary Fellowship Award of $1,200. Gladys Taylor, of Toronto, won a Ryerson Fiction Award for her first two books, *Pine Roots*, and *The King's Trees*.

Solange Chaput-Rolland, whose home is at Lac

Marois, Quebec, is the living incarnation of French Canada's cri de conscience, according to Hugh MacLennan who wrote the foreword for her *Reflections — Quebec Year One* published by Chateau Books of Montreal. Her writings make important reading for Canadians because they reflect French-Canadian views on Canadian affairs. A compassionate woman, she is an articulate journalist, broadcaster, lecturer and author. She collaborated with Gwethalyn Graham in writing the best-seller *Dear Enemies* and was named "Woman of the Year" in 1967 for her book *My Country Canada, or Quebec?* Mrs. Rolland spent six months travelling across Canada unsuccessfully trying to find a common denominator between French and English-speaking Canadians. Her books tell why.

A Detestable Mess?

"Possibly a genius" is the way U.S. critic Edmund Wilson describes Marie-Claire Blais, who says she writes out of an accumulation of suffering. Wilson got her a fellowship to work in the United States, and she now lives quietly in Cape Cod. Born 1940, by the time she was 18 she had written six novels, 12 plays and hundreds of poems, and had appealed to the Canada Council for help. Not hearing from the council she went to its offices to show her entire output. Very Rev. Georges-Henri Levesque called them stories of "utterly unpublishable relationships between human monsters," and told her to return with a simpler story. Two weeks later she brought him a new novel *La Belle Bête* which, when published in 1959, sold over 5,000 copies and brought her instant fame. It was certainly the most sensational book produced by French-Canada in decades, though the Jesuit magazine *Relations* penned it "a detestable mess." Her second novel *Tête Blanche* was called depraved.

In 1966 she won France's coveted Prix Medicis

for her internationally acclaimed *Une saison dans la vie d'Emmanuel,* and in 1969, she was given the Governor-General's Award for her seventh novel *Manuscripts de Pauline Archange.* Her plays have been produced over the CBC French network.

Marie-Claire — a round-faced, soft-spoken woman — was born in Quebec City, one of five children. While working as a typist, she wrote every evening for years. She composed her first poem at the age of six and her first book at fifteen. Mlle. Jeanne Lapointe says: "She writes by instinct, mostly about children exposed to cruelty and violence." Marie-Claire admits: "My characters grip my vitals so tightly that sometimes I think I shall die from giving birth to them."

Addicted To Writing

Margaret Laurence says: "Writing is an addiction with me . . . a novel demands everything I have and more." Writing children's books, she says, is pure pleasure, but writing novels is pure hell. Alfred Knopf, the American publisher, brought out three of her novels on the same day. Most have Canadian settings. *A Jest of God,* as the movie *Rachel, Rachel,* was a four-time nominee for a Hollywood Academy Award. This novel, along with *The Stone Angel,* has been translated into several other languages. Her latest novel *The Fire Dwellers* was serialized by *Ladies Home Journal.* Other books include *This Side Jordan, The Prophet's Camel Bell, The Tomorrow-Tamer* and *Long Drums and Cannons.* A volume of stories and a children's book were published in 1970. Her book *The Diviners* has been banned in some schools though it won a Governor-General's Award.

Margaret was born in Neepawa, Manitoba, in 1926, and graduated from University of Manitoba in 1947. She is passionately devoted to her husband, John, a civil engineer, daughter Jocelyn and son David. Her husband's profession has taken the family to England,

Somaliland and Ghana, providing Margaret with inspiration for writing; she also has written countless articles and short stories. Alternately elated and depressed, she is intensely emotional and deeply compassionate — qualities which give great vitality to her work. She won the Beta Sigma Phi First Novel Award in 1961, the President's Medal from the University of Western Ontario in 1961, 1962 and 1963, was made a Fellow of United College in 1966, and won the Governor-General's Medal in 1967. Mrs. Laurence accepted a post as writer-in-residence at University of Toronto for the winter of 1969-70. She was voted the most newsworthy woman in Literature, Art and Education in 1975. Mount Allison University conferred an honorary degree on Margaret Laurence in 1975.

The Fourth Estate

> *Once the itch of writing has seized a woman, nothing will cure it but the scratching of a pen.*
>
> (Anon)

Even as early as 1752 women were active in the field of journalism. Elizabeth Bushell was her father's mainstay at that time on the *Halifax Gazette*. An expert compositor, she set type by hand for him and inked and operated the printing press, each sheet being fed and drawn by hand.

Another Elizabeth, Elizabeth Draper, arrived in Halifax soon after the American Revolution, having won fame for her *Boston Newsletter*. Foundations set by her were carried on by her nephew, John Howe, the King's Printer and progenitor of the famed C. D. Howe family of the Maritimes. The family is known for its journalists and parliamentarians.

Resourceful Madame Fleury Mesplet made her contribution to early journalism in Montreal. Printing presses were banned throughout the French regime. In March 1776, Benjamin Franklin (founder of Canada's postal system in 1763, for King George III) and the French printer Fleury Mesplet and Madame Mesplet entered the city. The men planned to print pamphlets inciting the populace to join the American rebels. En route, during a bad storm at sea, precious papers and clothes had been washed overboard but Mesplet managed to salvage his hand-powered press, type and rolls of wallpaper. Mesplet set up a small printing shop on la rue Capitale but when the British recaptured Montreal

from the Rebels he was thrown into jail — both he and
his foreign money were regarded with suspicion. Penniless, Madame Mesplet promised to print a devotional
book for the St. Sulpice Order. She printed on the white
side of the wallpaper and used the flowered side for
covers. Illustrations were from wood blocks she had
drawn and carved. Fleury helped her finish the book
when he was released from jail, and it is now treasured
in the Toronto Library.

In 1776 Fleury founded the *Gazette* Printing Company and two years later, published the first hymns
printed in Canada — *Le Cantique Marseilles*. Working
by candlelight he published in French the first issue of
The Gazette, Montreal's first newspaper on June 3, 1778.
The Gazette became bilingual in 1785.

Power of The Press

The press, the greatest power in public life, has
served as both an informational and civilizing influence.
During the Crimean conflict it was the revelations of a
war correspondent about the scandalous state of the
wounded and dying soldiers that motivated Florence
Nightingale to initiate modern nursing.

Canadian Kit Coleman was the world's first
woman war correspondent. Her report during the Spanish-American war that there were no doctors or medi-
cines for wounded and malaria-stricken soldiers on the
transport ship *Comal* resulted in improved modern
military nursing. Dynamic, red-haired Kit was born in
Castle Blakeney, Ireland, in 1864. She was educated in
France, married at 16 and a penniless widow at 20. In
1884 she emigrated to Canada and in Toronto married
Edward Watkins. They had two children before he died
and Kit, again a penniless widow, was forced to find
work.

She met E. E. Sheppard, founder of *Saturday Night*, who persuaded her to write. Her articles intrigued Christopher Bunting, owner of *The Mail*, and he offered her a position on the paper in 1889. Kit became the first woman columnist of a paper — until then newspapers had had no regular women columnists or editors. Her first column, written in longhand was a 20-foot strip of items, but it proved interesting. Her "Women's Kingdom" soon became the paper's most popular feature.

She spent several months in England in 1892, writing of places made famous by Charles Dickens, and in 1893 covered the World's Fair in Chicago. In 1896 she was in London for Queen Victoria's Jubilee and accompanied Sir Wilfrid and Lady Laurier to a party at Buckingham Palace. Her articles were later published in a book *To London for the Jubilee*.

She charmed her editor, her fiancé (Dr. Theobald Coleman) and Russell Alger, U.S. Secretary of War, into allowing her to cover the 1898 Spanish-American War. She wrote rapidly and seemed oblivious of fatigue as a lone woman among 135 men whose consensus was "She's hot stuff!" Kit saw and reported the battle and surrender of Santiago to Shafter's army which most of the men missed. But when General Alger offered to sponsor her on a speaking tour, she replied angrily: "If I tell the women of the North American Continent what I have seen you will have a riot on your hands!"

She and thirteen other newspaperwomen, en route home in 1904 from covering the St. Louis Exposition, organized the Canadian Women's Press Club. Kit was first president. Fifty years later there were fifteen branches with a membership of over 600. In 1930 it became a member of the Imperial Press Union and in 1935 established annual members' memorial awards. Kit's closest colleague in founding the CWPC was Kate Simpson Hayes who succeeded her as president. For several years Mrs. Hayes edited the women's page of the *Winnipeg Free Press.* Her book, *Prairie Pot Pourri,* was the first written and published in the Northwest Territories.

After marrying Dr. Coleman, Kit moved to Hamilton and resigned in rage from her paper after being asked to write an additional front-page column for the same weekly salary of $35 — a salary which hadn't changed in the twenty years she had been writing her weekly page. She capitalized on her phenomenal popularity to write "Kit's Column" which she sold to a dozen papers at $5 apiece. She died suddenly in May, 1915. Mabel Burkholder wrote her biography and the Canadian Women's Press Club, Hamilton branch, awards an annual scholarship in Kit's honor.

* * *

Margaret Ecker Francis was Kit's modern counterpart. She was the only fully-accredited Canadian woman war correspondent overseas during World War II, and was the only woman present at the announcement of the German surrender by Gen. Dwight Eisenhower in a small, hot room in enemy territory. She had been one of the fifteen representatives of the world's press and radio summoned by the general. Mrs. Francis won the CWPC award in 1944, 1946 and 1947.

* * *

Elmina Atkinson (Mrs. J. E.) writing under the pen name "Madge Merton" was a pioneer woman journalist. She was on the staff of *Saturday Night,* later on the *Toronto Globe,* was women's editor of the *Montreal Herald,* then the women's page of the *Toronto Star.* The London Bookman prize was awarded her in 1915 for the poem *Green Gauntlet.* In 1892 she married Joseph E. Atkinson, and they had two children, Joseph Jr. and Ruth.

* * *

Today, thanks to pioneers, women fill an important niche on almost every newspaper throughout the land. More than 600 journalists do an indispensable job in social news, childcare, features, book reviews, cookery columns, general reporting, fashions and political news.

Among the pioneer political reporters is Mrs. Genevieve Lipsett Skinner. Graduating from the University of Manitoba, she studied law and then became a newspaperwoman. Gaining newspaper experience in Winnipeg and at the *Montreal Star,* she eventually joined Ottawa's Parliamentary Press Gallery.

Brilliant, beautiful Evelyn Tufts, born in Wolfville, Nova Scotia joined the Parliamentary Press Gallery in 1936 as political correspondent for the *Halifax Chronicle-Herald.* She championed Nova Scotia miners and fishermen, and had, earlier, covered the kidnapping of the Lindbergh baby, the subsequent Bruno Richard Hauptmann trial, and an Arctic murder case. Later, in London, England, she covered the murder trial of Reginald Christie, a modern "Bluebeard." More pleasant assignments included coverage of a royal Coronation and an Imperial Conference. Internationally known for clever, perceptive writing, Evelyn was equally famous for ultra-feminine hats and her effervescent personality. On her retirement she was the first woman to become an honorary member of the Parliamentary Press Gallery — thus she joined an exclusive illustrious company — Dr. Arthur Beauchesne, Senator Charles Bishop, Sir Winston Churchill, Arthur Ford and former Governors-General Vincent Massey and Viscount Alexander.

Helen Bannerman of Owen Sound, was the third woman to become a member of the Gallery, serving in 1946 and 1947. She spent a year in New York as staff-writer with *Canadian Press,* doing interviews, stories about the United Nations and a movie column. In Bermuda she met and married Richard Brimmell. Since then, now living in Guelph, she has tried painting, and has had pictures in several exhibitions. Helen is now Women's Editor of the Guelph *Mercury.*

Other Gallery members included: Kay Rex, formerly with *Canadian Press;* Tania Long Daniell, member of the husband-wife team which operated the *New York Times'* Ottawa bureau from the mid-fifties till the mid-sixties; Françoise Côte, representing Ottawa's *Le Droit* from 1957 to 1958; Ruth Campbell, Ottawa correspondent for St. John's, Newfoundland, papers; Frances Russell, *United Press International* representative from 1965-66; Brenda Large for *Canadian Press;* Joyce Fairburn of *FB Publication;* Joan Munn, representative of the *Canadian-American News Service;* and Ellen Neufeld, for the *Winnipeg Free Press* during the late 1950's.

A Person Without Peer

Warm-hearted Judith Robinson, who lived from 1899 to 1961, followed in the journalistic footsteps of her father, John R. "Black Jack" Robinson. Black Jack, a fearless crusader, was for 40 years editor of *The Toronto Telegram.* Colleagues said he wrote "not with ink, but with vitriol!"

A delicate child, Judith lacked formal education but was always an avid reader. She became a brilliant, dedicated writer with fierce convictions. Her reporting for the *Globe and Mail,* beginning in 1929, was interspersed with freelancing. During World War II, her courageous controversial column appeared in *News,* a weekly founded by Judith with the purpose of increasing Canada's war effort. In 1953 Judith started writing an influential political column for the *Toronto Telegram.* She was an ever-present member of the Ottawa Press Gallery. L. L. Golden once said: "It is not easy for a person as gentle as Judith to cut public men to pieces. It was done to serve a purpose, a purpose of *News'* beliefs." *Telegram* colleagues called her "The Public Conscience".

Judith also wrote *Tom Cullen of Baltimore* (a biography of a doctor) and *As We Came By*, a lively travel book. She edited John Farthey's *Freedom Wears a Crown* and in 1957 published *This is on the House*, a collection of her *Telegram* articles about Parliament. In 1954 she won the National Newspaper Award for spot news and was also awarded the Free French Commemorative Medal.

Roving, Ruthless Reporter

Jessie MacTaggart was born in 1904 in Toronto and was one of Canada's most competent women journalists. Jessie went to New York, met Harold Denny, the top foreign correspondent for the New York Times, and helped to write a book of Nicaraguan insurrection. This won her a job! She returned to Toronto in 1929 and joined the *Mail and Empire*. She would cover the police beat or go to the morgue to get a story, and wrote superbly. In 1935, near London, there was a terrible train wreck in which her father, engineer Malcolm MacTaggart, was critically injured. Jessie insisted the rest of the family drive to the hospital while she covered the story. Her father died.

Jessie married Henry Geissler of Tacoma and moved to the United States. During World War II, she was bureau chief for *Associated Press* at Tacoma, Seattle and when the Japanese shelled Estevan Point (near Vancouver) in 1942, the *Toronto Star* asked her to get the story out on a one-wire telegraph line which kept breaking down. She scooped everyone! The Geisslers moved to Toronto in 1957, and Jessie became women's editor for the short-lived *Sunday Telegram*. She joined the J. Walter Thompson Advertising Agency in 1960.

* * *

Although having little formal education, Bride

Broder of Picton was nevertheless an outstanding news-paperwoman on the *Globe and Mail*. Her Homemaker column, continued from 1944 to 1954 by Mrs. Mona Pur-ser, rated second in popularity; it was beaten only by J.V. McAree's column. Bride had great sympathy for the unfortunate and advised them on their problems.

Under the pseudonym "Cornelia" clever Lucy Doyle from about 1910 on, critic of the *Toronto Tele-gram*, stumped around Toronto with her cane, covered several royal tours, and wrote a book about the Prince of Wales. Later she also wrote one about Scarborough, where, thanks to the generosity of the Spencer Clarks, she lived in the Pioneer Cottage at beautiful Guild of All Arts.

Ottawa Journal columnist Alixe Carter has been a selling journalist since her teenage years in Calgary. She has won two national awards, the Canadian Women's Press Club memorial award 1956 for women newswriters, and the Media Club of Canada award in 1975 for columnists. Mrs. Carter has been a CBC direc-tor on the board, a British Columbia school trustee, a national director of the Canadian Women's Press Club and is past chairman of the Media Club of Canada, Ottawa branch. She represents women journalists in the Zonta Club of Ottawa. She is the mother of three chil-dren: Nancy, an elementary school teacher; Cpl. C.B. Carter, RCMP, and Rudi Carter, a producer with CBC Newsmagazine.

Jean Love Galloway (Mrs. Strome) took her B.A. at University of Toronto (Victoria College) in 1939 and Ontario College of Education with a specialist's certifi-cate in educational counselling and vocational guidance. She was on the *Varsity* newspaper staff, did special assignments for *Toronto Daily Star* and directed an extension course in journalism at Toronto YWCA.

During World War II Jean was press representa-tive of the Wartime Prices and Trade Board for Toronto and Central Ontario. She later headed her own publicity bureau. She wrote a paperback *Play for Pre-Schoolers* published by National Health and Welfare and edited the St. John Ambulance book *Child Care.*

Jean is a past president of the Toronto Women's Press Club and the Ottawa Media Club. She is a camerawoman and feature writer for the *Canadian Press Wire Service.*

Seller of Style

Top fashion editor Lillian Foster, born in Owen Sound, joined the *Toronto Telegram* in 1916, replacing a soldier. She wrote daily personality sketches of big businessmen. In 1930, blessed with an instinctive flair for style, she switched to the women's department.

After 40 years successful writing, Lillian could well afford mink but still looked like a fugitive from a rummage sale. However, she was the only Canadian journalist so popular that her colleagues gave her a dinner at the Royal York Hotel, plus a trip to Europe.

Prizewinners

Marie Moreau of the *Vancouver Province*, herself a fashion-plate, dyed her jet-black hair a platinum blonde so that she could write: *"What's It Like to Be a Blonde."* In 1961 she won first prize of $100 and a medal for her eye-witness report of the Cuban Revolt, in the annual CWPC contest.

To Maggie Grant's afficionados, who eagerly read *first* her delightfully humorous column in the *Canadian Magazine,* it will come as no surprise that the (then) Prince of Wales chose her as his "favorite dancing partner" on a Transatlantic crossing at the tender age of 14! This hit the headlines. Born Margaret Parker, in Toronto, in 1908, she claims to be uneducated, because school bored her. Maggie was married first at 19, which resulted in two sons and seven grandchildren! Life for

Maggie (writing, that is), began at 40, and for 10 years she produced a hilarious column for the *Globe and Mail,* thrice winning the CWPC Award. Clarke Irwin published these columns in book form. Since 1965 she has been brightening up the *Canadian Magazine.* Surely no one but our Maggie would live in a spacious converted pickle factory, or spend her second honeymoon (with newspaperman Frank MacEwan) baby-sitting two grandchildren!

Another prize-winning newswoman, Simma Holt of the *Vancouver Sun,* received a certificate of merit in the 1960 Bowater Awards for Journalism for a *Sun* series on the problems of unwed mothers. Her powerful book about the Doukhobors, *Terror in the Name of God,* further enhanced her reputation as a probing writer.

Blue Pencils

Armed with "blue" pencils, women have been editing newspapers, magazines and books in Canada for over a century.

Maritime pioneer poets Mary and Sarah Herbert of Halifax published *The Ladies' Acadian Newspaper* in 1851. In 1890, Mrs. William Lawson of Preston, Nova Scotia, edited a Halifax monthly magazine. Fifteen years later Mrs. Jean Fielding and Miss Antoinette Forbes jointly bought the *Windsor Tribune* and slaved to make it a success. Mrs. Fielding was elected a member of the Windsor Board of Trade, the first woman in North America to hold such a position. In 1957 Mrs. Edith Wallis, editor and publisher of the *Digby Courier,* became the first woman president of the Nova Scotia Weekly Newspaper Association. Then, in 1969, Mrs. Evelyn Rogers, editor and publisher of the *Athabasca Echo,* was the first woman elected president of the Alberta Weekly Newspaper Association.

Another first was scored by Madame Raoul Dandurand under the nom de plume "Josette". She founded and edited *Le Coin de Feu,* the first women's literary review in the Dominion, in 1892 in Quebec province. An eloquent speaker known as "The Female Laurier", she was the first Canadian woman elected a member of the French Academy. Vice-president of the National Council of Women, her community service was recognized in 1930 when she was appointed a Canadian government commissioner to the Paris Exposition.

Mrs. Annie Matthewson also scored a number of firsts. She worked 50 years on the *Daily Gleaner,* Fredericton, New Brunswick, first running errands and feeding paper into the manually-operated press and then becoming a reporter. In 1940 she was appointed the first woman city editor in Canada. For her community welfare work, she was made a Freeman of Fredericton, the first woman member of the Elks Order of North America and the first woman Boy Scout (she had organized the boy scout movement in New Brunswick). For service in World War II, she was awarded the O.B.E.

The World's Greatest Soothsayer

E. Cora Hind, beloved of western farmers, achieved her life's ambition when she became the first woman agricultural editor of a newspaper in North America. That was in 1909 when John W. Dafoe, newly-appointed editor of the *Winnipeg Free Press,* asked her to join his staff. She was to be acknowledged as Canada's most outstanding agricultural editor.

Born in 1861 in Toronto, Cora was orphaned early and was brought up by her Aunt Alice and her grandfather on his farm. After graduating from high school in Orillia, she went with her aunt to Winnipeg in 1882. Her aunt did dressmaking while Cora tried to break into the newspaper field. Indians and buffalo still roamed the prairies, and pails of water were delivered by ox-cart. A favorite pastime of young people was riding the horse-drawn street cars. Sometimes a band was provided.

Dr. Cora Hind

Applying to the *Free Press* for a job, Cora got a snort and a wave of dismissal. Undaunted, she nearly wore out two fingers practising on a new-fangled machine, the typewriter. "God guide my fingers!" she prayed when asked to demonstrate her new-found skill. She obtained a job with a law firm and by 1897 had saved enough to set herself up in business as the first public stenographer west of the Great Lakes. She was also writing agricultural articles which she insisted on signing "E. Cora Hind" to let people know a *woman* had written them.

In 1898 Cora made her first estimate of the Western Canadian wheat crop at the request of MacLean-Hunter Publishing. Cora disagreed with an American expert crop estimator who predicted only 35,000,000 bushels. Relying on childhood memories, she predicted between 50,000,000 and 55,000,000 bushels. The crop was almost 55,000,000. That was the first scoop for "The Crop Woman". Her phenomenal predictions, more accurate than either provincial or dominion estimates, were relayed all over the world and were anxiously awaited by dealers and grain speculators. Cora could have made a fortune by giving tips to speculators but never considered the idea. A Danish newspaper termed her "The World's Greatest Soothsayer". When Black Rust attacked western wheat in 1904, Eastern firms refused shipments of needed supplies for fear that farmers would be ruined. Cora's prediction of 55,000,000 bushels, which later proved accurate, induced resumption of normal trading. That same year she was the President of the Canadian Women's Press Club.

She was secretary of the Dairy Association and was a familiar figure at fall fairs, agricultural meetings and conventions, listening eagerly but never missing a stitch of her precious knitting. Her writing was terse and forceful and, before she was appointed to the staff, the *Free Press* eagerly bought her reports.

Cora loved cattle and in 1916 was presented with a purse of $1,300 by the Western Canada Livestock

Union. Two years later the wool growers presented her with a flock of sheep. One year she was accorded a unique honor — she was asked to open the Royal Winnipeg Fair. In 1922, the Canadian government sent her to London to persuade the British to lift the embargo on Canadian cattle — an embargo that spelled ruin for many western breeders. She succeeded where others had failed.

Cora had a waspish temper at times and both her speech and writing could be vitriolic. She made some enemies who called her "Calamity Cora" when she predicted poor crops; they said her method was "to march into a field, spin around three times with her eyes shut, and grab a stalk of wheat." In reality she climbed through barbed-wire fences, waded across muddy fields, tested wheat kernels with her teeth for hardness and chewed straw. She gave generously to charity, saying, "I have never forgotten what it is to be . . . down to one's last nickel." One admirer called her: "A battle axe with a heart of gold." Climax of her career was a two-year trip around the world from 1935 to 1937. A member of a roving commission, she visited 27 wheat-growing countries.

First woman to be given an honorary LL.D. by the University of Manitoba, she died in 1942. In her honor two scholarships in agricultural research were established. In 1948 she was one of three pioneers elected to the Manitoba Hall of Fame. Kennethe Haig, her colleague on the *Free Press*, was the first woman sent to a League of Nations Conference in Geneva by the Canadian Press. And it was she who wrote an exciting biography of Cora entitled *Brave Harvest*.

Literary Pioneer

Violet McNaughton says the West was opened up on hardship and hope. And she should know. As bride in 1910, her first home was a sod shack, cool in summer but cosy in winter. Grain was stored in her bedroom and once the roof leaked so badly that she and her husband went to bed under an umbrella. The well water was brown and very hard, so often skim milk was used to launder clothes. The first snowfall signalled a washing spree — using soft soap made from fat left from butchering and lye.

In 1914 Mrs. McNaughton was elected president of the women's section of the Saskatchewan Grain Growers' Association and the following year she drove a horse (harnessed with binder twine) and buggy all over the district getting signatures for a petition for women's suffrage.

Violet McNaughton became women's editor of the *Prairie Farmer,* Winnipeg in 1916, and from 1925 to 1950 was women's editor of the *Western Producer* in Saskatoon. She was appointed first president of the women's section of the Canadian Council of Agriculture in 1918. She helped build hospitals and libraries, form old age pensioners' Friendship Clubs and establish women's hostels throughout the country. In 1929 she went to the Prague Conference of the Women's International League for Peace and Freedom, then to the League of Nations Assembly. She was a delegate to the A.C.C.W. convention in 1956 in Copenhagen. Awarded the M.B.E. in 1934, she received an honorary LL.D. in 1951 from the University of Saskatchewan for "service to practical agriculture".

"Ma" Murray

Margaret Lally went west to "snare a handsome cowboy". Instead she married George Murray, a newspaperman and later Member of Parliament. Starting out as "office boy", Margaret rose to become George's secretary; he married her rather than lose her services. Of their paper, the racy *Alaska Highway News,* she admits: "It is a mess of misplaced metaphors and dangling participles but we've never yet lost a subscriber, except by death."

She turned down a $50,000 offer to keep the paper in the family. An ancient press outside Ma's office was used to print Robert Service's poems. Her daughter, Georgina Keddall, wrote a biography called *The Newspapering Murrays*.

* * *

Violet Pratt, widow of poet Dr. E. J. Pratt, was for 26 years editor of *World Friends*, the Women's Missionary Society children's publication. She published an anthology of her best writing, including a children's hymn, and wrote *Famous Doctors* for the Clarke-Irwin Canadian Portrait Series. Her artist daughter, Claire, was an editor for McClelland and Stewart. In 1956, Mrs. Pratt was the first woman to receive an honorary degree of Doctor of Sacred Letters from Victoria College. A sponsor said: "Long before the United Nations . . . Mrs. Pratt made *World Friends* a dynamic force in the dissemination . . . principles, the foundation-stone of the United Nations Charter."

Mary-Etta Macpherson (Mrs. Herbert McMannus) is beloved by writers across Canada for her kindly criticism and encouragement. Assistant editor of *Mayfair Magazine* and *Canadian Homes and Gardens* and managing editor of *Chatelaine*, she was for many years editor of the *Canadian Home Journal*. Twice president of the Association of Canadian Magazine Writers, she joined J. Walter Thompson Advertising Agency in 1956 as senior creative consultant for women. She wrote *Shopkeepers to a Nation* the story of the T. Eaton Company.

Robbin Fraser is a tall glamorous magnetic brunette who is a born promoter of worthy causes. She helped with publicity for the Ottawa Symphony Orchestra being organized in 1966, and helped with arrangements for the International Ballet Festival in Ottawa in 1965.

A widely experienced business manager, journalist, editor, travel writer, broadcaster and public speaker, she has, since coming from the West to Ottawa contributed greatly to the arts, tourism, Indian and Eskimo affairs, also public and international affairs. During ten years in the Canadian House of Commons she worked as Research Assistant and Private Secretary to Eldon Wooliams Q.C., M.P., also for Opposition House Leader, Gerald W. Baldwin, Q.C. M.P., and for four Cabinet Ministers — The Hon. Ron Basford, Hon. John Turner, the Hon. Hugh Faulkner and as Consultant to Canada's first Minister of Multiculturalism, the Hon. Stanley Haidasz.

Presently employed in the Department of Indian Affairs and Northern Development, she is also Canadian Bureau Chief of the *Magazine of World Diplomacy*, and Associate Editor of *Performing Arts* Magazine.

Inspired Editor

Elected "Newspaperwoman of the Year" in 1955, Kay (Mrs. E. H.) Marston knew nothing of newspaper work when she bought the *Elora Express* in 1940. She was a widow with four small children to support but soon became adept at every facet of journalism including linotype operating. Soon the paper's circulation doubled. No comparable paper has won so many awards — mainly due to her superb editorials. She is chairman of the advisory board of Grand Valley Conservation Authority, and the beautiful Elora Gorge Park is just one of the civic improvements for which she has been responsible. She won the Jack Sanderson Award in 1966.

* * *

Mme. Françoise Gaudet-Smet was originally a poet. A voluble French-Canadian, she founded *Paysana*, a magazine for countrywomen, in the early 1940's and it proved so popular she received over 2,000 letters weekly. At present she writes a column for *La Presse*, Montreal.

Pioneer Professor

Isabel Dingman, who died in 1960, was a pioneer journalism professor. Born in 1898, she was Canada's only syndicated lovelorn advice columnist, under the pen-name Elizabeth Thompson; in addition she pursued a career as freelance newspaperwoman and magazine writer. Her daughter, Jocelyn, also a newspaperwoman, married Robert Fulford of Toronto. In 1947 Mrs. Dingman was appointed assistant professor of journalism at the University of Western Ontario where George McCracken established an excellent course, and was professor of journalism for nine years. She was the first woman to hold such a position in the British Commonwealth.

* * *

In 1959 Winnifred Stokes celebrated her 40th anniversary with the Niagara Falls *Evening Review* — she had been hired in 1919 to write copy for the 40th anniversary issue of the paper. In early 1957 she was appointed managing editor, the first woman to hold the position in Canada. She was also the first woman chairman of the Public Library Board and the Greater Niagara Community Chest. In her city she has headed every women's club and community welfare project and has travelled the world in search of copy for her daily column, "Wit, Wonder and Wisdom".

Byrne Hope Sanders was so determined to be a writer that she learned typing in two weeks. She was successful as ghost writer, editor of a women's page, advertising copy writer and editor of *The Business Woman* until in 1929 she was appointed editor of *Chatelaine*. Thirteen years later she was appointed director of the Consumer Branch of the Wartime Prices and

Trade Board which she described as "not a job but a dedication". She was the only woman member of the Dollar Sterling Trade Board and in 1947 was awarded a CBE. She wrote *Judge Murphy, Crusader* and *Famous Canadian Women*. In 1952, in partnership with her brother Wilfrid, she became president of Sanders Market Research Organization.

Olive Dickason, director of information for the National Gallery, started her journalistic career in 1944 after graduation from the University of Ottawa with an arts degree in philosophy and French. She joined the *Regina Leader-Post,* then, *the Winnipeg Free Press,* before a three year stint of freelancing. In 1950 she joined *the Montreal Gazette* and in 1955 moved to the *Globe and Mail.* She was women's editor of the *Globe Magazine* before her appointment as women's editor of the daily. In 1956 Olive walked off with a first prize Elizabeth Arden award for fashion reporting. She also received two Judy awards (given in Ontario) for women's page work in 1965 and 1967.

Carol Lutes, after graduating in journalism from Carleton University, joined the *Ottawa Citizen* in 1962 as a columnist and feature writer. Three years later she became assistant women's editor, then in 1966 public affairs co-ordinator, first woman PR director in the Southam newspapers group. Miss Lutes was editorial consultant to the Canadian Interfaith Conference in 1967, and in 1969 completed editorial duties with the Task Force on Government Information. That year she served as executive assistant to publisher Clifford Sifton in organizing the International Press Institute annual assembly in Ottawa, and was appointed the first woman PR chairman for the Ottawa United Appeal campaign.

Sheila (Mrs. Jon) Kieran born 1930, is the daughter of S. R. Ginzler, for years first trombonist with Toronto Symphony Orchestra. She graduated with the Gold Medal in Journalism from Forest Hills High School in New York City, subsequently taking night courses at Columbia University. Mrs. Kieran has written articles on important issues of the day, for every major publication in Canada, her own seven well-cared-for children providing some source material. A staff writer for the *Globe and Mail* 1964-66, she is now with Canadian magazine *Star Weekly*. Author of *Going to Work* (a guide for working wives and mothers) she is presently researching a history book.

Editor of Chatelaine

Doris McCubbin (Anderson) became editor of *Chatelaine* magazine in 1958 and was married a week later to a Toronto lawyer. Now the mother of three sons, she is a well-known speaker who has served on the board of the Toronto Metropolitan Children's Aid Society and also on the board of directors of the Canadian Institute of Public Affairs. She was chairman of the CIPA's eighth winter conference. A trip to the Soviet Union in 1959 resulted in a *Chatelaine* magazine issue on the country; an issue on Australia was published in 1968 and in the autumn of 1969 she was planning to take a group from *Chatelaine* to Japan to bring out an issue on Japan and its world fair in February 1970.

* * *

Doyle Klyn, women's editor of *Weekend Magazine*, travels about 130,000 miles annually, writes lyrics for flashy nightclub revues, and is a popular lecturer who has to refuse about 50 speaking engagements monthly. She has the only North American collection of Welsh Loving Spoons, from which is derived the term "spooning", and also is a collector of unusual names.

* * *

Jean Sharpe Cochrane, born in Chatham, is the first women's editor of *Canadian Press*, the national newsgathering co-operative. She joined the CP staff in 1964 as a reporter. A graduate of Mount Allison University, 1953, Jean married Glenn Cochrane in 1965. Their son, Ralph was born in 1968.

* * *

Jean Danard, former president of the Canadian Women's Press Club, hails from Kirkland Lake but lives in Toronto where she is a feature writer and editor for the *Financial Post*. Jean won an honorable mention in an international contest for a series of articles on Eastern Europe. A graduate of the University of Toronto in science and economics, Miss Danard has been assistant editor with *Maclean's Magazine*, the *Imperial Oil Review* and travel editor with *Canadian Homes*.

After graduating from University of Toronto, Christina Newman had worked for a couple of years for *Maclean's Magazine* before marrying Peter Newman. For the next five years Mrs. Newman was associate editor of *Chatelaine* where, writing under several pseudonyms, she did general articles, news summaries, and a book column until the birth of her daughter in 1964. Then she was appointed editor of *Saturday Night* in 1967. Her articles include a scathing exposé of the Ottawa "man".

Mrs. Newman has also done some broadcasting and edited a collection of Ralph Allen's writing entitled *The Man from Oxbow*.

* * *

June Callwood, born in Chatham in 1924, after working as a reporter for *Brantford Expositor* and the *Globe and Mail*, married Trent Frayne in 1944. They have four children. This prolific writer has produced several hundred magazine articles, mostly for *Maclean's* and *Chatelaine*, as well as five books, including *Love,*

Hate, Fear, Anger and the Other Lively Emotions. Mrs. Frayne is also a well-known lecturer and TV personality. Sympathetic towards hippies, she champions them by pen and platform, and once was arrested for failing to "move along" in Yorkville, and spent a few hours in jail. She started a hostel called Yorkville Digger House for lost flower people, which is so highly regarded it is now supported by a government grant.

Mrs. Frayne is also vice-president of the Canadian Civil Liberties Association, treasurer of Citizens Housing Committee of Metro Toronto, member of Canadian Mental Health Association, a member of Citizens Committee to Support Farm Workers and World Federalism. She demonstrates that woman can successfully combine a career with marriage. She was chosen Woman of the Year in 1969 by B'nai B'rith Women.

* * *

So does Lotta Dempsey, widow of Richard A. Fisher, who was the first woman to fly in a jet plane that broke the sound barrier! Her enthusiastic curiosity about life and her likeable personality were essential ingredients to her highly successful career. Starting as a reporter, she was feature editor of *Chatelaine* for ten years, and is presently a columnist with the *Toronto Star*, sometimes discussing vital social problems, such as prostitution and prison reform. In 1948 she won the CWPC national award. Lotta Dempsey was named to the Canadian News Hall of Fame 1975. In 1976 her autobiography *No Life for a Lady* was published.

* * *

Doris French moved to Ottawa after marriage in 1941. As freelance writer, she had a popular daily radio program on CBC. From 1944 to 1949 she was a member of the Parliamentary Press Gallery. She wrote *High Button Bootstraps* and co-authored *Ask No Quarter* (the biography of Agnes Macphail) and *Faith, Sweat and Politics*, the story of trade unions in Canada. She now edits the *Canadian Welfare Magazine*.

Radio and television public affairs programs have been enriched by the talents of writer, commentator, editor Helen Dacey Wilson of Ottawa, who was born in Guysborough County, Nova Scotia. Her novels *Tales from Barrett's Landing* (1964) and *More Tales from Barrett's Landing* (1967) tell the tender, humorous story of her Maritime years. The author of numerous articles for national magazines and the editor of the federal government's Task Force on Information report, Helen won the 1966 CWPC Memorial Award for a satirical article in *Saturday Night*. Journalism students at Ottawa's Carleton University benefit from the creative writing seminars she has conducted for the past three years. Awarded a Canada Council grant in 1968, Miss Wilson is at work on her third book.

Women editors-in-chief include Mrs. B. S. McCool of Toronto, who for some years was editor-in-chief of W. J. Gage and Company; she was the first woman to hold such a position with a publishing firm in Canada, being appointed in 1957. Helen O'Reilly was chief Canadian editor for Longman's Green and Company and Gladys Neal of Toronto, was the first woman chairman of the Canadian Educational Book Publishing Company.

Miss Sheilagh Hickie is editor and publisher of *En Ville* a business family paper published in Montreal half in English, half in French. Sheilagh's perceptive, interesting style in her own column covers a wide range of subjects. It's a family affair with Mrs. Hickie in the circulation department.

Pioneer Women Publishers

Probably publishing is the most important busi-

404

ness in the world, for without books, civilization might perish. When her brother left, Irene Irwin Clarke became vice-president of their firm, Clarke-Irwin, and helped her husband Bill build up the business. Following his death, she carried on as president. Witty, capable Mrs. Clarke also lectured and did broadcasts on books.

May Ebbut Cutten — winner of first prize in the Centennial Commission Literary Competition for her book, *The Last Noble Savage* — is owner of the bilingual publishing house, Tundra Books in Montreal, which is one of two firms devoted exclusively to Canadian works. She published several small books about Expo '67.

Angelina du Tremblay was publisher of *La Presse*, the western hemisphere's largest French-language newspaper, from 1954 to 1961. This aristocractic, childless French-Canadian used to say: "My father had eight children, and always used to say *La Presse* was his ninth." Her father founded the newspaper in 1884 and she was secretary and a board member from 1935. Mme. du Tremblay was also president of *La Patrie* which ceased publication in 1957 (its Sunday supplement continued) and she owned radio stations CKAC and CHLP. The late Mme. Huguenin left the staff of *La Patrie* to found the successful *La Revue Moderne*.

Unique Wedding Gift

Maisie Hurley — "Ma" to the Indians of British Columbia — started publishing *Native Voice*, a monthly paper for Indians, in 1905 with just $150. to her credit. Her office was a mad mixture of Indian robes, hex sticks, medicine men's necklaces, an ancient typewriter, teacups and begonias. Her wedding gift from her husband, Tom Hurley, a criminal lawyer, was the mummified heart of her ancestor, the Marquess of Montrose, who was hanged and quartered by Cromwell in 1650.

Collector of Rare Volumes

Isobel Mackenzie is an avid collector of rare books, maps and prints pertaining to North America and has shuttled for years between Europe and Canada in search of material. She turned her hobby into a business in Montreal and is the only Canadian to be elected to the board of governors of the Antiquarian Booksellers Association of America, with headquarters in New York. She was first woman appointed a director of the Antiquarian Booksellers Association of Canada and is a member of the International League of Antiquarian Booksellers. She has exhibited collections in the Montreal Museum of Fine Arts, New York Public Library and the Rockefeller Centre among other well-known institutions, and divides her free time between Montreal bookrooms and her country home — North Hatley, Quebec.

Canadian Speakers' and Writers' Service

When Matie Molinaro came to Toronto as a war bride in 1946, she was appalled by the lack of literary agents in sparsely-settled Canada. After serving as a freelance editor for many publishing houses here, and reading fiction for *Maclean's Magazine* for several years, she started her own literary agency in 1950. Slow going at the start caused her to combine it with teaching languages and history at a private school, while managing her home and bringing up her children, Juliette and Paul. By 1959, her agency had such an impressive roster of lecturers and authors that she reorganized it under the name Canadian Speakers' and Writers' Service.

Matie was born in Brooklyn, New York in 1922. At Barnard College, Columbia University, she majored in political science and minored in languages, graduating in 1943. First she did public relations work for the North Atlantic area, American Red Cross. In 1944, she tried for an assignment overseas, but was rejected as "too young". So she joined the Psychological Warfare Branch of the United States Army, and, after a special training program, was sent to work in communications in Algiers. Assigned to Rome for a year, she met Professor Julius Molinaro, on leave of absence to do war work. They were married in the Cathedral of San Giusto, Trieste, and returned to Toronto where he taught in the Department of Italian and Hispanic Studies.

With the exciting advent of television, and increased interest in theatre across Canada, sparked by the advent of the Shakespearian Festivals at Stratford, Mrs. Molinaro was glad of an experience during college days. She worked part-time in the publicity department of the Theatre Production Service, headed by Broadway's Jean Rosenthal and Evelyn Peirce, once casting director for the brilliant company of Orson Welles. Now, in addition to many books published through CSWS, plays of all kinds were added. Properties by Lister Sinclair, Don Harron, Mavor Moore, Chris Wiggins, Ron Chudley, Diane Stapley, Aviva Ravel are among many colorful creations; and festivals all across Canada arranged for professional or amateur productions through the CSWS office. Forty of Canada's top public speakers (most of whom are also writers) are under CSWS contracts. It also makes available to Canadian audiences outstanding ecturers from the United States, as the CSWS is the exclusive booking office for Doubleday's Author Lecture Service. But Mrs. Molinaro feels that probably her greatest achievement has been in making "The law of literary property" meaningful to writers, publishers and producers.

Poets

> *Poetry is life transfused and irradi-*
> *ated.* (Audrey Alexandra Brown)

Like so many artists, Isabella Valency Crawford lived and died poverty-stricken, lonely and friendless; but years afterwards, was to be recognized as Canada's outstanding poet of the 19th century. She died in 1887, and recognition came in 1905, when John W. Garvin edited *The Collected Poems of Isabella Valency Crawford.*

Versatile poet Ethelwyn Wetherald edited the women's page of *The Globe* for years under the pen name Bel Thistlethwaite. As *Ladies' Home Journal* editor she helped Charles Dudley Warner edit 30 volumes of *The World's Best Literature.* Finding this drained her energy, she retired to her tree-top studio at Fenwick, Ontario, to write half a dozen books of poetry. She also collaborated with G. Mercer Adam in writing *An Algonquin Maiden.* She is the nation's leading nature poet.

Our Princess Poet

An air of expectancy pervaded an illustrious gathering in Buckingham Palace one evening in 1894. It was even more pronounced than that which had preceded the entrance of Queen Victoria, a few minutes earlier. All eyes were fixed on the door. Suddenly the guests were electrified by the entrance of a handsome woman in her early 30s with large luminous gray eyes and straight braided black hair through which slanted an eagle feather. Her buckskin dress was trimmed with ermine, two scalps dangled from her dagger-laden wampum belt, and she wore exquisitely embroidered moccasins. She glided first to the dais where Queen Victoria was seated. Though she curtsied gracefully, these two women met as equals. For she was Princess Tekonawika, or Pauline Johnson, daughter of the Chief of the Mohawk tribe. The Princess was there by royal invitation, and in answer to a request from Her Majesty, she declaimed, with dramatic gestures and deep thrilling voice, her poem, *The Cattle Thief.*

Pauline, Canada's most picturesque poet, born in 1862 proved immensely popular throughout England and North America, giving recitals for twenty exhausting years. Her poems are often fiery drama, set to lilting music. Her personality was magnetic. No stranger to romance, she never married. It was rumored that the man she loved objected to her Indian blood, of which she was fiercely proud. Today, even Pauline Johnson's signature would be worth $5, but for her most famous poem *The Song my Paddle Sings* she received only $3. When one magazine sent her a cheque for 75 cents for a poem, used as a magazine cover, she scornfully returned it. The wrongs suffered by her race was the theme of her first book *White Wampum* published in England 1894. *Canadian Born* was published in 1903. Later, she wrote prose, including *Shagnappi,* a book for boys, *The Moccasin Maker,* and *Legends of Vancouver,* 1911.

Broken in health, Pauline retired to Vancouver in 1909, spending her last two years in hospital. Writing against time, in agony from cancer, she managed to finish and proof-read *Flint and Feather.* Told that she could not recover, she accepted this verdict with brave Indian stoicism. When she died March 10, 1913 (the anniversary of her birthday) flags hung at half mast in Vancouver. There is a memorial fountain in Stanley Park, and in 1961 the Canadian Government issued a postage stamp honoring her. The National Film Board made a documentary of her life, and Chiefswood near Brantford, her old home, has become a national shrine.

Pauline Johnson

* * *

Mrs. S. F. Harrison, under the pseudonym "Seranus", was primarily a poet. She lived in Toronto and Montreal, but the impelling motive behind all her writing was interpretation of her beloved French Canada for her English compatriots. An example is *Pine, Rose and Fleur de Lis,* written in 1891. Seranus edited the first anthology of Canadian verse entitled *A Canadian Birthday Book,* in 1889. It contained the first French-Canadian poem ever written, some of Bliss Carman's early work, and a poem by the Indian Chief, Tecumseh.

Dorothy Dumbrille is a writer with a mission, trying to bridge the gap between the French and English, especially in her first novel *All This Difference.* Other books include *Deep Doorways, Up and Down the Glens,* and *Braggart in My Step.* Modest Miss Dumbrille, who says: "I have no standing as a Canadian writer," is also a prolific poet and article writer. Her fans included Mackenzie King, Eleanor Roosevelt and Lady Byng of Vimy. Dorothy Dumbrille is listed in Burke's Peerage.

Admirers in Montreal called Dorothy Sproule the "Lady Poet Laureate". Born in 1867, she was a specialist in verses commemorating historic events: her *Coronation Ode* won her a Coronation Medal. Her eight books of poetry won her the New York World Fair Gold Medal and the 1949 Schroeder Foundation Medal for Literature. (Other winners were Eleanor Roosevelt and Winston Churchill.) She died in 1963.

Poetry Prizes

Poetry prizewinners include "Fleurange" (Mrs. J. Lefevre of Brockville and Vancouver) who won a $100 prize for *The Italian Boy's Dream* around 1890; Kate MacPherson of Montreal, who won a prize for *Acanada* in 1897, and Annie C. Dalton of Vancouver, who in 1930 won a special Tweedsmuir Award for *The Neighing North.*

Agnes Austin Hill of Calgary, won the Governor-General's Silver Medal in 1941, and the same year another westerner, Anne Marriott, won a Governor-General's Award for her *Calling Adventures*. Elizabeth Garbutt, best-known for *Mount Eisenhower and Other Poems* won an award from the city of Calgary for "distinguished and exceptional public service in the field of Arts and Letters". In 1958 she was given a life membership of the Allied Arts Council.

P. K. Page, since her marriage to W. Arthur Irwin, publisher of the *Victoria Colonist,* has turned to art. However, in 1944, she won the Oscar Blumenthal Award for Poetry and 10 years later a Governor-General's Award for *The Metal and the Flower*. *Cry Ararat* is a distillation of poems published over 20 years, plus three new poems.

Author and poet Isabel Eclestone MacKay, who lived from 1875 to 1928, moved from Woodstock to the west. She wrote two novels, *Blencarrow* and *The Window Gazer,* and also penned the poems *Between the Lights* in 1904 and *The Shining Ship* in 1918. Her *Fires of Driftwood and other Poems* has been compared to Stevenson's *A Child's Garden of Verses*.

Marie Rina Lasnier of St. Jean, Quebec, member of the French-Canadian Academy, won the Prix David for her drama *Le Jeu de la Voyagere* in 1941, and 1943 was awarded a Canadian Government Overseas Fellowship by the Royal Society of Canada. In 1944, she collaborated with Dr. Marius Barbeau in *Madones Canadiennes*. Other books are mainly poetry. Twice winner of the Governor-General's Award, she also won the Lorne Pierce Medal of Royal Society for her "sustained and distinguished contribution to Canadian letters".

Anne Hebert's poems have wide readership in France and the United States as well as Canada. She has received awards also for fiction and plays, though her chief metier is poetry; prizes include a scholarship from the Royal Society for study in France, and a $15,000 Canada Council grant. Anne is on the staff of the National Film Board.

A Dryad in Nanaimo

Audrey Alexandra Brown, born in Nanaimo, B.C. 1904, is badly crippled. Suffering served to refine her noble spirit. Scholars such as Professor Pelham Edgar and Sir Alexander Macphail on reading her first book of poetry *A Dryad in Nanaimo* published in 1931, hailed her as a "star of the first magnitude". Their verdict was borne out by subsequent books, including her autobiography *Log of a Lame Duck* written in 1938.

*   *   *

Revolutionary writer, Dorothy Livesay, daughter of J. B. F. Livesay, general manager of the *Canadian Press*, and poet Florence Livesay, was born in 1909. For a lullaby she had a typewriter's tap-tap. During college days at the University of Toronto, she won the Jardine Memorial Prize for her poem *City Wife*; later she studied at the Sorbonne. In Paris she was greatly influenced by Henri Barbusse's League of Revolutionary Writers. In 1932, Dorothy graduated in Social Science from University of Toronto and did welfare work until her marriage in 1937 to Duncan MacNair. Her more mature work shows a highly developed social consciousness. Seven books of poems have been published, *Day and Night* and *Poems for the People* winning Governor-General's Awards. She was Writer-in-Residence at Ottawa University during winter 1976-77.

Anne Wilkinson has been compared to Elizabeth Barrett Browning. Her *Collected Poems of Anne Wilkinson*, edited and with an introduction by A. J. M. Smith, includes two brief books — *Counterpoint to Sleep* and *The Hangman Tied the Holly* — along with poems. She helped found *Tamarack Review* in which some poems appeared, and wrote *Swann and Daphne,* a book for children. Another of her works was *Lions in the Way,* an account of her relatives, the Osler family.

Jean Blewett has been called "The sweetest of Canadian poets" while Edna Jaques' homey verse has many admirers. Wilhemina Stitch is also popular. Witty "Willie" (Wilma M. Coutts) lives at Idylwilde in Durham, but her verses in *Sonnets from a Saugeen Farm* record her hilarious experiences of farm life. Published in 1951, many had been in the *Toronto Star* and were read over the CBC by Maurice Bodington. *Daily Dozen* appeared in 1954, and was promoted by the B and P Club of which Wilma was an active member. Singing and lecturing are other avocations of this beautiful blonde, who writes articles in her more serious moments.

* * *

Members of the Ottawa Canadian Author's Association include an active poetry group, under the leadership of Winnifred Horne (herself a poet of some stature), Lenore Pratt, a well-known poet, had her chapbook *Birch Light* published in 1956 by Ryerson press; and Thea Bennett, author of over four thousand lovely poems gathered some together in *Yesterday's Unicorn,* published in 1974. Thea has also given a great many readings of her poetry in connection with Medieval and Renaissance Music Groups.

Silver Light, a poetry book published in 1955 by Theresa and Donald Thompson of Ottawa, and *Myth and Monument,* published in 1957, are rare husband and wife collaborations. Theresa "Terry" Thompson had a chapbook of poems entitled *Silver Shadows* published by Ryerson and as well was co-author of three others with her husband. She also writes articles but her most important work was as executive-secretary of The Canadian Writers' Foundation, a position she held for 20 years. Dr. Lorne Pierce paid tribute to her as "The hands, the feet, the eyes, the ears, the tongue, and the

heart of the Foundation". The Foundation was organized in 1931, largely by Dr. Pelham Edgar. It obtained a
Dominion Charter in 1945 and exists to give financial
assistance to established authors in need because of illness or old age. William Arthur Deacon, who was at
first opposed to it, said: "I think Mrs. Terry Thompson
will be remembered in the far future as Florence Nightingale is." An accountant and writer, she is a Fellow of
the Royal Commonwealth Society. Both she and her
husband were awarded Centennial Medals.

Talent in the coming generation is indicated by
the fact that in February, 1955, 13 year-old Marie Jac-
ober of Fairview, won the International Literary Award
Gold Medal in the Shankar's Weekly annual competition in India, with her poem *The Fairy Queen*, against
24,000 entries by children from fifty-six countries.

Angel Shoes

"Whom the gods love, die young!" might have
been written of Canada's most gifted woman poet, Marjorie Pickthall. Born in England in 1883, she wrote, illustrated, and bound several books at the age of five.
Three early juvenile works, illustrated by C. W. Jeffreys,
are now collectors' items. Marjorie's family emigrated to
Toronto and at 16 she entered the annual story and
poetry competition in the *Mail and Empire*. She won
both story and poetry prizes for her *Song of the Nixies*.
"My hat still fits," she chuckled. She was awarded the
Globe's $200 prize for *The Pumpkin Seeds*, and at 11
was writing for quality magazines including *Atlantic
Monthly, Scribner's* and *Harpers*.

Drift of Pinions (1913), her first book of poetry,
was followed in 1917 by *The Lamp of Poor Souls and
Other Poems. The Woodcarver's Wife,* a verse-drama,
was published in 1922, the year of her untimely death.
Her distinctive style was probably the result of living in
a dream world. *Angels' Shoes* was published posthu-

mously, also two books, *Little Hearts* and *The Bridge*. She left an unfinished novel *The Beaten Man*. Her poetry has been compared to that of Elizabeth Barrett Browning and Christina Rossetti. Tribute has been paid her in biographies by Dr. J. D. Logan, Professor E. F. Pratt, and Dr. Lorne Pierce.

Today the poet's voice is lost in the wilderness, poetry is an extremely difficult product to sell to practical Canadians. However, many idealists still devote their time and talent to writing poetry, seeking only to communicate the song in their souls. Throughout the years, women writers of Canada have used their talent in delineation, interpretation, portraiture and inspiration to make a contribution to creative writing which adds greatly to Canada's literary heritage at home and to her cultural prestige abroad — a contribution which continues to flourish in contemporary times.

Chapter XIV

Centre Stage

Theatre

Dora Mavor Moore

An actor is a sculptor who carves in snow.

(Barrett)

Contemporary Canadian theatre took its cue from Stratford, with skillful off-stage prompting by Tom Patterson and Dora Mavor Moore to ensure that the house lights need never dim again. From modest beginnings in the original Tent theatre, the Stratford Shakespearean Festival which Tom Patterson and Mrs. Moore had dreamed of founding, took organizational shape in the hands of that Irish wizard of the theatre, Tyrone Guthrie.

Stratford shored up a Canadian theatrical foundation which had its roots in Port Royal when Marc Lescarbot's Neptune Theatre raised the curtain on North America's first drama production in 1606, performed on barges moored in the harbor. As was the custom in 17th century theatre, no women were members of the cast.

However, 350 years later, a woman, Mrs. R.H. Bond is credited with bringing the historic Lescarbot play out of mothballs. Working in co-operation with the Annapolis Royal Historical Association, Mrs. Bond and her colleagues, historian Mrs. Hortense Spurr Gilliatt; Mrs. H. Laura Hardy, for 30 years assistant curator of Fort Anne Museum; and Mrs. Connie Ford, of Quebec's charming Lachine Museum, presented the original Neptune play. Halifax's Neptune Theatre, which sprouted theatrical wings in the '60's under the direction of Leon Major, bears the proud name of Lescarbot's original theatre. A tablet reads: "This tablet placed here A.D. 1926 commemorates the Neptune Theatre at Port Royal in Acadia 1606, the birthplace of the Drama in North America."

Difficult Beginnings

Theatre has never been a viable full-time profession in Canada. Today, even with Stratford, the summer Charlottetown Festival, the National Arts Centre, such cross-country theatres as The Neptune, and itinerant work in television, promising young actors and actresses still find they have to move beyond Canada to expand artistically and to keep steadily employed.

Canadian theatre — both amateur and professional — has been nurtured by a series of "angels". One venture, the Canadian Repertory Theatre in Ottawa managed for a time by actress Amelia Hall, gave up its struggle for survival in 1956. During its eight-year existence it had fostered such talented performers as Anna Cameron, Kay Hawtrey, Margaret Griffin, Christopher Plummer, William Shatner, Eric House and Gerald Easton. Even such theatrical "angels" as Mr. and Mrs. Charles Southgate and the late H.S. Southam, publisher of The Ottawa Citizen, could not prevent its demise. Canadian theatrical history is marked by many peaks and valleys. A number of large theatres flourished in the heyday of 1920's vaudeville and musical comedy with sparkling productions of Rose Marie and the Student Prince and other favorites of the era. When the Depression hit theatres forced to drop live talent watched as performers drifted out to the U.S.

First Performance

In the early days of live Canadian theatre audiences thrilled to the vivid, emotional performances of Toronto's Clara Morris (1869-1925), the striking character impersonations of Hamilton's Jean Adair, born in

1873, and to musical comedy star Mabel Barrison.

Quebec's Lucille Watson made her debut at the old Ottawa Opera House in 1900 in *A Morning Call*. Two years later her New York debut was hailed by critics. A half century later as Madame Desmermortes in *Ring Around the Moon*, Lucille was still a stellar performer.

Eva Tanguay born 1876 in Marbelton, Quebec, was a stage queen for decades. At eight she played *Little Lord Fauntleroy;* then in 1904 became a star overnight for her acting in *The Chaperones*. Mitzi Gaynor starred in the film version of Eva's life story *The I Don't Care Girl*.

Toronto's Margaret Bannerman started acting in Winnipeg, gained fame in England, and returned home in Somerset Maugham's *Our Betters*. In Toronto she played in *Philadelphia Story* and did stage and film work in New York and Hollywood, playing the professor's mother in *My Fair Lady* which toured Canada.

Canada's Actress-Princess

Starting humbly, Eliza Joy, a farmer's daughter in St. Armand West, Quebec, left the New York stage in 1862 to marry Prince Z. Salm-Salm of Westphalia, Germany. After the Mexican Civil War, Prince Salm-Salm tried unsuccessfully to help Emperor Maximilian escape. Returning to Germany, Eliza was received by the Queen of Prussia. Her diary recorded pre-Nazi anti-Semitism: "These noblemen hate Jews, though not too proud to borrow money from them, or drink their champagne." Left penniless when her Prince died in battle, the Princess married a commoner, Heneager, and hopefully lived happily ever after.

Modern "Saint Joan"

"Temperament such as hers, beauty and voice

420

like hers, we associate somehow with ... Southern France, Spain, or Italy ..." said a critic, of Julia Arthur, born Ida Lewis in Hamilton in 1869. Her coach John Townsend put Julia onstage in *The Honeymoon* at the tender age of 11 and as Portia soon after. At 14, Mr. D.E. Bandmann gave her the role of Prince of Wales in *Richard III*. Leading roles in *East Lynne, The Corsican Brothers,* Shakespearean roles of Juliet, Desdemona and Ophelia followed. Before she was 20, Julia had toured North America. Following further study in Europe, she played leading roles in A.M. Palmer's New York Company.

At twenty-five without benefit of a publicity agent, she braved the English stage. "You might as well return home!" Henry Arthur Jones exclaimed. But her courage was richly rewarded by a place in Sir Henry Irving's company, with a debut at the London's Lyceum Theatre. Julia played with Ellen Terry as Hero in *Much Ado about Nothing* and Elaine in *King Arthur.* Her acting in Miss Terry's roles of Rosamond in *Thomas a Becket* and in *Cymbeline* were triumphs. Julia was human enough to gloat over seeing critic Jones among her enthusiastic audience! Later she toured America with Irving's company. Following her marriage to Benjamin Cheney in 1899, she practically retired, though kept one foot on the stage by starring in *The Eternal Magdalene* and *Macbeth* in 1915. As her swan song in 1924 at the age of fifty-five Julia Arthur toured Canada in Shaw's *Saint Joan,* a memorable performance.

Canada's Bernhardt

"One of the few dramatic geniuses of the day" was the immortal Sarah's description of Margaret Anglin, who was thrilled to be told she resembled Bernhardt. Margaret (1876-1958), a dainty, beautiful redhead, had the distinction of being the only baby ever born in Ottawa's Parliament Buildings. Her father Hon.

T.W. Anglin, Saint John, New Brunswick, was Speaker of the House of Commons. With a mother so fond of amateur theatricals it was logical that Margaret would study elocution.

Inspired by the voice of the inimitable Ellen Terry, Margaret became the star student at Nelson Wheatcroft's Dramatic School in New York. Engaged by Charles Froham, she made her debut in 1894, as Madeleine West in *Shenandoah*. Following a season in repertory, she joined E.H. Sothern's company in 1898 scoring successes in *Cyrano de Bergerac*, *The Only Way*, *Dr. Jekyll and Mr. Hyde* and *Virginius*. Her success was followed by seven seasons as leading lady in Froham's company; two years' touring; two successful Broadway seasons; a 1908-1909 Australian tour and a world tour a year later. Tragic career consequences followed her marriage in 1911 to writer Howard Hull, a much younger man. Insisting that Howard was also an actor Margaret tried to wangle parts for him in her plays. Quarrelling with managers, she walked out during production of two plays and was boycotted.

In 10 years Margaret Anglin played more than 30 roles. "My child, you must continue to play Shakespeare, you have the Irish seas in your voice," said actor James O'Neill (father of playwright Eugene O'Neill). She loved Shakespeare, but the public preferred her in such modern comedies as *Green Stockings* or dramatic plays like *The Awakening of Helen Ritchie*. Miss Anglin played *Mrs. Dane's Defense* in New York while another Canadian, Lena Ashwell, portrayed the role on the London stage. Forming her own company, Margaret successfully revived Greek plays. In June, 1916, Sophocles' *Antigone* and *Electra* was presented at Berkley University, California. In New York her performance in *Electra* was a stupendous success. "The Greek Tragedies", she said, "are for great moments; for the heights." In Canada's Diamond Jubilee Year, 1927, Margaret Anglin read the Confederation Ode on the first trans-Canada program broadcast internationally. University of Notre Dame in Indiana honored her that same year with a Laetare Medal. Years later New York welcomed her back in Ivor Novello's *Fresh Fields;* in 1943 she toured in *Watch on the Rhine.*

* * *

Many have called Toronto's Jane Mallett the heart of Canadian theatre. She helped found Canadian Actors' Equity Association and the Association of Canadian and Television Artists and was chairman of Actors' Fund of Canada which helps aged, sick and destitute actors. Her 40-year career has ranged over revue, plays, radio and television. She organized Jane Mallett Associates in 1955. Her revue "Fine Frenzy" actually made a penny or two of profit!

Queen of Clowns

"Beatrice Lillie fined five shillings for trying to be funny" — was the only unfavorable press notice she ever received. For many years she made $5,000 a week by being funny. This notice on the billboard backstage occurred when she was playing in the 1915 London *Not Likely.* Bored she slipped on-stage dressed as a man, twirling a handlebar moustache.

Born in Toronto 1898, Bea and her family went to England in 1914. Stagestruck and broke, Beatrice became discouraged. However, an audition with Andre Charlot resulted in a three-year contract at $60 weekly. Beatrice married Sir Robert Peel. Their only child was named Robert. Sick of society life, Lady Peel returned to the stage in *Up in Mabel's Room,* then Charlot's revue *Now and Then.* In 1922, the Peels produced *The Nine O'Clock Revue,* with pianist-sister Muriel composing the score. Bea went to New York in *Charlot's Revue of 1924* and played opposite Noel Coward in *This Year of Grace. At Home Abroad, The Show is On* and three movies, *Exit Smiling, Dr. Rhythm, On Approval,* were smash hits. Critics called her "a mistress of sophisticated slapstick."

Her husband died in 1934. In World War II Bobbie enlisted. Among the hundreds of congratulatory telegrams she received on the opening night of *The Big Top* in London was one saying her son was missing. She bravely "went on with the show."

Lady Peel appeared in Billy Rose's *Seven Lively Arts*, New York, winning the 1944-45 Donaldson Award. In England, *An Evening with Beatrice Lillie* proved a favorite. Indeed, to persuade her to return to America to star in *Inside U.S.A.,* Arthur Schwartz had to serenade her by long distance telephone, at $9.00 a minute!

Grand Dame of Canadian Theatre

Then there is that grand lady of Canadian theatre, Dora Mavor Moore, who became the primer for Canada's theatrical renaissance.

Before Stratford was developed Canadian theatre goers had to be satisfied with infrequent visits by British and U.S. companies for their taste of professional theatre which were scattered among a wide range of amateur little theatre productions. Dora Mavor Moore's far-reaching efforts paved the way for the encouragement and development of a pool of professional Canadian theatrical talent both behind the scenes and stage front and centre.

The daughter of Professor James Mavor, who founded the Department of Economy at the University of Toronto, Dora entered university at age sixteen. Later she studied at the Royal Academy of Dramatic Art and became the first Canadian actress to play at London's Old Vic — as Viola in *Twelfth Night*. Returning home, this enthusiastic, articulate actress toured North America with Ben Greet's Company, playing in everything from tents to magnificent auditoria. In 1938, Mrs. Moore launched The Village Players, among whom were her

son, Mavor, Barbara Kelly, (Mrs. Bernie Braden) and
Donald Harron, all internationally known today. On
Christmas that year she rented the Royal Alexandra
Theatre and put on an English Pantomime "for children
from five to 75".

The New Play Society, established in 1946 to produce works by Canadian authors introduced over 50 original plays, by such authors as Morley Callaghan,
Andrew Allan, John Coulter, Mavor Moore, Lister Sinclair, Pierre Berton and Harry Boyle, in addition to
twenty-two productions of *Spring Thaw*. Mrs. Moore
has trained three generations of Canadians in theatre
techniques.

Mrs. Moore came to the rescue of Tom Patterson
of Stratford, Ontario when he was contemplating the
Stratford Shakespearean Festival in the middle 1950's.
Dora Mavor Moore arranged the very important meeting
between her good friend Tyrone (Tony) Guthrie, and
Tom Patterson, through a telephone call to England,
from her office at the New Play Society in Toronto. During Stratford's first season two-thirds of the actors, and
most experts, were recruited from her New Play Society. Among its alumnae are Toby Robins, Jane Mallett,
Anna Russell, Diane Foster and Gisele Mackenzie.

Mrs. Moore lectures extensively on theatre and
has successfully used dramatic techniques as therapy in
mental hospitals. She received the honorary life membership in the Heliconian Society, the Woman of the
Year Award in 1967 from the B'nai B'rith, the Canadian
Drama Award in 1967, the Centennial Medal in recognition of "valuable service to the nation", and in 1970 the
Order of Canada. In June, 1969 she was awarded an
honorary Doctor of Fine Arts degree by Western College
for Women, Oxford, Ohio, in the same month that her
son, Mavor, received an honorary degree from Toronto's
York University. On November 31, 1971 the mayor of
Toronto declared "Dora Mavor Moore Day"; that evening 500 distinguished guests honoured her at a reception

to mark the close of a successful quarter-century run of her New Play Society School.

Anna Russell

* * *

In 1914 Nancy (Mrs. Charles B. Pyper) won a silver cup in Northern Ireland's "FEIS" (Irish Festival of Drama and Music). Marrying a Canadian soldier, she moved to the prairies with him in 1919. Her musical monologue hit the headlines, she produced and acted in dozens of plays and became drama director of University of Manitoba. Judith Evelyn was one of her students. In Toronto, in 1935, Nancy became the first woman director of Hart House Theatre, and produced the first pantomime, *Cinderella*, at Massey Hall. Joining the WRENS as public relations officer, she attained the rank of Lieutenant-Commander. In 1951 she became drama teacher at Bishop Strachan School, Toronto.

Splendid Monolith

"I went through agonies, trying to be a serious musician," Anna Russell recalls. "In Canada, in 1938, I twigged to the fact I am a comedienne." Born in England, Anna had an excellent musical education. She writes her own words and music and has made several hilariously funny records. Her book *The Power of Being a Positive Stinker* chalked up solid sales. Trying to crash Broadway, Anna almost starved. Roy Campbell coached her "for the carriage trade" and arranged a sell-out Town Hall Concert. Anna's star has zoomed upward from there and she has never looked back. Now living in Australia, Anna still tours the globe, keeping her faithful fans "rolling in the aisles".

Dramatic Wings

The '50's will be recalled as good years by the many Canadian actresses who got their dramatic wings on the stage and in radio and television. Kate Reid, Amelia Hall, Frances Hyland, Eleanor Stewart, Suzanne

Cloutier, Anna Massey, the late Catherine Proctor, Toby Robins, Corrine Conley and Barbara Chilcott to name a few.

Petite, pretty Amelia (Millie) Hall, was one of the first Canadians to earn a living in Canada solely by acting. Her training ranges from Toronto Royal Conservatory to "Q" Theatre in England to a stint of managing Canadian Repertory Theatre in Ottawa, from 1949 to 1954. Before its unhappy close in 1956, it was the only professional theatre in Canada playing a continuous winter season. Its production of *The Lady's Not for Burning* in 1952 broke attendance records. Miss Hall played leads in numerous plays, notably as Amanda with Christopher Plummer in *The Glass Menagerie,* and as Victoria in *Victoria Regina.* Miss Hall also founded the Children's Theatre.

Chosen by Tyrone Guthrie as the first actress to play at Stratford in 1953, Amelia took the role of Lady Anne in *Richard III,* opposite Alex Guinness. It was the start for her of a solid ten seasons at Stratford and tours with the travelling company to Edinburgh, Chichester and across Canada in 1967. During five seasons at Toronto's Crest Theatre from 1954 to 1959 Amelia played Maria Helliewell in *When We Are Married,* director Michael Langham's Canadian debut. Next year she played in New York in Tyrone Guthrie's production of Robertson Davies' *Love and Libel,* then on to the Stratford (Connecticut) Shakespearean Festival, for the role of Maria in *Twelfth Night.* Millie was a member of the foursome of Canadian Players along with William Hutt, Frances Hyland and Eric Christmas which toured in 1963-64 in *Masterpieces of Comedy* and *Private Lives* with Zoe Caldwell.

Her recent plays have included *Little Murders* in Theatre Toronto; *The Killing of Sister George* and *Death of a Salesman,* at Ottawa Town Theatre, in addition to several Stratford plays. Miss Hall starred in CBC Festival *The Spirit of the Deed* and played Mistress Quickly

428

in *Henry V* on CTV.

Eleanor Stuart of Montreal, played New York with George Arliss and Philip Merivale, toured with Ethel Barrymore, acted in the Comedie Française in Paris and in repertory theatre in Montreal and England, before bringing her students to the Stratford Festival.

Frances Hyland won an IODE scholarship to London's Royal Academy of Dramatic Art and made her professional debut there in *A Streetcar Named Desire.* Back home she toured with Canadian Players, playing title role in *Saint Joan,* and Ophelia in *Hamlet.* Her Stratford performances through the years have received wide critical acclaim. She is married to director George McGowan.

Wildcat Among The Pigeons

Critics have called Barbara Chilcott "The wildcat among the pigeons" so intense are her stage performances. Barbara often requires an osteopathic treatment before going on stage. She feels she is doubly handicapped by being "ugly" and having been brought up by maiden aunts to be "a perfect lady." Barbara is an exotic-looking brunette. Her early training was received at London's Central School of Speech Training and Dramatic Art. In England she played in *Dark Eyes* and *Young and Fair.*

In 1951 she joined her brothers Murray and Donald Davis and bought Crest Theatre, a cradle of Canadian talent in Toronto, Ontario. J.B. Priestly wrote *The Glass Cage* for the trio. It played Picadilly Theatre, the first company from an overseas and commonwealth country to be produced on the London stage. A mainstay of Stratford plays, she and husband Max Helpmann have also toured with Canadian players. She played Zenocrate in *Tamburlaine the Great,* on Broadway. She has also starred in numerous television dramas in both Canada and England.

* * *

Active in radio, television and stage work the late Catherine Proctor played "Gran" in *Whiteoaks* and achieved fame in New York's Belasco Theatre at the age of eighteen. Later she lectured to drama students on Romance of the Theatre.

In the '50s, Ottawa's Suzanne Cloutier flew to Hollywood to play a Parisienne in *Temptation*, toured France in stage plays, starred in *Au Royaume des Cieux* and the English film *Derby Day*. She played Desdemona opposite Orson Welles in 1950. Following her marriage to actor, writer, director Peter Ustinov in 1954, Suzanne exchanged the acting life for the role of wife and mother.

Shining Star

"I louse up everything . . . except up there, on the boards. The stage is security for me," says Kate Reid. Born in Oakville, Ontario, she was cursed with club feet, kept falling and breaking bones until an operation corrected the disability. Her mother, deserted by her husband, pinched pennies to send Kate to the Toronto Conservatory, where she won an acting award. At the age of seventeen, she gave a memorable performance in Dostoevski's *Crime and Punishment* at Hart House Theatre and not long after worked with the Straw Hat Players.

A teen-age marriage, and a later one to Austin Willis ended unhappily. "It used to be ghastly" she exclaims, bitter about having to raise her two children, Reid and Robin alone. But now they are the mainspring of Kate's life, she renounces many well-paying tours to be with them, spends a fortune on phone calls. Untidy and a poor organizer, warm-hearted Kate has kept her housekeeper for 13 years. Her health, figure, and finances are ever-present problems. In London, England, in 1955, Kate starred in *The Rainmaker* but rushed home when she learned her mother was seriously ill. Kate is an instinctive actress — a perfectionist. Some of her excellent television performances have been in Rebecca West's powerful *Salt of the Earth, Mother Courage, The Paper People* and *Little Women,* her work in the latter winning her the Canadian Authors and Artists Bronze Award.

Her Lady Macbeth and Katherine in *The Taming of the Shrew* at Stratford brought loud critical acclaim as did her roles with the touring Canadian Players. "Kate Reid has got tremendous stage power and finesse," says Arthur Miller, who had her play the lead on Broadway in his play *The Price.* Andrew Allan says: "She burns with an inner light" — a quality very much in evidence in her searing performance on Broadway as Martha in Albee's *Who's Afraid of Virginia Wolfe.*

Stage Hijinks

For stage front and centre hijinks few can match the rubber-faced versatility of comedienne Barbara Hamilton. Her memorable skits were bright spots of many a *Spring Thaw* revue earning her the undisputed title "Queen of Spring Thaw". More recently at the Charlottetown Festival, her touching portrayal of Marilla in *Anne of Green Gables* have brought kudos from critics. The long-run success of "Anne" — with its strong run in the opening weeks of the National Arts Centre in Ottawa followed by a booking in London, England — has prompted raves from such assiduous critics as Toronto's Nathan Cohen: "the most popular production in the history of Canadian musical theatre." Barbara was the toast of London, one admirer wrote "Award-winner" on her blouse with lipstick; all this acclaim for a play with little sex and no nudity.

* * *

The Charlottetown Festival sent the stage career of Diane Nyland soaring as critics lauded her sensitive portrayal of the deaf-mute Belinda in *Johnny Belinda*. After a successful several-season run at the Charlottetown Festival, Diane's "Belinda" won new hearts at the National Arts Centre in Ottawa in June, 1969.

The Canadian Players

Organized in 1954 by Tom Patterson and Douglas Campbell, the Canadian Players proved an important outgrowth of the Stratford Festival.

Faced with bankruptcy despite the financial support of Lady Eaton and later, Carl French, the company booked a stripped-stage production of Shaw's *Saint Joan* into Ottawa in October, 1954. The superb acting of Ann Casson (daughter of Dame Sybil Thorndyke and wife of Douglas Campbell) carried the show and brought the critical acclaim the company needed to survive at the box office. Later, an American tour proved both an artistic and financial success. They were the first Canadian company to appear on an American television program — playing *Hamlet* on Ford Foundation's Omnibus Series. More recently, the company has made seasonal tours of North America playing to appreciative drama buffs.

While Stratford and the travelling Canadian Players were breaking new ground, in Quebec Le Theatre de Nouveau Monde and Mme. Jeanine Beaubien's La Poudrière theatre were developing memorable theatre for French-speaking audiences. Outstanding French actresses such as the late Denise Pelletier and, more recently Denise Filiatrault, Louise Marleau and Yvette Brind-Amour have added depth to French language theatre.

Mme. Yvette Brind-Amour seems showered by her fairy godmother with beauty, youth, charm and, additionally, an acting and directing ability. She was founder of the successful Rideau Vert in Montreal in 1949.

In 1958 versatile Jeanine (Mme. Claude) Beaubien spent $160,000 and hundreds of work hours converting the old gunpowder magazine "La Poudrière" on Montreal's Ste. Helene Island into an international theatre producing plays in nine languages. She has supervised all 94 of La Poudrière's productions and acted in many of them, most memorably more than 100 times in the part written for her in *A Wife in the Hand*. Back in the '40s Mme. Beaubien founded La Société Dramatique d'Arvida, acting with the Quebec City Art Theatre and had a popular daily radio program. In Montreal stage and television work combined with National Film Board work in the '50s before La Poudrière. In 1964-65 she was the official narrator for the Montreal Symphony Orchestra matinees. She frequently lectures on theatre and is one of seventeen Board Members of the National Design Council. (Another woman member is Mrs. Thomas Bata of Don Mills, Ontario.) For Expo '67 Mme. Beaubien produced Médi-Théâtre in Man and His Health Pavilion.

Jeanine Beaubien was the first Canadian woman to receive a Fellowship from Royal Society of Arts, London, England and was invested Dame of the Military and Hospitaller Order of Saint Lazarus of Jerusalem in 1966.

Another of Montreal's recent dramatic ventures, La Comedie Canadienne, encourages both French and English playwrights, by producing their work. Ginette Letondal starred in the title role of its opening the Joan of Arc story *The Lark*.

Dominion Drama Festival

Before such developments as Stratford, La Poudrière and, more recently, the National Arts Centre, little theatre productions in scattered centres across the country kept alive interest in theatre. The best of these productions competed — as they still do — in the Dominion Drama Festival for the trophy established by former Governor-General Earl Grey. Amateur talent blossomed in such pioneer theatre groups as Hamilton's Players Guild founded in 1875 under the patronage of the Marquis of Lorne — one of the first amateur groups in North America. Following a hiatus in World War I the guild was revived by Caroline Crerar, president until 1938. For their production of *The Crucible*, the group won the Calvert Trophy.

In Quebec the Montreal Repertory Theatre was founded in 1929 by Martha Allan, daughter of millionaire Sir Montague Allan. She also assisted in organizing the Dominion Drama Festival. Her play *All on a Summer day* in 1934 won the Sir Barry Jackson Trophy. Miss Allan organized the theatre school and library and received the Canadian Drama Award. Her memory is perpetuated in the Martha Allan Trophy. Julia Murphy became resident director of MRT in 1959.

The Ottawa Little Theatre, Canada's oldest continuously-run theatre, started in 1913 as the Ottawa Drama League. At first, the group produced plays wherever they could — even in the Victoria Museum, until displaced by members of Parliament, who met there after the 1916 fire in the Parliament Buildings.

Mrs. Dwight Cruickshank was chairman of a fund-raising drive to raise $75,000 to buy the unused Eastern Methodist Church on the corner of King Edward and Besserer Streets, and convert it into a theatre. She recalls life-long friends who passed by on the other side, lest she ask for donations. Today the 500 seat theatre keeps one of the original pews in the foyer. Rich Little and Amelia Hall, later famous stars, got their theatrical stage training in the OLT. When Sara Bernhardt played there, OLT 'hands' searched frantically to find a French flag (which Bernhardt swiped!). However, today a bust of the great actress stands in the foyer.

The Ottawa Little Theatre was the setting for the first Dominion Drama Festival held in 1933, initiated by Governor-General Lord Bessborough over tea at Government House with Mrs. Cruickshank as one of the guests.

Patron Saint of Canadian Playwrights

Mrs. Roy MacGregor (Gladys) Watt, CDA, B.A., M.J.A. (U.S.A.) has been chairman of the national one-act playwriting competition sponsored by Ottawa Little Theatre for the past twenty-nine consecutive years. This is the oldest national competition in Canada and over one hundred plays are entered annually. A dedicated woman, Mrs. Watt has never received an honorarium.

After helping to found the Little Theatre in Dauphin, Manitoba, she moved to Ottawa in 1937. In thirty years, Gladys Watt has never missed a performance of prize-winning plays, including her own — *Sawdust*. She wrote, directed and produced *And So We Follow* for the St. John Ambulance Society. Two of her plays *Her Day* and *Values* were produced by the CBC; *Without Strings* by CKOY radio in Ottawa. Mrs. Watt was reappointed a governor of the Dominion Drama Festival for the 1967-1970 term.

Her many awards include honorary life membership of Theatre Canada DDF, a City of Ottawa award, a Canadian Drama Award, and the Canadian Centennial Medal in 1967. The coveted Margot Jones Award for outstanding achievement and contribution to live theatre in North America was presented to Mrs. Watt in Washington at the White House during President Johnson's tenure. She received the Order of Canada in 1973.

Prize-Winning Playwright

Prize-winning playwright Clare Foley Coupal (Mrs. J.L. Coupal) of Ottawa has been honoured in four

countries: Canada, the United States, Denmark and
Sweden. She is now at the crest of a dramatic career.
Her record of twenty-three awards, out of thirty-three
competitive entries for legitimate stage one-act plays,
began in 1949 when her first prize winner *When the
Bough Bends* was produced at the Ottawa Little Theatre.

Then in 1962 publisher Just Thorning of Denmark
requested this play, and later sent it up to Sweden,
where it was translated and produced at a Festival in
Stockholm, then produced across Sweden. Mr. Thorning, co-founder of DATS (Danish Amateur Theatre
Incorporated) and IATA (International Amateur Theatre Association) worldwide, authorized Mrs. Harriet
Kjerternes Secher, Secretariat of DATS Institute in
Charlottenlund, Copenhagen to translate fourteen Coupal plays. In 1973 a "Coupal Fond (Fund)" was established at DATS for continuing translations and
productions of Clare Foley Coupal's plays.

In 1975 Mayor Cervantes of St. Louis, Missouri,
presented Clare with the bi-centennial flag of St. Louis,
at City Hall, to commemorate her success in having won
the playwriting competition (two years in succession) of
the Theatre Guild of Webster Groves. Clare's many tributes include a silver tray presented by playwrights
entertained at her home "Clare Haven" and a 1967 citation as an honorary life member of Ottawa's Distinguished Citizen's Club. Mrs. Coupal, in addition to
writing, is currently cataloguing treasures in Dr. Coupal's private Museum of Canadiana. Their only daughter, Sandra, is a well-known pianist, composer and
teacher. Also in 1975 Dr. Dora Mavor Moore launched
Coupal plays in Toronto with productions at Royal
Ontario Museum and her New Play Society School.
Demands for scripts escalated across Canada after
Dora's Festival of Ten Best Canadian Plays. American
and Canadian universities asked for scripts as did
libraries and anthologists.

Mrs. Jean Bennett head of Canadian acquisitions, National Archives Library of Canada sent for some Coupal Danish copies to be filed with her English prize-winning plays published by the One-Act Playwriting Competition of the Ottawa Little Theatre, through a Canada Council grant in Volumes I and II.

Clare is a national member of the Canadian Author's Association, and in the Spring of 1977 she was guest speaker at Canadian Author's meetings in Ottawa and also in Montreal. Her topic was *Creative Writing for the Legitimate Stage*. Memberships include Theatre Ontario, Nova Scotia Drama League (which published *Cold Flame* in 1976), Canadian Child and Youth Drama Association. She has been a Governor on the Board of Theatre Canada D.D.F. since 1974.

A Gifted Dramatist

Also known to Ottawa audiences is the work of Alberta-born Gwen Pharis Ringwood, whose one-act play *Lament for Harmonica* won the Ottawa Little Theatre Birks Medal and was later produced on CBC television as was *The Deep Has Many Voices*. Of her play *Dark Harvest*, one critic said: "probably the best play that any native-born Canadian author has written ... she is a very gifted dramatist." For years the play was unpublished and unperformed. Finally, Thomas Nelson and Sons published it. Its first production was at the University of Manitoba and placed first in a playwriting contest in 1941. The play *Still Stands the House* became classroom drama text.

Mrs. Ringwood, a mother of four, has put her masters degree in dramatic art to good use by conducting speech and drama workshops in British Columbia and giving a course in speech arts to students at the Cariboo Indian School. She is a short story writer and published novelist as well.

* * *

During the '50s the plays of two busy authors, Mrs. Elda Cadogan and Mary Jukes were presented in skillfully directed productions. Good directors were a scarce commodity, according to adjudicator Pamela Stirling, who judged the 1956 Dominion Drama Festival. "The dominant need in theatres across Canada is stronger directors!" Her complaint was an echo of L. W. Brockington's comments of 1932 when he had adjudicated the Alberta Festival. "What this country needs is not so much a good 5 cent cigar but a good school of dramatic training," he maintained.

A year later, the Banff School of Fine Arts, organized by Dr. A.E. Corbett and Elizabeth Sterling Haynes, through a Carnegie Foundation grant, helped to ease the situation. Another Westerner who has contributed greatly is Mary Ellen Burgess of the Saskatchewan Arts Board. At drama festivals and regular productions, good directors such as Manitoba's Pauline Boutal, actress-directors Dorothy Davies and Dorothy Somerset, Joy Coghill and Myra Benson, all of Vancouver, also Newfoundland's Neala Griffin have given audiences memorable evenings of theatre.

Good directors must have good training and that is Dr. Betty Mitchell's department. A sophisticated mathematics and English teacher who also has a degree in botany, Dr. Mitchell's heart really belongs to theatre. Miss Mitchell spent a year visiting American amateur theatre groups on a Rockefeller Scholarship, then organized Workshop 14 at Calgary. She and Elizabeth Sterling Haynes jointly succeeded in establishing drama as an accredited course in Alberta schools, the first province in Canada to do so. More than 100 of her graduates are now in professional theatre.

Dr. Mitchell's group has won regional drama festival awards nine times. Their *The Lady's Not for*

Burning captured a plaque for best English-language play in one Dominion Drama Festival. Robert Speaight, British adjudicator, called Dr. Mitchell's production *Hedda Gabler*: "The best I have seen on six continents." In 1960, she was one of Canada's first Canadian adjudicators for the DDF in Toronto and two years later she helped found the Calgary Allied Arts Centre Theatre, dedicated in her honor. Winner of the Canadian Drama Award, Dr. Mitchell is the first person in Canada with an honorary degree in amateur theatre. In 1967, Workshop 14 became a professional theatre using the name Theatre Calgary.

Dedicated Director

When Mrs. Haynes produced *The Slave with Two Faces* at Institute of Pacific Relations conference at Banff, all the Asiatic delegates requested copies. She had two other plays produced, and directed *Tomorrow is no Island* in New York, where she invariably spent her holidays — seeing plays.

Thanks to Dr. George Hardy, famous novelist and head of the English Department there, the University of Alberta was so fortunate as to secure Elizabeth Sterling Haynes as Director of Dramatics. Starting with *Dear Brutus* (with Betty Mitchell) she helped direct twelve plays in two months! Her *Othello* won the Calvert Trophy in 1953. Starring in *Elizabeth the Queen* and *Madwoman of Chaillot* Elizabeth gave a thrilling performance. She was appointed director of Studio Theatre established in 1949 by the University.

She visited over 500 communities in five years, and never voiced a complaint about the rutty roads, terrible meals, and worse hotels. But wooden acting or poor directing infuriated her. She toured Canada for Canadian Clubs and University Women's Clubs, lecturing on Creative Theatre. The North American expert on this subject she trained dozens of actors, directors and playwrights, and wrote two valuable books. Recipient of Chamber of Commerce Citizenship Award, and Canada Drama Award, her death in 1957 was an irreparable loss to Canadian theatre. The Women's Theatre Guild Scholarship Fund honors her.

Versatile Student

Mrs. Norma Springford, of Montreal, was born in Saint John, N.B. and studied theatre with Elizabeth Sterling Haynes for three years. She is a producer, consultant, director, educator, adjudicator and remedial drama specialist. She first directed Montreal little theatre groups, including the McGill Player's Club's Theatre-in-the Round when it won the Martha Allan Trophy. She was production manager for Rosanna Seaborn's Shakespearian Theatre, then producer-owner, Mountain Playhouse Incorporated 1951-1961, associate-director, and company touring manager of Gratien Gelinas's English production *Bousille et les Justes*, assistant producer of two full-length films in French and television films in English. Since 1958 Mrs. Springford has conducted community theatre seminars in all provinces, and is now assistant professor, of drama Department of Fine Arts at Sir George Williams University, in Montreal. She has been awarded the "Congrès du Spectacle" and Canadian Drama Award for her great contribution to Canadian theatre.

* * *

Miss Vida Peene is a long-time generous patron of the arts in Canada. Among her interesting activities: an original member of the Canada Council, a president of Dominion Drama Festival, governor of National Theatre Society of Canada, member of Board of Canadian Music Centre, director Canadian Opera Association, director of Hart House Orchestra Committee, member of Canadian Centenary Council; in 1961 she was chairman of the editorial committee, Canadian Federation of University Women, who published *The Clear Spirit*, a book of biographies of Canadian women in 1966.

Workshop Promoter

Mrs. Dorothy White was the driving force behind Ottawa Little Theatre Workshop and in the '30s handled almost every OLT chore from actress to dishwasher, to costume designer and director. She won an award in 1939 for her direction of the play *French Without Tears*.

Another long-time OLT worker is Mrs. Douglas (Bubbles) Blair who was active in the Women's Liberal Federation, before her appointment as executive secretary to Judy LaMarsh in 1963. She was a director of Ottawa Welfare Bureau, a member of Canadian Welfare Council and was appointed hostess at the federal government's official guest house, Rideau Hall, in 1967 where she regularly welcomed Royalty and other celebrated official visitors.

Film Fame

It was poetic justice in the '50s when movies suddenly found audiences depleted, because millions of people stayed home to watch the new marvel, television. Talking pictures had wrought the same kind of havoc on live entertainment twenty years before. Movies lured patrons away from stage performances, inducing them to sit and watch flickering figures, listening to the pit pianist tinkle out "Hearts and Flowers," or "Horses, Horses, Horses".

Most theatres were converted into film houses and stages torn out. One of the early moving picture projectionists was a woman, Mrs. Eva Delaney, a talented musician. The Delaneys operated theatres in Pembroke, Renfrew, Smiths Falls and Picton. Moving to Gananoque, she was elected to City Council and in 1954 was named the town's outstanding citizen. Today, several women own and manage moving picture theatres, including Mrs. Helen Nesbitt of Edmonton and Mrs. J.

V. McLaughlin of Newcastle.

The steady flow of Canadian actresses in search of film fame to the United States and abroad began with Marie Dressler and Mary Pickford, who became America's Sweetheart.

Chairman of The Entertainment Committee

"My red hair is my own, but it was Alexander von Koerber who bequeathed me the T.N.T. that goes with it!" Marie Dressler would exclaim, speaking of her embittered, expatriate Austrian father, whose music talent she inherited. From her beloved Irish mother she inherited courage and laughter.

Born in Cobourg, Ontario, as a teenager she said ruefully: "I was born chairman of the entertainment committee!" At thirteen she began clerking in the underwear department of a store in Cobourg. She was fired for sending, by mistake, a suit of men's red flannel underwear to the primmest spinster in town!

She wangled the role of Cigarette in Ouida's *Under Two Flags*. Sick with stage fright, she admonished herself: "Here are folks . . . none too happy. They want to laugh and forget. It's my job to help them!" Marie practically lived in the theatre — an eager apprentice, at 23 she was acclaimed for her performance in *The Robbers of the Rhine* by Maurice Barrymore. Marie had memorized the whole show, which was fortunate — everyone else had stage fright and completely forgot their lines! Her prompting saved the show.

In 1896 she became the star in *Lady Slavery* and played the part for four years on Broadway. Marie became violently ill and Abe Erlanger, accusing her of faking illness, kept her off Broadway for four years. Later, turning to films, she made *Tillie's Nightmare* and *Tillie's Punctured Romance* for Quebec-born Mack Sennett and persuaded him to hire a Cockney lad — Charlie Chaplin.

Back on stage, in Proctor's Vaudeville House, Marie swaggered out to do her comedy routine with a basket of onions. Socialite, Mrs. Stuyvesant Fish, sitting in the first row got the full impact of the routine when an onion Marie tossed hit her tiara. Mrs. Fish, proved sporting, promptly invited Marie to a party and tossed a diamond bracelet at *her!*

In 1916, playing the *Century Girl on Broadway* for Florenz Ziegfeld, Marie tried to supervise rehearsals, but not for long — Ziegfeld fired her! Marie longed to be a tragedienne. George Edwards cast her in a dramatic role — then failed! Augustin Daly cast her in a tragedy — then died! Louis Calvert similarly died.

Moon-faced, six feet tall and weighting over two hundred, Marie was so homely that when she went cycling in Central Park with Lillian Russell — both in bloomers — they were nicknamed "Beauty and the Beastie." But everyone loved Marie. When *Anna Christie* with Greta Garbo in the title role was released in 1930, critics claimed: "A homely old woman has stolen the show from the beautiful star!" Marie played Marthy, an old waterfront "soak" in the film. During the depression years, Marie helped many keep their sanity by the healing power of laughter. In four years she made 24 movies so successful they grossed $50,000,000, the most memorable of which were *Min and Bill* and *Tugboat Annie.*

In 1931 she won an Oscar as best actress and was judged "Actress of the Year" a year later. She died of cancer in 1934 and was buried in Wee Kirk of Heather churchyard, New York, beside her enemy, Florenz Ziegfeld. Marie Dressler Restaurant in Cobourg, owned by Mrs. Lena Field Fisher, active in community welfare, has become almost a shrine. Thousands of fans each summer visit their idol's birthplace.

Mary Pickford

444

America's Sweetheart

Mary Pickford's acting career got a precocious start because her mother couldn't find a baby-sitter in turn-of-the-century Toronto. Mary's widowed mother, a part-time actress, brought her five-year old daughter along to the theatre on the very day the manager was searching for a child actress for *Bootle's Baby*. So began the career of *"America's Sweetheart"*. Young Mary, her sister Lottie and brother Jack, spent the next few years touring eastern United States with their mother, who understudied all the women in the cast. The family earned twenty dollars a week plus railway fare.

In New York, at 14, Mary charmed David Belasco into hiring her for *The Warrens of Virginia*. In 1909 Biograph Studios gave her the lead in *The Violin Maker of Cremona*. She was called "The Biograph Girl with the Curls"! (Even when she was famous, she always washed her hair herself with a raw egg followed by lemon rinse.)

In 1913, she returned to Belasco in a stage hit as the blind girl in *A Good Little Devil* which was later filmed. A year later, Mary had her first screen hit in *Hearts Adrift* for Famous Players; at 23 she was making half the profits of each picture, a guaranteed $10,000 a week — a king's ransom then. Mutual Studios offered a half million a year but she decided to stay with Zukor, who was like a father to her.

Seeing Mary Pickford walking by one day, Sam Goldwyn exclaimed: "My God, $10,000 a week and still she walks to work!" In *Friends* (with Lionel Barrymore and Henry B. Walthall) the great director, D. W. Griffith, took a close-up of Mary — a first for an actor. *Tess of the Storm Country*, a smash hit, was made in 1914.

At 16, Mary had secretly married actor Owen Moore much against her mother's wishes. In 1920 she divorced Owen and married Douglas Fairbanks. They enjoyed 15 years in their luxurious home "Pickfair" (loaned to USO as a troop-entertainment centre during World War II). Mary divorced Fairbanks and married band leader "Buddy" Rogers.

Around 1935 Mary Pickford returned to Toronto to supervise the sale of her old home on University Avenue (on part of the site of Sick Children's Hospital) and to aid the Toronto Star Fresh Air Fund. (Fond of children, she adopted two herself, Ronnie and Roxie Rogers.)

Mary Pickford did a great deal of philanthropic work, also earned a good income from her cosmetic firm in later years. In 1934 she made her debut as a writer with *Why Not Try God?*, and wrote several other books, including her autobiography.

Rags To Riches

In 1918, when Norma Shearer was 14, her father died, leaving the family practically penniless in Montreal. They sold their grand piano to go to New York, hoping Norma could get an acting job.

"We lived in a flat in Manhattan," she recalled; "Every time a train rattled past, it nearly shook the pictures off the wall! Summer heat was so unbearable we slept at Coney Island." First she played minor roles with Biograph. Success in *The Stealers* and *Channing of the Northwest* won her a contract with MGM in Hollywood.

Her contract was only four weeks — with an option for five years. In Hollywood she met Mayer's talented general manager, Irving Thalberg, and four years later they were married. In her first year in the film capital Norma made eight films. Both *He Who Gets Slapped* and Norma were hits. Her next film *Lady of the Night* and those that followed assured her stardom. Her performance in *The Divorcee* in 1929 won her the coveted Academy Award. However, *Smiling Through* was her most popular film.

After a hiatus in her career following the death of her husband in 1936, she resumed acting and became one of Hollywood's wealthiest stars. Her last screen appearance was as star in *Romeo and Juliet*.

Golden Voice

Deanna Durbin, the Winnipeg-born "girl with the golden voice" pulled Universal Studios out of almost certain bankruptcy with a string of hits from *Three Smart Girls* in 1936 onward. Her sister Edith financed Deanna's musical education. In 1935, at age 12, she played the role of Mme. Ernestine Schumann-Heink, as a child, in a film biography. Then Deanna was forgotten — until producer Rufus LeMaire of Universal needed a little girl. Starting at $350 a week, at 18 she was making $200,000 a year. Deanna had appeared with Leopold Stokowski in *One Hundred Men and a Girl*, and had won a junior Oscar in 1938 for *That Certain Age*. She retired wealthy. In 1955 she sang her hit number — Il Bacio — on television, then slipped back into her preferred quiet life in France as a wife and mother.

The Greatest Sinner

"She can't sing, she can't dance, she can't act — so we made her the star of the picture," groaned a Hollywood director when sultry Yvonne de Carlo arrived in cinema city. Vancouver-born Yvonne had won a contest as "The Most Beautiful Girl in the World" with the prize — the starring role in *Salome, Where she Danced*. (The Salome, in this case, was the name of a western town.)

Born in a charity ward of Vancouver Hospital, the daughter of impoverished stage troupers, Yvonne, at 13, had managed to study dancing and was playing bit parts in little theatre productions. Her first public performance as a dancer netted $3. In Hollywood, Yvonne worked hard to prove she had acting ability as well as beauty. Her many films included: *The Magic Fire* (Wagner's Life), *Captain's Paradise* with Alex Guiness; as Sephora, the wife of Moses in *The Ten Commandments*; as Mary Magdalene in *The Greatest Sinner*.

GIN AND TONIC

Probably the brightest star on the horizon is Quebec's Genevieve Bujold, a pixie brunette, trained in classical drama in Montreal who achieved prominence in three films shot in France in the late '60s. Work in CBC Festival dramas for two years with Toronto producer Paul Almond led to marriage. Widely acclaimed in a two-hour television dramatization of Saint Joan on CBC TV, she describes *The Act of the Heart*, a play produced and directed by her husband in which she acted the story of a modern saint.

When Richard Burton saw her pensive performance in the avant-garde French film *Isabelle* he chose her to play Anne Boleyn opposite his Henry VIII in the $6,000,000 movie, *Anne of a Thousand Days*. Canadian actress Katherine Blake plays Anne's mother in the almost completely Canadian film made in England. Burton says, " 'Gin' (she calls me 'Tonic'!) is remarkable, absolutely delicious. She has the quality of another Vivien Leigh." Indeed, film commitments mounted so quickly for Genevieve that she had to postpone her plans to play in *Caesar and Cleopatra* in the 1969-70 season of Theatre de Nouveau Monde, Montreal. Rather than cast another actress, Le Théâtre decided to book the play for the 1970-71 season, when Miss Bujold would be back to play the role. (Miss Bujold was chosen Woman of the Year in Stage, Screen and TV in 1969).

* * *

Although Canada has produced a good many prominent actors and directors, the country's feature film industry has, with certain exceptions, been notably

448

less productive. Documentary films and short features by both private companies and National Film Board have tended to dominate the film field — many winning international awards.

Crawley Films in Ottawa with husband and wife team Judy and "Budge" Crawley at the helm started modestly in 1943 and now has a giant slice of the Canadian film market, churning out versatile, creative films for both government and private clients, and grossing about $1,500,000 annually. More than 162 of the firm's 2000-odd films made in 22 languages have won national or international awards.

Another Team

After working several years for NFB, Alma Duncan and Audrey MacLaren combined in 1952 as Dunclaren Productions. The only independent producers of animated films in Canada, their films, in school and university libraries, also have been shown on television in Canada and the United States.

Versatility Personified

Versatile actress-producer Rosanna Seaborn Todd has produced several films distributed throughout Quebec including *Coeur de Maman* and *L'Esprit du Mal*, the most popular French-Canadian films ever made, the latter costing $150,000 and grossing $1,000,000. Because of austere moral attitudes of rural Québecois, sex was taboo, she therefore substituted cruelty and avarice, with righteousness finally triumphant! These films have been revived as recently as August 1969 with packed houses at double usual prices. An inveterate world-traveller, she finds an appalling ignorance of Canada which she hopes will be rectified by Canadian-made films. For health reasons, she now lives at Lyford Cay, Nassau, the Bahamas. Her unusual home there is built to resemble a Roman ruin with fortress walls, statuary and a sunken pool.

Daughter of noted bacteriologist Dr. John L. Todd, whose work is cited with Pasteur's and Lister's in an English Museum, lovely Rosanna is fully bilingual and is very proud of some Canadian Indian blood.

In 1947 she founded and acted in Montreal Open Air Playhouse, atop Mount Royal. At the Playhouse she directed Shakespearian plays for four years, once bringing in Theodore Komisarjevsky to stage *Cymbeline* in modern dress — Christopher Plummer's first starring role, playing "Posthumous" to Rosanna Seaborn's "Imogen". In recent years she has extensively researched the Papineau Rebellion of 1837 in Canada, London and Paris with a view to making a historical epic — a sort of Canadian *Gone with the Wind*.

Team Effort

The Canadian writer-producer team Marian Grudeff and Roy Jessel combined to create the Broadway hit *Baker Street*. Their latest musical, a light-hearted spoof on hippiedom, *Life Can Be — Like Wow* was on view at the 1969 Charlottetown Festival. Both live and work in New York, commuting to Canada for special assignments.

* * *

New York acclaim also came to Patricia Joudry whose *Teach Me How to Cry* was first produced in Theatre de Lys, New York then Toronto. It was presented by University Alumnae of Toronto and at the 1956 DDF in Sherbrooke. Hollywood paid $25,000 to film it as *The Restless Years*. The Steeles (Patricia's husband is photographer John Steele) went to London 1957 to produce *Teach Me How to Cry* (called *Noon Has No Shadows*) and *Three Rings for Michelle* in London's West End. *The Sand Castle*, *Walk Alone Together*, and *Song of Louise in the Morning* are other successful Joudry plays. *Noon Has No Shadows* received nine curtain calls.

Suzanne Finley, Toronto TV actress playing Melinda received the best actress award in the 1956 DDF. Glamorous Patricia Joudry once played the heroine of *Penny's Diary*, a radio serial and also *The Aldrich Family* for a U.S. network. In 1957 she tied with Gabrielle Roy as Canada's outstanding woman in literature and art. She shocked the world by announcing that from her alleged affair with George Bernard Shaw would come the second Christ.

World of Ballet

While an art in itself, ballet is closely allied with both music and theatre. Canada has produced a number of fine dancers but few as daring as Maude Allan whose "Salome" shocked polite society in 1908. Maude made her dancing debut in 1903, the start of a successful 14 year career as a pioneer of aesthetic dancing. In 1907 she danced before King Edward VII and the following year appeared at the London Palace Theatre in her *Visions of Salome* in transparent draperies, creating a sensation that has weathered the years.

Dancing Duo

A contemporary team, Blanche and Allan Lund, an outstanding pair of ballroom dancers are probably Canada's best known dancing duo. Together since high school days in Toronto, in the Navy Show during the War, the Lunds have danced on theatre stages, in supper clubs across America and Europe and at two royal command performances in London. A broken foot, a baby, even a severe attack of poliomyelitis have interrupted Blanche's career only temporarily. Always a team, the Lunds handled the choreography for "Caribbean Mardi Gras" at the Canadian Exhibition, Toronto in 1957 and most recently a number of successful revues and musicals including *Johnny Belinda*. They own and operate the Blanche and Allan Lund School of Dance.

* * *

Montreal's Spanish Gypsy, Sonia del Rio, is really French-Canadian. She was studying classical ballet when she saw Jose Greco dance in Montreal, was captivated and went back-stage to dance for him. He persuaded her parents to send her to Paris to study. Shortly after she went to Spain, where she was fortunate to have Hector Zaraspe teach her. Sonia now says: "I dance flamencos like a real gypsy."

* * *

Before Canada had a national ballet company, the Volkoff Ballet School founded in Toronto by a Russian expatriate, Boris Volkoff, and his wife, Janet Baldwin, trained promising dancers.

Melissa Hayden, for years Prima Ballerina of New York City Ballet, is one of its most famous graduates. At 15, in 1942, she got her start with night classes from Volkoff. Her professional career began in 1945 with the corps de ballet of Radio City Music Hall, whose ballet mistress is Canadian-born Florence Rogge. She was joined two years later by another Volkoff graduate, Patricia Drylie, later leader of the ballet in *My Fair Lady*. Melissa toured Europe and South America; was chosen by Charlie Chaplin to appear for Claire Bloom in *Limelight*. When she joined the New York City Ballet, she was accompanied by two other Canadian ballerinas, Maria Tallchief, an Indian, and Patricia Wilde.

In 1952, Miss Hayden, who for years suffered excruciating pain from a slipped disc in her back, was told by a specialist that her dancing days were over. Refusing to give up, she salvaged her career with painful exercises. In 1958 she danced at Brussel's World Fair; in 1960 toured for three months as Prima Ballerina of Ruth Paige's Chicago Opera Ballet; in 1963 received the annual award of Dance Magazine.

* * *

Canadians are extraordinarily successful in ballet, having two companies with international reputations. In 1939 Canada had only three ballet companies. By 1957 there were more than 20.

Royal Winnipeg

Englishwomen Gweneth Lloyd, S.M. director, and Betty Hay-Farally, ballet mistress, in 1938 founded the Winnipeg Ballet with a little cash and a lot of courage, accomplishing wonders. After a few years, they were able to support 20 Canadian dancers, among them ballerina Carlu Carter. Classes for professional teachers began in 1945. Jeanne MacKenzie, a graduate, teaches ballet in Vancouver. In 1951, the group received the prefix "Royal" when co-ordinating director, Lady Tupper arranged a performance for H.R.H. Princess Elizabeth during her first Canadian tour.

Miss Lloyd maintains: "We have no desire to follow slavishly the classical ballet. We want conceptions and interpretations that are Canadian." An example is *Kilowatt Magic*, a ballet telling the story of electricity, first produced in 1940. Miss Lloyd has created most of the group's modern ballets.

A 1954 fire destroyed everything but the spirit of the Royal Winnipeg Ballet. With no savings and no insurance, the group had to start from scratch again. An enthusiastic campaign to "put the Ballet back on its toes" was a quick success. Canada Council gave a small grant in 1957 which had risen to $170,000 by 1968. That year Arnold Spohr became artistic director. Principal dancers with the company include Christine Hennessy, Sheila MacKinnon and Alexandra Nadal. The Royal Winnipeg Ballet is a winner of two gold medals, one of them for *Best Company* at the 1968 ballet festival in Paris.

* * *

The most innovative contemporary company in Canada is Montreal's "Les Feux Follets" whose zestful spirited interpretations of Canadian history were a rousing success at Expo '67 and since then in both North American and European performances.

Ottawa's hard-working dance company, The Ballet Imperial of Canada is under the direction of Nesta Williams Toumine, a former member of the Ballet Russes de Monte Carlo in North American and European tours. Returning to Ottawa in 1946 to teach, she founded the Classical Ballet Company. The group has restaged many classics, and created original works such as *Maria Chapdelaine*, *Fadette*, *Gymnopedies* and the full-length *Cinderella*. In 1965, Miss Toumine enlarged the company and changed its name.

National Ballet

At the age of two, Celia Franca S.M., taken to a wedding by her parents, danced around the ballroom and when the orchestra started playing even tried to conduct the band. An outstanding dramatic dancer of Sadler Wells Ballet, she later became ballet mistress of London's Metropolitan Ballet.

When a group of Toronto balletomanes in 1951 asked Sadler Wells for help in organizing a national company, Ninette de Valois, founder-director, sent Celia Franca. She braved perishing cold, in both the literal and cultural sense, to ferret out dancers in circuses, one even from a law school. Celia organized the National Ballet of Canada in a lysol-reeking market loft, where Jenny Lind once sang, and which later had sheltered homeless vagrants. The twenty-four member National Ballet made its debut November 12, 1951 in Toronto's Eaton Auditorium.

In 1956 they staged the world premiere of *Swan*

Lake and since have presented *Coppelia, Winter Night, Casse Noisette,* and *Pineapple Poll* on television. That year, in Denver and again in 1958 in Mexico City, high altitude so exhausted the dancers' lungs, they had to be supplied with oxygen in the wings, by sympathetic firemen. Of 65 ballets, from classical to contemporary, two original Canadian ones, *The Fisherman and His Soul,* and *Postscripts* proved most popular. In 1958, Canada Council encouraged them with a grant of $100,000 and several large grants since, making possible luxuries like the Italian-made costumes costing $100,000 for *Romeo and Juliet.*

Grants also materialized Celia Franca's dream of a ballet school, where children can study ballet and academic subjects, patterned after Royal Ballet and Bolshoi Ballet Schools. Principal was Betty Oliphant, who was also ballet mistress. Academic principal was Mrs. Frank Haworth. A Toronto girl, Shirley Kash, in 1959, at nineteen, became assistant ballet mistress, a position held in 1969 by Carol Chadwick.

Lois Smith, prima ballerina of National Ballet Company is married to the male lead, David Adams. She danced with Vancouver's "Theatre Under the Stars" and the Los Angeles Light Opera Company, before joining the National Ballet. Due to several injuries she decided to resign to open her own ballet school.

Martine Van Hamel, daughter of a Netherlands diplomat, started ballet lessons at four in Copenhagen. She came to the National Ballet School in 1959, graduating at seventeen and becoming a soloist. Her rigid routine of six and a half hours daily practise and rigid dieting, paid off when she won three awards at the International Ballet Competition in Bulgaria and returned home a celebrity. The Ballet's TV production of *Romeo and Juliet,* in which she starred, was awarded first prize at Monte Carlo Festival in the spring of 1966. Martine was awarded an International Nickel Company of Canada Centennial Year scholarship in the performing arts. Martine left the National Ballet because of a personality clash with Miss Franca.

The year 1959 was eventful for Canadian National Ballet and its director. On its ninth North American tour, Ballet visited many centres that normally do not see ballet, playing in hockey rinks, converted barns, cinemas and school auditoria.

Celia Franca, who maintains that ballet is not an art but a way of life, inspires students to take "the artist's highway of hardship, hard work . . . even heartbreak." She was named "Woman of the Year" by B'nai B'rith women of Toronto, given an honorary LL.D. by Assumption University in Windsor, received the *Toronto Telegram* award for the most outstanding contribution to the arts in Canada, and became the first woman to receive a gold key to the city of Washington.

No other art form except opera provides such a vehicle for a nation's varied arts — as does ballet. Like the drama, ballet is the core of living theatre, both thriving on the two-way reaction between audience and performer that is the life-blood of all stage presentations. Theatre means much more than imposing "palaces of culture" such as Canada's $46,000,000 National Arts Centre. Living theatre means performers who can move audiences to laughter or tears, playwrights who write with power, and directors capable of interpretation. The theatre is "the temple of the passions", enabling mankind to forget its mundane problems and live gloriously for a few hours. When it accomplishes this, theatre is an art, even though it cannot leave such a permanent record as music, painting or writing.

Chapter XV

Media Messages

Radio and Television

Elizabeth Long

> *We found an important place in
> radio for women, presenting and
> interpreting the personal side of life.*
> (Elizabeth Long)

Livingroom Studio

"It was thrilling," said Flora Rogers, speaking of
the time she first heard a human voice over radio. That
was in Halifax towards the end of World War I when
radio operators on two American submarine-chasers
were testing equipment.

Flora, later president of CFCY radio and television, Charlottetown, was a radio pioneer. Her husband,
Col. Keith Rogers, built the first private radio station in
the Maritimes, working on a shoestring budget. He was
granted the first commercial licence in Eastern Canada
in 1924 and he and Flora arranged studio programs from
their livingroom, with the doorbell and telephone dis-
connected and their three children snickering from the
stairs. By 1950, CFCY had increased from the original
500 watts to 5,000 watts. When Keith died four years
later, Flora became president and continued his work. In
1958 the family built a television tower, a fitting memorial to a pioneer.

Popular Pioneer

Another popular pioneer of the airwaves is Jane
Gray, Canadian import from Croydon, England. After

45 years "on the air" she was still a fascinating broadcaster always ready to help raise money for the needy. Her programs on CHML and CHCH-TV originating from Hamilton have included numerology, hobbycraft, "Sunday school of the Air" and advice on contemporary problems of all kinds. Among her Jane Gray Players (CFCA) were the late Donald Gordon and Hart Wintrob, Bill Crampton and Gordon McLain, a few of many she inspired to attain greatness.

Jane was one of the mourners at the funeral of Kenneth Soble, owner of CHML and co-owner of CHCH-TV. Soble's charming and talented wife, Frances, has taken over his tasks as chairman of the board of Maple Broadcasting Co. Ltd. (CHML and CHML-FM) and president of Niagara Television Ltd. (CHCH-TV). Their daughter was one of the hostesses at Expo '67.

Grandmother of Radio

Mrs. Anna Dexter could be called the grandmother of radio. "I plan to stay in radio till I'm 120 years old," she used to say. Towards the end, till her death at age seventy-eight she broadcast from a hospital bed, protesting: "I'm not too old . . . can't get around much though . . . arthritis of the hip. Thank God it isn't my tongue!" She was the first woman to make regular scheduled broadcasts in North America. Her folksy tales were on the air six times weekly for 24 fan-filled years from 1928. She didn't even own a radio when she was approached by Major Bill Borrett, founder of radio station CHNS, Halifax.

Half-way through her first half-hour broadcast, she audibly tore up her script complaining: "It's unnatural." Doubtless the most informal program on radio, her talks ranged from gardening to government.

Twin Ambitions

Monica Mugan of Winnipeg had two consuming ambitions — to travel, to write — and she achieved both. For three years she travelled throughout Canada as a professional organizer for Chautauqua doing freelance writing. In 1930 she joined radio station CFAC, Calgary, when it had a staff of only three. During the next three years she took a whirl at everything, continuity and script writing, acting in plays, broadcasting news, playing the piano, singing and directing commercial programs. She launched the first women's program "Magazine of the Air" in 1930.

Moving to Toronto in 1936, Monica became one of the CBC's regular morning commentators and the first woman to broadcast direct to Britain. In 1949 she went to England to marry Norman Phillips. In addition to working for the BBC on school broadcasts and adaptations of radio plays — including Irwin Shaw's *Troubled Air*, translated into Persian — she emceed a show aired in Commonwealth countries and was also London correspondent for *Mayfair Magazine*. In Toronto in 1959 she did a series of talks on the CBC on the refugee problem. After her divorce, she went to Montreal in 1965 and took a position with Expo '67.

Chatelaine of the Air

Justina Rice could be called "Chatelaine of the Air." In Edmonton in 1930 her husband, G. R. A. "Dick" Rice, owner of radio station CFRN, persuaded her to initiate an hour-long women's daily program under the pseudonym "Susan Agar — Chatelaine of the Air." Besides the usual hints on cooking, beauty, fashion and music, Justina read outstanding literature and interviewed the authors. Justina was also the gracious chatelaine of her father's famous Springer Hotel before her marriage.

460

Incredible Canadian

In a private surgical ward of Toronto's Western Hospital an intern and a nurse were making their rounds when suddenly the intern stopped — dumbfounded. A grey-haired woman, propped up in bed and having her hair waved, was dictating radio scripts to two secretaries. "Good Lord," exclaimed the intern. "Working already? Surgery for breakfast, work for dinner?" "Why not?" laughed the nurse. "She's conscious isn't she?"

The incident is typical of Kate Aitken, a woman clever enough to realize radio's potential early in the game. Her philosophy — "There isn't anything you can't do if you keep trying" — took her from Beeton, Ontario, to Buckingham Palace; radio work won her an introduction to Queen Elizabeth as the "Best-loved voice in Canada."

The dynamic girl who sold cosmetics at twelve and halted stampeding wild horses at sixteen grew up to marry her childhood sweetheart, Henry Aitken. He ran the family mill while Kate raised chickens and their two daughters. For several years she was adviser to both the Ontario and federal agriculture departments. In 1923, as national secretary of the Federated Women's Institutes, she began twenty years as director of women's activities for the Canadian National Exhibition.

Four years later, she took a Canadian handicrafts exhibit to London, England, presided at an international wheat conference, and flew to Italy to discuss wheat with Mussolini. Labelled the "Winged Woman," Kate used planes more casually than taxis, flying over bombarded Madrid and Bilbao during the 1936 and 1939 Spanish revolution; to the Holy Land for Christmas; to Korea to interview Gen. Rockingham in 1952; and to Nairobi for the Mau-Mau trials in 1955. During her 25-year radio career, Kate travelled over 2,000,000 miles in 54 countries.

During World War II, as supervisor of the consumer branch of the Wartime Prices and Trade Board, she did a survey of Europe and Asia for the British Ministry of Food in 1943. Through radio appeals she provided clothing for thirteen British nurseries. Her broadcasting began in 1934 during a tour of Charlottetown with her cooking school. The regular commentator broke her hip and Kate filled in — she stayed on the air for 24 years, with CFRB, Toronto, and later CBC and CJAD, Montreal. She gave over 40,000 radio talks, receiving some 350,000 letters annually. From 1941 to 1951 she was women's editor of the *Montreal Standard*, helped by 12 secretaries and her daughter, Mary, and also wrote two major articles a month besides newspaper columns. Retiring from radio in 1957, she wrote half a dozen books constantly being revised, and, at 79, was owner of a steel firm.

For two years Kate Aitken represented Canada at the UN. She sponsored the International Association of Women Broadcasters Conference and in 1958 was appointed to the board and was CBC representative to the Canadian National Commission for UNESCO. Toronto columnist Jack Scott grudgingly admits: "This jet-propelled Grannie is the incredible Canadian." Kate Aitken's must have been a hard act to follow but Elsa Jenkins successfully managed to.

First Female TV Announcer

Elsa Jenkins of Peterborough has had a varied career, teaching handicrafts with the Canadian Red Cross and as editor and columnist for *Mayfair Magazine*. In 1951 she was appointed the first woman announcer in Canadian TV and was also a panelist on "Court of Opinion". She became manager of the women's division of the Canadian National Exhibition and organized all women's features, a job which involved considerable travelling to collect exhibits as well as radio and TV appearances. She was instrumental in the opening of the first women's building — the Queen Elizabeth Building — now housed in the Better Living Centre.

Just Mary

The love affair between Canadian children and Mary Grannon ended finally in 1960 with her retirement to Fredericton. For twenty-one years she had written, produced and told more than 1,200 stories on the CBC network, besides organizing children's programs. One early script for Hudson-Terraplane earned her just 75 cents. In 1936 she began working for CFNB and received $3. weekly for the comedy program "Aggravating Agatha." She joined the CBC in 1939. Her famous *Just Mary* and *Maggie Muggins* were broadcast by both CBC and the US educational networks, and immortalized in twenty books which have sold over 350,000 copies. In 1942 she won an award from the Institution of Education by Radio. She is an honorary member of the Mark Twain Society and in 1947 won a Beaver Award.

Claire for Courage

Claire Wallace was the first woman to broadcast nationally over CBC and in 1949 was at the crest of her career. As the radio personality with the highest audience rating in Canada, she signed a contract for $1,000 a week.

Born in Orangeville in 1906, shy Claire was excused from giving oral compositions at school. She had two great ambitions, both of which she realized, to have a son and to write. A year after she married, her son Wallace was born. Between fixing formulas, Claire wrote "fillers." She begged H. C. Hindmarsh of the *Toronto Star* for a staff position but he refused. She persisted until he finally relented. After a disastrous foray into London's Fleet Street, Claire returned to Toronto in 1935 but was unable to obtain a writing assignment

Claire Wallace

immediately. In desperation she started broadcasting Teatime Topics over CFRB.

In 1936 she switched to CBC with the program "They Tell Me" and became famous for offbeat stories. She interviewed a horse, broadcast from a salt mine 3,000 feet underground and from a volcano in Mexico. She was the only Canadian woman to report the formation of the United Nations in San Francisco. Her program became second only to the "Happy Gang" in popularity. The Six Nations Indians gave her the title

"Voice Heard all Over the Land," and she collected over $2,000 from fans for the Save the Children Fund.

She was nicknamed "Queen of the Castle" because she persuaded Toronto Kiwanis to make a tourist attraction of Casa Loma. The money raised helps underprivileged children and the elderly. When Claire joined "Hide and Seek" on television, fans saw their favorite radio voice as a tall, slim woman with a radiant smile and chic hats. In 1946 she won the Beaver Award as Canada's top woman commentator. Her etiquette guide *Mind Your Manners* was published in 1953 and revised with a travel section in 1960. For several years she headed the Claire Wallace Travel Bureau. Poor health in later life and the tragic death of her son resulted in a heart attack which killed Claire, one of Canada's best-loved broadcasters.

Never Marry A Nudist:

Pretty, honey-blonde Elsie Park Gowan had one recurring complaint during the years she wrote so prolifically for the CBC, that of radio scripts being ripped prematurely from her typewriter by over-eager producers. Elsie wrote many historical series and dramas for National School Broadcasts and for Columbia's School of the Air. However, her article *Never Marry A Nudist* probably attracted most comment. Both she and her husband, Dr. E. H. Gowan, were practising nudists.

Permanently stagestruck, she wrote award-winning plays such as *The Giantkillers, The Royal Touch,* and *Breeches from Bond Street.* She also wrote a highly successful pageant, *Who Builds a City,* for Edmonton's golden anniversary.

* * *

Mrs. Aline Fortier of CHRC, Quebec City, was in radio for almost thirty years. Widowed at twenty-five with five children to support, she took a position with the provincial government. She wrote over 2,000 radio scripts, including two that were broadcast for seven years. She wrote for a Murdochville newspaper as well as supplying a syndicated column to the Quebec papers, *Le Contact,* and magazines of the Business and Professional Women's and Altrusa Club. Also a stage comedienne, she won the Bessborough Trophy.

The Barthe's "Bernhardt"

Another stagestruck broadcaster, Marcelle Barthe, was jokingly called "The Barthe's Bernhardt" by friends. While studying at the School of Music and Elocution at the University of Ottawa she had a role in *L'Innocente* which won the Bessborough Trophy at the Dominion Drama Festival in 1933. Marcelle joined radio station CKCH in Hull, Quebec, and was heard in numerous programs. Rupert Lucas chose her to play in Lady Tweedmuir's *The Vision in the Inn.* In 1938 this completely bilingual and beloved broadcaster became CBC's first woman announcer. She was the only woman assigned to broadcast the Royal Visit in 1939, and by 1945 had achieved an ambition — to have her own program, "Lettre à une Canadienne." For the next 12 years she talked to more than 1,500 distinguished program guests including Mme. Chiang Kai-shek and Eleanor Roosevelt. She died in 1965.

Unique War Work

Another Ottawa area resident, Beatrice Belcourt, was the first Canadian woman to be named "Chevalier of the Legion of Honor" by the French government. On the CBC's public relations staff, she organized the first broadcast to France. As Canada had no shortwave at the time, Miss Belcourt made use of Boston's excellent facilities. Her broadcasts, heard even in the concentration camps, were credited with saving the Norwegian fleet from capture by the German navy. Miss Belcourt helped Princess Alice set up a Red Cross Committee in Canada to send supplies to the Free French.

Red Cross Lady

Also active in Red Cross work was Mrs. Mary Conquest who raised funds during World War I to build a veterans' hospital in Altario, Alberta where she was district superintendent of supplies. Moving to Calgary, she travelled extensively, lecturing to encourage support for the Red Cross and for crippled children. Despite the amputation of an arm, and later a leg, she continued her work of mercy through radio talks on CJCA and CFRN, Edmonton. Advice and help she gave listeners earned her the title of "Dorothy Dix of the Air." She was awarded the O.B.E. for outstanding service in 1943.

Public Service Programs

The Founder of the Alberta Friendship Clubs, Eve Henderson of Winnipeg, entered radio in 1938 via CKRC. Appointed the station's women's editor in 1945, her public service programs presented the work of the Red Cross, cancer research and the Shriners' Hospital for Crippled Children. She organized and was first president of Winnipeg's Women's Press Club. In 1947 she moved to Edmonton and took over CFRN's women's program. She organized Senior Citizen's Friendship clubs throughout Alberta. In 1948 she won a Beaver Award — her program was rated third in North America by Billboard — and a year later the Women's Advertising Club of St. Louis gave her the Emma Proctor Award for public service.

Power Behind the Microphone

The names of Kate Aitken and Claire Wallace immediately spring to mind as important women radio personalities. But the real power behind the CBC microphones for over fifteen years was an unassuming, pretty woman who is almost unknown. Elizabeth Long, as superviser of women's interests, was the first woman to hold an important executive position with the CBC. Thanks to her efforts, Canada is the only country in the world where women commentators have a year-round, five-day-a-week program. The broadcasts are a boon to lonely housewives in isolated areas — they take the place of a neighbor.

Miss Long presided over the first National Radio Conferences for Women Broadcasters in 1944 and three years later was elected convener of broadcasting for the International Council of Women.

Prominent Maritimers

Findlay MacDonald, manager of radio station CJCH, describes Abbie Lane as "the most prominent woman in the life of the Maritimes." For ten seasons Abbie broadcast "Mary Gillan, Farm Wife" for the CBC from Halifax, and she was a commentator on CJCH. She was president of the Welfare Bureau for six years, provincial president of the IODE and in 1951 was the first woman elected to Halifax City Council. Three years later she was appointed deputy mayor. In 1959 she represented Canada at a United Nations-sponsored women's seminar in Bogota, Colombia, which discussed women's participation in public life. In 1960 she succeeded in a drive to have women serve on juries.

Another Maritimes broadcaster, Joan Marshall of Moncton, N.B., began broadcasting at the age of six, and since 1942 has been CBC women's commentator in the Atlantic Provinces. Intensely interested in drama and sports, she also is radio and television convener for the National Council of Women.

Royal Tours

Maudie Ferguson of Ottawa began her radio career in 1949 as a CBC commentator and was often heard on "Trans-Canada Matinee" and "Roving

Reporter." She covered royal tours and was so popular that fans presented her with a car.

* * *

Physicist Mrs. Mattie Rotenberg of Toronto was nicknamed "The Madame Curie of Canada" by one admirer of her radio talks covering family living, human rights and current affairs. Ruth Harding was CBC consultant on consumer information for years and had a daily program heard across Canada on subjects of interest to women: food, child care and home-making topics were featured.

Eustella Langdon was known as "The Herb Lady" and qualified for the CBC ten-year club in 1955. Her popular program was "The Cooking School of the Air" and she worked closely with Dr. Elizabeth Chant Robertson, CBC's nutrition adviser with whom she collaborated in writing *Nutrition for Today*.

Voice from Europe

Westerner, Edna May, who now writes for radio, first was with the CBC as a commentator in Toronto in 1947. Two years later she became Montreal's first woman CBC commentator. She married Paul Guttman who was posted to the International Labor Organization in Geneva. From Europe she covered interesting meetings for the CBC and private stations before returning to CBC Toronto in 1954.

When the first Sputnik passed over Toronto she got up at 4 a.m. and taped a word picture, scooping the daily papers. She says: "Women nowadays aren't satisfied with a diet of recipes and household hints. They want to hear Sir John Gielgud on theatre, how housewives live in Tokyo and Caracas, and the latest in cancer research."

* * *

Margaret Howes joined the CBC in Montreal in

1948 as a talks producer and with the advent of television became senior producer of English language talks and public affairs. Interested in mental health, she received an award for her outstanding contribution. Her first award as a producer came for "Footloose in Deep South." She retired in January, 1966 and was succeeded at the CBC by Catherine McIvor.

Cross Country Check-Up

Betty Shapiro former moderator of Sunday night's "Cross Country Check-Up," Canada's only nation-wide open line radio program, is a human dynamo, with a sincere interest in people. The program is third most popular on the CBC radio ratings. Before taking over this program from Percy Saltzman, she wrote radio scripts for 15 years, and for three years had her own program "Let's Consider" discussing the Quebec problem.

Popular Performer

Marjorie Chadwick, radio and television actress-writer of Toronto, is a popular performer. She began her radio career in 1939 doing character roles and commercials. Her broadcast shows include *Dr. Susan,* the musical comedy *Ministering Maids, Voice of Victor,* "Lux Radio Theatre" and Victory Loan Shows. She wrote and broadcast *Beautiful Lady* on CKCL. Her daughter is assistant ballet mistress with the National Ballet.

Radio Veteran

Jean Hinds was a versatile radio veteran who, if asked how she started in radio, would answer: "By knitting socks." During World War II she was busily knitting when Elizabeth Long commissioned her to do a humorous program "Our Knitting Circle." Her background in teaching and journalism resulted in her becoming pioneer morning commentator of the prairies, broadcasting from Winnipeg in 1942. After freelancing for a few years she rejoined CBC in 1953 as morning commentator in Regina.

Florence Buchanan

Tuned In — Turned On

Florence Buchanan — "Mrs. B. of Brantford" — owns and directs the 10,000 watt station CKPC which was a gift from her father Cyrus Dolph in 1939. "I was such a greenhorn around the station, I didn't know a male plug from a female plug," she admits ruefully. "But I had my loyal staff." The staff consisted of five, including son Richard as managing director. Mrs. B. cooked the meals for the staff.

In 1946 she spent $75,000 to increase the station's power from 1,000 to 10,000 watts. By then the staff complement was twenty-four. At the height of racial trouble in Selma, U.S.A. her station's broadcast rallied such support for a memorial service that $500 was raised for the Martin Luther King Fund. Mrs. B. — a founding or life-member of at least twenty-five organizations including the Cerebral Palsy Association, the Canadian Cancer Society, the Zonta Club, an Indian Girl Guide company and another company at the Ontario School for the Blind — is generous with station time to aid worthy causes. Brantford Civitan club gave her their award as "Man of the Year" in 1960.

"Mrs. B." has been given an honorary life membership in the Canadian Cancer Society, and an award from the Sons of Italy.

Charlotte's Sister

Kathleen (Mrs. Frank) Whitton Ryan, with her wide, friendly grin, and delightful sense of humor, somehow managed not to be overpowered by her equally clever but more controversial sister, Charlotte Whitton. Kaye is probably the only woman in the world to erect a broadcasting tower on the top of a mountain. All TV and FM stations in Canada's capital are served, under long leases, by the 750 foot Ryan Tower on Skyline Ridge in the nearby Gatineau Mountains. When CFRA was built and operated by her husband in 1947, Mrs. Ryan broadcast daily, and was vice-president of the station. Following Frank Ryan's death in 1965, she became president of CFRA and CFMO, but later sold them.

A graduate of Queen's University in economics, a journalist and painter, Mrs. Ryan is active in the National Federation of Liberal Women, was the eastern Ontario chairman of the Women's Centennial Commission, an executive officer of the Regional Hospital Planning Council and a director of the Ontario Heritage Foundation.

Commission Chairman

Florence Bird, the pioneer political commentator, is a tall, white-haired, regal-looking woman who uses "Ann Francis" as her nom-de voix. Her married name is Mrs. John Bird. Graduating from Vassar, she spent three summers at Institute of Politics, William College, Massachusetts. She married John Bird a newspaperman in 1928. She believes that: "Any married woman who has no children should do volunteer work, or take on the discipline of a professional job."

She was on the Executive of the Central Voluntary Bureau of Winnipeg 1939-40 and wrote a weekly column about women's war work in Winnipeg for five years. Her first CBC series was "Headline History" under the auspices of the Manitoba Department of Education. She wrote a booklet about women workers of Canada for the U.N., another concerning the French and Flemish problem in Belgium, somewhat similar to Canada's bilingual problem (she herself is completely bilingual). In 1957 she prepared a masterly profile of Agnes Macphail, for the CBC Wednesday Night Broadcast.

From 1943 on, she was the first Canadian woman heard regularly on the CBC commenting on national and international affairs, over Trans-Canada Matinee, Press Conference, and Capital Report. An "independent broadcaster" not attached to any newspaper or political party, she was the only woman competing with men in this field.

Ann Francis has travelled extensively, on NATO tour of journalists to Greece, Turkey and Israel in 1955; as a member of the Canadian delegation to UNESCO conference in India; studied women of Pakistan and Lebanon in 1956; produced documentaries for the CBC in Germany, Denmark, France, Switzerland, Belgium, Netherlands, United States and Hungary between 1958 and 1966; was a special consultant to the Government of

Jamaica under CIDA 1975 and the government of Barbados 1976.

Mrs. John (Florence) Bird
"Ann Francis"

Women's clubs, particularly the NCW, FWUC, the B. and P. Clubs and the Committee for the Equality of Women in Canada, all were lobbying for a Royal Commission on the Status of Women in Canada. When the Canadian government finally acceded to their request and in 1967 appointed Mrs. Bird as Chairman of the Commission, some considered it "Just a sop to women voters." The Commission was instructed to recommend what steps the federal government could take to ensure female equality with men in all aspects of Canadian society. The Royal Commission on the Status of Women in Canada presented its controversial report in September 1971. In 1973 Mrs. Bird was in Sweden to discuss the report of the Commission with their government. She was consultant on the Task Force on the Status of Women in the CBC in 1974 and 1975.

In between other work, Mrs. Bird has written *Ann Francis - An Autobiography* published in Toronto in 1974 and *Holiday in the Woods* published by Clark, Irwin in 1976.

Honors include: two Women's national Press Club Awards; Companion of the Order of Canada, 1971; Honorary LL.D. York University 1972; Honorary D.Hum.L. Mount St. Vincent University 1974; Award of Merit, The Art Director Club of Toronto, 1973-4; Hon. LL.D, Carleton and Queen's Universities, 1975.

Televiews

> *Television is an instrument for progress second only to the printing press.*
> (Director of Iowa State College TV.)

Informal interviewer Elaine Grand was the first woman in Canada to emerge as an outstanding television personality — and she did so by just being natural. At seven, she starred in a radio series "The Adventures of Peter and Joan". She became a fashion illustrator in Toronto; she married social worker Soloman Grand. When Ross McLean began producing "Tabloid" in 1953 he had Elaine interview "Timmy" the Easter Seal Campaign symbol. McLean termed her "the best interviewer in North America". She had been on Tabloid nine months and her husband had just finished a multi-million-dollar campaign to build the new Mount Sinai Hospital when tragedy struck. The morning after a Christmas Eve party, Elaine woke to find Sol in a coma. He died soon afterwards.

In July 1954, Elaine became hostess of "Living", a half-hour CBC television program of demonstrations and interviews. Two years later she left for an expanded career in British television. She now lives in England, but commutes to North America occasionally for special assignments.

Joyce Was "Indifferent"

Beautiful Joyce Davidson made television history for her offhanded remark on Dave Garroway's "Today" show. With millions of Americans out there in television land watching, Joyce tossed off the remark: "Like most Canadians, I am indifferent to the forthcoming visit of Queen Elizabeth." The comment made prior to one of the Queen's visits to Canada in the '50's, brought Joyce international attention and headlines.

Married at 17, Joyce had two daughters before her divorce from R. D. Davidson in 1959. She worked as a welder in a Hamilton factory before getting a minor role in a cooking show on TV. The stunning blonde took a big step up when she started interviewing celebrities on CBC television's Tabloid program. Joyce had a talent for turning her charm and beauty to good advantage and in 1961 moved from the Tabloid program into big league U.S. television with commercial work on the Jack Benny show and later as co-host of the Mike Wallace show on ABC. Of TV work she says: "It's murder on the nerves and constitution or it's stimulation, excitement and satisfaction, depending on how you look at it."

Joyce worked as public relations officer for the New York company owned by David Susskind, millionaire television and motion picture producer. Then she married the boss. Now in her mid-30's, Joyce's first two daughters are almost grownup. She and her husband and their young daughter Samantha live in New York's most luxurious apartment, United Nations Plaza, overlooking the East River.

The Girl Who Can Do Anything

When the CBC fired popular singer Gisele, it may have hurt her feelings but it helped her career. Changing her name to Gisele MacKenzie — her real surname, LaFleche, was considered too theatrical — she began singing on Bob Crosby's Club 15 radio show in Hollywood in the '50's. Since then she has had several hit records, her own show on the NBC network in 1957-1958, a triumphant engagement at more than $5,000 a week at the luxurious Waldorf-Astoria Hotel in New York, and a successful tour of Great Britain. In 1956 the CBC paid Gisele $3,000 to sing four songs on its TV spectacular "Motorama" called by some critics "TV's longest commercial".

Born in 1927 in St. Boniface, Manitoba, she studied with Flora Matheson Goulden to be a concert violinist, making her debut at the Royal Alexandra Hotel, at age twelve. At two Gisele could play the piano by ear, but was a plump, shy, unpopular child. Next she studied with Kathleen Parlow on a Toronto Conservatory of Music scholarship. When her $3,000 Ceruti violin was stolen, she took it as an omen she was a singer rather than a violinist. Orchestra leader Bob Shuttleworth heard teen-age Gisele perform and signed her to sing with his band. Years later she married Bob, but they are now divorced. She had a CBC audition and soon was given her own show "Meet Gisele". By 1959, she was Canada's highest-paid vocalist. "Sensational!" was the verdict of critics, of the singer who had never had a singing lesson, who is also a comedienne, dancer, actress, pianist, and, of course, violinist. Gisele is also an excellent cook!

Gisele MacKenzie

Some say Gisele has acquired the hardness of a professional entertainer. An episode in Ottawa, around 1950, belies this. In town for a concert date, Gisele spent the afternoon (when she needed to rest) singing for war veterans in the Civic Hospital. The "up" cases clustered around the piano, applauding uproariously. Gisele asked diffidently: "Would the bed patients like to see me, perhaps, just to say 'Hi!'?" Smiling infectiously, Gisele went from bed to bed, making each man, for the time being, feel like a Clarke Gable.

So nervous she says she feels nauseated before each public appearance, and sometimes has even fainted back-stage. For the last few years she has played in many musicals, including *South Pacific, Annie, The Sound of Music, Auntie Mame,* interspersed with night club appearances. Her own musical-talk show had its debut in Hollywood in the summer of 1969. Gisele sang at John Diefenbaker's 80th birthday party in September 1975 in Ottawa.

Beautiful "Mother Bear"

Described as "the most beautiful girl on TV", Toby Robins complains that the compliment is a stumbling block to acceptance as a serious actress. Her acting career started in kindergarten when she played "Mother Bear" in *Goldilocks and the Three Bears.* At the age of eleven she enrolled in the drama course at Toronto's Royal Conservatory of Music while attending Harbord Collegiate. At seventeen Toby won an acting scholarship to Northwestern University, Illinois. While there she also managed to obtain a B.A. in 1952 from the University of Toronto — her twin sister (Ellen Cole of Toronto) attended lectures and sent the notes to Toby. She and Ellen keep in touch by telephone.

The year 1952 proved hectic! She played in summer stock, in radio dramas for CBC, in New York and married William Freedman, producer (Hadrian VII).

With the advent of Canadian television, she became master of ceremonies of The Big Review. She has been in dozens of radio and television plays including Patricia Joudry's *Teach Me How to Cry*. In the summer of 1954 she played Mariana in *Measure for Measure* at Stratford and later co-produced, with her husband, the London musical hit *Salad Days* at Hart House Theatre, Toronto. The play went on to success in Montreal and a brief New York run. For several years she was the only regular female panelist on TV's Front Page Challenge, which she left in 1961 because they refused to raise her weekly salary from $400 to $450.

Her colleague there, Gordon Sinclair, himself a frequent shocker but who resented her swearing on stage, would for once be rendered speechless had he seen her as the seductive, murderous nympho star of LeRoi Jones's *Dutchman;* her promiscuous performances in the comedy *The Flip Side;* or as Christine Van Dam, gorgeous, world's highest-paid call girl in Paddy Chayefsky's *The Latent Heterosexual.*

Canada's smiling "Miss Sunshine", like many others, had to go to London, England, to be taken seriously as an actress. The Freedmans moved there permanently in January 1964. Sophisticated, dramatically-dressed Toby has starred in *The Male Animal* for BBC-TV, is also a star of the Royal Shakespeare Company of London, in Vanbrugh's *The Relapse* which is a demanding role. She starred with Frank Sinatra in *The Naked Runner* saying, with satisfaction: "I looked terrible — *no make up* — but I was not ashamed of my acting." She turned down a musical part opposite Stubby Kaye, and a starring stage role opposite Rex Harrison, and another which involves appearing nude on stage. With Toby, acting is a fierce compulsion, and her consuming ambition is to be a *great* actress.

However, her family always takes first place. Her husband Bill is her best friend, their three children are at private schools in London. The family enjoys skiing and soccer football together. Toby neither smokes nor drinks, entertains little, and chooses to have few close friends, saving her strength for what she considers important interests, her family, her luxurious home, and her fabulous career.

Juliette, Perennial Pet

Juliette — still "Our Pet" is one of very few Canadians who have turned down a Hollywood contract — because it would have interfered with plans to marry handsome Tony Cavazzi, free-lance musician. Admittedly sentimental, her family still mean more to her than her career. This pretty, curvaceous blonde, now forty-ish, has one of television's sunniest smiles. Probably more personally popular than any other Canadian singer, Juliette has had her share of cutting criticism. The TV columnist of the *Globe and Mail* derided her "drab image of wholesomeness", another commented on her "wall to wall teeth".

She started singing in the Vancouver Hotel at thirteen, followed this with CBC's Sophisticating Strings, entertained servicemen across Canada, then in 1943 got her own show "Here's Juliette!" Her television shows included "Holiday Ranch", "Saturday Night", and the highly successful "Billy O'Connor Show". It was a jolt when CBC fired her in 1966, but she managed to make as much money with less work free-lancing. Juliette has been singing for 30 years. In a book about the CBC, the chapter on Juliette is called "The Queen".

Kennedy Horizons Unlimited

Betty Kennedy succeeded Toby Robins on "Front Page Challenge". Betty has been women's editor of CFRB, Canada's oldest and largest private radio station, since 1959 and has her own one-hour afternoon show which commands an audience greater than Toronto's next three stations combined. She has interviewed over

5,000 guests including Bennett Cerf, designer Oleg Cassini, and a woman who runs a flea circus. She flew to the Space Centre near Houston to interview Canadians who helped to make possible the 1969 moon landing. Careful and continuous reading of newspapers and magazines is essential for her work and in her spare time she records commercials, writes chatty columns, speaks at luncheons or dinners and opens bazaars.

Born and educated in Ottawa, Betty's first job was with the *Ottawa Citizen*. Later she moved west and on her return became writer, hostess and performer on the first women's program on CBC-TV. She married Gerhard Kennedy in 1948 and they had four children. Three days after the birth of the youngest, she went from hospital by ambulance to appear on "Front Page Challenge".

After Gerhard's death from cancer, Betty wrote: *Gerhard: A Love Story*.

In the autumn of 1976 she married Alan Burton, president of Robert Simpson Co. Limited, Toronto.

Personal interests include the humanities, world affairs, art, literature and education.

Rags to Riches

Perfectionist Adrienne Clarkson is hostess of the daily show "Take 30" and Canada's only woman television star. Her success story is inspiring. When only three she was brought to Canada by her parents, wartime refugees from Hong Kong. The family grew up in an Ottawa slum area. Adrienne escaped her environment with intensive reading and study. She graduated as head girl from Lisgar Collegiate and won a scholarship to the University of Toronto. In her third year she was vice-president of the Students Administrative Council. She succeeded in obtaining her M.A. in English literature.

She married Stephen Clarkson in Paris in 1962. Back in Toronto, she lectured part-time on poetry at Victoria College and did book reviews on the TV show, "Take 30". In 1965 she took over as the show's hostess. She still travels extensively to tape interviews, writes poetry and novels and in 1969 added motherhood to her list of accomplishments, then spent part of each afternoon and weekends at home with baby Kyra. For the future she is interested in television production and may turn to directing or writing film scripts. She also plans to write more books.

* * *

Marjorie McEnany (a sister of Dr. Mary Winspear, principal of Weston School in Montreal) is a top flight free-lance writer, editor, and producer of CBC Wednesday Night documentaries. She interrupted her career a few years ago to do public relations work for Dr. Norman Alcock's Peace Research Institute to emphasize her concern about the international situation.

* * *

At the Bal des Artistes in Montreal on February 26, 1957, the Canadian Council of Authors and Artists and L'Union des Artistes, celebrating its 20th anniversary, presented awards to members considered to have made outstanding contributions to Canadian radio, television or films during 1956. Among the Montreal women award winners were: Françoise Faucher (special French award for outstanding work), Yoland Guenard (TV silver award) and Claire Gagnier (radio work).

CRTC Term

Mrs. Pat Pearce of Montreal was appointed a commissioner of the Canadian Radio-Television Commission for a seven-year term in April, 1968. Born in Belfast, she was educated in Brussels and London. After a few years as a journalist on the *Sunday Dispatch* and *Daily Mirror* in London, she came to Canada in 1940

and the following year joined the *Montreal Star* as secretary to the editor. In 1947 she switched to the *Montreal
Herald* as entertainments editor responsible for movies,
drama, ballet and night clubs coverage and editing the
entertainment pages. In 1952 she added TV and radio
coverage. Returning to the *Montreal Star* in 1957 as TV-
radio critic, she wrote a demanding six columns a week
and from 1960 to 1962 also contributed a TV review to
the Canadian Annual Review. She has one daughter and
four grandchildren.

Flowers for the Living

Ruth Hancock's business career has been wide in
scope. Assistant accountant in a bank, owner of a secretarial service, later herself secretary-to-everyone at
CKKW Kitchener, she has worked in marketing and
public industrial relations, sold cars, and helped organize the Radio and Television Executives Club (now
BES). Mrs. Hancock also manages the Toronto office of
the Canadian Association of Broadcasters, helps the
Central Canada Broadcasters Association and the Sales
Representatives Association, and is executive secretary
of the Broadcast Executives Society. She sits on 14 different committees. On May 13, 1969 the BES celebrated
"Ruth Hancock Day". Ruth, completely taken by
surprise, exclaimed later to Dick Lewis, publisher of
Broadcaster: "I had to keep pinching myself to make
sure I wasn't dead!"

Barbara Frum:
Everyone's Favourite Broadcaster

Who do most Canadians eagerly listen to as they
relax before dinner, prepare dinner, or eat their dinner?
Their favourite broadcaster, of course, Barbara Frum.
Her program "As It Happens" keeps them in touch with
what's going on in the world. Consequently, her program's popularity is second only to news broadcasts.

484

Barbara Frum

Barbara at twenty-one had graduated in 1959
from University of Toronto with a B.A. in History, and a
clever husband, Dr. Murray Frum. They live in Toronto
with their three children. Part of her charm is her clear,
magnetic voice, and her enthusiasm. Despite a hectic

schedule, the family gets top priority with Barbara.

In the early 1960's Barbara wrote regularly for *MacLean's Magazine, Chatelaine, Saturday Night* and the *Toronto Star.* She also researched and wrote for CBC programs, and discovered a unique talent for interviewing people. So in 1967 she began doing television interviews for the CBC. She joined "As It Happens" in the Autumn of 1971, broadcast Monday - through - Friday from 6.30 p.m. to 8 p.m. She has worked with a variety of colleagues, but is now assisted by popular CBC announcer Alan Maitland.

In 1976 Mrs. Frum published *As it Happened*, the inside story of her current show. It was sensationally successful. In 1975 she was chosen Woman of the Year in the literature, art and education category by the Canadian Press. Among many other awards are two ACTRA Awards 1974 and 1975, the prestigious 1975 National Press Club of Canada Award, top prize in the Article category of the Memorial Awards, then in 1974 *As It Happens* was presented with the Canadian Broadcasting League CYBIL Award for "Being Instrumental in Upholding and Promoting the Public Interest in Broadcasting."

*   *   *

Despite such success stories, it is still extremely difficult for a woman to gain a top radio or television position in a serious program. Producers blame this on the latent hostility and jealousy of women viewers. Helping to change this attitude are Pauline Jewett, a frequent guest on TV, and Jeanine Locke who will work both behind and before the cameras on the new CBC-TV program 'Thursday Night'.

Thus today woman power is gradually breaking down barriers, to acquire both vocal and visual vent in radio and television — delivering media messages in far-reaching ways.

Chapter XVI

Will To Win

Sports

Barbara Ann Scott

> *We swear that we come to the*
> *Olympic Games in a chivalrous*
> *spirit, for the honor of our country*
> *and the glory of sport.*
>
> (Olympic Oath)

When the Olympic Games "the oldest show on earth" originated in Elis, Greece, in 776 B.C. women were barred, even as spectators! Disobedience was punishable by death. Women were also forbidden to compete. Years later, when the rules were slightly relaxed, a Macedonian woman, Betische, won the chariot race at the 128th Olympics.

Greek contestants lived solely on cheese and water during final training. First Olympic event was a 200-yard race but games now encompass every known competitive sport. Originally an olive wreath rewarded the victor; today a gold medal is awarded the winner, silver for second place and bronze for third. Today, officials may wrangle over amateur or professional status, but at an early Olympic, a boxer *killed* his opponent by trickery. The judges ruled him disgraced, and crowned the corpse!

The Olympic Games, held every four years, have done more to encourage sport than any other single factor. At first they also included fine arts and religious ceremonies. Abolished in 394 A.D. when Greece lost her independence, they were revived in 1896, appropriately in Athens. But the fair sex was still barred until finally admitted in 1912 in Stockholm.

In Amsterdam, in 1928, Canada's "Peerless Six" team beat all other nations, including a powerful 21 girl American team. They won seven medals. The gold medal winner, Myrtle Cook, captained a relay team of Torontonians which comprised Bobbie Rosenfeld, Ethel Smith and Florence Bell; they set a new 400-metre world record of 48.4 seconds. Bobbie Rosenfeld, along with Jean Thompson of Penetang, was also a finalist in the 800-metre race which has since been barred to women; the winner — Hitomi of Japan — dropped dead soon after his triumph. Bobbie, Ethel Smith and Myrtle Cook were also finalists in the 100-metre race, and Bobbie won second place in a photo finish with Betty Robinson of the U.S.

Saskatoon Lily

Then there was "Saskatoon Lily", the nickname given to statuesque Ethel Catherwood of Saskatchewan. Her high jump of 5'3" set a new Olympic and world record. She represented Parkdale Athletic Club operated by Teddy Oake, who moved girls' sports into the major league. The "Lily" always took a rag doll and ukelele with her and achieved more than fleeting fame. She was given a $50,000 trust fund.

Blackeyed Baby

Myrtle Cook, who later became a sports writer, was destined for sport from birth; the obstetrician's instruments slipped and she was born with a black eye. However, it was running, not boxing, that fate held in store for her. At five she won her first race — the prize was a free box lunch at a picnic on Center Island. Years later, in 1928, she was to set three world records, one of them in Halifax when she won the 100 metres in 12 seconds. The following year she won the Governor-General's Gold Medal at the International Games in Vancouver. Then she became the women's sports editor of the *Montreal Star* and married Lloyd McGowan. Today she still covers men's and women's major athletic events and chooses the women's outfits for the Olympic Games.

During World War II, Myrtle coached army, navy and air force personnel for inter-service championships in track and field. Always the only woman, she won the *Montreal Press* race several times. Her biggest thrill was beating the rarely-defeated Rosa Grosse and Bobbie Rosenfeld in the 1928 Olympic trials. Myrtle has nine Dominion medals (three gold), 10 diamond U.S. medals and others for basketball, tennis, war-canoe paddling, softball and ice hockey. As undefeated sprinter, she is still active in sports and has coached many prominent athletes. She chaperoned the women's team in Melbourne, Australia. Secretary of Canadian Amateur Athletic Hall of Fame and a member of the advisory board of the Canadian Olympic Committee, Myrtle Cook has received citations from the Canadian Amateur Swimming Association, and, from the Quebec Amateur Athletic Union.

Swift Landlubber

On her birthday in 1950, auburn-haired Bobbie Rosenfeld was named the Outstanding Canadian Athlete of the Half-Century in the Canadian Press poll. Born in Barrie, Ontario, Bobbie was an amazingly versatile champion; a winner in track, field, basketball, softball and ice hockey, successful at every sport — except swimming. As Pats Athletic Club's only entry in the Ontario Ladies' Track and Field Championship in 1925, Bobbie scored enough points to win the title. In Toronto she broke the 220-yard sprint world record. Wearing her brother's "Y" T-shirt and swim trunks and her dad's socks, she set three Canadian records in running and standing broad jumps and the discus throw at the 1928 Olympic finals in Halifax. She was also joint holder of the 100-yard world record of 11 seconds.

In 1929 she had to renounce sports, heartbroken because she was chained to her bed for eight months by arthritis. Upon her recovery she became the first woman insurance supervisor in Canada. She coached the Canadian women's track team in London for the British Empire Games in 1932 and four years later began writing "Sports Reel" for the *Globe and Mail*. When Canadian sportwriters and sportcasters held their first annual dinner in Toronto in 1952, with proceeds going to help crippled children, Bobbie was guest of honor.

In 1951 Bobbie, Florence Bell, Ethel Smith, Ethel Catherwood, Jean Wilson and Myrtle Cook were elected to the Canadian Amateur Sports Hall of Fame at the Canadian National Exhibition.

Interesting Assignments

Alexandrine Gibb, the outstanding basketball player joined the *Toronto Star* in 1928 as the first woman assistant sports editor of a metropolitan newspaper in Canada. For 13 years she wrote the popular "No Man's Land of Sport" and later the column "Have You Heard?" She managed Canadian women's Olympic Teams in 1928 and 1932 and covered Marilyn Bell's famous swim. Other interesting assignments were trips to Iran and Russia, both Quebec conferences during World War II, and Princess Elizabeth's cross-Canada tour. She died in 1958.

* * *

Among other Canadian Olympic medal winners were Jean Wilson who won a gold medal for skating in the 1932 Olympics at Lake Placid before her sudden death at the age of twenty-two, the undefeated champion of North America; Hilda Strike of Montreal, star softball and basketball player, who won a silver medal for sprinting; Mildred Frizell, Lillian Palmer and Mary Frizell who won silver medals on the relay team; and Frances Claudet, the Ottawa Minto Club gold medalist

who joined Shipstad and Johnson's Ice Follies and chor-
eographed the film *Ice Follies of 1939* starring Joan
Crawford and James Stewart. In the 1936 Olympics in
Berlin, Betty Taylor of Hamilton and a Miss Tally of
Italy clocked the same time of 11.7 seconds for the 80-
metre hurdles; however, Miss Tally received the gold
medal and Miss Taylor the silver.

Unbeatable Edmonton Grads

Dr. James Naismith of Almonte invented basketball in 1891 while an instructor at the International
YMCA Training School in Springfield, Mass. At that
time he used peach baskets to catch the ball. The world-
famous lady basketball players, the Edmonton Commercial Grads, were organized in 1915 by J. Percy Page,
later Alberta's Lieutenant-Governor. At four Olympic
Games — in Amsterdam, Paris, Berlin and Los Angeles
— the Grads won, scoring 1,863 points against their
opponents' 297. Once they took 147 consecutive games;
and they won seven of nine against men. In 25 years
they lost only 20 games out of 552 and captured the
Underwood Trophy repeatedly. Dr. Naismith called
them "The greatest team that ever stepped out on a basketball floor." Margaret MacBurney played 164 games
for them and other top players were Noel Macdonald,
Winnie Martin and Gladys Fry (captains), Babe Belan-
ger, Etta ("Y' Can't Catch Me") Dunn, Kate MacRae,
Mabel Munton, Elsie Bennie, Helen Northup, Mildred
McCormack, Kay MacRitchie, Connie Smith, the Johnson sisters and Eleanor Mountfield.

Sphairistike

Tennis, known as Sphairistike, was introduced to
North America in 1857 by Mary Outerbridge. Forty
years later, at the Championship games, the standard
attire was tight corsets, long sleeves, skirts and petti-
coats and floppy hats! Despite the impediments of her
clothing Ellen Hansill won. In 1957, 100 years after the

introduction of tennis to the continent, Hannah Sladek of Montreal was Canadian ladies' singles champion. A year later Mariette Laframboise, the Ottawa-born tennis champion in Montreal, became the first woman to win the Gil Ol Julian Trophy for the best French-Canadian athlete of Ontario and Western Quebec, the Four Hundred Club Tournament in Montreal, the Montreal Cup and the Province of Quebec championship.

Gymnastics

Ernestine Russell won her first international gymnast championship at the age of twelve and just two years later, in 1951, was chosen Woman Athlete of the Year. Born in Windsor, Ontario, she was seven times Canadian champion in gymnastics. At sixteen she won every event in the United States championships.

Another Canadian gymnast, Susan McDonnell, was a Pan-American Games gold medallist and won the Norman Craig Trophy as the top female athlete in 1967.

Born to Skate

Canada has been called the "country where every baby is born with skates on". Back in 1900, Edmonton had a ladies' hockey team which sported clamped-on skates, sweeping skirts, dashing toques, and turtle-necked sweaters — costumes more remarkable than their scores. Later Prince Edward Island had an outstanding women's hockey team called the 'Crystals'. Preston Rivulettes won the Lady Bessborough Trophy from 1935 to 1939 and as Dominion Champions established the most outstanding record of any ladies' hockey team in the world. Dominion skating champion Mrs. James McCaul received a medal from Lord Dufferin, then Governor-General.

"Ab's" Impersonation

Then there was "Ab's" impersonation. Abigail Hoffman's brilliant defense play won her a place on the All-Star Hockey Team in Toronto even after the terrible truth came out — that "Ab" was a girl! In 1960 she started sprinting and three years later won a gold medal in the 800-metre race in the Pan-Am Games in Brazil. Earlier, in New York in 1956, she had broken the women's indoor record for the half-mile. The top women's half-miler in North America, she won three gold medals for Canada at the eighth Maccabian Games at Tel Aviv in August, 1969; her record time for the 400 metre dash was a sizzling 57.3 seconds. Her success, matched with the silver medal won by Peter Bakonyi of Vancouver for fencing, upped the Canadian athletes' standing to 10th place. Ab won another gold medal in the women's half-mile race in Kingston, Jamaica, in 1966. She says: "If I must take a stimulant to win, I'd rather lose."

* * *

Another gifted Canadian athlete, brunette Linda Crutchfield Bocock not only tackled track and field but also swimming, diving, basketball, figure skating, soccer, skiing, golf and tennis, to name a few. "And for fun", she maintains. An Olympic competitor in several different sports, Linda is without doubt one of Canada's most gifted athletes — if not the most versatile woman athlete on the contemporary scene.

Conquering Queen

She Skated Into Our Hearts, a book written by Cay Moore, former social hostess at the Royal York Hotel, Toronto, records the conquering career of Barbara Ann Scott. By 1949, the twenty-year-old Barbara Ann of Ottawa, was ladies' senior figure-skating champion of Canada, North America, Europe and the world. She had also won an Olympic gold medal. Early in 1948,

494

after Barbara had won the European championship, it
was closed to all "western" contestants — forever.
Three times winner of the Lou Marsh Trophy, she is the
only honorary woman member of the Toronto Men's
Press Club. In 1951, she turned professional, replacing
Sonja Henie in the Hollywood Ice Review. Four years
later she married publicity director Tom King of Chicago.

* * *

First Canadians to win the World Pairs Figure
Skating Championship were Frances Dafoe of New
Brunswick, and her partner Norris Bowden; they
notched up the success at Oslo in 1954.

First pair to receive a perfect score in an Olympic
competition were Barbara Tope Wagner and Bob Paul
who won a gold medal and the Olympic title at Squaw
Valley in 1960. Representing the Toronto Skating Club,
they were Canadian champions in 1956, won the North
American and world championships in 1957 and the Lou
Marsh Trophy in 1959. Turning "pro", they joined the
Ice-Capades in 1960. Outstanding pair skaters in the
early 1960's were the brother-sister team, the Jelineks of
Oakville, Ont.

Hostess with the Mostest

Aidrie and Don Cruickshanks, a married couple,
were Canadian Figure Skating Waltz Champions for
five years. Aidrie also won a gold medal for swimming,
a bronze medal in slalom ski competition, the Matthew
Trophy for curling and a golf trophy at the Royal
Ottawa Golf Club. The sports-minded Cruickshanks
family altogether have 65 medals, innumerable ribbons,
and 48 cups. In her heyday as the Ottawa "Hostess with
the Mostest" as *Time Magazine* called her, Aidrie entertained the cream of Ottawa officialdom, including the
Governor General, with whom she shared a passion for
square dancing.

* * *

World Champion figure skater Petra Burka was born in Amsterdam — a premature baby, bow-legged as an Arizona cowboy. But she loved music and danced whenever she heard it, later taking ballet lessons. When the family came to Toronto, Mrs. Burka, the Dutch skating champion in 1945-46, taught the sport. She bought Petra her first pair of skates when she was six years old and began coaching her. Years of hard work and self-sacrifice paid dividends. At thirteen Petra was a gold medallist, at fourteen a double gold medallist and at fifteen a triple gold medallist. In 1964 she won a bronze medal at the Tokyo Olympics and a year later was at the pinnacle of her skating career. In one month she took the Canadian championship in Calgary, the North American title at Rochester, and the world crown at Colorado Springs. She was named Woman of the Year in Sports, and won the Lou Marsh Trophy.

For a time the hard-pressed Mrs. Burka refused tempting $100,000 offers, but in May, 1966, Petra finally turned professional and joined "Holiday on Ice." Petra toured for three years. For some years now she has been the commentator for all CBS and CBC television network coverage of international skating events. She has joined a Toronto film company as a research-production assistant, and eventually hopes to produce her own films.

Skating as Therapy

Skater Linda Carbonetto of Ottawa also turned professional. She broke both ankles at the age of five, and doctors recommended skating as medical therapy. Enjoying it, she took up the sport and dethroned Karen Magnussen in 1969 to win the Canadian figure-skating championship with an almost perfect display of free skating. She had finished third in North American and sixth in world championship contests. However, it was costing her parents about $3,000 annually for her training, so Linda signed up with the Ice Capades.

Karen Magnussen

Skating Star

Karen Magnussen's first public appearance as a skater was at age six, when she was a snowflake in a Vancouver carnival. Later, under the coaching of Linda Branckmann she became a world champion. When Petra Burka retired in 1968, Karen won the Canadian title. In the North American championships at Colorado Springs, Karen was found to have stress fractures in both legs. She watched from a wheelchair.

In 1970, Karen made a startling come-back, recapturing her Canadian title, which she retained until 1973. In 1971 in the N.A. Championships she won only a bronze medal, due to lack of skill in compulsory figures. But in 1973 she won the world championship. She triumphantly returned to a banquet chaired by Prime Minister Trudeau, and her hometown, Vancouver, gave her a warm welcome on her twenty-first birthday. Later that year she signed with Ice Capades. She started the Karen Magnussen Foundation to help young skaters. She was given the Order of Canada. Karen was married in June, 1977.

* * *

When Lyn Nightingale was three, the family moved to Victoria, B.C., and Lyn started skating. When the family moved to Ottawa, Lyn joined the Minto Skating Club. She started winning inter-club championships, then the Eastern Ontario Sectional Championships. In January 1972 she won the junior women's title at the Canadian championships. In November, competing in the Richmond Trophy in London, England, she came second in free skating and fourth overall. In January 1973 in Vancouver, Lyn came first in the compulsory free skating competition ahead of champion Karen Magnussen, who came second. Kim Alletson, another Minto Club member, finished second in the junior Ladies' Competition.

Twenty enthusiastic classmates of Lyn's from

Notre Dame High School were at Ottawa International Airport to meet Lyn, laden with flowers and banners reading "Nightingale Flies Again" etc. Her arrival was scheduled for 5:30 P.M. but freezing rain delayed the plane nine hours and the exhausted star arrived at 2:00 A.M. Lyn's secret of success is getting up at 5:30 A.M. and practising seven hours daily. Lyn has retained her title as Canadian champion in 1974, 75 and 76.

Lyn Nightingale

Novel Sports

Today, water-skiing enjoys phenomenal popularity. In 1950 Carol Ann Duthie won the Junior Girls' Trick Riding Championship after only two weeks practice. That year she also received the J. Edward Bays Memorial Award and by 1951 was Canadian junior women's champion. She won a host of trophies including the Overall Junior Women's Championship in 1953, and the World Water Ski Federation named her the world's outstanding junior skier. She headed her own water show at the Canadian National Exhibition and Columbia Pictures featured her in a sports' short. She also won a place in the Canadian Amateur Athletic Hall of Fame.

Or how about archery? If you're keen, there is a champion archer in Toronto who would be glad to teach you all the tricks of the William Tell game. She is Mrs. Alan Macdonald, Toronto's ladies' grand champion, a gal who is very handy with a bow and arrow.

Mrs. Eileen Learoyd of Victoria is the only Canadian woman privileged to wear "The Queen's Hundred Badge", the coveted honor given the top 100 marksmen at Bisley, England, which she earned in 1960 by placing 56th of 1,800 entries at Bisley. When she is not showing up the men at shooting, Mrs. Learoyd is busy writing a social column.

Diane Jones of Saskatoon won a gold medal in the pentathlon at the Pan-Am Games in Mexico City in 1975, which she resented as interfering with her training for the Montreal Olympics. Lucette Moreau of Vaudreuil, Quebec, won a bronze medal in the women's shot put, with Maureen Dowds of Winnipeg coming fourth.

Stars in two Sports

Sue Holloway of Ottawa is the first woman to

represent Canada in the Olympics in two widely different sports. Born May 19, 1955 in Halifax, Nova Scotia she studied ballet and judo as a child and ran long and medium distances for Brookfield High School with considerable success.

The year 1973 saw the beginning of her national cross country skiing and kayak successes. Sue became:

(1) Senior Canadian Cross Country Ski Champion
(2) Junior K1 Bronze medal winner
    in the World Championships, Poland.
(3) Junior K1 Canadian Champion
(4) Senior K2 Canadian Champion Crew
(5) Senior K2 Canadian Champion Crew
(6) Senior K4 Canadian Champion Crew

Sue was also awarded the 1973 ACT Trophy as Ottawa Athlete of the Year. She continued to win the Senior Ladies K1, K2 and K4 Canadian championships:

1974 Senior K1 North American Champion
1976 Sue competed in both winter and summer Olympics.
Cross Country skiing 5KM and relay Innsbruck.
Sue came 4th in the K1 semi-finals in Montreal.
Sue came 8th in K2 with Ann Dodge in the Finals.
                    (K1 means Kayak Singles)
                    (K2 is Kayak Tandem)

Sue is still training and hopes to continue in world competition in Kayak but in conjunction with studies at Simon Fraser University.

Winter Winners

Like skating, skiing is a great winter pastime in Canada and this country has produced some fine champions. The Wurtele twins held most North American honors from 1947 until 1952, including the coveted Harriman Cup; they were also winners in European meets. In 1952 Rhoda won the Norwegian title slalom — down-hill and combined — and her twin, the two American national crowns. Both were members of the Canadian Olympic team in 1948 and are in the National Ski Hall of Fame in Ishpeming, Michigan.

"Europeans have fight and drive to an almost startling degree," says blonde, green-eyed Lucile Wheeler, who was born and bred on ski slopes of Gray Rocks Inn, St. Jovite, Quebec. Her father, Harry Wheeler, has 25 ski instructors on his staff and Lucile began skiing at the age of two. For years she practised with a block of wood between her knees to avoid a knock-kneed stance — a natural hazard for women. She won the Canadian Junior crown at twelve and in 1949 the tough Taschereau women's race although handi-capped by a dislocated shoulder. Pepi Salvernmoser coached her. At the Olympics in Cortina, Italy in 1956, 50 skiers entered. Lucile just missed the silver but won a bronze, the first Canadian skier, man or woman, to win an Olympic medal. In 1958, at Bad Gastein, Austria, she won the downhill, accomplished the almost unprece-dented feat of winning the giant slalom (another gold medal) and beat the record of Italy's Carla Marchelli who was so furious when she fell that she lay and pum-melled the snow. In 1958, Lucile won the Velma Spring-stead Trophy as Canadian Athlete of the Year.

Success Secret

Ann Heggtveit at the age of seven won the Gatineau Ski Zone senior women's combined title. In 1954, she took the great slalom and Holmenkollen Gold cup and at the Ottawa's Sportmen's Dinner was awarded a scholarship and The Carling Trophy. Terrific determination is the secret of her success. She won the International White Ribbon Ski Tournament at St. Moritz, Switzerland in 1959 and also the combined women's title in the gruelling Arlberg-Kandahar race in Germany. In 1960 at Squaw Valley, she earned not one but three gold medals, including the Olympic. She was made an honorary Mohawk princess, as her friend Lucile Wheeler had been, and was presented with the Perry Medal, Great Britain's highest skiing award.

Reach for the Top

Little Nancy Greene of British Columbia was so thrilled at Ann Heggtveit's gold medal win at Squaw Valley in 1960 that she resolved she'd win one too. In fact, by the time she retired in 1969 she had won a couple of hundred downhills, slaloms and giant slaloms (including a gold medal for the giant slalom and a silver for the ladies' slalom at Grenoble, France) and was a World Cup winner. Both Ann Heggtveit and Nancy were born in Ottawa and both had skiing parents, but Nancy had lived in Rossland, B.C. most of her life. Between 1960 and 1969 she was encouraged by her many fans screaming "go, Tiger, go!" during competitions. Years of hard training, including mountain climbing and weightlifting, together with sprains, broken bones and humiliating falls were rewarded in 1967 by a winning streak. That spring at Jackson Hole, Wyoming, Nancy was determined to win both the giant slalom on Good Friday and the slalom on Easter Sunday. She was exhausted and the course was dangerous but in a raging blizzard she beat her nearest rival, Marielle Goitschel, by four points to become Canada's first World Cup champion. At the cocktail party celebrations, Nancy said she was "high on happiness". She was again World Cup champion in 1968 and won the Lou Marsh Award both years. She was named to the National Ski Hall of Fame in Ishpeming, Michigan, and her victory parade in Toronto in April, 1968, was the second largest ever. She was made an honorary citizen of Ottawa and given a $5,000 scholarship by British Columbia.

Nancy married Al Raine, coach of Canada's

national ski team in April, 1969, and her husband has set up the numerous Nancy Greene Ski Leagues for aspiring skiers aged thirteen and under. Patriotic Nancy chose Douglas Maxwell as her manager despite bids by Mark MacCormack, the United States sports entrepreneur. She reportedly earns around $100,000 annually from television and personal appearances and newspaper and magazine advertising for ski-wear and equipment. Premier W. A. C. Bennett of British Columbia termed her a "minister extraordinary" for tourism in his province. On her retirement she decided to devote her time to two books, an autobiography and picture album, as well as working as a member of the three-member task force appointed by the then health and welfare minister John Munro to investigate ways in which the federal government could help sportsmen improve their international competition performances.

* * *

Betsy Clifford, fifteen-year-old Ottawa skier, seemed most likely in 1969 to succeed Nancy as Canada's outstanding woman skier. In 1970 she scored an impressive series of wins, second in slalom at Bad Gastein, second in slalom at Grindelwald, and exciting first in grand slalom at Val Gardena, etc., against the best skiers in the world. Very independent, Betsy exclaims: "Maybe the other girls need psychological help, but I don't!"

At sixteen she was the youngest person ever to win a world championship, in 1970, the TIS World Championship at Val Gardena, Italy, in the giant slalom. Two years later, she cruelly broke both heels in a freak skiing accident in a World Cup downhill race at Grindelwald. Betsy retired. She staged a thrilling come-back in 1973 to become the first Canadian to win the Can-Am series at St. Moritz, Switzerland, then in the TIS World Championship 1974 won a silver medal, in downhill.

Another skiing star is Kathy Kreiner of Timmins,

Ontario, who won the World Cup Giant Slalom in 1974, then at Innsbruck in 1976 won another gold medal.

Epic of Endurance

Little Marilyn Bell of Toronto, knelt to ask God's help. It was near midnight on September 8, 1954, at Youngstown, New York. Then she kissed her parents farewell and plunged into the black, icy waters of Lake Ontario.

Marilyn Bell

Canadian National Exhibition officials and *The Toronto Telegram* had offered Florence Chadwick, champion U.S. swimmer who conquered the English Channel both ways, a sum of $2,500 to attempt to swim Lake Ontario, plus $7,500 if she succeeded. Gus Ryder urged the C.N.E. officials to allow Canadian swimmers to compete but they refused. However, the *Toronto Star* underwrote expenses of challengers and, besides sixteen-year-old Marilyn who was motivated only by patriotism, three other experienced swimmers entered.

Miss Chadwick, fighting 12-foot waves, stuck it out for 20 miles and was then pulled out half-drowned. Jerry Kerschner, an American professional swimmer, gave up during the night. Winnie Roach Leuzler, the first Canadian to swim the English Channel, covered 20 miles and was then forced out by the agonizing cramps she had endured for six hours.

Before starting, Marilyn had admitted fear of two things — darkness and eels and lampreys sucking her skin. Dawn brought battering waves and several times, stifling hysteria, she knocked eels off. Coach Gus Ryder, with whom she taught crippled children at the Lakeshore Swimming Club, extended a drink of corn syrup on a stick and then liniment to rub her pain-wracked limbs. She was enduring the agony of a strained tendon in her ankle.

By later afternoon, dozing, she appeared unconscious. Life-boats rushed out. Then her friend Joan Cooke, in panties and bra, jumped in and swam alongside Marilyn to urge her on. Marilyn revived but at dusk she stopped swimming and turned a pitiful, tear-streaked face to the boat. Her father ordered her out but, ignoring him, Ryder held up a blackboard message: "If you quit, I quit!" Marilyn thought of their crippled pupils. Her win might help them. Tapping some strange reserve of energy and endurance, she plodded on. Semiconscious when taken from the water, she was oblivious of the 300,000 madly-cheering fans. In the ambulance, when Joan exulted "Oh, Marilyn, you did it!", she first realized her ordeal was over. The slim sixteen-year-old was the first person to conquer Lake Ontario. The straight distance across was 20 miles, but she swam almost 40 miles. Her victory came one month after she had been the first of the women contestants to finish the 26-mile marathon race in Atlantic City; she was seventh of all contestants.

A year later she swam the English Channel, receiving congratulations from Gertrude Ederle, first woman to make the swim and in 1956 she swam the Strait of Juan de Fuca. *Swim to Glory,* by Ron McAllister, tells her story. She refused $100,000 worth of movie and television offers in order to finish school and teach crippled children, and insisted on sharing the money she did receive with Ryder who donated his portion to the Lakeshore Club. An orthopedic ward is named after them at Queensway Hospital.

Cheers for Courage

One of Canada's swimmers, little Irene Macdonald of Hamilton was bitterly disappointed when she was dropped from the 1952 Olympic team for lack of funds. However, she — along with all Canada's girl swimmers — placed in the 1956 Olympics in Melbourne, Australia. She entered the diving competition suffering agonies with bursitis, one shoulder frozen. Momentarily unable to raise that arm, she lost six points and therefore, the silver medal. Sobbing, she gritted her teeth and made two perfect dives. Her courage brought blasé newspapermen to their feet cheering. Her bronze medal was the first won by a Canadian girl for swimming at the Olympics.

Deep Sea Diver

"I just want to be first", explained Bette Singer,

the attractive young matron from Cooksville, Ont., when she descended 307 feet underwater in the Bahamas in 1961. She went 37 feet deeper than any other woman. A diver for eight years, she realized the risks.

Glamazon

Glamorous Jackie Macdonald of Toronto is a diving champion, basketball and shot-put ace. At the British Empire Games in Vancouver in 1954, where Robina Adams won the javelin throw, Jackie scored a basketball record of 38 points in one game. She also set a new Canadian record for the shot-put, winning a silver medal. Then in the 1958 Games in Wales she won a bronze medal for shot-put. At the Melbourne Olympics, as captain of the women's track and field team, she lunched with Prince Philip. This "glamazon" can lift 205 pounds in barbells. Now Mrs. William Gelling, she has two sons and is a consultant in the physical education department of the Ottawa Public School Board.

Danced with Delight

One of Canada's strongest women athletes is Nancy McCredie who, in 1963 at the age of seventeen, broke the Canadian shot-put record by 10 feet and set a new record for the discus. She danced with delight when she received her gold medals. In 1967 at the Pan-Am Games in Winnipeg she won another gold medal for the shot-put.

Winners Despite Difficulties

High altitudes made breathing difficult at the Pan-American Games in Mexico City in 1955 and 1956. However, Helen Stewart, British Columbia's outstanding athlete, won a gold medal for free style swimming and set a world record — a record she again broke in 1956. Beth Whittal of Montreal won four gold medals there, two individual and two relay, and was hailed as the outstanding athlete. She is a member of the Canadian Amateur Athletic Hall of Fame.

Best Dive

Beverley Boys, tomboy blonde diver of Pickering, winner of many awards, won a silver and a bronze medal at the Pan-American Games at Winnipeg in 1967.

At the 1968 Mexican Olympic Games, she completed a dive with a 2.9 "degree of difficulty" getting top marks for best dive, male or female, at the Games. Her brilliant performance pulled her up to a fourth place. Then in 1970, at the Commonwealth Games, Beverley won two gold medals.

* * *

Mary Stewart, the swimmer from Vancouver, holds the world record for the 100 metre butterfly, winning a gold medal in Australia at the British Empire Games. She also won four silver medals at the Pan-American Games in Brazil in 1963 and has twice been nominated Woman of the Year in sport.

Mighty Mouse

Mighty Mouse is the nickname fans have given Elaine Tanner, the Vancouver swimmer, but maybe "fish" would have been more appropriate. "I was born on February 22, which means I was born under the sign of Pisces, the fish," she laughs. She stunned the aquatic world by winning four gold and three silver medals at the 1966 British Commonwealth Games, setting world records in the 220-yard butterfly and the 440-yard free relay events. The next summer, at the Pan-Am Games in Winnipeg, she won two gold medals on two days in succession and three silver medals. At the 1968 Mexico Olympics, Elaine was a member of the relay team that brought home a bronze medal to Canada.

Learning to swim at the age of six, Elaine stayed afloat by using her own version of the backstroke. Her dad used to coax: "Elaine, do that funny little stroke," which her coach, Howard Firby, is now teaching his other swimmers. Elaine started winning medals at the age of eight, a habit she's kept up ever since. Her awards include the Velma Springfield Trophy and Lou Marsh Trophy for the outstanding Canadian Athlete of 1966, and the City of Vancouver's Order of Merit. She spent a week at Expo '67 as an official hostess at Olympic House and in the summer of 1969, she led a youth group of 3,000 at the opening parade of the Calgary Stampede.

Royal and Ancient Game

Mary, Queen of Scots, who lived from 1542 to 1587, is the first woman golfer on record, despite the fact that her grandfather, James IV, passed legislation forbidding the sport. Scottish officers who accompanied General Wolfe's army to Quebec in 1759 brought golf to Canada. Miss L. Young of Montreal won the first women's golf championship in 1901, but the legend of Canadian golf is Ada McKenzie.

In 1919 she won the Canadian Ladies' Open Championship and repeated the achievement five times. She founded the Ladies' Golf and Tennis Club in Toronto in 1924. Owned and operated by women for women, it is unique in the world. In 1953 she captained the first official women's team to represent Canada abroad in the British Open and a Commonwealth contest. Her team included Mrs. J. H. Todd and Babe Davies of British Columbia, Mary Gay of Alberta, Mrs. Graeme Pike and Daintry Chisolm of Quebec, and Marlene Stewart of Ontario. Ada MacKenzie was chosen Queen of Sports in 1933 and awarded the Toronto Centennial Championship's Athlete of the Year in 1934.

Little Miss Robot

Marlene Stewart is well-known in and out of

golfing circles. "You've got to do it!" she told herself firmly, as she adjusted her lucky Stewart Tartan golfing cap, on September 22, 1956. She was playing a difficult course in the United States Women's Amateur Championship against Joanne Henderson who had piled up a four-hole lead. Marlene won, the first Canadian-born woman to take this title. Born in Cereal, Alberta in 1934, Marlene developed amazing accuracy and phenomenal putting. She caddied to buy golf clubs. By 1951, she had won the Ontario Junior Championship, and 10 of the tournaments she had entered, including the Canadian Ladies' Open. In 1953 she won the British Open. Named "Outstanding Athlete of the Year" (1956-57) she won the Lou Marsh Trophy five times and in 1956 took eight major tournaments. The *Los Angeles Times* sports award board selected her as the outstanding woman golfer, and honored her with a dinner in Hollywood. Little Marlene, one girl among 1,000 men, was given a standing ovation.

In 1957 she won both Ontario Amateur and Canadian Women's closed titles. That June, following her marriage, she played and won the Ontario Open Championship. As Mrs. Streit, she won the Australian Women's Championship in 1963 and was Canadian Woman Athlete of the Year. The Ontario branch of Canadian Ladies' Golf Association set up a Marlene Stewart Streit trust fund and made a presentation to Mrs. Streit at the annual meeting in November 1966. In August, 1969 in Moncton, N.B., Marlene walked away with the Canadian Women's Championship for the ninth time in her startling career. The previous year she had captured both the Canadian Open and Closed Competitions.

* * *

Most likely to fall heir to Marlene's crown is Gail Harvey, who was Club Champion at Uplands in Ottawa. In 1956 she shot an 80 on the Metro Don Valley Course — a course which civic officials had condemned as too difficult, claiming it would be better as a zoo. Gail was Canadian junior champion in 1958, 1959 and 1960. She beat Marlene in 1965, to win the Canadian Women's Closed Golf Championship. Now Gail Harvey Moore, she was runner-up to Marlene in the 1968 closed amateur championship.

Marlene and Gail, along with Sue Hilton and Rae Milligan formed the winning Ontario team in 1963 taking the Interprovincial match and the R.C.G.A. trophy at Ottawa's Royal Ottawa Golf Club. Another hard-driving Ontario golfer, Pam Miller of Oshawa took the Ontario Women's Golf Championship in a tension-filled extra hole final in 1966, edging out Marlene Streit. Pam successfully defended her Ontario title in 1967.

Victory Ride

Canada's champion horsewoman, Shirley Thomas was born in 1935 and began falling off horses early at her parents' luxurious home, "Twin Gates", Aylmer, Quebec. In 1945, she gave her first public performance at the Ottawa Winter Fair. In 1953 Shirley won the Carling Trophy, the high jump competition at Toronto's Royal Winter Fair, the Pennsylvania National at Harrisburg, and the International Goodwill Challenge Trophy at the National Horse Show in Madison Square Gardens, New York. She was the first woman to represent Canada at international horse shows.

When Shirley visited Europe in 1954 as a member of Canada's Equestrian Team, she took her favorite horses, "Princess Midas" and "Revlon's White Sable". (Her father was president of Revlon Inc.) She won the ladies' championships in Belgium and Holland, suffering from a strained back and three broken ribs. The youngest competitor, Shirley outjumped 60 top horsemen at the Dublin Horse Show to win the Republic of Ireland Trophy. She won over 600 awards in three

years, yet she was not allowed to compete in horseman-
ship at the Olympic Games, as women are today.

The Weaker Sex?

The feminine invasion of masculine sports is
well-nigh complete. Granted few women play football,
once considered so dangerous that laws forbidding it
were passed in England. And today Brazil still prohibits
women from playing soccer. However, a Toronto girls'
team, the Canadian Belles, is one of four in a women's
professional football league which started in August,
1969; part of their takings will go to sponsoring charitable organizations. Even bullfighting has fallen to a
woman's hand; Carolyn Howard, of St. John's, studied
bullfighting in Mexico and this young matador's ambition is to introduce the sport to Newfoundland. Then,
there are lady wrestlers who earn around $20,000 annu-
ally. Promoter George Jacobs says his girl grapplers are
mainly university graduates, and one even renounced
an opera career.

Victoria, B.C. boasts two girl deep-sea octopus
wrestlers. Tiny Mary Aust also drag races and water
skis, but wrestling with octopi is her job as a display
diver for a Victoria Aquarium; she also enjoys tangling
with six-foot wolf eels. Elva Ware says, "Some divers
get their kicks eating bananas underwater, I prefer
something more challenging."

Meanwhile, other girls cheerfully risk black eyes
playing field hockey — a sport too rough for most men.

First Woman Jockey

Mary Cowan of Victoria, B.C., is Canada's first
woman jockey. She rode into the history books April 5,
1969, astride "Easter Jewel" at Victoria's Sandown Park
placing sixth. Her love of horses had prompted her to
save enough from her stenographer's salary to buy one.

Then she married a horse-trainer. Though keeping her steno job, she too became a trainer and exerciser and finally decided to make a career of racing. After testing her the B.C. Jockey Club issued her a license. When she first rode out in the red and white silks of the KJD Ranch the band played "For it was Mary, Mary. . ." and the crowd cheered.

Chapter XVII

The Space Age

New Fields for Women

Elsie Gregory MacGill

*We cannot expect to hold down
space age jobs with horse and buggy
training and education . . . we must
adjust our skills to the marketplace
of the future.*

(Margaret Ashdown, National
President of B and P Club)

War and Women

"One of the trends that impresses me most," said
Moira Guthrie, personnel selection officer of the Public
Service Commission, "is the diversity of skills and training women have chosen to acquire. At one time they
worked mainly as stenographers. Today they are administrative officers, economists, research scientists, foreign service officers, draftsmen, medical officers,
statisticians and customs examiners. War did much to
provide the occasion. Women have certainly risen to it!"

The two world wars boosted woman's drive for
equality. Work in World War I helped gain political
equality. World War II's critical man-power shortage
provided opportunities for women in traditionally male
domains. Labor-saving devices facilitated this trend,
and, more recently, the Pill made family planning truly
a matter of choice, not chance.

Among firsts for women in Canada is columnist
Lotta Dempsey's flight in a jet-plane — she was the first
female to break the sound barrier.

Some exceptional women have attained top positions, but many more serve as indispensable "Girl Fridays" to important executives. A shining example is Mary Macdonald, for 20 years the enthusiastic executive assistant to Rt. Hon. Lester Pearson, equally loyal whether he was in Opposition or leading the Government. Mary carefully avoided the limelight which surrounded her boss. Born in North Cobalt, Ontario she obtained her B.A. in political science at University of Ottawa. Following a stint with Metropolitan Life Insurance Company and overseas service with the Canadian Red Cross, she took a civil service job, a grade 4 clerk.

Her computer-like memory and friendly personality proved great assets. One highlight of a fascinating career came when she accompanied the Pearsons to Oslo, Norway for the presentation of Mr. Pearson's Nobel Peace Prize. Usually, however, Mary stayed close to Ottawa, keeping the office political fires burning, answering the mounds of mail and shoring up the political organization in Mr. Pearson's Algoma East riding. One Liberal wag commented. "Who would win if Mary Macdonald ran against Mike Pearson?" As his "Girl Friday", Mary's salary was reputedly around $14,000. Today she is a member of Prime Minister Trudeau's team, with a salary in the $18,000 range.

In 1956, an Equal Pay for Equal Work Act was finally passed; that same year, Canadian civil service gave "marrieds" the right to permanent appointment and pensions. Many had been "temporary" for 30 years!

Usually any woman with a top position today has had to work at least several years to get there. Many developed their skills and education along the way. Beautiful Phyllis Gregory Turner Ross, O.B.E., a brilliant economist, has enjoyed a successful career dotted with triumphs, among them, administrator of fats and oils, and economic adviser to the Wartime Prices and Trade Board — then Canada's highest paid woman civil servant, during World War II. She also has the honor of being the first woman university chancellor at the University of British Columbia, of which province her husband, Hon. Frank Ross, was Lieutenant Governor. Her son, handsome John Turner was a cabinet Minister in the federal government before he resigned.

Civil service commissioner, Ruth Addison of Winnipeg, a graduate of the University of Manitoba, worked her way from clerk in the civil service in Ottawa to Department of Trade and Commerce economist, executive assistant to the Minister of the Department of Defense Production, and in 1957 she was appointed first woman member of the Civil Service Commission. She is an inspiring example for 50,000 women civil servants.

Chairman of the Immigration Appeal Board is Janet V. Scott, a lawyer who was appointed to the Board in July 1967.

Marion Royce headed the federal Women's Labor Bureau in the '50's and '60's before her retirement. She also worked as consultant with the Economic and Social Council of United Nations considering such questions as the position of women, displaced persons and human rights. Miss Royce feels that everyone underestimates the "dignity of domesticity". Her special problems were married working women with children, and older women in industry. Her book *Women Who Work in Canada* was published in 1957.

Sylvia Gelber currently heads the Women's Bureau. Before her appointment she served on the International Labor Organization's panel of consultants dealing with the problems of women workers.

Miss Lita-Rose Betcherman, director of the Women's Bureau for the Ontario Department of Labor, specializes in advice to women who want to re-enter the labor force — "the re-treads" as they are termed.

In Ottawa, in 1965, Aideen Nicholson, psychiatric social worker, became Ontario's first administrator of adult female institutions. Agnes MacLeod, R.N., after distinguished overseas service, became director of treatment services, Department of Veterans' Affairs.

Among top women government scientists are Dr. Clara Fritz, pathologist with Forest Products Laboratories, Department of Resources and Development; Dr. Mildred Nobles, division of plant pathology, Department of Agriculture; Marie Rauter, first woman to graduate, Faculty of Forestry, University of Toronto, 1956, joined the Ontario Department of Lands and Forests as a specialist in research in genetics.

Dr. Eveline LeBlanc of Laval University, for years the only female chief of the Quebec Department of Education's home economics division, lectured across Canada. In 1959, she became dean of women at University of Ottawa.

Grace Nicholls took 30 years of varied extension courses after beginning her career as a junior-accountant-secretary. She became the first woman director and vice-president of an insurance company in Canada. Another woman, Willard Turner, Ph.D., F.S.S. served with her on the board. Grace joined the Soroptimist Club in 1937 and in 1950 was elected president of the American Federation.

Dark, striking-looking Nazla Dane, originally a Westerner, now living in Toronto, started out as a teacher, like many other career women. She is now public relations officer for Canadian Life Insurance Officers' Association. Intensely active in the B. and P. Club for many years, Nazla has served as national president and is now on the executive of the international club.

Miss Isabel Menzies, one of Montreal's best-known career women, served as secretary of a Montreal Insurance Company for over 40 years. She also was provincial, then national president of the Federation of B. and P. Women's Clubs. A world traveller, she sat in on the Status of Women Commission sessions at the UN in New York.

Grace Nicholls

Flying Fingers

Typewriters were first introduced in Canada in 1879, when a Remington was bought by a farm-machinery firm. By 1880, the YWCA taught English and bookkeeping; in 1884 classes began in phonography (shorthand). The first classes for typists were started at the Toronto YWCA in 1900. By 1906, Mary MacMahon, director of employment for Underwood, Limited, opened the first Canadian placement bureau for women in Toronto. In a half century, she placed more than a half-million stenographers, not many of whom would be able to match Margaret Hamma's output of 210 words per minute on an IBM electric.

Most women in business offices are stenographers or secretaries, none of whom wants merely to be a carbon copy of a man. Miss Merle Law, C.P.S. of London, in 1965 became the first non-American president of the 25,000 member National Secretaries' Association.

Her entire business career has been with London Life Insurance Company where she started as secretary. During 1957-58 she worked with Mary Gillespie, professor and head of the secretarial science department of the University of Western Ontario, to make available in Canada the Certified Professional Secretary examination.

Administrator Margaret Ashdown, F.C.I.S., says women can't expect to hold down space age jobs with horse and buggy training and education. She proved it herself; she started as secretary to the manager of a large manufacturing industry (one of their Coleman stoves once warmed the palace of the Shah of Iran), and studied her way up the ladder. Now Mrs. Ashdown is a member of the board of directors, corporate secretary, and office manager, administering a staff of 100 employees. "You name the course — I took it!" says this hardworking widow.

Once excluded from a dinner to celebrate the successful completion of a project she had worked on, Margaret joined the Business and Professional Women's Club to work through it for recognition of working women. For many years she has served the Club in many capacities, and through it has travelled extensively as a delegate to foreign countries. In 1966 she was elected a member of the board of the International Federation of Business and Professional Women, then in August, 1968 was elected president of the Canadian Federation.

Success stories like that of Toronto's Mrs. G. Douglas are hard to come by. She started as a bookkeeper for a thermometer company in 1935, became manager in 1939, bought the company in 1948, then hired her husband!

Feminine Preoccupations

Sewing was one of women's earliest occupations and history is threaded with its milestones. Mlle. Phaneuf was Montreal's first professional seamstress and the first Canadian woman to sew with silk thread. She was dressmaker to Mme. Louis Joseph Papineau, whose historic home forms part of the luxurious Seigniory Club at Montebello. The YWCA held the first classes in dressmaking from 1882 to 1892.

Versatile couturiere Cornelia Berceller, who cooked when husband Oscar first opened the famous Winston Grill in Toronto, started a dress shop featuring her originals. Later she opened an exclusive Bloor Street shop. Before the Bercellers fled Hitler, she was an opera singer in Vienna.

Joy McGillawee of Toronto heads the Wool Bureau of Canada.

Distinguished-looking Olga Cloke, of Hamilton, a woman with great executive ability, wed an uncle (by marriage) and brought up his large family after her aunt's death. When her husband Fred died, Olga took over the presidency of Cloke and Sons, Limited, once reputedly the largest and finest book store in Canada. Recently this firm has switched to become a complete office supply house. Mrs. Cloke who shares an apartment in Toronto with Helen Cleveland, has become a commuter and still serves as secretary-treasurer and a director of the family firm. For many years active in community clubs, Olga Cloke holds high office in the Zonta Club.

Beth Hammond of Montreal built a career as writer and administrator. She was women's editor of the *Family Herald*, director of the Footwear Bureau of Canada and in 1968 became director of the Leather Bureau of Canada. Among her many projects, she supervised a short film on Canadian fashions in leather.

Another well-known Montrealer, Doreen Day,

gained attention as Eaton's fashion consultant. Sophisticated and elegant, Doreen first did comparison shopping with Hudson's in Detroit. During World War II, she helped design the WRCN's uniforms and supervised Eaton's fashion and wedding bureau.

* * *

Florence Nightingale Graham lasted two weeks as a nurse, but the Woodbridge, Ontario, native's name will last many lifetimes in the memories of women. Miss Graham decided she'd rather make women pretty than well. A lady might pinch her cheeks to redden them, or, if daring, use a bit of beet juice in the late 1800's. But the ex-nurse, taking the name Elizabeth Arden, changed all this. In 1906 she became a partner in a cosmetic venture in New York. As Elizabeth Arden, she helped a young chemist "boil" a face cream. Borrowing $6,000 in 1909 she opened Fifth Avenue's first beauty salon.

Business boomed. Tiny Miss Arden, pounding her desk, would exclaim: "Fight! Fight! I only want people around who can do the impossible." A dress designer also, while in Europe on business, Elizabeth met Thomas Lewis, whom she married in 1915. She appointed him European sales manager. In 1934 she divorced him and Tom joined her rival, Helena Rubinstein. Elizabeth Arden was also famous for her prize-winning race horses. Theta Sigma Phi Fraternity gave Elizabeth Arden its Great Lady Award. When she died in 1966 she left an estate of $30,000,000.

Food and Seaweed

The Canadian Dietetic Association in 1950 established a joint memorial to Miss Violet Ryley and Miss Kathleen Jeffs, charter members of the association who devoted their lives to raising the status of their profession. Miss Ryley was most successful in military hospitals following World War I, in Eaton's under Lady

Eaton's sponsorship, in national organizations and philanthrophy. Kathleen Jeffs was her charming associate, supervisor of restaurants for the T. Eaton Company in Montreal. During World War II she organized food services for the armed forces, with the rank of Wing Officer in the RCAF; she was awarded the O.B.E.

Mrs. Norma Macdonald, gracious, hospitable hostess at her Oak Bay Hotel in Victoria, B.C., was first woman member of the International Hotel Association. Mme. Henri Berger's Restaurant in Hull, Quebec, specializing in French cuisine, has brought her international acclaim.

President of Morrison-Lamonthe Bakery Ltd. is Mrs. Arthur Piggott, the former Jean Morrison. Her sister, Mrs. R. B. Hale, is quality control officer for the company. Mrs. Piggott is also active in many community activities in and around Ottawa.

Belleville resident, Dorothy Batcheller, is director of home economics for the Poultry Products Institute of Canada Inc., a job which involves much travelling and public speaking as well as radio and television appearances.

A success story of fairytale proportions is that of Mrs. Ida Steinberg. In 1917 she opened the first Steinberg Store on Montreal's St. Lawrence Boulevard, with a capital of $300. Her aim was to furnish customers with quality food at low prices. A smile and a cheery word, sometimes also a rosy apple tucked in for good measure, always greeted patrons. Delivery was by hand cart, later by a wagon, with the Steinberg pony Nelly, pulling up front. Helpers were her five sons and a daughter. The tenth store, an experimental self-service "Wholesale Groceteria", opened by 1933 near the Forum. Telephone orders and free delivery were discontinued. Since then, stores have sprouted far beyond Montreal into a vast grocery and Miracle Mart empire.

"Queen of the Ramea", as Mrs. Marie Penney of

Newfoundland was called, has supervised both a fishing fleet and a fish processing plant since the death of her husband, Senator George Penney. Her only daughter, Mrs. Spencer Lake, is executive vice-president. Another president is Mrs. John Penney, head of a sales company in Boston, Massachusetts, and a refrigerated-transportation company. "Fish is served at least once a day in my house," Marie Penney says, proudly. As president of the Fisheries Council of Canada in 1967, she was the first woman to hold that office.

Connie MacFarlane, formerly principal of Mount Allison School for Girls, in New Brunswick, and later Dean of Women at University of Alberta, is marine botanist for the Nova Scotia Research Foundation. Her garden is the sea, and the treasure she hunts in a fishing boat is seaweed, worth sometimes $200 a ton. An international authority, she lectured to the British Association for the Advancement of Science, and at an international seaweed symposium in Norway. Well-known naturalist, Mrs. Eva Becket of Fort William, spent 25 years in the Arctic helping her husband. She has the honor of being the only woman in the world to have a saw-fly named after her. Mrs. John Lewis donned diving gear and helped her husband (director of Bellairs Institute) sweep the ocean floor for specimens. Mrs. Beatrice Barge, a McGill University meteorologist has conducted research on Meighen Island (700 miles from the North Pole) which hopefully will lead to more accurate weather forecasting.

Homemakers should be grateful to Mrs. Noah Cushing of Quebec who, in 1824 helped her husband invent a crude wooden washing machine, precursor of today's gleaming electric models.

Another enterprising woman who pioneered in an unusual job, especially one which has traditionally been filled by men, is Mrs. Audrey Seymour who, in 1957, became Canada's first licenced woman auctioneer.

Industrial chemist, Mrs. Dedie Dodds of Ottawa, was cook in an Arctic weather station, dietitian at an Indian Reserve and lighthouse-keeper at Gibraltar Point, Toronto Island. Toronto's Louise Girvan founded Girvan Travel Service, catering to an exclusive clientele, was a top-flight public relations gal for modern cruises by CPR's great Empress ships — she travelled 15 times around the world. In Canada, while manager of Royal Muskoka Hotel, she discovered the Horace Lapp Orchestra.

Therapist, Bernice Lurie, a chain-smoker of 50 cigarettes daily, launched a successful anti-smoking campaign at Royal Edward Chest Hospital in Montreal. Evaleen Dunlop, church soloist in Toronto for years, was appointed in 1963 as the only woman on Ontario's Board of Censors. She passes judgement on about 500 films annually. Mlle. Eduordina Dupont has operated a collection business in Trois Rivieres, Quebec. She is a director of the Quebec Association of Collection Agencies, Incorporated.

Gladys Beattie (Mrs. I. M.), a busy IODE worker in Fredericton, was asked by the Canadian Highway Safety Council to act as administrator for the New Brunswick Safety Awards. She helped organize the New Brunswick Safety Council in 1967 and helped to establish defensive driving courses across the province. She is the first woman to qualify as an instructor.

Mrs. Roger Percival of Ottawa breeds Siberian Huskies as a hobby. The granddaughter of philanthropist Jesse Ketchum, she is president of Ketchum Manufacturing Co. with affiliated offices in the U.S. and Great Britain. Her father taught her die casting and toolmaking maintaining that: "It is not enough for a girl just to be able to play the harp — not in this world anyway!"

Grave Business

When June Cullen's husband, Kingston under-taker R. B. Cullen died, she took a course and carried on his business, helped by her two older sons. Pretty Sharon Thompson of Parry Sound is an embalmer who dates other undertakers to avoid embarrassing explanations. Embalmer Mrs. Bruce MacKay of Don Mills, says: "I didn't lose any friends when I took up this work. Nobody thought I'd contaminate them." Her husband doesn't mind — he's in the business too.

Former Chief of Information Services Division at Indian Affairs and Northern Development Department is glamorous Mrs. Irene Baird. For years she says she had "One hand on the typewriter, the other in the kitchen sink". A brilliant newspaperwoman, she writes novels as well, including *Waste Heritage,* often called the Canadian *Grapes of Wrath.* She has been on the Canadian Film Board and was press officer at the Canadian Embassy in Mexico. At one NATO ministerial meeting, little Irene had the man-sized job of heading arrangements for the working press.

High Finance

Canada's first woman bank manager, Mary Pollack, once vowed the only place she didn't want to work was a bank. Then she landed a job as a secretary with the Bank of Montreal. She took an interest in her work, studied half a dozen subjects concerned with banking and later took courses in economics, banking history and commercial law. Within three years, she was a Fellow of the Canadian Banker's Association, leading a class of men in final exams. She became assistant accountant in 1942, then in 1957, assistant manager.

Petite, blonde Shirley Giles was warned, when she started working in the Bank of Nova Scotia in Toronto, that she couldn't hope to ever become a teller.

However, she was transferred from branch to branch, which gave her good experience, and she rose to be an assistant accountant. Then in September 1961 she and Gladys Marcellus were appointed managers. Shirley recently graduated to the Personnel End of the Systems Department.

Dr. Lucy Morgan became economics department manager of Bank of Nova Scotia, in Toronto, in 1954, and editor of the bank's monthly newsletter. A masterly report on Canada's economic prospects was her contribution in 1959. Walter Gordon termed it: "The best thing I've seen on the steel industry." Yet these women are rarities. Even today, few women make it to the top ladder as presidents or directors of firms. Early in 1968 Madame Pauline Vanier, a director of the Bank of Montreal, and Dr. Helen S. Hogg were appointed directors of the Bell Telephone Company.

Though in September, 1976, W. Earle McLaughlin, chairman and president of the Royal Bank of Canada, said the bank had been unable to find a qualified woman to serve on its board of directors, at the bank's annual meeting in November Mitzi Dobrin, vice-president of Steinberg's Limited and general manager of Steinberg's Miracle Mart Division, was named to the board.

More Than Purse Strings

Investment counsellor, Helen Cleveland of Toronto, was Canada's first woman to choose this career. She joined Wood, Gundy and Company and set out to study each department of the securities business from the ground up. She established Canada's first women's department for an investment firm. During 40 years with the firm she gave an annual lecture to women on the how-to of investment. On retirement in 1956, Miss Cleveland was the first woman in Canada granted an investment counsel licence and the first woman member of the Investment Counsel Association.

Brokerage firm president, Margaret Holland is a Dublin, Ontario native. Married to Jean-Louis Frappier of Montreal, Margaret was elected in 1969 to membership in the Canadian Stock Exchange, a "first" in the august world of finance. She purchased membership on the 100-seat Canadian Exchange for $5,500. As a point of interest only two women hold seats on the New York Stock Exchange.

Mrs. James Richardson of Winnipeg, on the death of her husband in 1939 became president of James Richardson and Sons Limited, one of Canada's largest and most important grain and investment firms. Her son Hon. James Richardson was named Minister of Supply and Services in 1969 and her daughter Agnes, the wife of Senator William Benidickson, is an active philanthropist and clubwoman. The firm celebrated its centenary in 1957 with cross-country birthday parties in 26 cities. From Winnipeg, Mrs. Richardson spoke by telephone to more than 1,000 employees, announcing the establishment of the Richardson Century Fund to provide books to libraries throughout Canada.

Dr. Alice Turner was born in the Norval manse where Lucy Maude Montgomery once lived. While with an investment firm in Toronto, in 1948 she wrote *Canadian Investors' Handbook*. She is assistant professor of mathematics at York University and 1969 was appointed to the financial advisory committee of the Ontario Development Agency.

Mrs. Irma Patterson of Charlottetown and Moncton, in June, 1954 became the first woman in the Maritimes to be elected president of the Institute of Chartered Accountants. In 1956, Nora Faulds, a chartered accountant, was elected director of Institute of Newspaper Controllers and Finance Officers. The same year, Alice Beauchesne of Three Rivers, was the first woman appointed an authorized trustee in bankruptcy, under the federal department of finance. In 1961, Violet Cook became the first full feminine partner in a Canadian brokerage house, Doherty, Roadhouse and McCuaig Brothers. She says: "I'm having a ball."

Myrtle Gray (Mrs. Clifford) of Toronto, who graduated from Queen's University with honors in Commerce and Finance, was a successful investment broker with J. H. Crang and Company.

Mrs. Sam Olan, New York-based wife of a wealthy Montreal businessman, is setting up her own brokerage firm and staffing it entirely with women stockbrokers. "After all, 60% of stockholders are women," notes Mrs. Olan.

A Titled Lady

Lady Maud Robinson's husband was the fifth Baronet. The first Baronet was Sir John Beverly Robinson, Chief Justice of Upper Canada 1829-1854, also First Chancellor of Trinity College, University of Toronto, who fought with Sir Isaac Brock and Tecumseh at the capture of Detroit in August 1812.

Born Maud Eva Coo, in London, Ont., her own ancestry is fascinating. In the reign of Queen Elizabeth I, Maud's first known ancestor was a highly successful pirate! He owned a fleet of ships, a fact which prompted the British Admiralty to invite him to join the British Navy. He rose to the rank of Admiral and eventually was knighted as Sir Charles Coo. The family crest displays an Admiral Bird and an anchor. Maud's father, William Charles Coo, who founded the Western Ontario Business Academy, was a court reporter and gentleman farmer. He is remembered in farming circles as the first person who succeeded in growing peanuts in Canada. Apparently the Coos had few financial worries — the children had sixteen ponies for their amusement and Maud's great-uncle Tom (Mrs. Arthur Roebuck's grandfather) often lit his cigar with a $10 bill.

After attending University of Toronto, Maud took a business course and became a court reporter and eventually became owner of a business "Coo and Thompson". Her most interesting assignment was the amalgamation proceedings of Toronto with its 13 neighboring municipalities in 1950-51. Her husband, Sir John, died suddenly in November 1948. Unfortunately, there is no son to carry on the title. But the children of intimate friends, Elsie and Louis Rice, are almost "family" to their "Aunt Maud". Of her dear friend, Elsie, Maud says: "Definitely her diploma is Motherhood." Maud herself is an artist, writer, eloquent speaker, clubwoman and philanthropist, whose creed is: "I believe in youth". To prove it she enrolled at York University for the 1969-70 winter term to finish her B.A.

Triumph of the Spirit

Pioneer aeronautical engineer, Elsie MacGill, victim of acute infectious myelitis, wrote final examinations in a wheelchair. She became the first woman aeronautical engineer in the world. Graduating in engineering from University of Toronto, she worked for Austin Aircraft Company, then did post-graduate work at University of Michigan. Elsie can scarcely walk with the help of two canes but it has never stopped her. Her only regret is that it's illegal for her to pilot a plane.

Born in Vancouver in 1905, daughter of Judge Helen MacGill, Elsie became assistant aeronautical engineer at Fairchild's Aircraft Limited, specializing in stress analysis. During her career she designed the Maple Leaf Trainer for the Mexican Air Force, the first plane designed by a woman. By January 1940 her skeleton staff of 120 mushroomed to 4,500 as the firm turned out more than 100 Hurricanes a month. Elsie also built 2,000 "winterized" Hurricanes, and Curtis-Wright Helldivers for the American Navy. Married to E. H. (Bill) Soulsby, youthful blonde little Elsie disclaims domesticity. She has no acknowledged hobbies but was active in the B. and P. Womens' Club as Ontario president. The club established an education grant called Elsie Gregory MacGill Bursary in her honor. In 1967 she was appointed a member of the Royal Commission on the Status of Women.

The Engineering Institute of Canada elected Elsie first woman member in 1938, and she is Associate Fellow of Royal Aeronautical Society, England. For her paper *Factors Affecting Mass Production of Aeroplanes,* the Engineering Institute awarded her the Gzowski Medal. She was first woman to serve as technical adviser to the international aviation organization at United Nations in 1948. "We're only three!" Elsie lamented early on, referring to the Women Engineers' Association.

* * *

In April 1953, Miss N. J. Moffatt was first woman engineer in the province of Quebec. Marion Seymour of Ottawa, graduated in civil engineering 1956 and became junior engineer with Ontario Department of Planning and Development. By 1957, Canada had only 24 women engineers, compared with Russia's 233,000!

Medical engineer Dr. Monique Arvisais was encouraged to change from a chemistry course to electrical engineering by her husband who was killed in a car accident a few weeks after their marriage. First woman to graduate in this profession from University of Ottawa, she first worked on communications systems for Northern Electric in Montreal. She was the second Canadian woman to win the Athlone Engineering Scholarship for advanced study in England, leading to a Ph.D. in medical engineering.

Grace Hutcheson (Mrs. W.G. Soloman) of Granby, Quebec was Canada's first woman pilot; Violet Milstead handled the difficult work of a bush pilot with ease; in 1951, Margaret Carson of Ottawa won the annual Powder Puff Derby over 10 crack American pilots. Dorothy Rungeling of Welland was first woman with a Class A instrument-rating licence (flying blind). In the National Air Show Race in 1953, she won the Governor-General's Silver Cup. Take-off time was written on the back of her dog licence, along with the day's grocery order!

Mrs. Evelyn Henson of Victoria succeeded her husband who was killed in a crash. He was president of Vancouver Island Helicopters. Marion Orr of Maple, Ontario, preferred flying lessons, at $9 an hour, to food. In 1950, she became the first woman to operate her own flying school. During World War II, she ferried Spitfires, Hurricanes and Harvards to Europe. "Prunehead!" she would shout angrily, at a student attempting to land downwind — the unforgiveable sin in flying. She trained over 600 successful pilots. Loraine B. Currie, Montreal, an employee of Aluminum Co. of Canada, in 1969 was the first woman elected president of a Wing (No. 306 — Maple Leaf Wing of the Royal Canadian Air Force Association).

Building Canada

Canada has few women architects. Alice Malhout of Calgary was the pioneer woman in this profession. Eric Arthur, University of Toronto School of Architecture, told a class that many woman architects drift into interior decorating because some feel handicapped in the supervisory areas of dealing with several trades on a job, or find it unappealing to work in all weathers and at all heights.

The biggest job Cornelia Oberlander, British Columbia's first woman architect, tackled was the International Airport at Philadelphia. Mrs. William Strange of Ottawa, joined Central Mortgage and Housing Corporation as an architect; Quebec's Mrs. Alfred Lavelee, a petite blonde with five children, built over $1,000,000 worth of homes. She designed, then hired a staff of 40 to build under her supervision.

Gwyneth Cooper-Jones resident architect of the $10,000,000 Lord Simcoe Hotel in Toronto, started early by building and furnishing doll's houses at the age of two. She matriculated from St. Catharine's Collegiate with draughting as an extra subject and studied architecture at McGill. In her class of 10, half were women. Miss Cooper-Jones has worked on homes, banks, schools, and hospitals. At business meetings, she takes a cigar when they're passed and saves it for a friend. She re-designed St. Mark's Anglican Sunday School at Niagara-on-the-Lake.

* * *

Women's concern with dust and dirt reaches far beyond the boundaries of the home in many careers. Geology, prospecting and mining are not exclusively the male's domain.

The first woman geologist in the world was Canadian, Dr. Alice Wilson, LL.D., M.B.E. She graduated in geology at Victoria College, then attained her Ph.D. in Chicago. Despite poor health, for over 30 years, she worked as a member of Geological Survey — tramping miles, climbing line fences. She hitch-hiked along the Amazon River, lectured on paleontology at Carleton University, 1954-58. She wrote *The Earth Beneath Our Feet*. The University Women's Club in Ottawa named a scholarship in her honor. Dr. Wilson was the first woman elected a Fellow of the Royal Society.

Mining Luck

Mme. Gilbertin was Canada's first woman gold digger. She discovered gold in the Chaudiere River in Quebec in 1823. As an infant, Mrs. Pauline Leary is said to have cut her teeth on rocks. Prospecting was her lifelong interest. Miss Gladys Clements of Elk Lake was the first woman mining recorder in Ontario. However, in

Canada it is illegal for women to work underground in mines.

* * *

"Dynamiting is just as safe as puttering around a kitchen, if you take the necessary precautions," Viola MacMillan maintained. Viola rose to control six mining companies and directed three others after a life of poverty and hardships in Northern Ontario. Born one of 12 children in Windermere, Ontario, she married George MacMillan in 1923 — their honeymoon was a prospecting trip.

In 1930, they heard of a gold rush in Hislop Township. Getting there at 4 a.m. they started driving claims by flashlight, stopping neither for food nor sleep until, aching from exhaustion, they had recorded 2,000 acres. By trading shares they acquired an interest in Hollinger Mine. Next, they bought the old Victor Mine in B.C. for $65,000, and scrambled over half the Rockies to find a second-hand compressor. When their mine "came in" they christened the $10,000,000 baby, "Viola C". Their office is a luxurious pink penthouse in downtown Toronto.

In 1934 the MacMillans joined the Prospectors and Developers Association, of which she was president 1943-65. In 1941, Viola was appointed a member of Federal War Metals Advisory Committee and managed to initiate much helpful provincial and federal mining legislation. Canada celebrates March 10 as Mining Day, this industry has attained such importance.

At the Summit

The highest post ever held by a woman in government service went to slim and serious brunette Sylvia Ostry in 1969 when she accepted a $25,000 a year job with the Economics Council of Canada.

Born in Winnipeg, she graduated with a B.A. in Economics from McGill in 1948, later obtained a Ph.D. from Cambridge University. For a time associate professor of economics at University of Montreal, Sylvia Ostry commuted to and from Ottawa two or three times a week. Finding this too exhausting, she took a position as assistant director of the labour division, Dominion Bureau of Statistics of which she later became Director.

Her published books include such weighty titles as *The Wage Structure of a Large Steel Firm* and *Inter-industry Earnings Differentials in Canada*. However, a gourmet cook, she says her own favorite reading is cookbooks.

Dr. Ostry was appointed Deputy Minister of Consumer and Corporate affairs in February, 1975 the year that Mount Allison University conferred on her an honorary degree.

Canada's First Woman Lieutenant-Governor

Pauline Emily Mills McGibbon was appointed Canada's first woman Lieutenant-Governor in March, 1974. That fateful afternoon she was in her kitchen preparing dinner when her husband called her away from the stove to talk to the Prime Minister. She accepted and was sworn in on April 10, in an impressive ceremony at Queen's Park.

This capable, graciously friendly woman, her light brown hair wound simply around her head in braids, fortunately enjoys excellent health. Her previous careers, she believes, helped to prepare her for her high office as the Ontario representative of her Majesty Queen Elizabeth II. Pauline was born in Sarnia, where her mother was Chairman of the Board of Education. She graduated in Modern History from Victoria College, University of Toronto, where she met her husband Donald McGibbon. He graduated in Economics, then worked for Imperial Oil, of which firm he is today

Treasurer. They were married in 1935 and moved to Toronto.

Her Excellency Pauline McGibbon

Pauline McGibbon's main interests have always been theatre and education, though she has done volunteer work for many other worthwhile organizations. She has been National President of the I.O.D.E., Chairman of the Board of Women's College Hospital, President of the Dominion Drama Festival, President of the Canadian Conference of the Arts, first woman President of the University Alumni Association, first woman member of the 75-year-old Canadian Club of Toronto, and the first woman Chancellor of the University of Toronto in 1971.

In her present position, Her Honor has the help of five secretaries and fifty aides throughout the Province, whom she affectionately dubs "the fuss and feathers." She is expected to travel widely in Ontario, but can't leave the Province without the consent of the Governor General or the Secretary of State. She must sign (by hand) two copies of every Act passed in Ontario during her term in office. She refuses to sign documents without knowing their contents. Our Lieutenant-Governor firmly believes that pomp and ceremony add interest to our daily life.

She wears her many honors lightly, including the Canadian Drama award, the 1967 Toronto Civic Award of Merit, The Canadian Centennial Medal, and an honorary doctorate from University of Alberta. In 1972 she received an honorary doctorate from the University of Ottawa, and is also an officer of the Order of Canada.

External Calls

Grace Hart, graduate librarian of McGill University, began as librarian in External Affairs in 1925. The longest service record is held by Marjorie Mackenzie, principal secretary to Dr. O. D. Skelton. In External's Commonwealth division, Miss Mackenzie often accompanied Canadian delegates to conferences abroad. Colleagues called her "a walking encyclopedia on Commonwealth affairs".

* * *

Mary Craig McGeachy Schuller of Sarnia, a graduate of University of Toronto, for 10 years was a member of the League of Nations secretariat in Geneva. When World War II broke out, she joined the United Kingdom Ministry of Economic Warfare and was appointed first secretary at the British Embassy in Washington in 1945. In the post-war period she helped set up UNRRA, became director of social welfare and president of ICW, living and working in New York.

* * *

Canada's foreign service was mainly masculine until 1947. Agnes McCloskey, Ottawa, joined the Department in 1925 as principal clerk and administrative officer; she was first Canadian woman to enjoy quasi-diplomatic status. In 1954 she was appointed vice-consul in New York, serving there until retirement in 1959.

* * *

When Louis St. Laurent became prime minister in 1948, he was faced with the critical Israel-Egypt war. His adviser was a gentle, hard-of-hearing lady, Elizabeth MacCallum. Though recognized as External's one-woman Middle East Division, it was a nine-day wonder when she was appointed Canada's first woman chargé d'affaires in Lebanon. Elizabeth, born in Turkey of missionary parents, was 14 before she saw any vehicle other than a wheelbarrow. At Queen's University, she and Charlotte Whitton were rivals. After obtaining her M.A. in 1919, Elizabeth studied European history at Columbia University. She joined External Affairs in 1942, serving as special adviser to the Canadian delegation at the United Nations founding conference in San Francisco.

* * *

Margaret Meagher in 1958 became Canada's first woman Ambassador with her posting to Israel. It was

Elizabeth MacCallum

tradition-shaking, but fitting, since Israel's foreign minister was a woman, Mrs. Golda Meir, later Israel's Prime Minister. Miss Meagher of Halifax, joined External Affairs in 1942. In 1962, she became ambassador to Austria and Canadian representative on the International Atomic Energy Agency in Vienna. In 1967, she

540

became high commissioner to Kenya and accredited to Uganda. She says of women diplomats: "We became legitimate!" 1969 Miss Meagher was given a key posting to Sweden in the midst of Canada-Red China negotiations for diplomatic recognition of the 700,000,000 communist nation.

Margaret Meagher

* * *

Miss Pamela McDougall, BSc., LL.D. (Mount Allison) was born and educated in Ottawa, but graduated from Mount Allison University in 1945, and continued her studies at University of Toronto. For a time she worked in the laboratories of the National Research Council, then in 1947-48 studied in Paris on a French Government bursary. She joined the Department of External Affairs in 1949, and served as Secretary at the Canadian Embassy at Bonn, and later (1959) as senior political adviser on the Canadian Delegation to the International Control Commission in Vietnam. After further postings in New Delhi and Ottawa, Miss McDougall was appointed Ambassador to Poland in January 1968.

* * *

On the political side of the coin, Elena Murdock (Da Costa) organized and became the first president of the Twentieth Century Liberal Club of Toronto. Elected to the Women's National Liberal Federation, Mrs. Da Costa took an active part in the 1963 federal election. A widow since 1951, Mrs. Da Costa purchased a 19th century stone house in Westport's Rideau Lake district in 1967, furnished it with family furniture carefully gathered over the years. During centennial year more than 2,000 persons toured the home which has been developed as a historic site.

With the speed of Canada's industrial development, the importance of the work women are doing in the field of labor relations cannot be over-estimated. There are now scarcely any restrictions on women's career opportunities. Biological responsibilities and mental capacities may now combine. Pioneering women have helped reform the structure of society. In the past, women had to make major sacrifices to succeed in a dual role. However, today, masculine understanding and science tend to be on their side.

Room at the Top

Vivacious Alberte Senecal of Hull, Quebec, knows what it takes to succeed as a space age career woman.

The red-haired widow from Valleyfield, Quebec, has climbed to the top in just about every job she has tackled. Awarded an M.B.E. for her World War II work with the Wartime Prices and Trade Board, Alberte joined the federal department of health and welfare in 1947 as officer in charge of French information services. The charming grandmother of several youngsters won the top award in the preventive medicine section of the first international festival of medico-surgical films for her translation of an NFB film. In 1963, Mme. Senecal was appointed assistant director of information services with the health and welfare department and in her spare time became the first woman to head a branch of the Canadian Public Relations Society, Ottawa — surrounded by an all-male team, of course.

Her fluency in French and English (she taught herself to speak English at the age of 34) was a big plus in bringing her out of retirement in Centennial year to head Secretary of State's special information services for state visits.

Labor Leaders

In Quebec, unionism had been discouraged by the parish societies and heavy religious influences from the turn of the century. The Duplessis regime in the province posed even greater barriers to the development of fraternities of workers with harsh legal punishments and social sanctions.

Thus it was particularly courageous work that wealthy socialite Madeleine Parent, a McGill graduate, carried out in the '40's. She met with manual workers and campaigned for free scholarships for needy students. In 1941 she married Vladimir Bjarnasson and while he served overseas, she organized brewery and tobacco workers into unions. Some textile workers had been trying to unionize since 1898. In 1942, they were paid only 19-20 cents per hour, half the workers were women and young children. They were given no holidays whatever. Mlle. Parent finally formed a union and had wage rates raised, child labor reduced and one week's annual holidays instituted.

"If any employer tried to make his employees work as long hours as I do, I'd call a strike!" exclaimed glamorous French-Canadian Huguette Plamondon, active labor leader at the national level. Huguette studied business management for a year, then English at

McGill University night classes. Completely bilingual, she completed her trade union education in CCL labor schools.

A devout Catholic, Huguette is theoretically a Rabbi — the only woman member of the United Packinghouse Workers Association Chapter of Ritual slaughterers, "The Rabbi Local". Other members are all Hebrews, 60 to 80, whose religion forbids them to attend meetings as delegates.

Huguette Plamondon

She joined the Packinghouse Workers of America as secretary in 1945, by 1953 she was the official representative, organizing, drafting and negotiating contracts for 28 Quebec and Maritime locals. During a brewer's strike in 1945, she joined the picket line. "When workers are suffering, there is no such thing as a rival union," she said. In another strike in 1947 she spent Thanksgiving Day in jail. Huguette made history in 1955 when she defeated Charles Devlin by a two to one vote to become the Montreal Labor Council's first woman president. She was re-elected by acclamation. Later, Huguette was elected one of 13 vice-presidents of the Canadian Labor Congress.

Mrs. John Mayne in 1949 became first woman president in Canada for the Oshawa Labor Council. Mrs. Marion Kushner was elected in Port Arthur six years later. In Quebec Mme. Guillemet became president of ILGWU's Local 262 and Yvette Charpentier was made director of educational and recreational activities. Mme. Annette Renault, once deputy administrator of the dress industry's parity committee, became a member of Quebec's Unemployment Commission. Yolande Valois became vice-president of Canadian Federation of Labor. Mrs. Alma Gosselin, for 20 years manager of a pharmacy, in 1950 became a management consultant. She set a precedent when named negotiator for Montreal on a contract dispute with 3,000 white-collar workers.

Grace Hartman of Ottawa, national secretary-treasurer of the Canadian Union of Public Employees since November, 1967, and now president has held an impressive number of union offices. She helped prepare CUPE briefs presented to the Status of Women Commission. She thinks that job evaluation is crucial to the improvement of women's job status. A Winnipeg native Jean Edmonds, helps direct Canada's expansive Manpower program. An economics and English major in college, she took part in the CBC schools' Broadcast series on children's art which, when published, won an international competition. Jean's voice was heard as news commentator for 10 years on a national network. Simultaneously, she wrote four weekly editorials for *The Financial Post,* for which she also covered the inauguration of the European Common Market in Brussels. An economist for Central Mortgage and Housing Corporation for two years, she joined the Department of Manpower and Immigration as an assistant director in 1966, becoming a director two years later.

The Selling Game

In the contemporary world of psycho-suggestion, sales promotion of thousands of commodities is slanted towards women buyers. Consequently, the field is a fertile one for bright career gals on the move. Grace Wilson Guiness, who started out as a typist became the second woman director of the Association of Canadian Advertisers by 1956, In 1958 she was named Advertising Woman of the year.

Mabel Stoakley of Toronto, was the first woman agency director. She completed 28 years with R. C. Smith Advertising Agency in 1950. A Mabel Stoakley Scholarship is donated annually by the Toronto Young Women's Canadian Club.

Miss Mary Cardon, McGill graduate, taught advertising and market research at Sir George Williams in Montreal. With J. Walter Thompson Co. from 1930-55, she was chiefly responsible for organizing media and research. She and Toronto's Cecilia Long in 1957 were co-winners of the first Woman of the Year in Advertising Award. Cecilia Long also became the first woman president of the Federation of Advertising and Sales Clubs. Graduate from University of British Columbia, she did post-graduate work in journalism at University of Washington. After work on *The Vancouver Sun* and *About Town* magazine, she took a train to Toronto with a return ticket as unemployment insurance. But she never needed to use it. Her career was a success story by any standard. By 1955 she was director of women's promotions for Ronolds Advertising Agency. During World War II she had worked on the national war finance radio committee. 'Cec' says: "Women own 70% of all private wealth, they'll soon say: 'If I own them, why can't I help run them?'".

She is a past president of both the Women's Advertising Club of Toronto and Zonta Club, a member of National CWPC and was first woman chairman of public relations for the United Appeal of Metropolitan Toronto. In 1966, she was made an honorary member of the Canadian Sunshine Club (which helps shut-ins and disabled people) in recognition of her tangible assistance and sustained interest. She is vice-chairman of the Metropolitan Zoological Society and was president of the Board of Governors of Women's College Hospital 1966-70.

* * *

Fashion authority Mairuth Sarsfield of Ottawa combines a career as writer and homemaker. Her work has been in advertising and promotion fields with advertising agencies, as well as boutique designers. She is an authority in the fashion field, about which she writes and lectures. She acted as co-ordinator of the popular "People Tree" at the Canadian Pavilion at Expo '70 Japan.

"I enjoy being a Canadian Negro . . . I don't understand all this fuss about identity . . . I just enjoy being me," says Mairuth, with typical charming candor. She was born and educated in Montreal, did extension studies at University of Montreal after a journalism course at Columbia University. Her first husband was photographer Rudolf Haas; she is married again to Dominick Sarsfield.

*   *   *

Miss Madelaine Levason, formerly of Montreal, an attractive brunette, was news editor for CBC International Services, women's editor of *Montreal Herald* before she became associated with Canadian Industries Limited public relations department. Later she served as manager of advertising and public relations of Canadian Chemical and Cellulose Company. In June, 1956 she started her own public relations business, along with freelance writing, which, as she admits, is "an extremely mixed bag of activities." One of them is producing monthly columns under the heading "Texstyles" that appear in more than 20 daily newspapers and 30 odd weeklies across Canada. Miss Levason is an active member of the CWPC. Her headquarters is now Ottawa, where she works for John Doherty and Co. Limited, besides writing a weekly syndicated column.

*   *   *

Miss Mary Joliffe's work latterly has been mainly connected with theatre. For six years she was responsible for the publicity programs of Stratford Festival, the O'Keefe Center, Toronto; Fathers of Confederation Centennial Center in Charlottetown, Metropolitan Opera National Company, Tyrone Guthrie Theatre in Minneapolis, the Atlanta (Georgia) Arts Center, and the World Festival of Expo '67. Miss Joliffe was director of public relations for the National Arts Center in Ottawa from October 1968 until her resignation in July 1969.

Top PR Post

Mrs. Barbara Kilvert, executive assistant public relations officer with Hudson Bay Company in Winnipeg, has probably the best position of any Canadian woman in the PR field. She travels more than 25,000 miles annually for the company. "I have bought underwear for a poet going North and obtained polar bears for a zoo!" she says, recalling some of the offbeat requests her PR department has handled.

Film Firm

Handsome Hani Benjamin, born in Riga, Latvia, came to Canada around 1950, and has made a considerable contribution to her adopted country, as have many other women of varied ethnic origins. After graduating in Pharmacy, Hani married wealthy George Benjamin. In Toronto the Benjamins first started a building business, later they established the highly-successful Benjamin Film Laboratories, which initiated colored processing film in Canada. Previously all colored film had to be sent to the United States for processing. Hani, vice-president of the firm, and her husband have won many international film awards and have been featured in *National Geographic Magazine*.

* * *

Much has been accomplished in the related fields of medicine and animal care thanks to several women pioneering in these fascinating fields. Possibly Dr. Dorothea Erxleben is the pioneer woman physician. She graduated in medicine from the University of Halle, Germany in 1754. Swinging down the centuries, Emilia Bonneville of Quebec became Canada's first woman Bachelor of Pharmacy. Better known is pretty Nell Martin of Windsor and Ottawa, who was a capable pharmacist before marrying her front-ranking, bilingual politician husband, Senator Paul Martin, now Canada's High Commissioner to London, England.

* * *

Western Canada's Dr. Gladys E. (Mrs. Merrill) Muttart, a diabetic herself, helped found and was first president of the Canadian Diabetic Association, incorporated in 1953. Through lecturing on this disease, she established numerous branches throughout Canada.

Through the Gladys and Merrill Muttart Foundation, the Muttarts have contributed thousands of dollars to research in this disease, and to many other charitable causes. Mrs. Muttart is vice-president of Merrill D. Muttart and Associates, a booming construction business.

Mrs. Muttart was made a Serving Sister of the Venerable Order of St. John of Jerusalem, given an honorary degree by Mount Allison University, and awarded a Centennial Medal.

Feminine Veterinarians

Dr. Anne Currier, first woman veterinarian in private practice, graduated from Ontario Veterinary College, Guelph in 1948. No male veterinarian would hire her, so she was forced to go to the United States (like many women before her) to start her career. Returning with $350 and a carload of equipment, she started her own practice near Manotick.

Dr. Audrey Fyvie became the provincial lands and forests department's first woman veterinary officer; Dr. Elizabeth Pocock headed veterinary services in the public health department, Port Credit, Ontario. Dr. Jean Belcher was the first woman on staff at Ontario Veterinary College.

* * *

History's pages and the annals of the space age list the names of many active in widely diversified fields. This was literally true in the case of Dr. Margaret Newton, whose deep concern with the health of Canadian wheat gave her a place in Canada's history books.

In 1665, wheat was legal tender. By 1813 Selkirk settlers were planting the grain in the West. In 1947, the first year the championship was offered, Mrs. Amy Grace Kelsey of Erickson, B.C. won the world wheat crown, the most important of eight world titles, with her Reward Wheat. In 1958, Gail Adams, a member of the 4-H Club of Drumheller, Alberta, won the world championship with her Chinook Wheat. Mrs. Margaret Jenkins of Kelvington, Saskatchewan, was named the only

Robertson Associate of the Canadian Seedgrowers Association.

Unsung Heroine

Canada's wheat stem rust fighter, scientist Margaret Newton, won her battle with the dreaded wheat disease but lost her health in the process. What she had thought was a tiresome case of asthma was diagnosed as the incurable Miner's Lungs. She was told she must either live in a warm climate or in an iron lung for the rest of her life. Pioneers in new fields often pay a high price for the honor of taking the first painful steps along the path of human progress. Dr. Newton's vital research into wheat stem rust, which saved Canada millions of dollars, had ruined her health.

Born in 1887, Margaret sought admission to Macdonald Agricultural College, Ste. Anne de Bellevue and was brusquely refused because of her sex. Finally Margaret, who studied plant pathology, and Pearl Stanforth, were admitted, and were the first female graduates of any agricultural college in Canada. Margaret graduated in 1915, winning the Governor-General's Gold Medal and a fellowship to proceed with her Master and Ph.D. degrees.

Following further study, she was appointed assistant professor of pathology at Saskatchewan University. There she isolated 14 different varieties of rust. In 1916, a magnificent crop filled Western farmers with optimism, which later turned to dismay when over 100,000,000 bushels of wheat were suddenly ruined by rust. Discouraged, the farmers threatened to stop growing grain. An alarmed federal minister of agricultural promptly had a rust laboratory built at Winnipeg in 1925, with Dr. Newton appointed senior plant pathologist.

In 1943, Dr. Newton was elected a member of the Royal Society, which later awarded her the Flavelle Gold Medal. She was the first graduate of any agricultural college to receive this high honor. Other recipients include Sir Charles Saunders (Marquis Wheat), Sir Frederick Banting, and Dr. Wilder Penfield. In February 1956, University of Minnesota presented her with its Outstanding Achievement Award.

*   *   *

Today, as woman power makes itself felt in the space age in diverse fields, Magistrate Emily Murphy's prophetic words ring down the centuries, as she foresaw the enduring challenge:

"Because the world has become a unit, as never before, our moral concerns can no longer be looked upon as men's problems or women's problems. These are now problems of humanity, and may be solved only by the two sexes and the different nations acting in co-operation. There is still a terrific need for pioneering women possessed of wide-eyed courage, with vision to perceive the dire fate that threatens mankind . . . the valour to deal with it effectively. The cause of mankind cannot afford to wait."

Bibliography

Adult Education in Canada, J. R. Kidd (Garden City Press) Toronto

A Temperate Dispute, Dr. Hilda Neatby (Clarke Irwin Company) Toronto

American Women, edited by Beverley B. Cassara (Beacon Press) Boston

And His Charming Lady, Lucille Iremonger (Martin, Secker, Warburg) London, England

A History of Montreal General Hospital, H. E. MacDermot (the Hospital) Montreal

A History of Nursing, Nutting and Dock (G. P. Putnam's Sons) New York

Maude Abbott: A Memoir, H. E. MacDermot (Macmillan) Toronto

A Woman Doctor Looks at Life and Love, Dr. M. Hilliard (Doubelday Co. Inc.) New York

A Bonny Fechter (Lady Aberdeen), Lady Marjorie Pentland (Batsford) London, England

Ask No Quarter (Agnes Macphail), Doris French and Margaret Stewart (Longmans Green) Toronto

Albani, Forty Years of Song (Mills and Boon) London, England

A History of Emily Montague, Frances Brook (London, England) republished (McClelland and Stewart) Toronto

Barbara Heck, Blanche Hume (Ryerson Canadian History Readers) Toronto

Brave Harvest (Cora Hind), Kennethe Haig (Allen) Toronto

Builders of Fortunes, George Lonn (Pitt Publishing Company) Toronto

Carrie Chapman Catt, Helen H. Miller (Suffrage Movement in United States) New York

Canadiennes, Albert Tessier Fides, Montreal

Canadian Poets, (edited) J. W. McGarvin (McClelland and Stewart) Toronto

Canadian Wild Flowers, Catherine Parr Traill, Montreal

Culture in Canada, (edited) Albert A. Shea (Can. Association for Adult Education)

Catalogue of Canadian Composers (edited) Helmut Kellman (Garden City Press) Toronto

Courageous Women, L. M. Montgomery; Marian Keith; M. B. McKinley; (McClelland and Stewart) Toronto

Campaign Echoes, Letitia Youmans, Toronto

Clearing in the West, Nellie McClung (autobiography) (T. Allen) Toronto

Dr. James Barrie (Her Secret Story), Olga Racster (Home) London, England

Dictionary of Biographies (Consolidated Book Publishers, Inc.) Chicago

Emily Carr as I Knew Her, Carol E. W. Pearson (Clarke Irwin) Toronto

Emily Murphy: Crusader, Byrne Hope Sanders (Macmillan) Toronto

Famous Doctors, Viola W. Pratt (Clarke Irwin, Canadian Portrait Series) Toronto

Famous Musicians, Louise G. McCready (Clarke Irwin Canadian Portrait Series) Toronto

Famous Women, Byrne Hope Sanders (Clarke Irwin Canadian Portrait Series) Toronto

Famous Women of History, W. H. Browne (Arnold) Philadelphia

First Ladies, Jane and Burt McConnell (Thomas Y. Crowell Co.) New York

For the Greater Glory, Dorothy M. Henderson (Ryerson Press) Toronto

Florence Nightingale as Seen in Her Portraits, Dr. M. Abbott (Boston Medical Journal)

Flame of Power, Peter C. Newman (Longmans Green) Toronto

Give My Heart (Dr. Marion Hilliard), Marion O. Robinson (Doubleday) Garden City, N.Y.,

Growing Pains, Emily Carr, autobiography (Oxford University Press) Toronto

Great Composers, Henry and Dana Lee Thomas (Garden City) New York

Geologists and Prospectors, Margaret M. Shaw (Clarke Irwin Portrait Series) Toronto

Heroines of Canadian History, W. S. Herrington (William Briggs) Toronto

House of All Sorts, Emily Carr (Oxford University Press) Toronto

Hamilton General Hospital, Marjorie Freeman Campbell (School of Nursing) (Ryerson Press) Toronto

Hospitals of Ontario, A. A. Allan (King's Printer) Toronto

History of the Women's Medical College, Dr. Gulielma F. Alsop (J. B. Lipincott Co.) (Philadelphia 1850-1950) Philadelphia, London, Montreal

History of Medicine in Province of Quebec, Dr. Maude Abbott, Montreal.

Illustrated Minute Biographies, W. A. Dewitt and S. Nisenson (Grosset and Dunlap) New York

Jeanne Mance, Wm. H. Atherton (Catholic Hospital Association) St. Louis

Jeanne Mance, Katharine Hale (Ryerson Canadian History Readers) Toronto

Kateri of the Mohawks, Marie C. Buehrle (Bruce) Milwaukee, United States

Lady Into Woman, Vera Brittain (Dakers) London

Life of Letitia Youmans, Mrs. H. G. Willes (booklet)

Life in the Clearings, Susanna Moodie (De Witt and Davenport) New York

La femme canadienne française, A. Levesque, Montreal

Medical Practice in Canada Under the British Regime, Dr. J. J. Heagerty (The Macmillan Company), Toronto

Medicine in Manitoba, Dr. Ross Mitchell (Stovel-Advocate Press Ltd.) Winnipeg

Medical Profession in Upper Canada (1783-1850), Wm. Canniff (Wm. Briggs) Toronto

Mary of the Incarnation (An Ursuline of Quebec) Quebec

My Seventy Years, Martha Black (told to Elizabeth Bailey Price) (Nelson) London

Music in Canada (edited) Sir Ernest MacMillan (University of Toronto Press) Toronto

Massey Report (chief commissioner Vincent Massey) (Queen's Printer) Ottawa

Men and Mines, George Lonn (Pitt Publishing Co.) Toronto

Mère Marie de l'Incarnation, Blodwen Davies (Ryerson Canadian History Readers)

Marguerite Bourgeoys, Frank Oliper Call (Ryerson Canadian History Readers)

Memory's Wall, Lady Flora Eaton (Clarke Irwin) Toronto

My Mother, the Judge, Elsie McGill (Ryerson Press) Toronto

My Travels and Findings, E. Cora Hind (My articles on Europe collected into a book)

Never a Day So Bright, Kate Aitken, autobiography (Longmans Green Company) Toronto

National Council of Women of Canada Yearbooks (1895-1964) (National Councils)

Proud Heritage (story of N.C.W.) Rosa Shaw (Ryerson Press) Toronto

Portraits de femmes, Madeleine C. Huguenin (Editions La Patrie) Montreal

Pause, autobiography; Emily Carr, (Clarke Irwin) Toronto

Roughing it in the Bush, Susanna Moodie (autobiography) (McClelland and Stewart, republished) Toronto

Ringing the Changes, Mazo de la Roche (autobiography) (Little, Brown) Boston, Toronto

She Skated Into Our Hearts, Cay Moore (Barbara Ann Scott) (McClelland and Stewart Ltd.) Toronto

So Little for the Mind, Dr. Hilda Neatby (Clarke Irwin Co.) Toronto

Seeing for Myself, E. Cora Hind (Articles on Europe collected into a book)

The Lily of the Mohawks (Kateri Tekawitha) Ellen Walworth

The Church and the Secular World (United Church Report) (Educational Books Inc.)

White Angel of Tokyo (chapter in *They Went Forth*) (Caroline Macdonald) Dr. John McNab (published 1933 McClelland and Stewart, Toronto, revised 1955)

Types of Canadian Women, Henry J. Morgan (Wm. Briggs) Toronto

The Canadian Men and Women of the Time (Vol. I) (Wm. Briggs) Toronto

The Woman — Bless Her, Marjory MacMurchy (Gundy) Toronto

The Stream Runs Fast, Nellie McClung (autobiography) (T. Allen) Toronto

The Story of L. M. Montgomery, Hilda M. Ridley (Ryerson Press) Toronto

The Strange Story of Dr. James Barrie, Rae Isabel (London, England), (Longmans) Toronto

The Strickland Sisters, Blanche Hume (Ryerson Canadian History Readers) Toronto

Ten Canadian Poets, Desmond Pacey (Ryerson Press) Toronto

The Writing of Biography, Catherine D. Bowen (The Writer, Inc.) Boston

Three Centuries of Canadian Nursing, M. S. Mathewson, R.N., and J. Murray Gibbon (Macmillan Company) Toronto

The Women Pioneers of North America, Sophy L. Elliot (Garden City Press) Quebec

The Feminine Mystique, Betty Friedan (Dell Publishing Company) New York

The Bold Women, Helen B. Woodward (Farrar, Strauss and Young) New York

The School of Femininity, Margaret Lawrence (Frederick A. Stokes Company) New York

The Woman Suffrage Movement in Canada, Catherine L. Cleverdon (University of Toronto Press) Toronto

The Pioneer Women of Vancouver Island (1843-1866) Lugrin (Women's Canadian Club) Victoria.

The Macmillan Dictionary of Canadian Biography, W. S. Wallace (Macmillan Co.) Toronto

The Jesuit Relations (edited) E. Kenton (McClelland and Stewart) Toronto

The Loyalists, Selwyn Banwell (Ross and Mann Ltd.) Toronto

Unusual Facts of Canadian History, Wm. L. Styles (McClelland and Stewart) Toronto

Unfold the Years, Mary Quayle Innis (Y.W.C.A.) (McClelland and Stewart), Toronto

We Twa, Lady Aberdeen (Her Canadian Journal) (Champlain Society) Toronto

Women Doctors of the World, Dr. Esther P. Lovejoy (Macmillan) New York, Toronto

Wives (Portraits American Women) Gamaliel Bradford (Harper and Brothers) New York

Women Today (edited) Elizabeth Bragdon (Bobbs-Merrill Company) New York

Women of Canada (Their Life and Work) by the N.C.W. compiled for the Paris International Exposition in 1900, republishd by N.C.W. in 1976

Women of Red River, W. J. Healey (Russell Lang) Winnipeg

Women in the Nineteenth Century, S. M. Ossoli (J. P. Jewett) Boston

Women's Who's Who of America (1914-1915) American Commonwealth Company N.Y. (1914)

Women of All Nations (edited) Joyce T. and Thomas N. W. Athol (Cassells) London

The Report of the Royal Commission on the Status of Women in Canada, Florence Bird, Chairman, published by Queen's Printer, Ottawa, in 1971.

Various encyclopedias

Acknowledgments

My grateful thanks to numerous helpful librarians and archivists across Canada. Particularly Dr. W. Kaye Lamb, former National Librarian and Archivist; Norman Fee, former Assistant Archivist; Mr. Erik Spicer, Parliamentary Librarian; Mr. Claude Aubrey, Director, and the staff of Carnegie Library, Osler Medical Library; Dr. W. Ireland, Victoria; Miss Margaret Hardy and other Western and Maritime librarians and archivists. To the nuns of the Ursuline Convent, Quebec; the Grey Nuns, and those of Hotel Dieu and Marguerite Bourgeoys College, Montreal.

The National Council of Women, Women's Institutes, W.C.T.U., I.O.D.E., the Canadian Association of Nurses, Federation of Home and School Associations, and other women's associations and service clubs, and their magazines, especially the annual lists of women of the Business and Professional Women's Magazine — all have supplied me with useful information, as have Alixe Carter's column and many others.

While Dr. John Robbins was compiling the Encyclopedia Canadiana, we exchanged information about Canadian women's work, a case of the lion and the mouse!

Knowledgeable friends who helped with criticism or advice include Walter Herbert, R. York Wilson, George McCracken, Dr. John McLeish, Col. Ted Bullock, Myrtle Gray, Dr. Jack Firestone, Kenneth P. Kirkwood, George Lonn, Bernice Coffey, Gordon Burns, William Arthur Deacon, Sir Ernest MacMillan, Alan Jarvis, Dr. Lorne Pierce, Hugh MacLennan and Vera Britten.

Most important of all, my heartfelt thanks to my beloved husband (who cheerfully "Did Dishes") and to my son, for their unfailing encouragement and steadfast faith.

List of Illustrations

PICTURE CREDITS

The author's appreciation is extended to the many individuals and institutions who have willingly supplied pictures for this book.

Andrews-Newton, Ottawa p. 198
Archives of the United Church of Canada pp. 43, 51
Ashley and Crippen, Toronto p. 160
Audio-Visual Services, Alberta p. 231
Ballard and Jarrett, Toronto p. 514
Capital Press, Ottawa p. 281
Cavouk of Ottawa pp. 6, 536
C.B.C. Toronto pp. 301, 477
Central Office of Information, London p. 5
Charlie Binks p. 498
College Marguerite Bourgeoys, Montreal p. 29
Dassel, Ottawa p. 105
Department of External Affairs, Ottawa p. 539
Edmonton Journal, Edmonton, Alberta p. 213
Federation of Home and School Association, Toronto p. 65
Gaby, Montreal p. 270
Health and Welfare Canada p. 496
Hospital for Sick Children, Toronto p. 92
Hotel Dieu, Pavillon du Bullion p. 24
James B. Hardy, Toronto p. 463
Joe Roseminial p. 425
John Evans, Ottawa p. 540
John Street United Methodist Church, New York, p. 37
Karsh, Ottawa p. 235
Maclean's Magazine, Toronto p. 416
Marguerite d'Youville Centre, Montreal p. 33
Mark McClung, Ottawa p. 224
Mary Pickford p. 443
Matthews Studio p. 456
Michael Bedford, Ottawa p. 7
Milne Studio, Toronto p. 519
Miss Roy, p. 371
Montreal General Hospital Archives p. 86
Municipal Archives, Ottawa p. 486

Mrs. Fairclough, p. 249
Mrs. Gordon Conant, Oshawa p. 140
Mrs. Hugh Scully, Ottawa p. 219
Orillia Public Library p. 319
Osler Library, McGill University, Montreal p. 115
Panda Studio, Toronto p. 152
Patricia E. Stowe p. 106
Paul Horsdal, Ottawa p. 125
Posen, Montreal p. 315
Powell, p. 146
Provincial Archivist, Victoria, B.C. p. 349
Province of Quebec p. 273
Public Archives of Canada pp. 174, 183, 189, 245, 257, 285, 353, 358, 409
Radio and T.V. p. 484
Recard Photo p. 394
The *Telegram*, Toronto p. 504
Toronto General Hospital p. 82
Ursuline Convent, Quebec pp. 17, 19
Victoria Order of Nurses p. 96
Winnipeg Free Press, Winnipeg p. 392
W. C. T. U. Toronto p. 210
Women's Law Association of Ontario p. 150

Jean Bannerman

Jean Bannerman

Tragedies and triumphs highlight the life of Jean Bannerman. Born in Leamington, Ontario, Jean was educated in Hamilton. Nursing her mother through a prolonged illness, able to attend school only part-time, Jean managed to pass her Senior Matriculation examination with honours.

Love of humanity motivated her fixed determination to be a nurse, and she started her training that Autumn at Hamilton General Hospital. Interrupted by a critical illness in her final year (Jean is a hemophiliac), she returned and finished her training after two years' convalescence at home.

Graduating, she was offered an excellent position lecturing and supervising at the hospital (she had a record 93% in her R.N. examinations). Instead she married Glen Bannerman in December 1928, on condition that he allow her to nurse during the summers and attend university during the winters until they had a family.

Jean enrolled in a Public Health Nursing course, but contracted encephalitis. Recovering, she changed to an Arts Course. Four years later, she had a beautiful nine-pound baby boy, Glenny Alexander (whom she nearly lost through hemorrhaging). Friends, joking, said she got her "MA" instead of her "B.A.!"

In 1946, the Bannermans moved to Ottawa, when Glen became Director of the Canadian Government Exhibition Commission, and lived in a charming Penthouse, complete with roof-garden. With son Al studying at St. Andrew's College in Aurora, Jean resumed studies for her B.A. at Carleton College.

Winning a scholarship in Spanish, in June 1949 she went to Santander, Spain, to study, while Al visited friends in Italy. Joining Glen in London, England in early September, she spent two months travelling with him in seven different countries. Fortunately, she kept a diary.

Returning to Canada, she won the weekly prize for an anecdote in *Over the Teacups,* and Bernice Coffey, women's editor of Saturday Night, asked her to write a travel article. Previously, her writing was confined to winning a provincial essay contest, aged thirteen on "How to Avoid Motor ACCIDENTS." and an article in the Globe entitled "The Humble Housewife."

Saturday Night accepted her article and asked for more, and Jean has been writing ever since. She sold one poem and one short story, but mainly articles on travel, personality sketches, health and safety. In 1954 she started writing her book *Leading Ladies-Canada-1639-1967* which took twelve years. Jean spent one summer in the West and another in the Maritimes, interviewing women and doing research in libraries and archives.

In 1958, Glen was appointed Commissioner General for Canada at the Brussels World Fair, with the rank of an Ambassador. Jean says their nine months in Brussels was like a fairy tale come true. "Hostessing" she loves, and at the closing dinner the Bannermans were voted the most popular couple. The Toronto *Telegram* had an article calling Jean "The Hostess with the Mostest."

Back home that dreary November, Jean felt like Cinderella back in the chimney corner! After Christmas, Glen had the first of several eye operations, for cataract. Then, in July 1960, Al was nearly killed in a terrible car accident, and spent the next five years in various hospitals. That November, Jean had a very serious cancer operation. In September, the Bannermans had a dreadful fire, which took six months to recover from.

The Seattle World Fair, at which Glen was again Commissioner General, was a bright spot. Then in March, 1964, the Bannermans moved to Montreal, where Glen was a Special Advisor to Expo '67. That Spring Jean's book was finally published, friends calling it "The Bannerman Centennial Project." Numerous talks to women's clubs, radio and television interviews followed.

In April 1958, the Bannermans moved back to Ottawa. The next day, Jean drove Glen back to Montreal for his second cataract operation. This was successful, but a subsequent operation for a detached retina was not, and Glen is now blind in one eye, and rapidly losing his sight in the other. Doctors consider it too risky to operate.

Jean has been occupied the last ten years with club work, the study of graphology, an article for *Chatelaine* about Al's accident, an anecdote for *The Reader's Digest,* a prize-winning recipe in the *National Enquirer,* and the revision of *Leading Ladies-Canada* now being published in a new and expanded edition.

Name Index

Forgues, Dr. Laura Coleman 121, 122
Forrester, Jane 278
Forrester, Maureen 291, 292
Fortier, Aline 464, 465
Foster, Diane 424
Foster, Lillian 389
Fowke, Edith 293, 307
Franca, Celia 452, 455
Francis, Ann (Florence Bird) 472-474
Francis of Assisi, Sister 69
Francis, Margaret Ecker 384
Frankel, Ruth 135
Fraser, Mrs. Kaspar 134
Fraser, Robbin 396, 397
Freedman, Harry 307
Freedman, Ray 90
Freedman, William 478, 479
Freiman, Mrs. A. J. 125, 127
French, Doris 402, 403
French, Maida Parlow 365
Fritz, Dr. Clara 518
Frizell, Mary 490
Frizell, Mildred 490
Frum, Barbara 483, 484, 485
Fry, Gladys 491
Fyvie, Dr. Audrey 549

Gagne, Claire 292
Gagnier, Claire 482
Gale, Annie 275
Gale, Carrie 276
Galloway, Jean Love (Mrs. Strome) 388, 389
Garbitt, Betty 71
Garbutt, Dr. Elizabeth 119, 411
Garland, Eileen 74
Garrett, Elizabeth 107, 108
Gaudet-Smet, Mme. Françoise 397
Gaudreault, Laure 70, 71
Gaultier, Rose 166
Gauthier, Cecile 302
Gauthier, Eva 290
Gay, Mary 509
Geddis, Mrs. John 45
Geiger-Torel, Dr. Herman 306
Gelber, Sylvia 517
Gendreau, Mariana 70
Genereaux, Georgina 96, 97
Genereaux, Leontine 96, 97
Gibb, Alexandrine 490
Gibb, Mrs. Beniah 87, 88
Gibbons, Mrs. Elsie 277
Gilbertin, Mme. 533

Gilbride, Louise (Mrs. J. Stuart) 199
Gilbride, Mrs. R. G. 199
Gilchrist, Joan 166
Giles, Shirley 526, 527
Gill, Margaret 81
Gillespie, Mary 520
Gilliatt, Hortense Spurr 417
Gilstorf, Eveline (Mrs. Reginald) 57, 58
Girard, Alice 102, 103, 104
Girdleston, Eloise 205
Girvan, Louise 525
Glover, Rev. Geoffrey 53
Goddard, Adelaide 207
Godfrey, Mrs. John M. 306
Goggins, Jessie Muriel (Mrs. Merril Denison) 371, 372
Gordon, Daniel M. 62
Gordon, Dr. Margaret 110
Gordon, Dr. Wilhemina 62
Gosling, Mrs. A. G. 267
Gosselin, Alma 544
Gostick, Edith 268
Gouin, Yvette (Senator Leon) 347
Goulden, Flora 306
Goulden, Flora Matheson 476
Gowan, Elsie Park (Mrs. E. H. Gowan) 464
Gowdy, Mary 90
Graham, Rev. Anne 54
Graham, Betty 55
Graham, Dorothy Frances 118
Graham, Florence (Elizabeth Arden) 522
Graham, Gwethalyn 375, 376, 378
Grand, Elaine 474, 475
Grannon, Mary 462
Grant, Maggie 389, 390
Grant, Sylvia 307
Gray, Jane 457, 458
Gray, Dr. Jessie 122, 123
Gray, Myrtle 529
Greene, Nancy 502, 503
Grenier, Cecile 71, 72
Grescoe, Mrs. G. H. 311, 312
Grey, Elizabeth Benson 307
Griffen, Margaret 418
Griffin, Neala 437
Grimson, Sybil 80
Grosse, Rosa 489
Groves, Edith L. 64
Gruchy, Lydia 51-53
Grudeff, Marian 449
Guerin, Bellelle 39

580

DATE DUE

GAYLORD			PRINTED IN U.S.A.